The Birth of the Penitentiary in Latin America:
Essays on Criminology, Prison Reform, and
Social Control, 1830–1940

D1258863

**iLAS** New Interpretations of Latin America Series

# The Birth of the Penitentiary in Latin America:
# Essays on Criminology, Prison Reform, and Social Control, 1830–1940

Edited by
Ricardo D. Salvatore
and
Carlos Aguirre

University of Texas Press, Austin
Institute of Latin American Studies

First Edition, 1996

Requests for permission to reproduce material from this work should be sent to Permissions, University of Texas Press, P.O. Box 7819, Austin, Texas 78713-7819

♾ The paper used in this publication meets the minimum requirements of American National Standard for Information Sciences—Permanence of Paper for Printed Library Materials, ANSI Z39.48–1984.

**Library of Congress Cataloging-in-Publication Data**

The birth of the penitentiary in Latin America : essays on criminology, prison reform, and social control, 1830–1940 / edited by Ricardo D. Salvatore and Carlos Aguirre.
    p.  cm. — (New Interpretations of Latin America Series)
    Includes bibliographical references (p. ) and index.

    ISBN 0-292-77707-8 (pbk. : alk. paper)
    1. Prisons—Latin America—History   I. Salvatore, Ricardo Donato.
II. Aguirre, Carlos. III. Series.
HV9510.5.B57 1996
365'.98—dc20

                    96-3851
                    CIP

"En realidad se trata de una usina, de un gigantesco laboratorio, en el cual la materia prima con que se trabaja e investiga no es ni el metal, ni la lana, ni el algodón, sino que otra mucho más noble, y de más difícil manipulación, como es la materia humana viciada o degenerada, desgraciada o sufrida. Ahí se transforma a los carcomidos por el vicio y el crimen, en seres útiles a la sociedad."

[It is actually a factory, a gigantic laboratory, in which the raw material they work with and investigate is not metal, wool, or cotton, but one much more noble and of much more difficult manipulation: humans, corrupted or degenerated, unfortunate or long-suffering. There, those ruined by vice and crime are transformed into human beings useful to society.]

—Israel Drapkin, *Actualidades penales y penitenciarias del Brasil* (Santiago, 1939)

# Contents

Photo section following p. 159.

# Introduction

In 1834, Brazilian authorities began the construction of the Casa de Correção in Rio de Janeiro, the first institution of confinement in Latin America to be built following the penitentiary principles. During the next one hundred years or so, within different time frames and with varied degrees of commitment and success, most Latin American countries adopted the penitentiary project; that is, they decided to build penitentiaries and reformatories and, more generally, embarked on successive attempts at prison reform. The general aim—as it was presented in the rhetoric of authorities and reformers—was to eradicate the ruinous, unhealthful, inefficient, and inhumane jails that existed all over the region and to replace them with modern, "scientific," and rehabilitative institutions for transforming the criminal into an obedient, hard-working, law-abiding subject. Reformers embraced the new criminological science (heavily influenced by positivism), placed anthropometric research facilities in their carceral institutions, enhanced the power of experts (criminologists, physicians, teachers) within the prison, generated the statistics needed to analyze the problems of crime, and gradually induced changes in their penal legislation in order to incorporate the most recent European and North American innovations in the "science" of punishment. By doing so, Latin American elites and public authorities sought to offer "civilized," scientific, and effective solutions to the "criminal question."

As with so many imported cultural, political, social, and technological devices, the adaptation of Western penal institutions in Latin America was controversial and complex. With so many factors impinging upon the process, the ultimate outcome of this adaptation was bound to diverge from the original design, despite all the hope and energy invested by the reformers. A number of factors hindered the progress of penitentiary reform: scarce state revenues, unsuitable legislation, prevailing patterns of social control, and the hegemony of discourses that justified traditional ways of interaction between classes, sexes, and races. In spite of poor results, the penitentiary ideal was never really challenged, and it remained throughout this period as the prima donna of the whole process of penal reform. It epitomized all the dreams and obsessions of Latin American state officials, local authorities, scientists, lawyers, and of course ruling elites. It established itself as both the solution to their concerns about crime and social disorder and the ultimate symbol of modernity and civilization. While the basic penitentiary principles were shared by each country's respective reformers, each case required different adjustments due to specific local conditions and to concrete political and ideological configurations.

This volume attempts to shed new light on the protracted, multifaceted, and ambiguous process of modernization in Latin America by analyzing the fate of prison reform and its connections with broader social issues. By analyzing the multiple factors influencing the building, operation, and reform of carceral institutions in Latin America, the essays in this collection try to address a topic rarely explored in the historiography of modern Latin America. The long century that elapsed between the beginning of the construction of the Casa de Correção in Rio de Janeiro (1834) and the year in which Cuba finally adopted the penitentiary system (1939) is the time period chosen for this study, a period that, as any student of the modern history of Latin America knows, witnessed dramatic changes in the social structure, economic development, political forms, and ideological trends of Latin American countries.

This book grew from an initial encounter between the editors in Minneapolis, Minnesota, in November 1990. Plans for an AHA panel first and then an edited collection of essays developed after we realized that some of our common research interests had been inadequately dealt with in the existing literature. We were struck by the fact that in spite of all the symbolic and political importance of prisons in modern Latin American history and the rather dramatic situation of the region's prisons during the 1980s (several major prison riots broke out in some of the most important Latin American cities), the attention the subject had received from the scholarly community was rather limited. Consequently, we set out to organize a collection of papers that could stimulate discussion about the history of prisons, penitentiaries, and reformatories in the context of changing social structures and ethnic, class, and gender identities and relationships, as well as shifting discourses about society.

The study of the history of institutions of confinement was propelled by the publication in 1975 of Michel Foucault's *Surveiller et punir*.[1] Although valuable work had already been done, it was this book which sparked the interest of historians on this topic, and it was this book which placed the issue of the birth of carceral institutions at the center of the debates around the notion of modernity, its antinomies, and its legacies. Foucault placed his conceptualization of the birth of the prison within a more ambitious explanatory scheme: he put the prison at the center of the construction of "modern" societies, thus attempting to show the ways in which discipline, power, and surveillance became constitutive elements of modernity.[2] While Foucault's elaborations on the history of the prison, his arguments about the connections between modernity and "panopticism," and his broader theoretical and methodological assumptions have all been subjected to various forms of criticism, there is no doubt that *Surveiller et punir* is still a source of inspiration for a whole range of studies on institutions of incarceration all over the world.

Although this collection of essays was not conceived as a "test" of Foucault's thesis for Latin America, the cases we study here will furnish new and interesting materials that should enrich the debates about these issues. In Latin America there has been scant interest in the history of prisons until very recently, a neglect that is indeed unfortunate. This situation arises in part due to the fact that many Latin American historians, trapped in the net of old concepts and theories, see the prison as just one more institution of the state, probably the least remarkable and appealing. Unable to draw the connection between the prison and the objects of study of more fashionable areas of social, intellectual, and political history (the state, labor, ideologies, political parties, social conflict, women, the family), historians do not consider the study of prisons to be crucial for the understanding of our past. The recent explosion of studies on hidden and obscure spaces, subordinate social groups, day-to-day forms of social control, the construction of hegemony, and subaltern resistance makes us view with optimism the prospect of increasingly sophisticated scholarship on the history of prisons, reformatories, and other similar institutions in Latin America.[3]

Penitentiaries, prisons, and reformatories were—and still are—crucial institutions within the overall strategies of control and discipline and the construction of hegemonic visions of society by ruling groups. They were also conceived as sites for the observation, classification, and normalization of subaltern groups in general, not only the so-called criminal class. In addition, prisons and penitentiaries played a central role in the social *imaginaire* of both the elites and the lower classes, thus offering an enormously promising terrain for exploring the processes of cultural and ideological contention. For these reasons, we believe that the study of carceral institutions in Latin America provides fertile ground for advancing our understanding of the region's past and present.

The first essay, "The Birth of the Penitentiary in Latin America," offers an interpretive framework for understanding the connections between the successive waves of prison reform and major changes affecting the region during the period from 1830 to 1940. Using a multidimensional approach, the essay argues that the birth of the penitentiary in Latin America was a process that has to be viewed against the backdrop of institutional changes, contested processes of nation and state formation, struggles over power and social discipline, and shifting discourses about society. The penitentiary, we argue, was an imported device whose fate has to be explored in the context of Latin America's hybrid modernity. The new theories embodied into the penitentiary model added a modern "punitive city" to the existing punitive repertoire but did not displace, by themselves, private justice and brutal punishment. Imitation of foreign models and the importation of liberal/positivist/scientific ideas served to strengthen or refashion traditional forms of domination and personal dependence. In other words, the highly costly venture of building penitentiaries became part of a process that has been described as "traditional modernization," that is, a process of modernization that did not replace the old social structures, forms of interaction, or racial and gender hierarchies but, instead, reinforced them. Prison reform in Latin America—unlike the European and North American experiences—became part of a process of state and nation formation in which a rhetoric about modernization and innovation was generally contradicted by the continual—and usually violent—exclusion of the majorities from the exercise of democratic rights and citizenship.

In chapter 2, Carlos Aguirre explains how the imitation of Western models and existing social tensions led to the adoption of the penitentiary in Peru, while prevailing patterns of social control and traditional mentalities undercut the accomplishments of the reform. The search for order and stability after a period of social dislocation found in the penitentiary the apparent ideal solution. Yet the failure of the penitentiary in realizing the dreams of controlling crime, reforming prisoners, and transforming them into useful and productive citizens speaks of persistent (colonial) social hierarchies and mental settings in Peruvian soil. The project itself was colored by inherent contradictions (such as the blunt racism displayed by reformer Paz Soldán), and not even those in charge of realizing the project seemed convinced of its suitability. Aguirre's essay also shows the close connection between the adoption of the penitentiary and the development of a modern state and renewed efforts at social control. Equally important, it shows how the adoption of European and North American innovations resulted from the elite's general fascination with them, regardless of their feasibility, a topic that speaks more about the elite's obsessions and mental settings than about social realities.

María Zárate Campos reviews the functioning of the Santiago Women's Correctional House during the second half of the nineteenth century, offering important elements to analyze the construction of gender categories within penal discourse. The transition in the administration of the Correctional House from a lay benevolent association to a religious congregation served to preserve the disciplining of women within the spheres of home and religion. The new religious administrators gendered the reformatory principle, understanding reform as redirecting the inmates from the path of vice to the path of virtue. Religious instruction and personal interaction between nuns and inmates were central to the disciplinary process. The work of inmates (sewing, embroidering, washing, spinning) contributed to consolidate the ideal of domesticity held by the Chilean elite. Internal methods of classification and separation of inmates also replicated elite prejudices: prostitutes, thieves, and serious offenders were separated from the apprentices of vice ("helpless girls" arrested for vagrancy). Devoid of the scientific underpinning characteristic of the experiment of reformation in male penitentiaries, the Correctional House reinforced a quite traditional project: safeguarding women's attachment to God, husband, and children.

Marcos Luiz Bretas approaches the study of Rio de Janeiro's prisons through the analysis of representation. In a truly innovative manner, he studies the ways in which different types of witnesses (journalists, lawyers, convicts) reflected upon prison and prison life, showing the multiple meanings and symbolisms associated with the carceral institutions. In many ways, these writings contributed to the "invention" or the "apprehension" of the criminal. By portraying prison populations as essentially made up of recidivists, true criminals, and the like, they disseminated an image of the prison as a "world apart," hidden from public scrutiny. This tended to alleviate the anxieties felt by the free population and helped to stress the importance of having these criminals behind bars. The overall result was the "naturalization" of the image of the "savage criminal," a notion shared by those "scientists"—the criminologists—whose task was to decipher the intricacies of the criminal mind. These visions, by portraying criminals as "unreformable," ultimately offered pessimistic judgments about the overall performance of the reformed prisons. The inmate, construed as peaceful and obedient in appearance but violent and brutal in essence, reinforced the pessimism of reformers on the possibilities of rehabilitation.

Kelvin Santiago-Valles discusses methods of punishment in relation to the economic and labor structures of Puerto Rico during the late colonial period. Combining discourse analysis with a solid dissection of the economic and social realities of the island, Santiago suggests that the colonial and noncapitalistic character of the island's economy and society undermined the possibilities of building a "modern" system of punishment. Moreover, the perceptions of Puerto Rican peasants as essentially lazy, ignorant, and primitive sabotaged the likelihood of more democratic and liberal social and institutional practices. Forms of peasant resistance translated, in the memories of the colonizers, into a discourse about the *jíbaro* (the word used by the colonialists to refer pejoratively to the country folk of Puerto Rico) that conflated race, class, and "vice." Given the weaknesses of capitalism in Puerto Rico, it made no sense to develop a penitentiary system, and thus the solution was to foster the development of penal colonies that better fitted the economic necessities and mental assumptions of colonial elites. Hard labor in penal colonies, Santiago argues, was the colonial government's brutal response to a population considered naturally recalcitrant about supplying labor to others. This chapter is an important addition to the growing literature on colonial penal regimes as both extensions and refashionings of metropolitan ones.[4]

The chapter on Mexico by Robert Buffington deals with the relationship between prison reform and the political and ideological debates from the Porfiriato to the Mexican Revolution. The essay demonstrates the centrality of the penitentiary for the construction of a national state and the search for political hegemony, showing the continuities in the discourse about prison and punishment between both periods. These continuities find their rationale in the fact that both regimes, in spite of major differences in other respects, considered the state to be the major regulator of social life and were prepared to use the penitentiary as a metaphor for the political system. The penitentiary, promoted by both the *científico* Porfirian community and the congressmen of the 1917 Constitutional Convention, was conceived as a modern instrument for the control of crime, but above all it was a powerful symbol of state power that promised legitimacy to each regime. In addition to the continuities, Buffington notices key differences in the discourse of these two sets of policymakers. While Porfirian *científicos* stressed the need for political centralization, the revolutionaries at the 1917 convention were much more concerned with preventing the emergence of a new autocracy. Thus penitentiary reform in Mexico was not just an instrument of "modernity" but rather a contested terrain on which alternative visions of the Mexican state confronted each other.

The chapter by Ricardo Salvatore compares positivist criminology in Argentina and Brazil and its influence in shaping the discourse of prison and penal reform in these two countries. The language of criminologists provides insights for studying the interconnection between prison reform and contending discourses about the social—what the author calls "visions of class"—in two countries experiencing rapid integration into the world market. Argentina and Brazil, both facing new social problems associated with the emergence of a predominantly immigrant, urban, and mobile working class, responded differently to the challenges of "criminality." While Brazilian criminologists found the category "race" useful for explaining the country's economic backwardness and the lack of integration of the peasant majorities into the project of progress, Argentine criminologists emphasized the influence of the social environment of the city and the psychopathological traits of individuals to explicate criminal behavior. Endowed with the new powers of observation gained from the penitentiary-as-clinic, criminologists proceeded to interpret the "social question" and to evaluate the consequences of export-led growth on social control. As a result, a similar type of knowledge served to construct two different "criminalities" and two distinct "social questions."

In the last essay, Steven Palmer analyzes the emergence of penal reform as part of a broader attempt to implement liberal welfare policies in early-twentieth-century Costa Rica. The transition between early experiments with agricultural penal colonies in the 1880s and the subsequent emphasis on penitentiary reformation was related to the emergence and consolidation of a project of "social hygiene" between 1906 and 1924. He argues that, rather than constituting a mere reaction to already existing social problems, the move toward prison reform anticipated the emergence of the "social question" in modern metropolises. As such, the penitentiary formed an integral part of the whole project of building a liberal welfare state that had, among its major tasks, the molding and shaping of the lower classes' behavior and morals. Curiously, prison reform and scientific policing coexisted with the expansion of the state's role in social protection (infant care, maternity benefits, and social workers). The metaphor of the state as a loving mother who was supposed to provide care, education, and protection to her citizens encapsulated deep concerns about the dangerousness of the working class and the desire to prevent future social unrest. Even if the project of the penitentiary did not work as its founders planned, Palmer argues, it nonetheless played a key role in increasing vigilance, control, and observation of the lower classes. In many ways unique in relation to the experience of other Latin American countries, Costa Rica also appears unique in the issue of prison reform: an early experiment in penal/welfare state intervention developed here, much earlier than in any other country of the region.

In spite of their differing methodological assumptions and thematic foci, the essays in this collection are linked by several common threads. First, they attempt to place the development of prison reform within a context of the move toward "modernization," shifting social realities, and conflicting discourses about class, gender, race, and nation. Borrowing from methodologies developed by the new social history, discourse analysis, gender history, and subaltern studies, the essays of this collection try to overcome the limitations of a literature that relies only on the prison's design and the reformers' wills, that is, a literature centered on "social control." The contributors have made a conscious effort to avoid the reductionism of polarities such as structure-superstructure, factory-prison, center-periphery, and ideology–class interest for the benefit of a more culturally contextualized and historically meaningful analysis. Whether or not they succeed in this attempt, the chapters in this book suggest connections among different layers of social construction and systems of power (crime, social conflict, export economies, state ideologies, popular culture, patriarchy, colonialism) rarely explored.

The story of the birth of the penitentiary, the essays seem to imply, cannot be told with a simple, unambiguous, and unidirectional narrative, for the penitentiary project itself was a multivalent creature and was cast in a complex system of power relations and significations. Attempts at prison reform served as catalysts for conceiving and effecting new forms of state. Criminology supplied an interpretive system of the "social question" which directly affected the way the state dealt with the subaltern classes. The hope in the reformation of delinquents was also tied to propositions about the nature of political representation and professional power. Racial, gender, and colonial prejudices and biases about the criminal—developed in the context of contested social processes—informed the projects of penitentiary regeneration. Thus notions of expiation, motherhood, race, colonial prerogative, and class propriety permeated the ambitious ventures of social control.

Second, these essays engage, directly or indirectly, the leading interpretive paradigms about the birth of the penitentiary and the spread of prisons in modern societies. The connections between prison reform and state formation, class struggle, export economies, ideological innovations, and the broader process of constructing modernity in Latin America allow fruitful comparison and contrast with the European and North American experience. The adoption of these quite European and North American "innovations" in the technology of punishment was not a belated replication of developments at the center nor a functional matching between economic realities and social systems. The birth of the penitentiary required a collective interpretive work by which elites could construct simultaneously the need to modernize prisons and methods of punishment, the criminal class, the threats facing the nation's progress, and, more generally, the technologies of classification, observation, intervention, and cure constitutive of the modern states. The essays in this book, by placing the study of the birth of the penitentiary in Latin America within the historical peculiarities of the region and the evolution of discourses about crime and punishment that were, at the same time, specific and alien, offer a set of propositions that will enrich our understanding of the history of confinement in postcolonial societies.

A few remarks are needed, however, about the limitations of this collection. First, the question of the prisoner. Some time ago, both Michael Ignatieff and Michelle Perrot called for a multilayered "social history of prisons" that looked at both sides of the prison wall—the "inside" and the "outside," the "carceral" and the civil society—in their complex interrelationship.[5] They urged historians to put the history of prison life back into the picture. Prisoners' experience of discipline and their struggle for greater control of their bodies and their rights had to become part of the social history of prisons. "It is precisely the real, the daily life of this group—the prisoners—that we must try to capture at its most hidden level, the level that lies behind and beyond the serene statements and the conventions of the discourse of the penitentiary," Perrot tells us.[6] More recently, Peter Linebaugh and Pieter Spierenburg, departing from distinct perspectives, have actualized this project, adding new dimensions to the intricacies of the prison. For Linebaugh, the reconstruction of the prisoner's experience led to the uncovering of hidden dimensions of working-class life in eighteenth-century London.[7] For Spierenburg, the reconstruction implied examining the workings of the "civilizing process" into its practical dimensions, thus questioning the basis of elite views about the savage delinquent.[8] This dimension—prisoners' lives and experiences—receives less emphasis in this collection. In part, this neglect obeys our focus on the discourse of reform, its appropriation, and its uses. In part, it reflects the state of research on this field in Latin America: a similar collection based on visions "from below" (or, rather, "from the inside out") would have been very difficult—if not impossible—to assemble at this point.[9]

Second, the question of gender. Though conceived as a project to confine and reform male delinquents, women in Latin America were affected, and in not insignificant ways, by the arrival of the penitentiary. First, the project tended to reinforce a delineation of sexual spheres that assigned women to the domestic, private, and "nonwork" spheres and men to the public and productive ones. The penitentiary, because it emphasized the centrality of reformation through industrial work, was conceived as a disciplinary or reformatory project for men. When reformers spoke of the "inmate" they often had in mind a male inmate. Women, reformers believed, might also benefit from the therapy of work, but the tasks they had to perform were different: the "correctional" had to prepare them for reproductive work at home rather than for productive work at workshops and factories. Second, the criminological ideas that supported the penitentiary (particularly in its second phase) tended to separate two types of criminality: one for women, another for men. Female criminality belonged to the terrain of morality; male criminality, instead, resulted from the "struggle for life." Women were conceived either as not responsible for committed crimes (like children) or as mere "auxiliaries" to them, not "real" delinquents. Even sexual offenses, with the help of the new medical knowledge, could be relegated to the terrain of mental illnesses or abnormalities. Consequently, the "fall" of women into "vice" could be either tackled by the old method of remorse, repentance, and cloister (priests and nuns were better prepared for this task) or, alternatively, treated in separate institutions for the insane. Third, in terms of symbolic capital, women appeared as a bad investment. While the exemplar mother could be used to foster ideas of nationhood, little could be gained by confining prostitutes and other "vicious" women within a modern penitentiary. If reformers were skeptical of the possibility of turning male delinquents into honest citizens, the disbelief was total when dealing with "vicious women": how were they to regain "virtue"?[10]

More research is needed in both dimensions: the prisoners' experiences and the workings of gender. The full incorporation of both issues into the study of prisons and reformatories will greatly enrich the debates about the history of prisons in Latin America. Other country studies will also improve our understanding of the impact of the penitentiary project. The issue of the reception of the penitentiary by popular culture requires much greater attention from historians. Similarly, as we suggest in chapter 1, the enormous literature on prisons (novels, poems, travelers' reports, journalistic accounts, etc.) still awaits its historians. This collection only claims to be an introduction to a theme that we believe is central to the understanding of the construction of Latin American modernity. The introduction of new technologies of punishment into the region produced, rather than a humanization in penal treatment, new interpretations of economic development, race and social relations, the foundations of state power, and popular culture. A diverse region, Latin America interpreted in many ways the penitentiary or reformatory project and used it for multiple purposes: to sustain certain views of state building, to warn about the "social question" and the risks it posed to export-led growth, to legitimate elite prejudices about racial, sexual, and other social differences, and to build new forms of authority (scientific, medical, professional). Our emphasis on the multiple interpretations and uses of the penitentiary might serve as a guide, as an initial step, to look deeper into the relationship between prison and society and between technologies of punishment and culture in Latin America. This collection aims at opening the field for new interdisciplinary work and new questions that could realize our expectations of an interpretive social history of prisons. Our hope is that other researchers will join us in this effort.

During the time this book was in preparation we received encouragement and constructive criticism from a number of scholars to whom we would like to extend our appreciation: William Beezley, Eduardo Cavieres, Clive Emsley, Mary Gibson, Donna Guy, Martha Huggins, Peter Linebaugh, Robert McCaa, Stuart Schwartz, Paul Vanderwood, Mary Kay Vaughn, and Charles Walker. We are indebted to our respective institutions (the Universidad Torcuato Di Tella and the Department of History of the University of Minnesota) for the facilities provided to carry this project to its conclusion, as well as to those institutions which provided funding for research and writing (the Institute for Advanced Studies at Princeton, the Program of Agrarian Studies of Yale University, the MacArthur Interdisciplinary Program at the University of Minnesota, and the Harry Frank Guggenheim Foundation). The patience and kindness of Theresa May at the University of Texas Press and Virginia Hagerty at the Institute of Latin American Studies deserve special mention. So also do the people who helped us assemble pictures, improve our untidy manuscript (our copyeditor, Mary M. Hill, did a superb job), and communicate over thousands of miles. To all of them, our warmest thanks.

*R.D.S./C.A.*

### Notes

1. Michel Foucault, *Surveiller et punir: naissance de la prison* (Paris: Editions Gallimard, 1975). The book was translated first into Spanish by Aurelio Garzón del Camino as *Vigilar y castigar: nacimiento de la prisión* (Mexico City: Siglo XXI Editores, 1976) and then into English by Alan Sheridan, *Discipline and Punish: The Birth of the Prison* (New York: Pantheon Books, 1977).

2. The literature on this topic has become abundant during the last two decades. See, for instance, Christopher Dandeker, *Surveillance, Power, and Modernity: Bureaucracy and Discipline from 1700 to the Present* (New York: St. Martin's Press, 1990); Darius M. Rejali, *Torture and Modernity: Self, Society, and State in Modern Iran* (Boulder, Colo.: Westview Press, 1994); Thomas Dumm, *Democracy and Punishment: Disciplinary Origins of the United States* (Madison: University of Wisconsin Press, 1987); William G. Staples, *Castles of Our Conscience: Social Control and the American State, 1800–1985* (New Brunswick, N.J.: Rutgers University Press, 1991); Michel Foucault, *Power/Knowledge: Selected Interviews & Other Writings, 1972–1977*, ed. Colin Gordon (New York: Pantheon Books, 1972).

3. Among the most recent literature on popular culture and the day-to-day workings of nation and state formation in Latin America, see especially Gilbert

Joseph and Daniel Nugent, eds., *Everyday Forms of State Formation: Revolution and the Negotiation of Rule in Modern Mexico* (Durham and London: Duke University Press, 1994); William H. Beezley, Cheryl E. Martin, and William E. French, eds., *Rituals of Rule, Rituals of Resistance: Public Celebrations and Popular Culture in Mexico* (Wilmington, Del.: Scholarly Resources, 1994); and Florencia Mallon, *Peasant and Nation: The Making of Post-Colonial Mexico and Peru* (Berkeley and Los Angeles: University of California Press, 1995).

4. Of special importance is the literature on penal regimes in Australia, Africa, and India, of which only a sample can be mentioned here. See, for example, Alastair Davidson, *The Invisible State: The Formation of the Australian State, 1788–1901* (Cambridge: Cambridge University Press, 1991); Stephen Nicholas, ed., *Convict Workers: Reinterpreting Australia's Past* (Cambridge: Cambridge University Press, 1988); David Arnold, *Police Power and Colonial Rule. Madras, 1859–1947* (Delhi and New York: Oxford University Press, 1986); David Arnold, "The Colonial Prison: Power, Knowledge and Penology in Nineteenth-Century India," in David Arnold and David Hardiman, eds., *Subaltern Studies*, vol. 8 (Delhi: Oxford University Press, 1994); Linda Chisholm, "The Pedagogy of Porter: The Origins of the Reformatory in the Cape Colony, 1882–1910," *Journal of African History* 27, no. 3 (1986); Linda Chisholm, "Education, Punishment and the Contradictions of Penal Reform: Klan Paton and Diepkloof Reformatory, 1934–1948," *Journal of Southern African Studies* 17, no. 1 (1991); David Killingray, "The 'Rod of Empire': The Debate over Corporal Punishment in the British African Colonial Times, 1886–1946," *Journal of African History* 35, no. 2 (1994); William Worger, "Contesting Power in the Workplace and the Prison: Diamond Miners and Convicts in Late Nineteenth Century South Africa," Paper, Northwestern University, 1990.

5. Michael Ignatieff, "Historiographie critique du système pénitentiaire," in Jacques G. Petit, ed., *La Prison, le bagne et l'histoire* (Geneva: Librairie des Meridiens, 1984); Michelle Perrot, "Delinquency and the Penitentiary System in Nineteenth-Century France," in Robert Forster and Orest Ranum, eds., *Deviants and the Abandoned in French Society: Selections from the Annales, Economies, Societies, Civilisations* (Baltimore, Md.: Johns Hopkins University Press, 1978).

6. Perrot, "Delinquency and the Penitentiary System," p. 217.

7. Peter Linebaugh has carried out this possibility. Based on the reports of the Ordinary of Newgate containing confessions of prisoners sentenced to capital punishment, he has reconstructed overlooked dimensions of London's working-class life in the eighteenth century: customary direct appropriation, the experience of transportation, the underground circuits of commodities, the expressions of conflict within manufactures and workshops, the multiracial solidarities of the "picaresque proletariat," and the underpinnings of crowd protest against Tyburn. Linebaugh, *The London Hanged: Crime and Civil Society in Eighteenth-Century London* (Cambridge: Cambridge University Press, 1992).

8. See Pieter C. Spierenburg, *The Prison Experience: Disciplinary Institutions and Their Inmates in Early Modern Europe* (New Brunswick, N.J.: Rutgers University Press, 1991).

9. A recent book by Peruvian anthropologist José Luis Pérez Guadalupe, *Faites y atorrantes: una etnografía del penal de Lurigancho* (Lima: Centro de Investigaciones Teológicas, 1994), an "ethnography" of the largest penal institution in Lima, is an outstanding example of an approach that privileges the prisoners' experiences and "agency" in the study of carceral institutions.

10. The literature on women's carceral institutions in Latin America is almost nonexistent. See Jennifer M. Pearson, "Centro Femenil: A Women's Prison in Mexico," *Social Justice* 20, nos. 3–4 (1993): 85–128, for a study of a women's penal institution in contemporary Mexico. In a larger context, a recent book by Adrian Howe offers an intelligent and provocative assessment of the historical and sociological literature on "penality" from a feminist point of view. Adrian Howe, *Punish and Critique: Towards a Feminist Analysis of Penality* (London and New York: Routledge, 1994). For further—and more empirical—work on institutions of confinement for women, see Nicole Rafter, *Partial Justice: Women, Prisons, and Social Control*, 2d ed. (New Brunswick, N.J.: Transaction Publishers, 1990), and Lucia Zedner, *Women, Crime, and Custody in Victorian England* (Oxford: Clarendon Press, 1991).

The Birth of the Penitentiary in Latin America:
Essays on Criminology, Prison Reform, and
Social Control, 1830–1940

# 1. The Birth of the Penitentiary in Latin America: Toward an Interpretive Social History of Prisons

*Ricardo D. Salvatore and Carlos Aguirre*

In Europe and North America, modern penitentiaries and reformatories added important dimensions to the project of modernity. The new prisons, in addition to their explicit goals of humanizing the treatment of inmates and providing more rational means of reformation, presented the possibility of changes in attitudes, sensibilities, and perceptions that were deemed necessary for the construction of modern market economies, republican governments, and stable and harmonic social relations. These changes extended far beyond the confines of the prison, where new technologies of punishment tried to instill capitalist work habits, honesty, and thrift among inmates, projecting onto the social and political body new policies, principles, and authorities. Whether we consider the prison as part of a gradual civilizing process, as the central element of a grid defining a carceral, disciplinary society, or as a self-improving institution that mimicked the goals of the industrial bourgeoisie, the effects of the prison on European and North American societies have been recognized as pervasive and long-lasting.

In Latin America, little is known about the process that gave birth to the penitentiary.[1] Available evidence (the compilation of fragmentary studies) suggests that this was a protracted process encompassing more than a century (1830–1940) and uneven in its evolution and nature. Clearly, the nature of the penitentiary project embodied in the Casa de Correção of Rio de Janeiro in the 1850s was quite different from that incorporated into the Penitenciaría Nacional of Buenos Aires in the 1910s. Hence, any attempt to understand the emergence of the penitentiary in Latin America must pay attention to questions of periodization and regional diversity. The reasons why some countries adopted the penitentiary project earlier than others are not always clear, constituting in fact one of the questions we attempt to explore in this essay.

The purpose of the penitentiary project, as it was conceived by different countries in the region between 1830 and 1940, seems to differ from the European and North American experience, adding difficulty to the task of understanding the experiences of prison reform in Latin America. In addition to their functions as loci of social control, penitentiaries in the region served various other purposes. New prisons acted as catalysts of a clinical, "scientific" view of social problems, provided the experimental grounds for the consolidation of the new sciences of crime and punishment (criminology and penology), and pioneered professional interventions that reshaped the relations between the state and the lower classes.

In the political terrain, the effect of the penitentiary was also significantly different. Rather than contributing to imagining a democratic polity (as in Europe and North America), the various efforts at prison reform in Latin America were predicated upon nondemocratic conceptions of the political order. Instead of a foundation for a new political order or the imaginary (*imaginaire*) that sustained that order, the penitentiary in Latin America served as either a symbol of modernity or as an instrument of social differentiation and control. Regarding the connection between the new disciplinary power and the construction of the social, the penitentiary project gave birth to a diversity of discourses about the lower classes (immigrant workers, blacks, indigenous peoples, mothers, and infants) that tried to interpret the challenges facing the emerging export economies of the region.

In part, this was the effect of quite different transformations affecting Latin American societies during this period: the consolidation of centralist nation-states, the rapid integration of their economies to the world market, the sudden changes in the composition of the working classes associated with mass immigration, regional displacements of population, and important changes in the social relations of production. To this extent, the discursive formation that supported the different movements toward prison reform can be considered as attempts to interpret Latin America's ambivalent economic, political, and social modernity.

This essay is an attempt to address these issues in a rather exploratory way. Given the scant attention these issues have received in Latin American scholarship (nothing compared to the richness and sophistication of the debates on criminal justice history in Europe and North America), this essay has very modest goals. It should be read as an initial effort at ordering information, contrasting the Latin American experience with that of other regions (where prisons and penitentiaries were actually invented), and proposing a number of hypotheses about the institutions of confinement, the recurrent efforts for their reform and modernization, and their connections with the broader Latin American societies.

First, we describe the development in North America and Europe of new technologies of punishment and locate in this context the uneven and ambivalent "adoption" of the penitentiary in Latin America. We then discuss the problem of the different timing of these "adoptions" and the shifting ideological and sociopolitical environments from which they emerged. Next, we examine the discursive formations that produced the enunciations that supported and conditioned the march of prison reform, differentiating a period of liberal constitutionalism (1830–1860) from a later period marked by the influence of positivist criminology (1880–1910). In this second period, we argue, discourses on prison reform served to construct and interpret different problems and projects related to building the nation-state, the integration of national economies to the world market, and the "social question."

## Approaching the History of the Penitentiary

The history of the penitentiary can be narrated in at least three alternative or complementary ways.[2] First, it can be regarded as a series of institutional innovations which coalesced in the formation of a specialized kind of knowledge ("penology"). In this sense, the emergence and diffusion of the house of correction, the cellular prison, the penal colony, the method of "congregated" work, the Irish system of classification, and the reformatory could be seen as stages in a "progressive" path toward more sophisticated and effective prisons. Thus, the penitentiary appears as a combination of techniques of control applied onto the prisoner's soul and body and as a set of blueprints generally developed abroad ready to be transferred, adopted, and improved. Second, the history of the penitentiary can be described as a genealogy of discourses and practices about crime and criminals that engendered—along with new disciplinary techniques—certain forms of authority, identity, and rationality characteristic of "modernity." In this second approach, the penitentiary is located at the intersection of modern ways of looking, classifying, isolating, and understanding the poor, the working class, the colonial subject, or the subordinate. Seen both as the manufacturing site of individuation, regimentation, and self-containment and as a clinic or laboratory for the understanding and treatment of "social problems," the penitentiary acts upon (that is, actualizes) a discursive formation containing enunciations about the "criminal class" and about the national, racial, or gender character of delinquency.[3] Third, this history can be seen as an account of the new technologies of discipline—its promises and its failures—as experienced by the prisoners themselves. In addition to the systems of rules, the architecture, the administration, the lessons, and the sermons within the penitentiary, the historian committed to this type of history must examine the secret communication and barter among prisoners and between them and their guards, their protest against rules and their enforcers, as well as their sufferings, frustrations, and silences. From this perspective, prisoners' experiences serve to illustrate the development of social classes, gender divisions, and racial tensions in society at large.[4]

Each alternative narrative strategy promises a different periodization and poses its own difficulties. We concentrate on the first two approaches and their interrelationship. The former, the "progressive" history of "innovations," provides us with a context and reference in which to locate the history of Latin America's adoption of new methods of punishment in relation to wider international practices. This was the perception of the Latin American "specialists" who traveled to Europe and the United States in search of the best available technology of punishment. Isolated from the historical context in which they emerged and from the sufferings they inflicted, these "innovations" appeared as additions to the stock of accumulated knowledge about the reformation of prisoners, as "improvements," and as "modernizations." The reformers' attempt to bring their countries up to the standards of the more industrialized nations necessarily replicated and naturalized the "progressive" history of penal institutions as conceived by European and North American experts.[5]

Our intention is not to measure the modernity or backwardness of Latin America in relation to Europe and the United States but rather to examine the question of why certain regimes and groups within the elite, at given conjunctures, found it necessary to modernize the methods of incarceration and the treatment of prisoners. This implies an examination of the rhetoric of reformers, the multiple forms through which they argued for the "innovations," the different references and authorities they invoked to assert their claims, and the ways in which the penitentiary was connected to imagined political and social communities. It is in this connection that we pursue the second approach: the genealogy of discourses about crime, punishment, and prison reform and the emergence of criminology. We are concerned with the local appropriation and uses of internationally circulated discourses about crime, punishment, and confinement. Aware of the similarities in the rhetoric and intent with which European, North American, and Latin American elites looked at, discredited, and criminalized their respective "lower classes," we want to understand the connections between "national" perceptions of prison reform and the set of contentious processes that characterized the region's history in the period under study (1830–1940): class formation, nation building, labor gendering, and racial/ethnic conflict.

In our view, the discursive articulation of international technologies of punishment to fit the needs of national or local debates about revolution, political reform, the "social question" posed by immigrants, or the nature of colonial peasantry was part of a process of interpreting and appropriating modernity. The Latin American experts who visited the prisons of Europe and the United States looking for innovations replicated in their reports the idiom of modernity in which the community of penologists cloaked the new methods. Determined to spread more humane and effective methods of rehabilitation, these experts, in their communications with government officials and the public in general, presented certain methods of imprisonment as the most modern, scientific, and efficient.

The relation between discourses of reform and the diffusion of the penitentiary model presents us with additional questions, for neither the "original" model nor its replicas in Latin America had the diffusion that penologists and prison administrators expected. Consequently, the discourse of reform included also a pessimistic strand: a set of propositions aimed at explaining the failure of reform which connected naturally with "explanations" concerning the "character" of the lower classes, the habits of ruling groups, or the nature of the political system. By exploring these "explanations" we can understand better the interpretive and symbolic benefits derived from a project—the penitentiary, the reformatory—that failed to fulfill its promises of humanizing punishment and disciplining prisoners.

Another intriguing dimension concerns the construction of a new form of power/knowledge. By the end of the nineteenth century a growing pool of prison managers and experts came to claim monopoly to a new kind of knowledge: a set of propositions about the efficacy of methods of confinement, isolation, religious instruction, agricultural work, and so forth disseminated through specialized journals as well as through national and international congresses. While Latin American reformers had the possibility of selecting among competing, practical methods of prison administration, penology, the new science of punishment, guided their choice in a certain direction. Similarly, visions of the "criminal class" were shaped by the new science, criminology, heavily influenced in the late nineteenth century by positivism. Thus, the search for and the adoption of modern technologies of punishment in the region were closely associated with new attitudes of elites and governments toward science.

## New Technologies of Punishment

In Europe and the United States, the period between American independence and the Franco-Prussian War produced momentous transformations in the organization and role of prisons. The most significant of these transformations was the conception of the penitentiary. The humanitarian campaigns conducted by Howard and other reformers of the late eighteenth century to turn prisons into clean, incorrupt, and healthful environments led to the development of institutional machines predicated upon the principle of reformation through solitude, silence, and regimentation.[6] Early penitentiaries (the one designed by Howard and Blackstone in 1779 or that planned by Eddy for New York State some years later) pointed to existing "houses of correction" as their closest antecedent.[7] But houses of correction (even those like the Maison de Force at Ghent, which used industrial work) lacked the main principle that distinguished early penitentiaries: correction through isolation. Cellular confinement, mandated in the English act of 1779 and implemented on American soil in the penitentiaries of Auburn, Sing-Sing, and Philadelphia, became the center of the new punitive approach. The cell was seen as a site of both repentance and segregation—the requirements of noncontamination and introspection basic to the reformatory project found a "solution" in a single architectural design.[8] Isolation, it was believed, could produce remorse, and this, when combined with the habit-forming power of work, could lead inmates to regeneration.

The panopticon (a central tower with radiating pavilions) imagined by Bentham added to the legitimacy of the project by promising surveillance at a minimum cost, but the cell was the imagined center for the "fabrication of virtue."[9] The debate during the period 1820 to 1840 between the two American systems (Auburn and Philadelphia) focused on variations of the same principle: isolation. In the former model inmates were isolated at night and worked "congregated" during the day. They were, in addition, forbidden to communicate (verbally or otherwise) with their fellow inmates while working, eating, or staying in their cells. The Philadelphia system, on the other hand, isolated each prisoner through permanent cellular confinement. The prisoner was supposed to eat, work, and sleep alone, and, of course, any contact with other prisoners was entirely prohibited. As David Rothman argues, however, the two models presented more similarities than differences. Given that the two systems actually strove to avoid any communication among the prisoners, the actual difference centered on "whether convicts should work silently in large groups or individually within solitary cells."[10] Across the Atlantic, the masks and the cellular oratory of Pentonville (1843) reflected the same assumptions and beliefs underlying the banning of conversations among inmates at Auburn and other American penitentiaries.[11]

Other innovations were later added to this model. The "progressive system of classification" developed out of England's colonial experiences in South Africa, Ireland, and Australia was disseminated all over the world.[12] Inmates had to pass through a period of solitary confinement before they could enter a second period of rules learning; this, in turn, was the prerequisite for other stages leading toward increasing privileges and, ultimately, freedom. By the middle of the nineteenth century penologists had begun to consider group work, lectures on morality, and elementary instruction as necessary complements to solitary confinement, a recognition that reformation required the active and willing involvement of inmates. The constant criticism of "outside" reformers together with the experiments of prison administrators converged toward the combined use of techniques of punishment and "moral suasion," giving concretion to the "reformatory ideal."[13] All these innovations moved penitentiary discipline from its earlier emphasis on isolation and work toward a more complex regime that facilitated individualized treatment.

In this process, the 1870 Cincinnati Conference marked a point of synthesis. Organized by Enoch Wines and Zebulon Brockway, it asserted the predictability of criminal behavior and the renewed belief in reformation through appropriate techniques. More important, it acknowledged the consensus among American reformers about the best available system: the Elmira Reformatory was now the model, representing a combination of proven techniques and the synthesis of long debates and arguments.[14] The Elmira Reformatory used common industrial work, cellular isolation, the Irish classificatory system, individual follow-up and treatment, economic rewards for good conduct, advisory councils recommending parole or probation, professional wardens, and religious and elementary education. With evangelical zeal American reformers tried to spread this model internationally as the finest achievement of the science of punishment.

This technological package preceded the advent of positivist criminology by over a decade. By the time the works of Lombroso, Ferri, and Garofalo had initiated a crusade against classical penology, rallying for individualized treatment, rehabilitation instead of punishment, and clinical detection of dangerous elements, penologists had already developed the techniques of institutional control which could make this theory work.[15] Ironically, the new criminology served to discredit the exaggerated optimism of prison reformers, presenting new categories of criminals that were immune to treatment. Lombroso's notion of an inborn or atavistic criminal and the more sociologically oriented theories of Ferri and Tarde put in doubt the ability of the penitentiary to reform delinquents.[16]

Optimism in the penitentiary revived in the 1890s and 1900s, when psychological/psychiatric knowledge began to challenge the simpler versions of crime and criminals proposed by "criminal anthropology" and medical expertise was given a new tutelage over the reformatory process.[17] This time, the penitentiary project, no longer captive to the project of moral reform, became part of a larger design of interventions— a more complex medico-legal-police machine involving the assessment, classification, and differentiation of potential delinquents. In its new incarnation, the penitentiary had to operate within a network of institutions specializing in the diagnosis, prevention, and treatment of crime (mental asylums, child reformatories, agricultural colonies, police systems of identification, criminological research institutes, and social welfare initiatives that targeted ex-convicts). As a clinic and social laboratory, the penitentiary extended its functions to a hitherto unknown terrain: the validation of new forms of authority, the classification of the lower classes, and the production of knowledge about "deviance."

Unlike the early penitentiaries, whose impulse derived from religious and philanthropic movements and Enlightenment ideas, the efforts to reform penitentiaries in the period 1890 to 1920 derived strength from a new scientific discipline: criminology. The new theories of "social defense" not only destabilized classical conceptions of crime and criminals, but they also created new instances for expert intervention and police surveillance in the lives of the poor.[18] The massive collection of criminal statistics and the introduction of dactyloscopy for identification purposes were part of these developments. These innovations anticipated important changes in the relations between the lower classes and the state. Not surprisingly, penitentiary reform in the early twentieth century became associated with the normalizing powers of the incipient welfare state—what David Garland calls the "penalwelfare" complex.[19] The attempt to integrate a cohesive and organized working class under the wings of the state, the efforts to guide the socialization of children in a direction compatible with a stable national community, and the classificatory/investigative enterprise conducted within the penitentiary became part of a common project aimed at normalizing, segregating, and correcting the subordinate.[20] As a technology of punishment, the penitentiary did not change much between the 1830s and the 1930s (a few gears were added to the machinery); what changed were the perceptions that structured the reception of this disciplinary technology: from religion to science, from the laissez-faire state to the welfare state, from a generalized class prejudice to a taxonomical, hierarchically ordered, and racial view of the "dangerous classes."

## Latin America and Its Penitentiaries

The introduction of European and North American penitentiary models into Latin America was an uneven and protracted process. The process of "adoption" of the new regime proceeded through short spurts of enthusiasm and activism, usually followed by periods of pessimism and indifference. Over a century elapsed between the time Brazil (1834) and Chile (1843) made their first plans for building penitentiaries and the time latecomers like Colombia (1934) and Cuba (1939) decided to take the path of reform.[21] Over this prolonged period the nature of these "innovations" certainly changed, as did the supporting ideas and conceptions which reformers used to justify their adoption.

Brazil, one of the early adopters of the penitentiary, went through a typical process of enthusiasm, disbelief, and renewed interest. Two periods of political renovation, the Regency and the Republic, brought about flashes of modernization, if not in the carceral institutions, at least in the rhetoric about the need to improve prisons. In the early 1830s reformers trying to adapt prison facilities to the new legal system (penal and civil codes, trial by jury, locally elected justices) embraced Bentham's panopticon as the model to be followed.[22] Between 1834 and 1850 the government built the Casa de Correção in Rio de Janeiro, while other states (Bahia, Goiás, Minas Gerais) rushed to initiate the construction of similar facilities. Soon, however, the impulse lost momentum and pessimism set in. Lacking funds, the states used the so-called penitentiaries for multiple purposes, including the "correction" of unruly slaves. The Casa de Correção, conceived as the pioneer of the reformatory project, turned into a house of disease and death.[23] Reports drafted in 1879 and 1890 presented the Brazilian prison system as "primitive" and unreformed; in the eyes of prison administrators, little had been achieved since the 1850s.[24] Mounting criticism during the last two decades of the century led to some improvement in the prisons of Fernando de Noronha, Rio de Janeiro, Bahia, and Recife, but a general consensus prevailed among administrators about the inability of existing prisons to reform delinquents.

Renewed interest in the modernization of prisons came with the enactment of a new criminal code in 1890 which mandated the introduction of the Irish "progressive system" of classification and with the spread of positivist criminology in the 1890s and 1900s.[25] Based on the pioneer work of physician Almeida Valle in Rio, new cadres of reformers sprouted in Bahia, Recife, and São Paulo, initiating a drive toward the "medicalization" of the treatment of inmates. The penitentiary of São Paulo, built at the end of the nineteenth century, underwent a significant transformation after 1914 (its new name, Instituto de Regeneração, was a good reflection of its managers' intentions). Its vast silent pavilions, its school, its active workshops, its anthropometrical institute, its gymnastic exercises, and its internal regime geared to individualized treatment all made this giant three-pronged panopticon both the envy and pride of Latin American prison reformers.[26]

Chile was another pioneer in penal reform in Latin America. Santiago's penitentiary, built between 1844 and 1849, closely followed the Philadelphia model. In fact, its architectural design was a replica of the latter, with its octagonal form and seven rays radiating from a central tower. The triangular spaces between the rays were used for workshops, the hospital, and other facilities.[27] Its internal regime borrowed heavily from the Cherry Hill facility: silence and cellular isolation were thought to be the keys to the reformation of the inmates. While blaming the past Portalian regime for its harsh and arbitrary treatment of prisoners, Chilean liberals (among them Benjamín Vicuña Mackenna) thought of the penitentiary regime not as a modern, rule-guided institution for behavioral control but as a site of repentance and spiritual conversion.[28] Religious metaphors pervaded the discourse of reformers about the purpose and methods of the penitentiary. In practice, the penitentiary of Santiago fell short of its promises. Overcrowding, limited budgets, and inadequate separation among inmates severely incapacitated the institution, preventing it from fulfilling its mandate.[29]

The reformatory impulse in Chile extended to a few other facilities and localities. In 1864, the restructured Casa Correccional de Mujeres (Women's Correctional House) was inaugurated and put under the administration of the Congregation of the Good Shepherd.[30] Two years later, the new penitentiary at Talca began construction. The penal colony on the island of Juan Fernández, viewed as the most salient example of the corruption and brutality of the ancient regime, ceased to receive prisoners in 1852 and gradually turned into an agricultural colony.[31]

Peru can also be considered a case of early adoption of the penitentiary project. Mariano Felipe Paz Soldán, commissioned by President José Rufino Echenique to visit penitentiaries in the United States, wrote at his return (1853) an extensive report recommending the adoption of the Auburn system. Like Howard in England, Paz Soldán's personal crusade was motivated by the horror and demoralization that existing prisons and jails produced in inmates.[32] The new penitentiary was completed in 1862. Built from blueprints copied from the most modern North American penitentiaries, the *panóptico* of Lima was considered a model for its time.[33] But, as Aguirre argues in this volume, the idea of reforming criminals through confinement, work, and moral sermons was not really embraced by the authorities nor shared by the ruling groups, turning the whole project into a failure.[34] Soon, overcrowding and scarce budgets led to inadequate clothing of inmates, disease, and mutinies. Administrators, feeling powerless to control the prisoners, obtained a few years later the legal restoration of corporal punishment.

Mounting criticism of old prisons and jails in Ecuador during the regime of Gabriel García Moreno (1860–1875) led to the construction of the Penitenciaría de Quito, a project completed in 1874. Also a *panóptico*, its design combined modernity with terror. Its walls were painted black so that inmates would live in the shadows; its rules severely punished any violation of silence. Repetitive work performed during a large part of the day aimed only at the creation of habit, not at the production of useful goods or services.[35] In 1893, a progressive system similar to the one created by Crofton was introduced. Still, the regime within the penitentiary did not facilitate the individualization of treatment: the *panóptico* housed unruly minors and servants sent by their parents and masters as well as common delinquents.[36] Conditions did not improve during the liberal regime (1895–1910). A reform of the penal code in 1906 allowed deportation as punishment and ordered the creation of agricultural colonies in the Colón archipelago, which became a reality in the 1920s.[37]

In 1877 the Penitenciaría de Buenos Aires was inaugurated. This facility, with a layout similar to that of Pentonville and an internal regime resembling that of Auburn, was to become a model in South America. It was double the size of the Lima panopticon and triple the size of the Santiago penitentiary. It was considered a symbol of the province's progress along with the new railroads, port facilities, banks, waterworks, and other public works (its blueprints together with the handicrafts produced by its inmates were sent to the Paris Exposition of 1878).[38] Inside the penitentiary, on the other hand, changes came more gradually. Managed by military personnel and with scant resources, the penitentiary remained for over two decades a mixed facility housing sentenced and unsentenced prisoners, men as well as women, and minors. To the public, the penitentiary was a place of penance rather than a site for reformation.[39]

It was the positivist reformer J. A. Ballvé who brought the institution up to the standards of the penitentiary ideal in the period 1904 to 1914. During this time, workshops and a school were organized, a *reglamento* more attuned to the principle of individual treatment was passed, and the new Instituto de Criminología was created.[40] José Ingenieros, the leading criminologist of his time, gave so much international exposure to the work of the Buenos Aires penitentiary that the building became an attraction to foreign "progressive" visitors. The example of the Penitenciaría (now called "Nacional" in accordance with the new political status of Buenos Aires) was not readily followed by other facilities. The Correccional de Mujeres (Women's Correctional), managed by nuns and upper-class women, remained beyond the reach of positivist reformers.[41] Under the rigors of cold weather, privation, and hard labor, the Penal de Tierra del Fuego served as a place of retention—hardly a site for the reformation—of dangerous criminals and political offenders.[42] With the exception of the Penitenciaría de Córdoba, undergoing modernization, provincial *cárceles* remained "places of pain . . . sites of unhealthy fermentations. Overcrowding, promiscuity, and the lack of hygiene, work, discipline, instruction, and organization [were] their common characteristics."[43] By the end of the 1920s positivists could only boast as their accomplishment (besides the Penitenciaría Nacional de Buenos Aires) the reformatory and agricultural colony of Marcos Paz.[44]

We know less about the Uruguayan path to penitentiary reform. Criticism of existing jails and prisons had increased by the late nineteenth century as part of a broader process of change in "sensibilities" that included the rejection of corporal punishment.[45] In 1879 the minister of government ordered that inmates should be treated "with all the consideration and equality they deserve," for prisons were not places for the "mortification of the delinquent." In November 1882 the commission for the elaboration of a new penal code presented a report on contemporary penitentiary systems. On the commission's recommendation, the Congress passed a new penal code in 1889, adopting the "mixed" (Philadelphia-Auburn) system. Particularly important were the emphasis on obligatory work, the establishment of the gradual system, and the use of a combination of rewards and penalties in the reformation process. In 1912 cellular individual reclusion was abolished. Penitentiary reform gathered momentum along with mounting criticism against the death penalty, which was abolished in 1907. Explanations regarding criminal behavior also gradually changed. As in Argentina and Brazil, medical metaphors replaced explanations based on individual responsibility.[46]

Mexico reached consensus on the need for a penitentiary system as early as 1848, but its prisons remained largely unreformed until the Porfiriato.[47] Despite the liberals' insistence on the necessity for modern penitentiaries, little could be done before the wars of the reform ended and the national state consolidated its finances.[48] By 1879, the prison of Belén in Mexico City represented what reformers despised most about the ancient prison system: men, women, and children shared the same facilities (common halls with humid walls and scarce sunlight), and some inmates worked voluntarily in ruinous workshops while others taught themselves in an improvised Lancasterian school. The prison provided socialization and entertainment rather than correction.[49] It was the Díaz administration, with its emphasis on "order and progress" and its organic intellectuals, the positivist *científicos*, that furnished the impetus to reform. The new penitentiary of the Distrito Federal began construction in 1885 and was inaugurated in 1900; in 1902 the prison of Belén was modernized and assigned only to those awaiting trial; in 1905 the government bought the Marías Islands with the intention of establishing a penal colony; and by 1907 the new correctional for women was completed. Other states soon joined the effort, and penitentiaries were built in Guadalajara, Guanajuato, and Puebla.[50] The abolition of the death penalty, a liberal promise that was captive to the building of penitentiary facilities, could then be effected.

Venezuelan prisons showed little change from the colonial period to the late 1930s and early 1940s. During the administration of modernizer Antonio Guzmán Blanco (1870–1887), a crafts school was introduced to the *presidio* of San Carlos and a decree was enacted in 1876 that mandated the construction of three regional penitentiaries (at San Carlos, Puerto Cabello, and Santiago).[51] For a long time, Guzmán Blanco's initiatives existed only on paper. In 1881 a report indicated that no penitentiary worthy of the name existed in the country. An 1896 law completed this paper reform: the act advocated the principle of regeneration, created a system of criminological files, and instituted oratories, infirmaries, and workshops in each penitentiary.[52] No institution, however, corresponded to this ideal. During the dictatorship of Juan Vicente Gómez (1908–1935), the reformatory project was relegated to a less-important position as the old prisons became depositories for political prisoners. As various memoirs of incarcerated politicians make clear, old prisons (the Castillo at Puerto Cabello, the infamous Rotunda at Caracas, the Castillo at Maracaibo) served well the dictator's political goals: they were places of death and torture where exorcising the sin of political dissent was more important than reforming delinquents.[53] In fact, common delinquents, politicians argued, did not deserve to be in prison: the prison must be the privilege of the literate and articulate.[54] The model penitentiary of Caracas was built after the fall of Gómez, during a short period of "democracy." Its construction seemed to be the realization of the old ideal of reformation adopted by the modernizing state in the 1870s.

Colombia was another latecomer: only in 1934 did it join the party of penitentiary reformers. Decree 1405 of that year established the basis of the new system: confinement for the purpose of moral regeneration, compulsory work as the best instrument of correction, and treatment according to the scientific study of each inmate. A Department of Prisons was formed to control an impressive carceral network—nine penitentiaries, eighteen *cárceles*, two agricultural colonies, and numerous local jails—as part of a system of social defense similar to that proposed by Ingenieros in Argentina. Before the end of the decade, new buildings were erected (the penitentiaries at Picota and Palmira, the agricultural colony at Acacias) and existing facilities were modernized, in particular the Penitenciaría Central and the Reformatorio de Menores at Bogotá. Francisco Bruno pioneered these reforms at the Central Penitentiary. In addition to farming plots, he established "industrial" workshops and provided the penitentiary with a school, a hospital, modern kitchens, a disciplinary council, and a research facility (the Instituto de Antropología y Pedagogía Penitenciaria).[55]

In Cuba, both criticism of the old carceral system and calls for building new penitentiaries and reformatories escalated by the turn of the century.[56] Years later, following Governor Alfredo Zayas Bazán's efforts to modernize existing prisons, an impressive Presidio Modelo (Model Prison) was inaugurated in 1926 on the island that for years had served for the banishment of common delinquents and political opponents: Isla de Pinos.[57] The Presidio, a massive *panóptico* made of five circular buildings and heralded as the symbol of Cuba's modernity, promised to regenerate delinquents through individual treatment, work, and study. The project encompassed both industrial and agricultural labor and a criminal laboratory or clinic, following the model of similar institutions in Buenos Aires and São Paulo.[58] The creation of this laboratory resulted from the efforts of the renowned Cuban criminologist Israel Castellanos, another key figure in the country's penal reform.[59] In actuality, the penitentiary served to hold political opponents of the regime of Gerardo Machado—the students and workers who participated in the 1933 revolution knew this emblem of modernity quite well. In 1938 the new government tried to improve the image of the penitentiary, appointing a council of social defense formed by university professors, judges, and representatives of benevolent organizations.[60]

We know comparatively less about the adoption of penitentiaries in other republics of Central America and the Caribbean. Before 1879 Guatemalan rulers did not feel the need for a penitentiary as numerous local prisons seemed to keep the indigenous peasantry quiet.[61] Hygiene, religious instruction, handicraft work, and military rigor seemed to be sufficient for the purposes of social control. Costa Rica, exceptional in many regards, showed also a surprising modernity in its policy of crime control. In the 1870s and 1880s the government built a system of confinement and regeneration centered around two agricultural penal colonies (San Lucas and Coco). After 1890, government emphasis shifted toward control of the new urban working class. Between 1902 and 1909 the San José penitentiary was erected, showing all the amenities of similar institutions in Europe and the United States.[62] Puerto Rico, due to the persistence of a colonial relationship with Spain during the nineteenth century, failed to adopt the penitentiary as a central institution of reform. The Spanish administration used penal colonies and forced labor as a means of terrorizing a too independent and "indolent" peasantry.[63] Only after 1933 did Puerto Rico inaugurate the Penitenciaría Insular at Río Piedras.

These differences in the timing of the adoption of the penitentiary system posit interesting questions concerning the motivations, the context, and the meaning of the reforms. Early adopters like Chile and Brazil had to choose between European houses of correction, Bentham's panopticon, or the more rigid American models of the 1820s. For them, a belief in the reformatory powers of solitary confinement and work was all that was required. The adoption was, to a certain extent, independent from the cultivation of a particular discipline or of a "scientific" way of perceiving the criminal problem. For those joining penitentiary reform during the period 1890 to 1910 (Argentina, Mexico, and again Brazil), on the other hand, positivist criminology influenced definitively their views and decisions. The language of criminology served to renew the criticism of old prisons and to accelerate the path of penitentiary reform, but, at the same time, it posed new problems of interpretation and debate. The penitentiary became part of a wide spectrum of state disciplinary and preemptive interventions against the poor, policies that were supported by "scientific" portrayals of the "criminal class." Late adopters of the twentieth century (Colombia, Cuba) must have had other motivations in mind. By that time, positivism had begun to lose ground, and the reformatory ideal gave way to the more active and skeptical penal policy. Having failed to fulfill its promises to constrain within limits the "social question" (as the revolutions of the 1930s in Colombia and Cuba made clear), the penitentiary lost its privileged position in the elite's imaginary of social control.

The reformers' dissatisfaction with the results is perhaps one of the common elements among these otherwise dissimilar reform efforts. Once introduced, the penitentiary failed to produce the expected results, or, more frequently, the new disciplinary technique was not replicated in the rest of the prison system. Various penitentiaries initially heralded as symbols of progress became over time the center of criticism by the next cadre of reformers.[64] Various factors could explain these shortcomings. Scarce revenues and traditional legislation presented important obstacles to the introduction of the new disciplinary methods. Implementing individualized treatment, prolonged confinement, and the "grading system" required significant modification of the existing criminal codes. Early efforts in penal codification, inspired by classical penology, carried their own inertia into the courts and national assemblies.[65] Building and maintaining penitentiaries was also a costly endeavor which strained the limited fiscal resources of the new republics.[66] Brazil's commitment to the Crofton system in 1890 remained a paper reform until sufficient cells could be built inside the penitentiaries to implement the first stage of isolation.

But perhaps the greatest hurdle to the spread of penitentiary reform—and above all, to its successful implementation—was prevailing patterns of social control and discourses that justified traditional ways of interaction between classes, sexes, and races. Slavery, peonage, domestic servitude, and other forms of personal dependence still informed the pattern of social relations in most parts of Latin America by the time penitentiary reforms were enacted. Accustomed to the use of corporal punishment and arbitrary arrest, slaveholders, *hacendados*, functionaries, and the military did not actually welcome penitentiary reform. The modernization of punishment tended to delegitimize private forms of justice, threatening the landowners' and the military's social and political position.

A *relatório* signed by Judge Albino José Barbosa de Oliveira in 1847, for instance, blamed slavocracy for the slow pace of prison reform in Bahia, a situation that was no different from that found in the American South. Slaveholders' belief in private correction on plantations was shared by the local police, who customarily rounded up abandoned children and sent them to *fazendas* (plantations) in the interior.[67] Further skepticism about prison reform stemmed from the use by Brazilian authorities of forced enlistment in the army as a way of punishing criminals and instilling fear in the lower classes.[68] Similarly, the reforms pioneered by Paz Soldán in Lima found skepticism and disbelief among coastal landowners and urban proprietors. A punitive structure inherited from colonial times proved enduring. The death penalty survived several attempts at abolition, whipping remained the preferred "corrective" tool in dealing with servants, and cruel and swift punishment was perceived as the only way of preventing lower-class insubordination.[69] Mexico's debate about the convenience of retaining or abolishing capital punishment during the Porfiriato speaks of the widespread belief among the elite in the deterrent power of executions on a people "naturally violent." Disillusionment with the penitentiary revived the "need" for capital punishment to discipline the lower classes.[70] In Puerto Rico, a discourse that portrayed independent peasants as idle and vicious served to justify the continued practices of arbitrary arrest and penal servitude.[71] In Argentina, the military kept corporal punishment as a form of disciplining soldiers long after the inauguration of the country's model penitentiary.

Ultimately, it was the very character of Latin American modernity which explained both the adoption and the failure of the reform and the hope and disillusionment of the elites. Imitation of foreign models and the importation of positivist ideas accompanied the strengthening or refashioning of ancient forms of personal dependence, not their elimination. The new theories embodied into the reformatory model added a modern "punitive city" to the existing repertoire, but it did not displace private justice and brutal and inhumane punishment.

## Competing Discourses about the Social

The work of Michel Foucault suggests a different way of ordering the history of punishment. Rather than narrating the adoption and implementation of reforms, he sees three distinct discursive formations that center around the question of punishment: the monarchical mode (the scaffold, punishment as a ceremonial of sovereignty); the enlightened mode (gentle punishment to restore the legitimacy of the law); and the institutional mode (training of bodies into obedience to rules). The penitentiary was located at the intersection of the latter two discursive practices. It emerged in Europe and North America as a critique of brutal punishment and the scaffold and also as the legitimating force of classical, utilitarian penology and its legal pedagogy.[72] The technology of controlling bodies and minds through confinement, solitude, and work developed at a crossroads with the doctrine that privileged many theaters of punishment (prisoners working at public roads) for the education of the common citizen.[73]

Prison discipline was thus a collection of principles about human nature, authority, and criminal behavior as well as certain techniques of power in an institutional context. These principles and techniques (isolation, work, individualized treatment, degree of dangerousness as a classificatory criterion, and separate penal power) can be found in the practice of the Elmira Reformatory and in the theories of positivist criminology of the late nineteenth century. What Foucault calls the "carceral" is nothing but the projection of the reformatory ideal into a system or grid[74] whose final function was to construct delinquency, to make acceptable the existence of a "criminal class," and to naturalize state interventions geared to differentiate "dangerous" elements among the working class. The penitentiary, in this view, constructed delinquency at the same time that it tried to reform delinquents.

Applying this particular approach to the history of Latin American penitentiaries is at the same time illuminating and problematic. It is problematic because with such a broad characterization of punitive discourses we run the risk of collapsing into a single construct practices and ideas that belong, in time and nature, to different pigeonholes. The Benthamite ordering of society according to utility and the liberal constitutionalism of the early independent leaders cannot be easily appended to the imaginaries developed under the aegis of positivist criminology. They arrived at the region at different periods and served to produce distinct discourses about the social, despite the fact that they served to justify the same corrective principle, the penitentiary. In fact, it could be argued that the erosion of the ideals of egalitarianism and social democracy in the period from 1830 to 1850 facilitated constructions of the lower classes as "barbarians" in need of retributive punishment—classical penology served here to feed a less humane and enlightened social imaginary. Similarly, the advent of positivism in a context of abolition, republican government, and immigrant labor (1880–1914) gave way to conceptions of the "criminal class" that betrayed in part the reformatory project: certain races, political agents, and social types remained unreformable.

The spread of modern conceptions about crime and criminals throughout the region merits, then, a different periodization. In Latin America, the new punitive models were predicated upon a multiplicity of arguments which not only departed from European and North American debates but whose nature changed significantly over time. The adoption of European constitutionalism and codification in the postindependence period and the diffusion of positivist criminology in the last decades of the nineteenth century appear as important landmarks in our periodization. If the fear of popular protest or social disorder was constitutive of discourses favoring prison reform, this phenomenon was more typical of the era of European immigration, foreign capital, and positivism than of the postindependence period. In Latin America the disorganization and social havoc created by the wars of independence did not produce a reformist ethos similar to that experienced by urban societies of the U.S. Northeast.[75] It is quite difficult to imagine the pioneer reforms of Brazil and Chile emerging from the threat of social disorder (something similar to what Ignatieff calls the "ideological origins" of the penitentiary). Before 1850 enunciations about penal reform appear almost invariably as gestures of governmental power and of the assumed modernity of the ruling group.

In Latin America the age of humanitarian critique of existing prisons and the utilitarian designs for rationalizing punishment according to an all-embracing penal code passed by without leaving enduring institutional traces. The idea of a social, egalitarian, and moralist state embodied in Bentham's panopticon was certainly adopted by postrevolutionary leaders (Santander, Rivadavia, Del Valle) but very rarely produced movements for the amelioration of prisons similar to those experienced in Paris, London, and New York. Indeed, Latin Americans were more impressed by Bentham's comprehensive code than by his panopticon.[76] Even more influential than Bentham were writers like Benjamin Constant, whose constitutionalism could be traced in the writings of many of the region's liberal reformers.[77] The pursuit of a system of law that could guarantee individual liberties was, however, independent of the choice of a punitive technology. Each of them applied to different parts of the social body: liberties were to be granted to landowners, politicians, intellectuals, professionals, and merchants while punishment served to control the excesses of the "barbarian" rural masses.

Postindependence Latin American countries, immersed in intestinal struggles over power and in dramatic accommodations of their economies to the world market, were an unfertile terrain for imaginaries of total institutional control. Ideological affinity, the exploits of pillage, slavery, and press-gangs served as chief mechanisms to mobilize labor power to war in organizations that could be best described as unregimented and premodern.[78] Moreover, the disillusionment of different ruling groups with the first egalitarian and democratic experiments made them accept less-democratic solutions to the social and political order: *caudillismo*, *coronelismo*, private punishment of slaves, coercive recruitment into armies and militias, and vagrancy laws.[79]

The restoration of a system of law after the upheavals of independence demanded the consolidation of old forms of punishment, not so much its criticism. Significantly, the Brazilian empire, the Portales republic in Chile, and the Rosas autocracy in Argentina tried to rebuild the "rule of law" with the use of old ways of punishment. Whipping, the stake, public works, and deportation were inscribed into the codes of the new republics as legitimate ways of disciplining the rebellious, disordered, and often self-marginalized "lower orders." Exemplary executions, without the riotous environment of Tyburn, were common to all three "strong" states, as well as to other "weaker" states such as Peru. Consequently, instead of the critique of old colonial prisons (now serving for the detention of prisoners of war and political offenders), new concerns developed about the safety and efficiency of the primitive detention facilities available. Efficient containment when not banishment of "dangerous" elements replaced the European and North American concern for reformation. Escape of the detainee was the most important prison-related problem reported by justice officials in Argentina and Brazil, two countries experimenting with systems of justice which extended the arm of the state deep into rural and urban landscapes.

With the ascent of a liberal-conservative state after the middle of the nineteenth century, some Latin American countries opted for punitive solutions that were at the same time old and new. Their conception of the retributive nature, publicity, and diversity of punitive sanctions was proper to classical penal policy (they preferred the stake to the prison, execution or banishment to redemptive work), but the principle of proportionality between offense and penalty was rarely applied. Two basic assumptions guided this common approach to the disciplining of the social body: the deterrent effect over potential criminals of visible state violence (public executions and torture) and the unreformable character of the rural masses. Within this discursive field, the modernization of punishment appeared as a necessary sign of "civilization" quite independent from the state of development of each country and, in fact, independent from the belief in the reformatory principle. The separation of women, juveniles, habitual delinquents, and lunatics, a major concern among European and North American prison reformers, was less pressing in the new Latin American states. The overwhelming concern was to maintain class and social difference, the separation between master and slave, white and colored, "civilized" and "barbarian," all within a social compost that was already too egalitarian and too mixed. As the *povo baixo* (lower classes), *gentes de color* (colored people), and Indian peasantry were considered idle, ignorant, and vicious, separating the honest citizen from the criminal element made little sense.

The idea of individual reformation through solitude and introspection had already been well tested in Catholic convents. Similarly, the Jesuit missions had made a valuable contribution to the practice of disciplining bodies and spirits with the help of common work, music, and language instruction. But this knowledge was rather dispensable for the new states, now maintaining unstable and often conflictive relations with the Catholic Church. The triumph of secular state power—most notably in the case of Mexico after the War of Reform—ushered in attempts to "pacify" the countryside by means of a rural police rather than by the construction of penitentiaries.[80] It is clear, then, that the progress of penitentiary reform—after the pioneer efforts failed—necessitated a prior reconstruction of the ways of seeing the lower classes and imagining the social and political order. The penitentiary's future rested upon the construction of a reformable criminal class, the Herculean task of the new European discipline: criminology.

Whereas earlier prison reforms came unsupported by any scientific doctrine, prison reformers of the late nineteenth century had at their disposal a powerful instrument, the scientific or positive approach to the study of delinquency. The works of Lombroso, Garofalo, and Ferri were rapidly absorbed by the intellectuals, who formed the first associations for the study of "criminal anthropology" in the 1880s (we find these associations in Mexico, Brazil, Argentina, and Peru). From specialized journals, university lectures and theses, and government positions, positivists began to spread the principles of the Italian School: penalties aimed at reformation, not retribution; individual states of "perilousness" being determined by biological and environmental factors; the society's right to separate "dangerous" elements for its own defense and also its duty to reform them; different penalties according to the inmate's progress toward reformation; and so on. Though few of these principles went into law, in many cases positivists were able to influence official circles in the direction of penitentiary reform. The penitentiary could serve as a catalyst to positivist penal policies and also as a laboratory to further study criminal behavior. It was due to this positivist impulse that new ways of looking at and reporting crime became available to policymakers: statistical tables of arrests and sentences, personal identification procedures, clinical reports of inmates, and other novel sources of "evidence." With greater haste than wisdom, positivist criminologists contributed this "evidence" to ongoing discussions about the alleged rising criminality of each country of the region.

Positivist criminology impinged upon the Latin American imagination with stronger force than it ever did in Europe, but its contents were immediately translated, modified, and adapted to account for the region's diverse social problems. Some readers of Lombroso, Ferri, and Garofalo fully appropriated their masters' insights (Dellepiane and Veyga in Argentina, Nina Rodrigues in Brazil, Guerrero in Mexico), while others challenged the premises of crime as a biologically plus environmentally determined phenomenon. These critical readers (José Ingenieros in Argentina, Justo Sierra and Carlos Roumagnac in Mexico, and Tobias Barreto and Afrânio Peixoto in Brazil) worked to displace the doctrines of the Italian School toward a more psychological and cultural dimension.[81] In this "medical" incarnation, criminology turned the penitentiary into a clinic or laboratory, inmates into patients, and the working poor into the endangered population of a disease called crime. As Lombroso's notion of atavism presented few possibilities for national variation (except of course for those who privileged racial explanations), other notions of dangerousness were considered more useful.

As Leopoldo Zea has argued, positivism served to support quite an array of political and social programs in the region, from the defense of autocracy to the support of individual liberties, from the defense of *indigenismo* to the construction of theories about the racial inferiority of mestizos.[82] Similarly, the ideas of the Italian School suffered substantial modifications as they were used to explain local conditions. Living in a society obsessed with intemperance, Mexican positivists presented the problems of alcoholism and violence as central to their nation's criminality. Peasants in arms drinking pulque and beer and easily aroused and led to violence by a *machista* sense of honor constituted the object of study and of reform.[83] Not surprisingly, the birth of the penitentiary took place in the midst of a debate about the convenience of abolishing capital punishment—could the total institution replace the death penalty in a country prone to violence? Brazilian positivists, on the other hand, presented the question of race as central to the understanding of Brazil's criminality. The abolition of slavery, the expansion of the white frontier at the expense of Indian ways of life, and the millenarian revolts of the *sertão* created the need to look at Brazil's "criminal class" as the historical result of miscegenation and obsolete social institutions. Reformers had to try to integrate this racial compost into the new republican road to progress and, at the same time, distinguish and isolate those who could not be integrated. Later on, the arrival of new collectivities (immigrants and their radical political expressions) shifted reformers' attention to the urban "mass" and the problems of modern social protest.

In Buenos Aires at the turn of the century, the new science, aided by new developments in legal medicine and social hygiene, tended to "medicalize" the criminal problem, leading to the construction of a "criminal class" (*mala vida*) made up of professional delinquents— usually dropouts from the labor market or the victims of orphanages and "bad companions." This in turn engendered comprehensive plans of social defense which included quite modern techniques of surveillance, individuation, and the isolation of agitators, the morally weak, and the unindustrious.[84] In Costa Rica, Steven Palmer tells us, criminology also served to construct a modern view of the urban working class with an emphasis on fostering abandoned children, educating inmates, and selecting problem makers among San José's artisan working class.[85] In Peru, "scientific" criminology put great emphasis on the study of Indian criminality, searching for the "innate" and "environmental" causes of crime. Criminologists—including well-intentioned *indigenistas*—portrayed Indians as degenerate people in need of education and "civilization" as a prerequisite for their full acceptance as citizens of the Peruvian nation.[86]

## Building the Nation-State

Changes in the forms of organizing and perceiving the political system should also be part of the history of the penitentiary. The French revolution meant the fall of the Bastille in more than its literary sense: it anticipated a mode of government whose authority to punish was encoded in law and whose treatment of bodies and souls had to comply with the prescriptions of "humanity." No longer the territory of regal arbitrariness, the hidden space within the prisons' walls was to be subjected to public scrutiny. Similarly, the building of a republican government in the United States coincided with the emergence of a reformist ethos resting on the "institutional hypothesis" (the idea that institutions like asylums, penitentiaries, and houses of refuge could manage growing social problems). As Thomas Dumm has argued, the penitentiary idea developed with the new republic. "The penitentiary became a primary institution through which a new set of techniques of pedagogy developed. These techniques, by which the action of citizens might be assessed, managed, and controlled, became an integral part of creating a constitutional republic."[87] The new political order demanded "republican machines," institutions which could produce self-governing individuals as well as principles of authority legitimating republican rule. The penitentiary and the asylum were such institutions: they embodied new techniques of power geared to the production of a "moral community" made up of abstinent, obedient, honest, and industrious citizens.

In England, too, the consolidation of the penitentiary ideal paralleled the struggles for the extension of political and civil rights. Not only were Howard's followers deeply committed to the cause of parliamentary reform, they also saw a necessary connection between the extension of rights and the increased regimentation within the penitentiary. A more democratic political order could no longer consent to the paternalistic laxity and toleration with which aristocratic government related to the lower orders: under a reformed political system, rich and poor should bend to the power of the law. Besides their belief in Nonconformist asceticism and human improvability through discipline, reformers from Newgate to Pentonville shared a vision of a state based on the rule of law and its undisputed authority to punish. Rational and humane punishment was seen as a major legitimator of the liberal state.[88]

Can we establish a similar connection between the emergence of the penitentiary and such political transformations as the revolution of independence, republican government, and the ascent of the liberal state in Latin America? The scarcity of the available scholarship on these issues allows only incomplete answers to this question. Differences in the language of penitentiary reform among the several Latin American cases further complicate these answers. The information provided by the essays included in this book, however, permits us to point out significant differences between reform movements in North America and Europe and those in Latin America. The language of penitentiary reform addressed the question of state formation, but in a quite distinct fashion.

Unlike European and North American reformers, who posited the penitentiary as the institutional foundation for a democratic society, reformers in Brazil saw in the penitentiary first a symbol of modernity and later an instrument of social differentiation. The period during which the Casa de Correção was built (1834–1850) coincided with the transition between the "republican experiment" of the Regency and the conservative restoration under Pedro II, which put an end to an era of nationalistic and republican regional insurrections.[89] After 1850 there followed a period of peace and economic growth during which "democracy" became synonymous with the ritualistic contention between liberals and conservatives and the "rule of law" a territory exclusive to free, propertied men. On the grounds of peasant and lower-class unpreparedness for self-government, a reduced political class excluded the participation of the majority and learned to live, amidst occasional criticism, with racial privilege and slavery. Brazil's modernization of the justice system, which included the establishment of trial by jury and coincided with the building of provincial "houses of correction," paralleled the enactment of slave penal codes which consolidated the "peculiar institution" and strengthened the masters' private authority to punish.[90] The penitentiary, therefore, could not represent the fears of an elite concerned with the opening up of the political system. The Casa de Correção was first and foremost a symbol of modernity. The emperor could boast of the modernization of his prison facilities in front of foreigners while masters retained their right to punish their slaves. As a result, the reformed Casa de Correção continued to "correct" slaves with whips, chains, and other instruments of torture.

With the advent of the Republic, the "institutional hypothesis" began to recapture the imagination of reformers. The new political regime, responding to a long-voiced criticism, abolished in 1890 all "cruel and humiliating" penalties, including the galés (galleys) and capital punishment, and incorporated the Irish system of classification into the penal code. The new code extended the use of cellular confinement to most felonies.[91] But actual conditions in prisons changed too little and too slowly: after three decades only the penitentiary of São Paulo could be taken as an example of republican progress. Reformers, however, found in the Republic a more permeable environment for the spread of their ideas about crime and punishment. Concerns about the unrestrained or unwise use of political rights by groups that had been kept at the bottom of the social structure during the Empire underlined reformers' efforts to identify the problem of crime with lower-class/ethnic culture. The language of penitentiary reform, now geared toward the separation of offenders by types, the application of indeterminate sentences, and greater institutional power, served not to enhance democracy but to call attention to possible threats to the republican order: peasant rebellions, workers' "riotous behavior," and the violent and irreformable character of blacks and Indians.[92] Penitentiary reform provided a terrain for discourses that favored social and political containment and exclusion.

As Robert Buffington reminds us in his essay, penitentiary reform can produce enunciations about the political order that organize unclear political positions and legitimate a given political regime.[93] In his analysis of the discourse of Porfirian and revolutionary reformers, he sees the penitentiary as a metaphor for the relations of power and legitimacy that characterized the Mexican state. Issues like state autonomy versus centralization, strong executive versus congressional and judicial checks, and the need to reconcile civil liberties with national peace clouded the 1917 debate over the nature of penitentiary reform. Divergences between Porfirian and revolutionary prison reformers reflected different assumptions and fears about the functioning of the political system. Porfirian *científicos'* commitment to reformation hinged upon the necessity of replicating in the prison the strong "order" gained in politics. A centralized control of the prison system, a powerful director, and scientifically trained experts could lead inmates toward reformation. Revolutionaries saw it differently: in order to avoid the abuses of presidential despotism, the states should administer their own prisons. In other regards, convention delegates' discourse upheld the tradition of "moral improvement" initiated by the Porfirian *científicos.* By annexing prison reform to education (a combination emphasized by the *científicos*) and to new social programs (agrarian reform and workers' rights), delegates attempted to provide legitimacy to a government which claimed to represent "the people."

The continuity of a tradition of prison reform (liberal-Porfirian-revolutionary) under quite distinct cultural and intellectual environments tends to undermine the role of "ideology" in the making of reform and to strengthen the presumption that prisons were part and parcel of a long-lasting debate over the formation of the nation-state. If this is so, attempts at prison reform should be closely associated with efforts at national reconciliation, political centralization, and the construction of a national identity. The Mexican case fits this description. Ambitious plans for a penitentiary system emerged after two civil wars, the War of Reform and the Revolution. The penitentiary symbolized a future commitment to peace and national reconstruction, its actual building representing the success of government in taming the passions that undermined national reconciliation.

The Costa Rican case also speaks of a close relationship between prison reform and the formation of hegemonic visions of the state.[94] The lawyers/statesmen who, between 1880 and 1930, built the foundations of the liberal state shared an organic conception of society and a medical view of its problems: "parasites" (disease, malnutrition, poverty, abandoned children, and criminals) were infesting the social body of the nation and required comprehensive state interventions in matters of police, prison, and health reform. Thus, the penitentiary became part of a program of social hygiene built to police the urban working class and the laboring poor, a program that included foster homes for destitute mothers, "scientific" police training, and an army of teachers and social workers who inspected sanitary conditions, precisely because the liberal state was conceived of as a loving mother caring for the physical and moral health of her people. Behind this conception were fears about the reproduction of the Costa Rican working class, the anticipation of the criminal problem of European metropolises, and the need to sustain the seemingly participatory politics of the liberal oligarchy. Social and political imperatives contributed to produce an educator and social protector state by the 1920s that was unique in Central America. While the neighboring countries were entering the path of military despotism, Costa Rica was anticipating the emergence of a welfare state. The same pool of ideas (positivist criminology) that served in Mexico to support the autocratic state produced here an entirely different result.

In these three cases (Brazil, Mexico, and Costa Rica) the correlation between democratization and penitentiary reform is at best ambiguous. The equation between strict regimentation, silence, and intense work and the democratization of society experienced in the American Northeast in the 1820s and 1830s has very few parallels on Latin American soil. The Mexican Revolution, perhaps the greatest democratic movement in the region before 1930, simply carried through a program of prison reform initiated by an elite which had supported Porfirio Díaz's autocracy. Costa Rica's liberal oligarchy, which, facing the challenge of an increasingly active urban working class, built the educator protector state, was in no sense of the word concerned with democracy. Similarly, Brazilian reformers, whose criticism became more visible and urgent after the advent of the Republic, had to take as a given the existence of oligarchic government. The penitentiary was rarely imagined as a pedagogy in civil participation and republican government. In the cases where a true belief in reformation could be said to guide reformers' efforts, observation, cure, and ultimately social control were the accepted goals of the penitentiary. Few saw in the new disciplinary technology the possibility of building a "moral community" capable of self-government. Indeed, moralizing the working poor was often the response to elite fears about working-class or peasant challenges to oligarchic regimes.

## Penitentiaries and Export Economies

The penitentiary, a project of disciplinary power developed between 1770 and 1830, carried with it the promise of a double reconstruction: that of the moral subject by means of isolation (reflection and remorse) and moral suasion; and that of the *Homo economicus* through the operation of redemptive work and the system of incentives and penalties associated with it. The penitentiary was to reinsert individuals into the world of labor once they had lost their "love for work." In a sense, this was a response to a quite modern problem: the conflict within and without the factory over the imposition of "industrial discipline" in the way that E. P. Thompson defined it: the difficult task of changing workers' preindustrial notions of time, work, and authority in a way that would make continuous, monotonous, intense, collective, and regulated work possible. The penitentiary was thus predicated upon an existing "proletariat" who seriously challenged, or at least conditioned their acceptance of, the hegemony of the "industrial order." Reformation within the penitentiary assumed the existence of problems in the reproduction of the work ethic and the obedience and salability of labor power.

Melossi and Pavarini's book *The Prison and the Factory* deals precisely with this relationship.[95] The industrial takeoff of the American Northeast and the corresponding growth of commercial agriculture were accompanied by a new valuation of the social order. Moral and social reformers found individuals to be responsible for their own poverty (the result of indolence, vice, and intemperance) and recommended granting poor relief only to the "deserving poor"—the rest were to be institutionalized. The poor, the idle, and the vagabond, reformers believed, had to be confined and educated through work in farm schools, orphan asylums, and prisons.[96] Penitentiaries organized like factories became the model of industrializing America: they could "produce" proletarians (disciplined, mechanical subjects) out of criminals and legitimate by these means the logic of the labor market. "Solitary confinement of the prisoner-worker highlights the bourgeois desire for an isolated worker, that is, an unorganized worker . . . an unproblematic factor of production."[97] Auburn was first and foremost an experiment in industrial-capitalist relations of production.

How could this problem appeal to Latin American reformers? The ubiquity of the penitentiary project throughout the continent undermines the credibility of any association of the penitentiary with the process of industrialization. In fact, the existence of factories did not seem to condition the acceptance and diffusion of the penitentiary model. As the Argentine case makes evident, the penitentiary's workshops were a model of organization to which no private establishment could aspire (few private workshops were as large, as productive, and as disciplined as the Penitenciaría Nacional). Similarly, penitentiaries in Brazil developed almost simultaneously in Recife and Bahia, places with very little manufacturing, as well as in São Paulo, the center of early textile manufacturing. The prison of Puebla (where the Mexican textile industry had settled) was hardly more modern than that of Mexico City.

Moreover, Latin American reformers denied the very assumption of the penitentiary model: the existence of a waged proletariat integral to a market society. Reformers saw the prevalence of wage labor and of a market economy as ideals beyond their horizon, as realities more proper to Europe and North America than to the republics that emerged after the dissolution of the Spanish Empire. For many of them, the generalization of market relations, particularly in the sphere of work, belonged to the future. Relations of personal dependency—the heritage of slavery, the hacienda system, and *caudillo* politics—had prevented the spread of autonomy and market behavior among the lower classes. Hence, the idea of the self-regulated worker identified with the work ethic and struggling within a system of incentives and penalties demarcated by the market was, in their view, not the rule but the exception. As a corollary, they could not imagine their intervention as a reconstruction of *Homo economicus* until the diffusion of market relations became more visible or until the power of science and of imported ideas could replace the old imaginary of unyielding barbarism projected onto the lower classes.

The first condition required a context different from that faced by earlier prison reformers. Those who built the Casa de Correção, the Lima penitentiary, and the Buenos Aires penitentiary had to contend with a social body predominantly rural and with few connections to the world market. Reforming peasants turned into bandits, black slaves, and defiant indigenous peoples reaffirmed the existence of a radical other, the "rural masses," whose integration into exchange relations was ignored or discounted by the reformers. In the views of Sarmiento, Bilbao, Vicuña Mackenna, and others, the peasantry was an unreformable, barbarous subject defined more by its passions than by its economic interests.[98] Building a national market from these resources was, if not impossible, at least a path with numerous hurdles. Not surprisingly, those enthusiastic about prison reform also supported immigration plans which promised to reconstitute the social (and ethnic) makeup of their nations.

The second condition is closely related to the first. A reorganization of the lower classes, from an undifferentiated rural mass into a modern urban proletariat and its opposite, the delinquents, created the possibility for the penitentiary project. Criminals had to be construed as a distinct subspecies within the urban fauna, as a modern type of "city barbarian," for the punitive model embodied in the penitentiary to make sense. As Foucault has argued, the penitentiary created the delinquent as the subject of criminology, penology, psychology, and other sciences in opposition to a normality defined by the figure of the honest and obedient worker. The conflictive nature of industrial society and its challenging subject—the working class—were thus subsumed and normalized into a series of pathological anomalies that defined criminal behavior. This process of marginalization of the delinquent from its "natural" milieu—working-class neighborhoods—paralleled the construction of a punitive power acting behind the secrecy of high walls.[99]

Our suggestion is that the construction of the polarity criminals/ workers could proceed only in societies on the way to "economic modernization," that is, in those countries where, because of their rapid integration into the world economy, the mercantilization of social relations was well advanced. Thus, export economies with an intense process of adaptation of market institutions (exchange markets, banks, ports, insurance companies, etc.) represented a more secure referent for the diffusion of the penitentiary model. Flourishing export economies, not because they demanded more free labor, brought forth a reconstruction of the elite's conception about their country's social fabric. A new belief in the market as a mediator of social relations and in the central state as the guarantor of market relations among honest proprietors and workers favored the birth of the penitentiary. The construction of the "world of crime" demanded the assumption of a majority made up of honest and obedient workers. The project for the reconstruction of *Homo economicus* could not proceed from a social imaginary dominated by images of peasants, landlords, and personal dependency.

How did reformers influence the construction of this new confidence in the market? First, through the very experiment of prison reform. Ingenieros, who used the prison as a clinic for the observation of the lower classes, discovered the "materialism" (pecuniary motivation) among their subjects. He indignantly reported of fathers who sold their children at a price which discounted anticipated wages, prostitutes who earned more than a man's wage, and delinquents who applied the best entrepreneurial talent to their "antisocial" activities. The materialism of the "criminal class" reinforced the reformers' conception of social interactions as an endless *lucha por la vida* (struggle for a living), a symptom of the penetrating work of markets into the social fabric. Second, confidence was built through the spectacle of vibrant markets. Bursting activity at the exchange, the observation of railroad workers and of stevedores lining up for daily jobs, the emergence of new forms of advertising, and the new wealth accumulated by planters, middlemen, bankers, and shippers must have provided reformers with ample motifs to anticipate the coming of a class-divided, market society. The social theaters of export economies in conjunction with the newly discovered "world of crime" were tangent evidence of a tendency toward the generalization of exchange relations.

Before industrialization, criminologists and prison administrators could begin to treat the social body *as if* industrial conflict had arrived. As Steven Palmer suggests, the criminologists and statesmen who promoted penitentiary reform in Costa Rica anticipated the development of urban criminal problems that did not yet exist, drawing on their knowledge of European metropolises. In fact, the transition from agricultural to industrial labor as a form of prison therapy stemmed from the failure of prior agricultural colonies more than from a dramatic change in the proportion of industrial workers. Similarly, Ricardo Salvatore has argued that, since factory relations were not common among the Buenos Aires working class (small workshops, labor contracting, and outputting comprised the majority of employment in the "modern" sector), the penitentiary could not have developed out of concerns for a militant industrial proletariat. The penitentiary was motivated by a sense of social danger constructed out of the observation of a mobile and heterogeneous working class tied to the export economy.[100] The penitentiary's industrial workshops anticipated a discipline tailored to a collective worker that did not exist in the "outside."

Latin America's integration into the world market altered social structures and institutions and created new problems of social control. The coming of European immigrants, the freeing of slaves, and the increasing migration to the cities of indigenous peasants changed the nature of the working classes and affected elite perceptions of social antagonisms. As the "social question" moved to the forefront of political debates, the search for alternative means of social control intensified. Compulsory elementary education, universal male suffrage and military draft, public health campaigns, labor codes, and modern prisons presented variants of the same impulse to modernize the relations between the state and the working poor. But all these reforms cannot be simply imputed or ascribed to the changes in social relations of production. Between the promise of the penitentiary and the social and political problems of export economies lay an assortment of enunciations that organized "reality" and tried to foresee "solutions." *Interpretation* mediated all reformers' perception of the social question. Though European and North American institutions provided the model for most Latin American adoptions of this novel disciplinary technique, the penitentiary arrived in each country with a rhetorical garb that reflected the reformers' obsessive concern for "national" peculiarities. In this, positivism and criminology played an important role. Penitentiary reformers, using the vocabulary of positivist criminology, addressed the "social question" in a novel fashion, providing new interpretations to problems of national fragmentation, economic backwardness, and gender and racial inequalities. Perhaps these "interpretive interventions" were their most lasting contribution.

## Resonance and Wonder

In a well-known article, Stephen Greenblatt proposes two criteria for analyzing the interplay between literature and culture: "resonance" and "wonder."[101] A historian should be attentive to those instances of cultural production that create a sense of amazement and "wonder"; something that seems not to fit the self-representation of a culture promises to illuminate better its most intimate and dark aspects. The importance of any aspect of that culture, Greenblatt argues, should be measured against its resonance in other aspects of social life. A motif performed at the theater is just a motif until we see its logic deployed in multiple manifestations and circumstances—in public and private life, informing the reason of the state and the arguments of a peasant protest, influencing "scientific" researchers as well as consumers. To the historian of prisons this imposes yet another task: that of looking outside the prison walls for evidence of the "resonance" in society—in its *mentalité*, in its *imaginaire*, in its understanding of modernity—of the "wonder" created by the penitentiary. Here, the discourse of reformers must give way to other types of representations that express alternative visions of the prison or replicate in a different syntax and for different purposes the reformatory ideal preached by prison administrators, statesmen, and criminologists.[102]

Marcos Bretas's essay in this collection comes close to this objective. He focuses on the reception of prison reform in the public imagination of Brazilians.[103] Like Dumas's novels, various narratives from "outside" the prison tried to restore the centrality of the prisoner in the drama of reformation, a centrality that is not found in the works of the reformers. These narratives presented different scenarios: to political prisoners, the prison was a place of unjust suffering; to prison administrators and other bureaucrats, it was a tranquil place where a criminal class passively learned the rules of an institution; to journalists writing for mass audiences, the prison appeared as a place of lost innocence, as a school of crime, a city of barbarians grotesquely resembling the civilized urbanity outside the prison walls. Implicit in all these narratives was the failure of the reformatory project. The two personas of the inmate (the peaceful and obedient exterior versus the brutal and passionate interior) prefigured the existence of a criminal class for whom there was neither reformation nor redemption. The other inmates, the innocent ones who had fallen into the trap of the criminal system, were soon to learn in this common school, this "world of its own" built beyond the public eye. Rather than contributing to the imaginary construction of the modern state, narratives of prison tended to undermine the foundations of the reformatory project.

Cuba provides another interesting case that explores this connection. In Cuba politics and prisons seemed to have been more closely associated than in other Latin American countries (with the exception of Venezuela). The Presidio Modelo at Isla de Pinos (built in 1926) could not erase the old image of the penal colony which preceded it.[104] This was in part the product of history and representation: the fact that Machado used this monument of modernity to incarcerate students and other malcontents during the troubled years of his regime would have passed unnoticed if the prisoners themselves (most of them students) had not put their experiences into memoirs and made them available to the public. A variety of narratives served to associate in the perception of readers the Presidio Modelo with cruelty, corruption, arbitrariness, and suffering.[105] The revolutionaries of 1933 only had to recall that the island had been the site for the incarceration of famous patriots fighting for Cuba's independence (the most famous being José Martí) to counter the influence of the regime's official rhetoric that portrayed the Presidio as an example of progress and humanity. The Presidio Modelo, the student prisoners claimed, was truly a "model of atrocities."

In 1953 another group of revolutionaries—Fidel Castro and the small group that conducted the assault of Moncada—was arrested and sent to the Presidio of Isla de Pinos. There, in the hospital wing of the complex, they also wrote impressive and well-publicized memoirs of their prison experience in which they recounted not the horrors of prison life but the ways in which they attained a new understanding of the situation of their country, of their struggles, and of the strategy needed to bring about radical change.[106] The prison for them was a revolutionary school; within the high-wall halls they read widely, discussed philosophy and politics, and drafted pamphlets that reached far into towns and countryside.[107] The strategy of mass insurrection and the long march to Havana were devised within the prison. Not surprisingly, those who participated in the revolution rushed to destroy Machado's infamous prison. The symbolic role played by this prison in the making of Cuba cannot be overemphasized. From a bulwark of Spanish colonialism, the island became a place of imprisonment and torture of the leaders of independence, a land whose repossession had to be negotiated with Washington,

D.C., later the hidden and obscure site of the Machado dictatorship, and afterward the place for the incubation of a revolution against the Batista regime. In the place where the Presidio used to be, the new revolutionary state built schools, hospitals, and cooperative farms and renamed the island the Isla de la Juventud (Island of Youth). The medical power that in the 1920s and 1930s was used outwardly to preach modernity and inwardly to poison the inmates could now serve to benefit the people. As in 1789 France, a prison was the site where the history of a nation was reinscribed and the possibilities of a new beginning imagined.

## Conclusion

In this essay, we have suggested an approach to the history of penitentiaries and prison reform in Latin America that privileges the overlapping of diverse and seemingly complementary points of view. Our point of departure has been the assumption that any attempt to analyze the history of institutions of confinement should be attentive to the specificities of the Latin American experience and that any such attempt needs to reexamine the validity of the categories and relationships well established in the historiography of European and North American prisons. We have argued for (and experimented with) an interpretive social history of prisons in Latin America. Such an approach seems to throw new light onto questions concerning the spread and adaptation of European ideas, the conflicting perceptions of discipline, social order, and appropriate behavior, and the tensions between tradition and modernity in the shaping of primary-exporting economies.

Following this perspective, we have related the history of institutions of confinement in the region to changes in social relations, state building, and the economy. A special effort was made to interpret prison reform movements within the context of contending discourses about class, gender, and race during the formative period of export economies, centralized national states, and the constitution of the "social question."

The specificity of these problematic processes separates the Latin American experience with prison reform from that of Europe and North America. Discourses, policies, and institutions "invented" in those regions for dealing with the "criminal question" were not only adopted but also adapted to local conditions in Latin American countries. The history that we are trying to reconstruct thus finds its place at the intersection of ideological, political, social, and cultural developments.

The introduction of new technologies of punishment into the region produced, instead of a humanization of penal treatment, new interpretations about economic development, race and social relations, the foundations of state power, and popular culture. A diverse region, Latin America interpreted in many ways the penitentiary (or reformatory) project and used it for multiple purposes: to sustain certain views of state building, to alert ruling elites about the "social question" and the risks it posed to export-led growth, to legitimate elite prejudices about racial, sexual, and other social differences, and to build new forms of authority (scientific, medical, professional). Our emphasis on the multiple interpretations and the multiple uses of the penitentiary might serve as a guide, as an initial step, to look deeper into the relationship between prison and society and between technologies of punishment and culture in Latin America.

## Notes

1. Though there has been a growing interest in the history of crime and criminal justice in Latin America (banditry, peasant rebellions, and urban delinquency commanding central attention), few studies have concentrated on the region's prisons. Of the vast literature on these themes, only a sample could be mentioned here. On urban crime and policing, see Lyman L. Johnson, ed., *The Problem of Order in Changing Societies: Essays on Crime and Policing in Argentina and Uruguay, 1750–1940* (Albuquerque: University of New Mexico Press, 1990), and Thomas Holloway, *Policing Rio de Janeiro: Resistance and Repression in a 19th-Century City* (Stanford, Calif.: Stanford University Press, 1993). On rural banditry, see Richard W. Slatta, ed., *Bandidos: The Varieties of Latin American Banditry* (New York: Greenwood Press, 1987); Carlos Aguirre and Charles Walker, eds., *Bandoleros, abigeos y montoneros: criminalidad y violencia en el Perú, siglos XVIII–XX* (Lima: Instituto de Apoyo Agrario, 1990); Paul J. Vanderwood, *Disorder and Progress: Bandits, Police, and Mexican Development*, 2d ed. (Wilmington, Del.: Scholarly Resources, 1992); Maria Isaura Pereira de Queiroz, *História do Cangaço* (São Paulo: Global, 1982); and Jaime Valenzuela, *Bandidaje rural en Chile Central* (Santiago: Centro de Investigaciones D. Barros Arana, 1991). On peasant revolts and rebellions, see Friedrich Katz, ed., *Riot, Rebellion and Revolution: Rural Social Conflict in Mexico* (Princeton, N.J.: Princeton University Press, 1988); Scarlett O'Phelan, *Rebellions and Revolts in Eighteenth Century Peru and Upper Peru* (Cologne: Böhlau, 1985); Steve Stern, ed., *Resistance, Rebellion, and Consciousness in the Andean Peasant World* (Madison: University of Wisconsin Press, 1987). Of related interest are also Donna J. Guy, *Sex and Danger in Buenos Aires: Prostitution, Family, and Nation in Argentina* (Lincoln: University of Nebraska Press, 1991), and Fernando Picó, *1898—la guerra después de la guerra* (Río Piedras: Ed. Huracán, 1987).

2. For a discussion about contending approaches to the study of prisons, see Robert P. Weiss, "Humanitarianism, Labor Exploitation, or Social Control: A Critical Survey of Theory and Research on the Origins and Development of Prisons," *Social History* 12, no. 3 (October 1987): 331–350; Michael Ignatieff, "State, Civil Society, and Total Institutions: A Critique of Recent Social

Histories of Punishment," in Stanley Cohen and Andrew Scull, eds., *Social Control and the State: Historical and Contemporary Essays* (Oxford: Basil Blackwell, 1985), pp. 75–105; by the same author, "Historiographie critique du système pénitentiaire," in Jacques G. Petit, ed., *La Prison, le bagne et l'histoire* (Geneva: Librairie des Meridiens, 1984), pp. 9–17.

3. Michel Foucault, *Discipline and Punish: The Birth of the Prison*, trans. Alan Sheridan (New York: Pantheon, 1977). For French reactions to Foucault's book, see Michelle Perrot, ed., *L'Impossible prison: recherches sur le système pénitentiaire aux XIXe siècle* (Paris: Editions du Seuil, 1980). For a discussion of "disciplines" and "discursive formations," see Michel Foucault, *The Archeology of Knowledge* (New York: Pantheon, 1971), pp. 178–195. An excellent study of Indian prisons as sites for the construction of colonial power/knowledge is David Arnold, "The Colonial Prison: Power, Knowledge and Penology in Nineteenth-Century India," in David Arnold and David Hardiman, eds., *Subaltern Studies*, vol. 8 (Delhi: Oxford University Press, 1994), pp. 148–187.

4. This is precisely the type of history suggested by M. Ignatieff in his "Historiographie critique du système pénitentiaire." Patricia O'Brien calls this "a history of the prison from the inside out." A recent book by Fernando Picó, *El día menos pensado: historia de los presidiarios de Puerto Rico* (Río Piedras: Ed. Huracán, 1994), offers a reconstruction of Puerto Rican carceral institutions from the point of view of the prisoners' experiences.

5. It was common for these official travelers to simplify the history of European and American prisons into a collection of alternative or complementary "systems" ranked according to their novelty and degree of perfection. For examples of these reports, see Mariano Felipe Paz Soldán, *Examen de las penitenciarías de los Estados Unidos: informe que presenta al Supremo Gobierno del Perú* (New York: S. W. Benedict, 1853); Octavio Beeche, *Estudios penitenciarios: informe presentado al gobierno de Costa Rica* (San José: Tipografía Nacional, 1890); Mucio Valdovinos, *Ensayo sobre los diversos sistemas de cárceles conocidos bajo el nombre de penitenciarías y algunas reflexiones respecto al que debe adoptarse en la República Mexicana* (Mexico City: Imprenta de Cumplido, 1852); Armando Claros, *Informe del delegado al Congreso Penitenciario de Washington* (Buenos Aires: N.p., 1911); Adolfo S. Carranza, *Estado de algunas cárceles en Europa: informe* (Tucumán: N.p., 1921).

6. John Bender argues that the conception of the penitentiary owed a great deal to the literature on crime and lower-class life. See John B. Bender, *Imagining the Penitentiary: Fiction and the Architecture of Mind in Eighteenth-Century England* (Chicago: University of Chicago Press, 1987). Peter Linebaugh, on the other side, challenges traditional interpretations by locating Bentham's design in the context of workers' struggles against the elimination of customary perquisites and against capital punishment. See Peter Linebaugh, *The London Hanged: Crime and Civil Society in the Eighteenth Century* (Cambridge and New York: Cambridge University Press, 1992), pp. 360–373.

7. The following is based on Max Grunhüt, *Penal Reform: A Comparative Study* (Oxford: Clarendon Press, 1948), pp. 23–42; and William J. Forsythe, *The Reform of Prisoners, 1830–1900* (New York: St. Martin's Press, 1987). Adam Hirsch has emphasized the strong continuity between earlier forms of punishment, including houses of correction, and the penitentiary. See Adam J. Hirsch,

*The Rise of the Penitentiary: Prisons and Punishment in Early America* (New Haven, Conn.: Yale University Press, 1992).

8. According to Forsythe, the "reformatory project" stemmed from two different traditions or perspectives: the "evangelical," which emphasized the confidence that persuasion, good example, religious instruction, and introspection would reform prisoners; and the "associationist" (the Benthamite project), which trusted that a combination of incentives and penalties would stimulate the development of the good aspects of human behavior while curing its most violent and obscure features. See William J. Forsythe, *Penal Discipline, Reformatory Projects, and the English Prison Commission, 1895–1939* (Exeter: University of Exeter Press, 1991), chap. 1.

9. Robin Evans, *The Fabrication of Virtue: English Prison Architecture 1750–1840* (Cambridge: Cambridge University Press, 1982).

10. David Rothman, *The Discovery of the Asylum: Social Order and Disorder in the New Republic* (Boston and Toronto: Little, Brown and Co., 1971), pp. 81–83. For additional information on the rival American penitentiary systems, see Alexis de Tocqueville and Gustave de Beaumont, *On the Penitentiary System in the United States and Its Application in France* (Philadelphia: Carey, Lea & Blanchard, 1833), and Lawrence M. Friedman, *Crime and Punishment in American History* (New York: Basic Books, 1993), pp. 77–82.

11. See Michael Ignatieff, *A Just Measure of Pain: The Penitentiary in the Industrial Revolution, 1750–1850* (New York: Pantheon, 1978).

12. For a history of penal transportation, see A. G. L. Shaw, *Convicts and the Colonies* (London: Faber and Faber, 1966); and George Rudé, *Protest and Punishment: The Story of Social and Political Protesters Transported to Australia 1788–1868* (Oxford: Clarendon Press, 1978).

13. For the contributions of American reformers Z. Brockway, E. Wines, and T. Dwight to the development of the reformatory project, see Anthony M. Platt, *The Child Savers: The Invention of Delinquency* (Chicago and London: University of Chicago Press, 1969). On the European side, Alexander Maconochie and Walter Crofton are credited with the original development of techniques of individual treatment and progressive classification.

14. Enoch C. Wines, "The Present Outlook of Prison Discipline in the United States," in *Transactions of the National Congress on Penitentiary and Reformatory Discipline Held at Cincinnati, Ohio, Oct. 12–18, 1870* (Albany: Weed, Parsons, 1871), pp. 15–20. Significantly, the essays presented at this conference were rapidly translated into Spanish and circulated in Latin America: Zebulon Brockway and J. R. Bittanger, *La cuestión penal* (Toluca, Mexico: Martínez, 1871). In a recent book, Alexander W. Pisciotta studies the disparities between theory and practice in the Elmira reformatory. Instead of being the model institution that foreign observers tended to portray, Pisciotta finds that "Elmira was, quite simply, a brutal prison." The Elmira project, according to the author, was full of promises rather than of achievements. Alexander W. Pisciotta, *Benevolent Repression: Social Control and the American Reformatory-Prison Movement* (New York and London: New York University Press, 1994).

15. We are referring here, of course, to the well-known Italian and French criminological theories of the late nineteenth century. A list of a few key works

should include Cesare Lombroso, *L'uomo delinquente: studiato in rapporto alla antropologia, alla medicina legale ed alle discipline carcerarie* (Milan: Hoepli, 1876); Raffaele Garofalo, *Criminologia: studio sul delito e sulla teoria della repressione*, 2d ed. (Turin: Fratelli Bocca, 1891); Enrico Ferri, *Sociologia criminale*, 4th ed. (Turin: Fratelli Bocca, 1900); Gabriel Tarde, *La criminalité comparée* (Paris: F. Alcan, 1886). An excellent analysis of the criminological program of the positivists can be found in David Garland, *Punishment and Welfare: A History of Penal Strategies* (Aldershot: Gower, 1985), pp. 73–111. On the intellectual origins of the project, see Marie-Christine Leps, *Apprehending the Criminal: The Production of Deviance in Nineteenth-Century Discourse* (Durham, N.C.: Duke University Press, 1992), and Piers Beirne, *Inventing Criminology: Essays on the Rise of Homo Criminalis* (Albany: State University of New York Press, 1993). Still informative are Hermann Mannheim, *Pioneers in Criminology* (London: Stevens, 1960), and Ian Taylor, Paul Walton, and Jock Young, *The New Criminology* (London: Routledge & Kegan Paul, 1973).

16. In England, between 1890 and 1910, the confluence of eugenics with the youth movement blended well with the new criminology, adding pessimism to the reformatory project. The Gladstone Committee (1892–1894) gathered the mounting criticism against the penitentiary system—a system that, according to its critics, had failed to provide humane treatment and to rehabilitate inmates. Forsythe, *Penal Discipline*, pp. 9–30.

17. The discovery of many classes of delinquents and the curability of some of these types helped to constitute a new "medical power" with the authority to admit and release prisoners. Ibid., p. 12. On the emergence and consolidation of medical power in the English prison system, see Joe Sim, *Medical Power in Prisons: The Prison Medical Service in England 1774–1989* (Milton Keynes: Open University Press, 1990). See also Stephen Watson, "Malingerers, the 'Weakminded' Criminal and the 'Moral Imbecile': How the English Prison Medical Officer Became an Expert in Mental Deficiency, 1880–1930," in Michael Clark and Catherine Crawford, eds., *Legal Medicine in History* (Cambridge: Cambridge University Press, 1994), pp. 223–241.

18. Positivist criminology challenged well-established concepts such as individual freedom, responsibility, rationality, and rights.

19. Garland, *Punishment and Welfare*, pp. 231–264.

20. For the history of the project for normalizing families, see Jacques Donzelot, *The Policing of Families* (London: Hutchison, 1979).

21. For a chronology of this adoption, see Rosa del Olmo, *América Latina y su criminología* (Mexico City: Siglo XXI, 1981), table pp. 131–132; and Negley K. Teeters, *Penology from Panama to Cape Horn* (Philadelphia: University of Pennsylvania Press, 1946), p. 26.

22. Patricia A. Aufderheide, "Order and Violence: Social Deviance and Social Control in Brazil, 1780–1840," Ph.D. diss., University of Minnesota, 1976.

23. See Bretas's essay, chapter 4, this volume; and Salvatore's essay, chapter 7, this volume.

24. *Le Congrès Pénitentiaire International de Stockholm* (Stockholm: Bureau de la Comission Pénitentiaire Internationale, 1897), 2: 431–436. See also Salvatore, chapter 7, this volume.

25. See Salvatore's essay, chapter 7, this volume.

26. Juan Silva Riestra, "La cárcel modelo de São Paulo," *Archivos de Medicina Legal e Identificação* 6, no. 13 (June 1936).

27. Vicuña Mackenna, who visited the Philadelphia penitentiary in 1853, noticed the similarity between the two buildings. Benjamín Vicuña Mackenna, *Memoria sobre el sistema penitenciario en jeneral i su mejor aplicación en Chile* (Santiago: Imprenta del Ferrocarril, 1857), pp. 12, 21.

28. Eduardo Cavieres, "Aislar el cuerpo y sanar el alma: el régimen penitenciario chileno, 1843–1928," unpublished manuscript. We are thankful to this author for making available to us his work in progress.

29. Ibid.

30. See Zárate's essay, chapter 3, this volume.

31. Though still the stage of rebellions and a bandits' paradise in the 1850s, with time the island acquired the tranquility of an agricultural colony. It had its first election of municipal authorities in 1862 and was given in contract to an ex-officer of the Austrian army, Alfredo de Rodt, in 1877. See Benjamín Vicuña Mackenna, *Juan Fernández: historia verdadera de la isla de Robinson Crusoe* (Santiago, Chile: R. Jover, 1883; repr. Santiago, Chile: Ediciones Universitarias de Valparaíso, 1974, 2 vols.); and Mario Orellana Rodríguez, *Las Islas de Juan Fernández: historia, arqueología y antropología de la isla Robinson Crusoe* (Santiago de Chile: Universidad de Chile, ca. 1975).

32. Paz Soldán, *Examen de las penitenciarías*, passim.

33. See *Le Congrès Pénitentiaire*, p. 438; see also Carlos Moreyra Paz Soldán, *La obra de los Paz Soldán: bibliografía* (Lima: Talleres Gráficos P. L. Villanueva, 1974), pp. 37–55.

34. See Aguirre's essay, chapter 2, this volume.

35. Santiago Argüello, *Prisiones: estado de la cuestión* (Quito, Ecuador: El Conejo, 1991).

36. Only in 1903 was a section of "temperance" for habitual drunks established within the penitentiary.

37. Eduardo Espinoza, "114 años del penal García Moreno," *Ruptura* (Quito) 32 (1988): 233–236; and Ana María Goetschel, "El discurso sobre la delincuencia y la constitución del estado ecuatoriano en el siglo XIX (períodos Garciano y Liberal)," Master's thesis, Facultad Latinoamericana de Ciencias Sociales (FLACSO), Quito, 1992, esp. pp. 67–86.

38. J. Carlos García Basalo, *Historia de la Penitenciaría de Buenos Aires, 1869–1880* (Buenos Aires: Servicio Penitenciario Federal, 1979). See also Ricardo D. Salvatore, "Criminology, Prison Reform, and the Buenos Aires Working Class," *Journal of Interdisciplinary History* 23, no. 2 (autumn 1992): 279–299.

39. This is at least the conclusion of the *gaucho* Martín Fierro, who thought that the neologism *penitenciaría* stemmed from the old Christian word *penitencia*.

40. José Belbey, "Antonio Ballvé, un precursor del moderno tratamiento de los delincuentes," *Archivos de Medicina Legal* (1950): 51–72; see also Beatriz Ruibal, *Ideología del control social: Buenos Aires, 1880–1920* (Buenos Aires: Centro Editor de América Latina, 1993).

41. See Graciela Vivalda and Gabriela Dalla Corte, "La mujer y el Asilo del Buen Pastor en Rosario, 1898–1911," paper submitted to the "Jornadas sobre los trabajadores en la historia del siglo XX," Fundación Simón Rodríguez, Buenos Aires, July 17–18, 1991. This division between a religious administration of

female prisons and expert criminological guidance in male prisons was also the case in Chile. See Zárate's contribution, chapter 3, this volume.

42. J. Carlos García Basalo, *La colonización penal de la Tierra del Fuego* (Buenos Aires: Marymar, 1988).

43. Adolfo S. Carranza, "Cárceles argentinas y chilenas," *Revista Argentina de Ciencias Políticas* 10, nos. 57–59 (1915): 10.

44. Not surprisingly, positivist criminology oriented the efforts of reformers toward the new cog in the machinery of "social defense": the socialization of "children at risk."

45. José Pedro Barrán, *Historia de la sensibilidad en el Uruguay*, vol. 2: *El disciplinamiento (1860–1920)* (Montevideo: Ediciones de la Banda Oriental, 1991).

46. Now the criminal was considered "morally sick" and his behavior determined by the "functioning of a sick brain." This was the view of Julián Álvarez Cortés, physician of the Montevideo Penitentiary. Other, more social explanations were also offered, like that of Héctor Miranda, for whom it was social injustice that bore responsibility for the delinquent's illness. Ibid.

47. See Buffington's essay, chapter 6, this volume.

48. This was the explanation given by Mexico to a visiting commission in 1870: "Though all our statesmen and philanthropists have of late become aware of the importance and convenience to the public of the establishment of the penitentiary system, the financial difficulties, the little stability of our governments, and the constant necessity in which we have been placed to defend our existence against the attempts of revolutionary bands, an object which has almost exclusively absorbed our attention, have until now prevented the realization of this great social reform. Consequently, great criminals and petty offenders being indiscriminately mixed in our prisons, the contact, the bad conduct, and the example of the former, have exercised a baneful influence on the latter; and generally those who, having offended against the law, are sent to our prisons, and those who have remained some time in them, far from being reformed, leave the gaol considerably worse than when they first passed under its gates." Quoted from Edwin Pears, ed., *Prisons and Reformatories at Home and Abroad* (London: Longmans, Green and Co., 1872), pp. 164–165.

49. Daniel Cosío Villegas, *Historia moderna de México*, vol. 4, *El Porfiriato, vida social* (Mexico City: Editorial Hermes, 1957), pp. 439–445.

50. Ibid., pp. 441–444; and Manuel Carrión Tizcareño, *La cárcel en México* (Mexico City: N.p., 1975), pp. 26–31. See also Laurence J. Rohlfes, "Police and Penal Correction in Mexico City, 1876–1911: A Study of Order and Progress in Porfirian Mexico," Ph.D. diss., Tulane University, 1983. Prison reform in Puebla has been extensively studied by historian Nydia Cruz. See, for instance, "Los encierros de los ángeles: las prisiones poblanas en el siglo XIX," in Carlos Contreras, ed., *Espacio y perfiles: historia regional mexicana del siglo XIX* (Puebla: Centro de Investigaciones Históricas y Sociales de la Universidad Autónoma de Puebla, 1989), 1: 223–242, and "Reclusión, control social y ciencia penitenciaria en Puebla en el siglo XIX," *Siglo XIX: Revista de Historia* (Instituto Mora, Mexico City) 12 (1992): 119–146.

51. The impetus for reform produced little more than nominal changes: old *fortalezas* were given the name of penitentiaries without major modifications in their internal regime.

52. Emilia Troconis de Veracoechea, *Historia de las cárceles en Venezuela (1600–1890)* (Caracas: Academia Nacional de Historia, 1983); and Myrla Linares Alemán, *El sistema penitenciario venezolano* (Caracas: Instituto de Ciencias Penales, 1977).

53. See Jesús Sanoja Fernández, "Largo viaje hacia la muerte," in Elías Pinto Iturrieta, ed., *Juan Vicente Gómez y su época* (Caracas: Monte Ávila, 1985), pp. 141–155; and "Historia de presos y alcaides," in Ramón J. Velázquez, ed., *Memorias de Venezuela* (Caracas: Ediciones Centauro, 1991), pp. 245–248. Pereira's account of life in prison is a good example of this type of narrative: students opposing Gómez were sent to Puerto Cabello first and then to Las Colonias. Pedro N. Pereira, *En la prisión (los estudiantes de 1928)* (Caracas: Ávila Gráfica, 1952). The practice of incarcerating political adversaries continued after the fall of Gómez. See Rigoberto Henríquez Vera, *De la tiranía a la democracia: memorias 1958–1983* (Caracas: Ediciones Centauro, 1989).

54. Sanoja Fernández, "Historia de presos y alcaides," p. 247.

55. Colombia, Departamento de Prisiones, *Realizaciones y proyectos para la Reforma Carcelaria y Penitenciaria, 1938–1939* (Bogotá: Imprenta Nacional, 1939); and *La Reforma Carcelaria y Penitenciaria en Colombia* (Bogotá: Imprenta Nacional, 1936). See also Jesús A. Muñoz Gómez, "Notes toward a Historical Understanding of the Colombian Penal System," *Crime and Social Justice* 30 (1987): 60–77.

56. See, for instance, Gabriel Pichardo y Moya, "Nuestras cárceles," in *Memoria oficial: Tercera Conferencia Nacional de Beneficencia y Corrección de la Isla de Cuba* (Havana: Librería e Imprenta "La Moderna Poesía," 1904), pp. 261–265. See also Antonio Miguel Alcover, "Necesidad de una nueva cárcel pública en Sagua y como su construcción puede servir de modelo para nuevas penitenciarías en Cuba," and Domingo Urquiola, "Sistema penitenciario irlandés," both in *Memoria oficial: Octava Conferencia Nacional de Beneficencia y Corrección de la Isla de Cuba* (Havana: Librería e Imprenta "La Moderna Poesía," 1911), pp. 245–261. According to Alcover, Cubans had to efface the current carceral regime and build modern penitentiaries if they wanted to get rid of the "depressive concept" in which "truly civilized peoples" held Cubans: that of being "Indians in frock coats," that is, only superficially "modern." In other words, penitentiaries would not only bring *true* modernity to the island, they would also have helped to overcome this image of Indianness and backwardness.

57. "Síntesis de la historia de Isla de Pinos," in Thelvia Marín, *Condenados: del presidio a la vida* (Mexico City: Siglo XXI, 1976), pp. 17–38.

58. The Laboratorio Central de Antropología was founded within the prison in 1928. It was in charge of examining, registering, and classifying the inmates, as well as studying the medical and anthropological causes of each type of crime.

59. In an earlier pamphlet, "Un plan para reformar el régimen penal cubano," Castellanos provided a gruesome portrait of existing Cuban prisons, suggesting that the reform of the criminal required not only better buildings but also the classification of the inmates and their individualized treatment. See Mariano Ruiz-Funes, "La antropología penitenciaria en Cuba," in *El delincuente y la justicia* (Buenos Aires: Librería La Facultad, 1944), pp. 114–119.

60. Federico de Córdoba, "El nuevo sistema penitenciario cubano," *Revista Penal y Penitenciaria* 18 (October–November 1940).

61. "Guatemala," in *Le Congrès Pénitentiaire.*

62. See Palmer's essay, chapter 8, this volume.

63. See Santiago-Valles's essay, chapter 5, this volume.

64. São Paulo's Casa de Correção, built in 1852, was found in the 1870s and 1880s to be unhealthful, overcrowded, and quite inferior to the more modest *cadeias.* Evaristo de Moraes, *Prisões e instituições penitenciárias no Brasil* (Rio de Janeiro: Liv. Cândido de Oliveira, 1923), pp. 26–27. The penitentiary of Lima, once a source of pride for Peruvian reformers and authorities, was found in 1890 in such a condition that for an official inspector "it was preferable to return to the old and hateful carceral regime." See Aguirre's essay, chapter 2, this volume.

65. Many efforts by Argentine positivist criminologists to change their country's codes, for instance, resulted in compromising solutions with an assortment of penalties and ambivalent concepts of crime. See Salvatore, "Criminology, Prison Reform."

66. The case of Mexico is symptomatic: the disarray in government finances and the wars of reform prevented for decades the implementation of the 1848 law mandating a penitentiary system. See Rohlfes, "Police and Penal Correction."

67. Moraes, *Prisões e instituições penitenciárias,* pp. 29–30, 79.

68. See Peter Beattie, "Discipline and Progress: Brazilian Army Reform and Changing Strategies of Social Control, 1870–1916," paper presented to the Brazilian Studies Meeting at the American Historical Association Conference, San Francisco, January 1993.

69. See Aguirre's essay, chapter 2, this volume.

70. Having abolished the death penalty earlier, various states of Mexico reestablished it between 1895 and 1900, when it was clear that the penitentiary would not contain the "dangerous classes" and that immigration might bring additional social disorder. Cosío Villegas, *Historia moderna de México,* 4: 415–453. See also Alfonso Quiroz Cuarón, *La pena de muerte en México* (Mexico City: Editorial Botas, 1962).

71. See Santiago-Valles's essay, chapter 5, this volume.

72. Pieter Spierenburg has emphasized how increasing repugnance toward public violence led to the spread of incarceration as a means of punishment in eighteenth-century Europe. See *The Spectacle of Suffering: Executions and the Evolution of Repression: From a Preindustrial Metropolis to the European Experience* (Cambridge: Cambridge University Press, 1984).

73. The "punitive city" among the free (the restoration of a juridical subject respectful of the law through a process of education) had as its necessary complement the clean, uncorrupted, and moralizing prison for the unfree. Foucault, *Discipline and Punish,* pp. 128–130.

74. This grid "combine[d] in a single figure discourses and architectures, coercive regulations and scientific propositions, real social effects and invincible utopias, programs for correcting delinquents and mechanisms that reinforce delinquency." Ibid., p. 271.

75. The absence of a Protestant tradition, the lesser impact of immigration, the economic crisis of the post-Independence period, and the reduced numbers of its enlightened class can be cited as reasons for Latin American lack of concern, prior to 1850, with issues like temperance, moral reform, poor relief, and the work ethic.

76. On the influence of Bentham's panopticon and codification proposals on the region, see Miriam Williford, *Jeremy Bentham on Spanish America* (Baton Rouge and London: Louisiana State University Press, 1980).

77. See Charles Hale, *Mexican Liberalism during the Age of Mora, 1825–1853* (New Haven, Conn.: Yale University Press, 1968); and David Bushnell and Neill Macaulay, *The Emergence of Latin America in the Nineteenth Century*, 2d ed. (New York: Oxford University Press, 1994).

78. See, for example, Ricardo Salvatore, "Reclutamiento militar, disciplinamiento y proletarización en la era de Rosas," *Boletín de Historia Argentina y Americana Dr. E. Ravignani* 5 (1992): 25–47.

79. We refer here to the critique of "democracy" by the Argentine generation of 1837 and to the prevailing elitist conceptions of "democracy" under the Brazilian empire. See José L. Romero, *Las ideas políticas en Argentina* (Mexico City: Fondo de Cultura Económica, 1946); and Emilia Viotti da Costa, *The Brazilian Empire: Myths and Histories* (Chicago: University of Chicago Press, 1985).

80. Vanderwood, *Disorder and Progress.*

81. Justo Sierra, "Problemas sociológicos de México: discurso [pronunciado] en la clausura de los concursos científicos, 18 de agosto de 1895," in *Obras Completas del Maestro Justo Sierra* (Mexico City: Universidad Nacional Autónoma de México, 1948), 5: 197–219; Carlos Roumagnac, *Los criminales en México: ensayo de psicología criminal* (Mexico City: Tipografía Fénix, 1904); on Brazilian and Argentine positivism, see Salvatore's essay, chapter 7, this volume, and Ruibal, *Ideología del control social.* See also José Luis Peset, *Ciencia y marginación: sobre negros, locos y criminales* (Barcelona: Crítica, 1983), pp. 202–207.

82. Leopoldo Zea, *Dos etapas del pensamiento en Hispanoamérica: del romanticismo al positivismo* (Mexico City: El Colegio de México, 1949). See by the same author, *América Latina en sus ideas* (Paris and Mexico City: UNESCO–Siglo XXI, 1986), and *Apogeo y decadencia del positivismo en México* (Mexico City: El Colegio de México, 1944).

83. Cosío Villegas, *Historia moderna de México*, 4: 415–453; and Sierra, "Problemas sociológicos de Mexico."

84. See Salvatore's essay, chapter 7, this volume.

85. See Palmer's essay, chapter 8, this volume.

86. See Deborah Poole, "Ciencia, peligrosidad y represión en la criminología indigenista peruana," in Aguirre and Walker, eds., *Bandoleros, abigeos y montoneros*, pp. 335–367.

87. Thomas L. Dumm, *Democracy and Punishment: Disciplinary Origins of the United States* (Madison: University of Wisconsin Press, 1987), pp. 87–111, passim.

88. Ignatieff, *A Just Measure of Pain*, pp. 212–215. See also V. A. C. Gatrell, "Crime, Authority and the Policeman-State," in *The Cambridge Social History of Britain, 1750–1950*, vol. 3 (Cambridge: Cambridge University Press, 1990).

89. See Clarence H. Haring, *Empire in Brazil* (New York: Norton, 1958), chap. 3.

90. See Viotti Da Costa, "Liberalism: Theory and Practice," in Viotti Da Costa, *The Brazilian Empire*, pp. 53–77. The enactment of specific legislation to penalize slaves' crimes is discussed in Maria H. Pereira Machado, *Crime e*

*escravidão: trabalho, luta e resistência nas lavouras paulistas, 1830–1888* (São Paulo: Brasiliense, 1987), pp. 28–37.

91. Moraes, *Prisões e instituições penitenciárias*, pp. 48–74.

92. See Salvatore's essay, chapter 7, this volume. On the connections between racist thoughts and perceptions about the criminal in Brazil, see Lilia Moritz Schwarcz, *O espetáculo das raças: cientistas, instituições, e questão racial no Brasil, 1870–1930* (São Paulo: Companhia das Letras, 1993), pp. 159–168.

93. See Buffington's essay, chapter 6, this volume.

94. See Palmer's essay, chapter 8, this volume.

95. Dario Melossi and Massimo Pavarini, *The Prison and the Factory: Origins of the Penitentiary System* (Totowa, N.J.: Barnes and Noble, 1981), part 2.

96. Ibid., pp. 117–123.

97. Ibid., p. 157.

98. See E. Bradford Burns, *The Poverty of Progress* (Berkeley and Los Angeles: University of California Press, 1980).

99. Foucault, *Discipline and Punish*, p. 274.

100. Salvatore, "Criminology, Prison Reform."

101. Stephen J. Greenblatt, *Learning to Curse: Essays in Early Modern Culture* (New York: Routledge, 1990).

102. Interesting work has been done on prison writing, especially the way writers, politicians, and intellectuals in general portrayed their experience in the prison. See Mary Ann Frese Witt, *Existential Prisons: Captivity in Mid-Twentieth-Century French Literature* (Durham, N.C.: Duke University Press, 1985), and Ioan Davies, *Writers in Prison* (Oxford: Basil Blackwell, 1990).

103. See Bretas's essay, chapter 4, this volume.

104. Since 1794 the island had been used to banish all sorts of offenders (vagrants, thieves, murderers, etc.). In the 1820s and 1830s, the island became a haven for pirates—not in vain was it associated with Stevenson's novel *Treasure Island*—until it was recolonized by the Spanish military in the 1840s and used later as a place of detention of political opponents. In 1879 José Martí was sent to this prison. Additional evidence suggests that the facility was also used to terrorize peasants into compliance with the local *caciquillos*.

105. The pioneer of this genre was José Martí himself, who published his *El presidio político en Cuba* in Madrid in 1871 (reedited in 1938 in Havana by the Asociación Protectora del Preso). Among the narratives of the revolutionaries of the 1920s and 1930s, see Pablo de la Torriente, *Presidio modelo* (Havana: Editorial de Ciencias Sociales, 1969). Some of these works were widely distributed in the form of political literature. See, for example, Comité de Jóvenes Revolucionarios Cubanos, *El terror en Cuba* (Madrid: Editorial Castro, 1933). A recent historical novel—Thelvia Marín, *Condenados: del presidio a la vida* (Mexico City: Siglo XXI, 1976)—brings all these accounts into new light.

106. See Mario Mencia, *La prisión fecunda* (Havana: Editora Política, 1980); Carlos Franqui, *Diario de la Revolución Cubana* (Paris: Ruedo Ibérico, 1976); and VV. AA., *26: historia de héroes* (Caracas: Fondo Editorial Salvador de la Plaza, 1973).

107. Mencia, *La prisión fecunda*, p. 145.

# 2. The Lima Penitentiary and the Modernization of Criminal Justice in Nineteenth-Century Peru

*Carlos Aguirre*

As the Peruvian criminal justice system began to shift toward a "modern" layout by the middle of the nineteenth century (a transformation strongly influenced by European and North American developments in the art of punishment), prisons became the center of a system of punishment allegedly oriented toward redemption and reform. While early-nineteenth-century Peruvian jails were only places for seclusion and were not intended for the reform of the criminal, by the 1850s the rhetoric of penitentiary reform and of the redemption of the criminal began to inflate the language of state authorities, policymakers, and other "experts." The Lima penitentiary, inaugurated in 1862, became the masterpiece of the new punitive apparatus. It was regarded as a major step toward the redemption of the deviant and the elimination of crime. Rather than looking at criminals with hate and abhorrence and inflicting upon them vengeance and suffering, society should now make an effort to display humanitarian attitudes, which, it was thought, would become the best instrument for correcting and readapting the deviant into the social body. The penitentiary was considered to be the state-of-the-art device for healing the injuries crime caused to society as a whole.

While both the anxiety growing from the perceived rising levels of crime and criminals' impunity in Lima and the humanitarian sentiments of Peruvian reformer Mariano Felipe Paz Soldán were instrumental in the decision to promote prison reform in Peru, the fascination with foreign (i.e., European and North American) cultural and social "achievements" facilitated the election of the penitentiary as the appropriate solution. By adopting the penitentiary, it was thought, Peru was to join the privileged group of civilized countries. Beyond Paz Soldán's own convictions and some statesmen's rather rhetorical support, however, the whole idea never really inspired a lot of enthusiasm among Peruvian policymakers and authorities. The fashionable attraction enjoyed by such an enormous and costly enterprise was matched only by the lack of discussion about the adaptability of the penitentiary model to Peruvian society. Unlike other similar proposals—notably the adoption of the jury system—which sparked a heated and antagonistic debate among Peruvian intellectual and social elites, the penitentiary was adopted as if Peruvian society were naturally prepared for it. To reach civilization—a key element in the imaginary of nineteenth-century elites—the erection of a penitentiary was required, so no question was raised about the necessity of having one. This lack of debate was then followed by a lack of commitment to the true changes in attitudes and behavior needed to implement the whole penitentiary model. As we will see below, the complex, all-embracing penitentiary design was progressively abandoned, thus reducing its impact and undermining its final objectives. In addition, although plans for expanding the system were issued, reformist efforts did not really reach the rest of the carceral complex until much later and with much less strength.

In the end, then, as in almost any other society, the Lima penitentiary failed to accomplish its goals, prison reform did not reach the entire carceral system, and the living conditions of the inmates did not really improve. But, equally important, the purpose of having a controlled, disciplined, rigorously managed institution for instilling obedience, allegiance to the law, and order was also undercut by the persistent ability of the inmates to create their own rules, to manipulate the weaknesses of the system, and to build informal procedures both among themselves and with guards, employees, and prison authorities.[1]

This essay focuses on the adoption of the penitentiary in Peru. It explores how and why Peruvian authorities decided to build a penitentiary in Lima by the middle of the nineteenth century. It starts with a review of the state of prisons and jails in Lima during the initial decades of the nineteenth century; it then analyzes the project and construction of the Lima penitentiary and recounts its vicissitudes during the initial years of operation. Finally, it establishes the connections between prison reform and broader processes of social and political change in nineteenth-century Peru. It tries to show how the adoption of the penitentiary reinforced the authoritarian nature of the Peruvian state. The search for order after a period of social dislocation (the age of *caudillismo*) and the desire to preserve traditional social relations generated the necessity for a strongly repressive and centralized state. The penitentiary was, in addition, a clear symbol of modernization in Peru. As this essay argues, however, modernization in Peru was of a rather ambiguous and contradictory character, which was clearly reflected in the fate of penal reform.

Prisons and penitentiaries have been one important focus of attention in recent scholarship concerning criminal justice history. We can identify three major paradigms for explaining the historical changes that led to the emergence of confinement as the quintessential form of penalty and the role of carceral institutions in modern societies. First, scholars working within the Marxist tradition have explained the emergence of carceral institutions as a process directly linked with the development of capitalism. Rusche and Kirchheimer, for instance, in a book published in 1939 but only "rediscovered" in 1968, hypothesized the need for a disciplined labor force and for control over the labor market as the central element leading to the adoption of carceral institutions.[2] Other Marxist scholars such as Michael Ignatieff, on the other hand, emphasized the political and ideological components behind the emergence of the penitentiary during the transition to a new industrial order which brought a concomitant need for new methods of control over the poor.[3] Second, there is the Foucauldian paradigm. In his classic *Discipline and Punish*, Foucault presented the birth of the prison as the result of increasing control from "disciplinary power," a process linked with the emergence of bourgeois society. As many critics have noticed, however, he overemphasized the opposition between "ancien régime" and "modern" societies, leaving aside the elements of continuity and interchange between them, and his portrait relied almost entirely on prison design rather than on actual operation. In addition, as Ignatieff (among others) has pointed out, Foucault remains rather vague about the real location of the "disciplinary power" and the concrete actors exerting "control" over others.[4] Third, there is the "history of mentalities" approach. Pieter Spierenburg, borrowing ideas from Norbert Elias, has hypothesized a change in European cultural values and mentalities as the main catalyst for the shift in punitive methods from torture and public executions to imprisonment.[5]

All these interpretive frameworks have been formulated according to the European and North American experience.[6] Much less concern has been shown about similar institutions in other areas of the world whose study may yield valuable insights into current historiographical debates. Latin America is particularly interesting in this regard, for the adoption of the penitentiary in the region proceeded within a context dominated by the discourse of liberalism, the tensions of state building, and a set of mental structures formed during centuries of colonialism and its practices of social and racial segregation. After independence in the early nineteenth century, the breaking into the open terrain of politics and social relations of some forms of plebeian resistance (against authority, property, and racial discrimination) challenged the elite's absorption of "modernity" and complicated its project. The social disruption that followed independence affected the sensibilities of both the elites and the poor, introducing new dimensions to the disciplinary project imagined from the state. In this context, the humanitarian and legal project embodied in European and North American penitentiaries had to come to terms with the authoritarian *mentalité* that permeated productive landscapes, state structures, and everyday life.

Penitentiaries are generally thought of as an example of what Goffman has called "total institutions."[7] According to O'Brien, they are "self-contained places of work and residence for specially designated populations," a definition that is commonly applied to a whole variety of institutions, including penitentiaries, workhouses, juvenile reformatories, and insane asylums.[8] The Lima penitentiary was clearly devised as one of these total institutions. It was designed not only to host inmates but, more centrally, to act upon them ceaselessly through work, religious sermonizing, education, vigilance, and a strict rules-learning process. As many scholars have argued, however, total institutions never really work as they are projected to. If this is true, we cannot reconstruct their history using only their design, bylaws, and blueprints. On the contrary, we should try to reconstruct, as deeply as possible, the realities of everyday life inside the prison, the multiple informal arrangements, and the myriad acts of resistance and negotiation that take place inside the walls of these "total institutions." This essay thus tries to contrast the design with the actual operation of the Lima penitentiary during its early years.

## Punishment in Early-Nineteenth-Century Lima

During the period inmediately following independence in Peru, methods of punishment, the workings of the judicial system, and the normativity of the law all reflected a strong continuity with the colonial period. On March 17, 1821, a *Reglamento provisional* issued by the new independent government stated that colonial laws were still valid for the new republic except when they opposed the principles of independence and liberty that sustained the republican order.[9] This meant that the penal laws contained in the *Código de las siete partidas* and a series of other colonial codes were still applicable. The punitive structure derived from this legislation was based on vengeance and cruelty and included penalties such as mutilations, public executions, and the gallows.[10] Aware of ongoing penal reforms in Europe, republican lawyers and legislators rejected some elements of this penal system, and after 1821 some rather slow changes began to take place. But the adoption of new penal criteria (humanitarian treatment, equality under the law) was not easy. Attempts to limit the use of debasing and cruel punishment failed either because they were never enforced or they included mere formal changes. A decree abolishing hanging in 1822, for instance, ordered that those sentenced to death would be shot, and if they were guilty of treason or sedition, their bodies would be hanged on the gallows to make their punishment "more impressive."[11]

The perceived increase in urban crime and disorder led to the adoption of drastic measures. In July 1823, for instance, it was decreed that any theft over two reales would be punishable by death.[12] In November authorities decided to take measures against "the multitude of malefactors that infest the capital and continually invade its inhabitants' properties and persons."[13] Some years later, the Prefectura demanded that military jurisdiction should be extended to criminals whose activities were on the rise, it was believed, due to the lack of punishment.[14] Another recourse frequently used was the reposition of the Tribunal de la Acordada, an old colonial institution viewed as severe and effective enough to control crime.[15]

The death penalty also survived throughout the period under study.[16] It was legally restricted to punish both serious crimes committed by really "dangerous" criminals and political subversion, but in fact it was broadly used in periods of intense instability. Criminals and highway robbers were summarily and illegally executed in the place of their capture[17] and, during critical moments, the death penalty was issued even for slight crimes. More important, the spectacle of death did not disappear as a means to inspire terror.[18] The traveler Radiguet witnessed the execution of a criminal in the main plaza of Lima surrounded by a multitude whose "necessity of emotions moved them to feel the terrible voluptuousness of terror." The regiments and their bands brought an air of festivity to the ceremony that disappeared right after the arrival of the accused and his execution by firing squad. The festive atmosphere evolved into a "painful emotion," and "the crowd, pale and breathless, started to run in all directions, with a wild agility."[19]

Partly due to the fact that the colonial social structure remained largely untouched during the early republican period, attitudes toward penal repression did not significantly change. Elites showed little interest in adopting new methods of punishment more in harmony with the republican discourse on "progress" and "civilization." While new challenges emerged, political and social elites were prone to respond in ways that revealed more their willingness to preserve social relations than a commitment to true republicanism. Liberal ideology did not receive a particularly enthusiastic reception in Peru.[20] Permanent political and social agitation impeded any durable project of change, and the day-to-day urgency of confronting disorder and crime made preferable the use of already known cruel and severe punishments instead of attempting to introduce substantive reforms. Impotence encouraged extreme and immediate solutions. During the first decades of the nineteenth century, an extended (and socially accepted, thus immune) subsystem of private and unofficial punishment was in place. Rural workers being held in hacienda prisons, disobedient slaves sent to work in bakeries as punishment, students castigated in a school's own dungeons, and highway robbers illegally executed are just a sample of the variety of victims of this informal and arbitrary type of "justice."[21]

To fully understand this process we have to take into account the increase in ethnic and social divisions and its corresponding ideology: the supposed existence of superior and inferior races, the former naturally inclined to "progress" and "civilization," the latter to "barbarism" and crime. The diffusion of a racist discourse and practice formerly embedded in colonialism contributed to shape an extreme and authoritarian punitive mentality.[22] The impossibility or impracticality of exerting humanitarian or compassionate attitudes toward "inferior" groups, expected just to obey and properly behave, was a common upper-class belief in Peru during this period. One extreme but not uncommon case was that of Ramona, a twelve-year-old *cholita* (girl of Indian descent) who worked as a domestic servant for one Manuel García. She was accused of the theft of twelve reales, and, "by virtue of her continuous thefts of money," the master decided to punish her. The beating started at seven in the morning and ended seven hours later, when Ramona died. The master's wife, doña Josefa Vásquez, exclaimed while Ramona was being beaten: "Dénle duro que no siente."[23] She also told a neighbor that if Ramona did not die after the punishment, it would be necessary to stab her, because "*cholos* must be punished this way."[24]

This case illustrates the close links between the permanence of colonial racial and social hierarchies and the continuity in punishment methods during the early republican period. Profound convictions about how to punish in order to obtain submission were reinforced during this period, and they undoubtedly influenced the way penal repression was conceived and practiced. The direct relationship between skin color and social position reinforced discriminatory notions about supposedly inferior racial groups. The case of Ramona underscores the need to look at the connections between formal justice—tribunals, courts, jails, prisons—and widespread patterns of social behavior.

Although other forms of punishment did not disappear in early republican Peru, incarceration gradually became the most common penalty applied by the formal justice system. Criminals sentenced by the courts were sent to prison for almost any crime, though sometimes reclusion was combined with other forms of punishment, like whipping or public works. An examination of the conditions in which imprisonment took place in early-nineteenth-century Lima's jails is a necessary step for understanding responses to crime, the need for hidden and private forms of punishment, and the process leading to the adoption of the penitentiary.

By the time Peru gained its independence from Spain there were a few jails in Lima, each one worse than the next. The two most prominent were the Cárcel de Pescadería, named after the street in which it was located, and the Cárcel de Cabildo, or city jail, both situated in the main plaza of the city. The conditions in which the inmates lived were highlighted during a little-known but in some ways remarkable visit that the Liberator José de San Martín—the first postindependence Peruvian ruler—made on October 15, 1821, less than three months after the independent government was established.[25] Accompanied by ministers, court judges, prosecutors, lawyers, the mayor, and other authorities, San Martín listened to the prisoners' complaints and eventually ordered the release of some. The symbolism of the act needs to be emphasized: these prisoners had been suffering from oppression inflicted on them by the colonial situation, so, by liberating them, the leaders of the new independent republic stressed its difference from the old regime. The publicity given to this incident shows that it was not a prosaic administrative act but instead a very significant maneuver. For San Martín, at least, a true republican order had to go hand in hand with a humanitarian and just judicial system. During the visit, he was especially shocked by the existence of dungeons known as *infiernillos* (little hells), where, according to the *Gaceta del gobierno* report, "men were buried, got desperate, and died during the old regime."

Shortly after his visit, San Martín implemented some changes. First, he ordered the demolition of the *infiernillos*; second, he announced his decision to transform these jails into places where inmates could "be converted, through moderate and useful work, from immoral and vicious men into industrious and honest citizens." Third, San Martín announced the conversion of the old Convent of Guadalupe into a new prison "which will not be used for fruitlessly oppressing the disgraced but for correcting them and making them feel that the laws of a free people could sometimes be severe, but never cruel."[26] A mixture of humanitarianism with a clear condemnation of the old regime's system of justice and some traces of the ongoing reforms in Europe can be found in this packet of (attempted) reforms. The most important feature was the implicit program for reforming the criminal through work inside the prison, which reflected the appeal that European enlightened reforms had for Latin American liberators. But San Martín's endeavors were not followed up: work in the prison was never established, the new Cárcel de Guadalupe, inaugurated under such inspiring auspices, was later to become as horrendous and as fruitlessly cruel as the old jails it replaced, and even the *infiernillos* survived for decades to come.[27]

As can be noticed in the preceding paragraph, a language of humanism and reform merged with a rhetoric of freedom and republicanism. San Martín envisioned a Peruvian republic made up of free people under the empire of the law. The conditions of the jails and, by extension, the operation of the judicial apparatus were perceived as the denial of those enlightened principles. But this was a rather isolated attitude. The builders of the new independent country were much more concerned with securing their property, keeping Indians and blacks under political and social control, assuring the provision of labor for their haciendas, and guaranteeing the military victory over Spain. As many studies have emphasized, order and social control were far more important than equality and justice in the agenda of the republican leaders.[28]

An echo of San Martín's preoccupation with prison conditions is found in a couple of legal enactments issued by his successor, the marqués de Torre Tagle. Torre Tagle issued the first prison bylaws (*Reglamento de cárceles*) for independent Peru on March 23, 1822. Most of the rules were simple administrative regulations, and the best the *reglamento* did for the prisoners was to grant them one hour in the morning and one in the afternoon to leave the cells and get some sunshine and fresh air. In addition, it mandated separation between sexes and ages. Both measures were rather difficult to implement, and in most Peruvian jails they were never really enforced.[29] Neither was the elimination, also ordered by Torre Tagle, of the prison fee, or *derecho de carcelaje*, that the inmates had to pay at their release.[30] This was a clearly discriminatory practice, because most of the inmates were poor people who could not afford the fee, and thus they remained indeterminately in prison. As late as 1853 Paz Soldán found that the fee was still being charged in some Peruvian jails.

There were in Lima other prisons or sites for transitory confinement. The Presidio de Casas-Matas, an old and pestilent jail located inside the Fortress of Callao, the jail called Carceletas, placed in the old Inquisition building, and some military or police headquarters such as Santa Catalina or Dragones de Policía were all used for long-term or temporary arrests, while a barrack on San Lorenzo Island was used to house criminals— especially black slaves—sent out to cut stones. Overcrowding, lack of ventilation and sanitary facilities, deficient food, and continuous darkness were the general characteristics of these places.[31] The Casas-Matas jail, for instance, was described as a "horrendous" place. Two underground rooms of seven by fifty yards each hosted no fewer than sixty and sometimes as many as two hundred inmates. There was no internal vigilance or work, and a minimum maintenance of hygiene was almost impossible. It projected, according to Paz Soldán, "the most lively picture of human corruption [*envilecimiento*]."[32] Women and "distinctive" prisoners occupied a contiguous room, separated from the rest of the inmates, but no division was allowed between sentenced and unsentenced prisoners. Gambling and consumption of tobacco and alcohol took most of the twenty-five cents the government provided the prisoners for their daily feeding, and the prisoners developed systems for both introducing banned items such as tobacco or alcohol and accumulating money for "purchasing" their freedom from corrupted guards. Carceletas, on the other hand, located in a central plaza of Lima, was considered a true "tomb for the living" (*sepulcro de los vivos*). Security and surveillance were almost impossible, because the building was made up of a series of dungeons, hallways, and other smaller rooms. In spite of San Martín's efforts to abolish the *infiernillos*, Paz Soldán still found one in Carceletas in the early 1850s, where prisoners faced "situations proper to hell." However, Paz Soldán admitted that food was good and abundant, and he thought this might be the reason why prisoners did not riot frequently.[33]

The authorities' main concern was the ease with which prisoners could escape, especially when they were taken out for public works. This situation elicited complaints like that of the governor of Callao in 1827, who informed the Lima prefect that the escapes occurred because the troops were few in number and made up of men without morals. He asked that the prisoners be sent to public works in chains, a petition that had been discarded before, "perhaps for the sake of maintaining the liberal benignity, which, the governor assured him, could never be welcome or useful with such people."[34] Public works were a source of constant uneasiness and panic for some sectors of Lima's population due to the proliferation of escapes. They increased feelings of impotence among the authorities and ruling groups. Lima was still a small and walled city, without the clear distinctions and physical separation between social groups typical of contemporary cities.[35] According to Paz Soldán, fewer than ten out of one thousand prisoners sentenced to eight years in prison completed their terms without having fled two or three times.[36] Prisoners dressed in yellow uniforms were demoralized, guards and soldiers were suborned by the inmates, and opportunities for escape were readily available. The benefits of having prisoners working in public works, Paz Soldán must have been thinking, were severely lessened by the alarm and suffering that the escaped prisoners generated among the city's inhabitants. Paz Soldán considered public works to be a true hotbed of bandit gangs; thus, they had to be abolished: "prisoners' work is imperfect, the trial costs are greater, and, even worse, demoralization spreads among all the social classes."[37]

Early-nineteenth-century Lima's jails were thus both infernal and insecure places for confinement. Very little interest was shown by authorities and ruling groups in improving the conditions of these institutions. The prison did not play as important a role in their strategy of containment as it did in other societies.[38] While in the United States, for instance, the penitentiary actually paralleled the building of an independent democratic-liberal society and the enlargement of individual rights, in Peru independence accentuated division and hierarchies. The rule of law was restricted to the ruling social and racial elites, while the rest of the population—mostly Indians and blacks—was targeted as barbarian and criminal and thus received punishment and discrimination instead of rights.[39] Given this situation, it would have been surprising to see republican leaders deeply concerned with the conditions of prisons and the rights and welfare of the prisoners becoming a priority for authorities. In fact, authorities and ruling groups placed greater confidence in the severity and cruelty of private punishment and in humiliating sanctions—whipping, public executions—than in incarceration as a means of discouraging disorderly behavior. The idea of reforming the criminal remained alien to the elite's mentality during this period, and so was the even more exotic notion of prisons as places of redemption. Any concern for prisoners' conditions was viewed as a mere liberal "weakness," a pedagogy inappropriate for corrupted and stubborn criminals. This situation relates to basic social and cultural features of nineteenth-century Peru, a society where violence and cruelty were used without guilt or shame. Profound social and ethnic divisions, the permanence of slavery and domestic servitude, the use of private punishment at haciendas and *chacras*, and the way in which children were treated at home and at school all produced an authoritarian consensus on the efficacy of violence.[40] Within this context, a true reformer or advocate for humanizing the treatment of prisoners would have been navigating against the current. In some ways, this is what happened to San Martín and his attempts to reform Lima's jails.

There were, however, some isolated reform projects during the early decades of independent Peru. In 1827 there was a request to set up workshops inside the Carceletas jail and to have the prisoners working while completing their sentences, but funds were unavailable or insufficient. The director of the Sociedad de Beneficencia Pública (public welfare agency), the institution in charge of prisons at the time, decided to wait until the jail was transformed into a "house of correction or panopticon."[41] That transformation never occurred. In 1832 the newspaper *El Telégrafo de Lima* launched a similar idea. In order to end "tolerance" of beggars, vagabonds, and gamblers, the newspaper proposed building public workhouses administered by private individuals in which prisoners would be forced to labor.[42] The inspiration for this idea came clearly from English and Dutch workhouses, designed to instill labor discipline among lower-class and criminal groups in order to meet the needs of nascent capitalism.[43] Even if none of these projects was actually effected, they are evidence that European developments in penology were already being perceived as the most advanced devices by some illustrated minds, too concerned with what they perceived as rising levels of criminality and the weakness of the criminal justice system.

Even more interesting was a brief experiment with prison reform that took place in Cusco (in the southern Andes of Peru) in the mid-nineteenth century. In order to avoid unnecessary suffering by Indian criminals being sent to Lima, a *presidio* was established in Cusco, first inside an old fortress, then at the jail in Aquira, and finally in a renovated Jesuit convent in Cusco. The Cárcel de Aquira gained a reputation as the most horrifying of all Peruvian jails. It was built inside a natural cave, and according to Paz Soldán, "it deserves to belong to the centuries of barbarism." Since most prisoners became ill and many of them died, the *presidio* was moved to Cusco. General Miguel Medina, the department prefect, ordered the old Jesuit convent in Cusco to be converted into a prison. Concerned about the welfare of the inmates, Medina established a work regimen inside the prison. Although very little was actually accomplished, according to Paz Soldán, this should be considered an important step in the direction of "prison reform." On July 1, 1850, the government issued a *Reglamento interno para el presidio del Cusco*. It mandated obligatory work for all the inmates; police supervision of contracts celebrated between the inmates and outsiders; classification of inmates into five categories according to sentence and further divided by sex, age, origin, and occupation; and a system of rewards for those observing good behavior that even included the reduction of the sentence.[44] This *reglamento* incorporated several elements of the ongoing trend in European prison reform, but according to the sources it was not really enforced.[45]

Attempts to turn Lima's jails into workhouses failed, but coercive labor was not absent from penal repression during this period. Penal servitude, which had served since colonial times to supply a labor force for *obrajes* (textile workshops), bakeries, and mines, continued during the early republican period, along with the use of prisoners in public works and on the guano islands.[46] In these cases, it was assumed that prisoners had a debt to society which could be repaid by providing labor in activities which, due to their particularly negative work conditions, did not attract sufficient laborers. The aim of this form of punishment was not to teach labor discipline to prisoners but to exploit prisoners as laborers.[47] The absence or weakness of belief in the redemptive capacity of work for criminals explains the lack of enthusiasm for the system of workhouses. It was not until the arrival of the penitentiary that the teaching of labor discipline became a central purpose of penal correction.

During these decades, prisons were under the supervision of different branches of the state: municipalities, local political authorities such as prefects and subprefects, or the Sociedad de Beneficencia Pública. Disputes over who was going to pay for the inmates' living expenses were common and were exacerbated by a general context of fiscal poverty. The lack of any sense of the direction the carceral system was going to take, the scarcity of money, and the general unconcern with prisons and prisoners' conditions all created a true "hot potato" which nobody really wanted to keep in their hands. In a context of permanent political turmoil and the general weakness of the Peruvian state, this is not a surprise, but it does epitomize the difficulties facing the emergence of a new attitude toward criminals. In 1854 a new *Reglamento de tribunales y juzgados* tried to put some order in the administration of the country's carceral system.[48] It reiterated that the prisons were "places of security and not of punishment" and prohibited "every useless severity in the custody of inmates." The conditions within the prisons were put under the authority of the judges. The *reglamento* mandated separation between men and women and between *reos* (criminals waiting for a sentence or sentenced to corporal punishment but still waiting for execution) and *detenidos* (criminals already sentenced to prison). It also stipulated mandatory assistance to any prisoner needing medical intervention. Finally, it sanctioned the already customary weekly visit to the prisons (*visita de cárcel*) to check the general conditions of the prison and to listen to the prisoners' complaints. Twice a year, during the Christmas and Easter holidays, the *visita de cárcel* was to be presided over by the president himself, accompanied by the full cabinet and the rest of the local authorities.[49] But, significantly enough, the whole issue of prison reform, rehabilitation, and prisoners' work was completely absent from this new legislation.

## Paz Soldán and the Plan for Adopting the Penitentiary

The report written by lawyer and former judge Mariano Felipe Paz Soldán in 1853 on the conditions of prisons and jails throughout the country marked the beginning of genuine concern with prison conditions and the search for prison reform in Peru. Unlike previous rather timid initiatives, this time the whole endeavor was inscribed within an intellectual and political context marked by a powerful impulse toward "modernization" and "progress."[50] Paz Soldán believed he was acting as "the physician who describes the disease with its most lively colors in order to catch the patient's attention and take him out of indolence and to later apply the remedy." His was a painful yet necessary task, and it was not only a question of humanitarian sentiments, for he also claimed to be following scientific developments in Europe and North America.

He proudly defined himself as being part of the reformist trend in penal justice which had started in Europe by the mid–eighteenth century. In ancient times, he explained, criminals were executed, tortured, or mutilated. Later came the penalty of confinement, but it only added to the prisoners' degradation. Before the reforms, the prison was generally "a hateful and repellent place by its sole appearance and by the vices settled in the mud of its pestilent cells." Prisons, he reminded readers, used to be "schools for the corruption of the body and the infection of the soul."[51] The reform changed this by implementing mechanisms and institutions aimed at reforming the criminal—instead of exerting vengeance upon him[52]—and recovering him for society. The penitentiary was to occupy the central role in achieving this purpose.[53]

After reading the report, President José Rufino Echenique took an interest in this issue and decided to send Paz Soldán to the United States with the explicit duty of examining both the Auburn and the Philadelphia penitentiary systems—the two most conspicuous penitentiary models in vogue during that time—and of evaluating which one would be the most suitable for Peru.[54] The Auburn system placed an emphasis on productive work and attempted to resemble a real factory. Prisoners worked together during the day and were separated at night.[55] The Philadelphia regime, on the other hand, was based on complete isolation both day and night. The prisoner was segregated not only from the external world but also from any other person inside the prison. The prisoner was masked any time he had to leave his cell. Religion played an important role in this system and it became "the favored instrument in the rhetoric of subjection."[56] Paz Soldán compared both systems and finally chose the Auburn one for Peru. The system of absolute solitary confinement, he thought, was very expensive and did not result in any benefits, and absolute isolation could never be achieved. He distrusted the reformative power of isolation: rehabilitation of the criminal would be easier "in the company of his peers, motivated by the good examples." As it turned out, the penitentiary that was built based on his advice totally contradicted Paz Soldán's early assessment. Isolation was the ultimate goal in both systems, and the differences between them were, in spite of all the polemics involved, more apparent than real.[57]

Paz Soldán's choice of the Auburn system was also based on his perception of the peculiar nature of the Peruvian population. The main obstacle to the success of the Philadelphia system was considered to be Peruvian ethnic diversity. Racial prejudice shaped his characterization of the white, black, and Indian populations of Peru—not an uncommon attitude of Peruvian social and intellectual elites.[58] The white man, he says, "is humanitarian and, consequently, sociable by excellence, [has] moral inclinations, [is] attached to progress, honorable, and sometimes frivolous; it is easy to drive him into the bad path, only because he likes to yield."[59] Indians, on the contrary, were portrayed as "indolent by nature, nothing can move them to improve their physical condition, and they do not comprehend that their morality could be different; they are indifferent to ignorance, because they do not perceive the advantages of knowledge."[60] The main cause of their miserable condition was laziness. "Idleness is their major happiness, their normal condition; from it they only come out to do the strictly indispensable for satisfying their needs, which are reduced only to animality."[61] His description portrays the Indian as a beast, reduced to instincts and without any disposition to change; taciturn, reserved, distrustful, and unable to rebel. "They like and enjoy solitude; they consider themselves happy being in a desert taking care of their cattle."

Paz Soldán's inference was that the Philadelphia isolation regime would have no punitive effect on Indians, who made up the majority of the Peruvian population at that time.[62] Solitude would be for them "happiness and pleasure," and their "natural" vices would find, in the cell's isolation, an unyielding refuge. Considering their "natural laziness," work in common was thought to be the best choice—for Indians as well as for whites, though for different reasons.[63] To propose the adoption of the penitentiary, a symbol of nineteenth-century modernization, and to embrace this kind of racist ideology did not seem contradictory or exceptional to Peruvian liberals. In fact, it was not. As many studies have demonstrated, the construction of a liberal nation-state under Creole leadership in nineteenth-century Latin America was pursued without consideration of the Indians as an integral part of the national community. Indians were also considered to be obstacles to progress and modernization. The language of modernization and progress in nineteenth-century Peru was used precisely as a way to differentiate and exclude. The way Paz Soldán and others imagined the penitentiary and its future inmates was, thus, coherent with the broader process in which penal reform was immersed. This perception of the Indian was also to permeate, decades later, the way the Indian criminal was constructed by Peruvian criminologists.[64]

Physician José Casimiro Ulloa was one of the few public figures who explicitly objected to the choice of the Auburn system, although he generally supported Paz Soldán's efforts to modernize the Peruvian prison system.[65] For Ulloa, an "immense revolution" was under way in the Peruvian criminal justice system which was to have "a transcendental influence on the physical and moral conditions of our people and, consequently, on public health." But his objections were also colored by racial prejudices. He believed the Indians to be docile and shy, attributes that would counterbalance their indolence and passion, especially when "the precepts of the authority are dictated upon them and enforced through severity." Ulloa favored the Philadelphia regime, and at least one of his arguments proved to be true: he was afraid that the Auburn system, which relied heavily on the guards for surveillance and control, was virtually inapplicable in Peru because of the lack of discipline among those who usually performed those duties.[66] If there was still any doubt about what purposes a penitentiary should serve, Ulloa ended his article by quoting French philosopher Alexis de Tocqueville: the best penitentiary system is the one "which is the most suitable to repress crime and to secure the life and fortune of the citizens."[67] It seems clear, after reading Paz Soldán's and Ulloa's remarks, that the issues of public order, social control, and the protection of property were far more important in their expectations than the redemption of the criminal or the welfare of the prisoners.[68]

The blueprint, following Paz Soldán's indications, was drawn by architect Maximiliano Mimey. It included some basic principles of reformation: the building had to offer a good location, security, and ventilation in order to provide an aseptic, orderly, and controlled environment. The prison had to transform the prisoners' attitudes, their criminal "instincts," as well as their everyday habits. Cleanliness, order, and hygiene were to be instilled. Severity started with the building's external appearance. The penitentiary's facade had to look "firm, solid, durable, but never attractive: rather, it must present a serious, severe, and somber appearance."[69] Despite his preference for the Auburn system, Paz Soldán adopted many features of the Philadelphia system, especially the strong emphasis on religious instruction as the basis for reformation and discipline. The chaplain was to play a crucial role in instilling obedience, submission, and repentance. The *Reglamento de la penitenciaría*, drafted also by Paz Soldán,[70] mandated that the chaplain give the prisoners a daily talk around purely moral issues and a sermon on Sundays, after Mass. He had to make the prisoners understand that "work serves as a consolation, and it is a necessity rather than a punishment; that silence, obedience, and work are their main duties, and that their escape is impossible." Religion would give the prisoners consolation and help them to accept the rigid discipline of the penitentiary.

Strict disciplinary measures were also designed. In a reversal of Paz Soldán's previous suggestions, prisoners were prohibited from talking among themselves. "Every conversation, whatever its purpose is, must be severely prohibited, and profound silence must be kept in every act."[71] Silence was required for meditation and could be broken only for confessing to the chaplain. The purpose was to separate the prisoners, to avoid any contact among them, and to preclude the revealing of their sentiments or emotions: prisoners were to learn to live in solitude and segregation. "Even if the bodies are together, the souls have to be in absolute isolation."[72] This was the supreme penitentiary ideal: silence enforced not only as an opportunity for meditation and repentance, but also as the condition for better and more effective control. "It is more useful and easier to govern when there is silence," said Paz Soldán, referring to the penitentiary order, but his statement could also be understood as a metaphor for what was being perceived and pursued outside the penitentiary as an ideal social order.[73]

Obligatory work was another supporting column of the penitentiary regime. It was thought of as an effective instrument to reform criminals, transforming them into subjects inclined to "useful and profitable work"; thus, a series of workshops were to be set up inside the penitentiary. For the first time in the history of Peruvian prisons, penal work had the explicit purpose of teaching labor discipline. The penitentiary would be a sort of "factory of men";[74] it would transform disorderly people into industrious workers. The factory—not a common feature yet on Peruvian soil but projected onto Peru's future as the ideal outcome of progress and civilization—was conceived as an extension of the prison. Actually, order and discipline were the objectives of the reform, regardless of the prisoners' insertion in the labor market. Work inside the prison complemented the "domestication" of the inmate, convinced through religious preaching that work was necessary and virtuous and trained in its practice through the daily regimen in the prison workshops.

The emphasis on the redemptive nature of work must be understood against the backdrop of elite perceptions about the laziness of the Peruvian, particularly the lower-class, population. The creation of the image of Indians, blacks, and other nonwhite people as naturally resistant to hard work had a centuries-long history.[75] Developmentalist projects throughout the nineteenth century, and especially after the 1850s, emphasized the need to create a disciplined labor force as a precondition for progress.[76] Rather than posing the problem in moral or religious terms (laziness and idleness as sin or proof of demoralization), it was now depicted as an impediment to progress and a proof of the lack of commitment to the "true" needs of the Peruvian nation. The penitentiary thus promised to overcome one of the most disturbing nightmares of the Peruvian elites.

Total obedience was a fundamental part of the penitentiary regime. Paz Soldán's understanding of the concept of obedience is worth quoting: "[obedience] must be blind . . . men must have their volition dead and must obey without doubt everything that is ordered. Without obedience there will be no order, and the first factual or verbal disrespect will open a breach in the institution."[77] The central purpose of the penitentiary, according to Paz Soldán, was to make people docile and obedient, without any volition. The prisoner had to yield before any superior order. The penitentiary project entailed much more than the sole repression of criminal or deviant behavior; it implied the eradication of any conduct that showed disrespect for superiors. It was a promise of the restoration of social order and racial hierarchy. To accomplish these goals, the penitentiary incorporated as a fundamental principle a strict system of vigilance. It had to be "constant, equal, never interrupted," so that observation could reveal "the proper mind of the prisoners, if possible."[78] The architectonic principle of Bentham's panopticon, which was used by Paz Soldán as an inspiration, appeared as paradigmatic: complete and constant observation to contain disrespect.[79] The corresponding principle of Bentham's legal order—the balance of pain and pleasure in the inducement of proper, legal behavior—was replaced by a military conception: blind obedience to rules to produce order.

The penitentiary, in brief, responded to very concrete needs. It was a punitive design that pursued efficacy in repressing crime by confining criminals. It was predicated on the inmates' reformation into useful, docile, industrious, and controlled subjects. But the discipline of silence and blind obedience spoke more to the anxieties about social disorder common among the Peruvian elites than to the promise of reformation. The ideal of an orderly and disciplined institution producing obedient subjects had its appeal in a society where "disorderly and disrespectful" lower classes were challenging elite hegemony. The penitentiary was thought of, in fact, as a laboratory for the whole society.

Reformist approaches to the penal question have been generally interpreted by revisionist scholars as little more than hypocritical attitudes, masking real purposes of political and social control.[80] This extremely instrumental vision has been criticized, among others, by Ignatieff, Garland, and Forsythe.[81] Forsythe reminds us that reformers "sought to base their action upon a more independent ethic of very high importance, an ideal of social inclusion and human value of prisoners which stood at the heart of many of their endeavors."[82] Statements like this help us counterbalance the most extreme claims made by revisionist scholars, who assign reformers certain obscure, hidden, and ad hoc motivations that most of the time cannot be documented. But we still share with the revisionist scholarship the persuasion that individual reformers' endeavors are inscribed in broader processes of social change, political hegemony, and ideological contention. We have no reason to doubt that Paz Soldán was sincerely motivated by humane feelings and that he genuinely believed that penal reform would benefit both society and the criminal. His project, however, went beyond individual motivations, so we need to look at it as part of the broader purpose of improving mechanisms of social and political control and of consolidating the state's central authority.

Since the early 1850s a number of social and political changes had been taking place in Peru. Political stabilization under liberal hegemony led to a process of state consolidation. Many political and social reforms were initiated, notably the abolition of both slavery (1854) and Indian tribute (1855). Penal and police reforms were part of this process. The purposes of building a modern state and of rationalizing the administration, at a time when guano revenues permitted the expansion of the state apparatus, required centralization in the exercise of justice and control, an efficient system of penal justice that could repress with efficacy, and certain mechanisms of social vigilance that could preclude the continuation of misgovernment. It was within this context of increased needs of social control, a great impulse toward modernization, and the growth and consolidation of a nation-state that the project for building a penitentiary was formulated. Not less important, guano provided the resources necessary to build the penitentiary.[83] This made Peru different from Mexico, where financial tightness prevented for many decades the building of a penitentiary.[84]

The erection of the Lima penitentiary started in 1856 under the direction of Paz Soldán and lasted for more than six years. For political reasons the project had been discarded by President Echenique, but his successor, Ramón Castilla, who took office in January 1855, decided to start the project.[85] The labor force used in its construction included foreign skilled workers for cutting and carving the stone, local free workers for hauling the stone, some skilled artisans (carpenters, blacksmiths), and, of course, prisoners.[86] The final edifice, located at one of the city's extreme edges,[87] framed a total extension of more than 40,000 square yards and was first designed to house 350 inmates. The building was certainly impressive, and for several decades it was the most visible and monumental edifice in Lima. Foreign travelers testified to the impression the penitentiary left on them.[88] The final report by Paz Soldán shows his great pride in what he considered "one of the best buildings in South America." All the architectural principles included in the blueprint were successfully incorporated in the building: the severe facade, the central observatory nucleus, the underground corridors. The prison was surrounded by a high wall. At the center of the facade was a two-story, sober edifice where the administrative offices were located. It connected with the rotunda, at the center of the construction, from which the five branches of the penitentiary extended "like radii from a common center." Three of the five pavilions contained departments of prisoners, and each of them had cells, administrative offices, a kitchen, workshops, storage rooms, patios, restrooms, and other facilities. All these departments, each of them made up of two rows of twenty-six cells each, connected to a central observatory which, following the architectonic principle of the panopticon, was built to assure constant and centralized surveillance. An underground corridor was also constructed to allow the director to go directly from his office to any of the inmates' departments. The departments occupied the first and second floors of the building, and on the third floor there were apartments for the director, subdirector, and chaplain, an elegant room for receptions, a nursery, a pharmacy, and the chapel, which was built so that the inmates attending Mass would not be able to look at each other. On the first floor, the sidewalk between the two rows of cells was used as a dining room. At the end of the row there was a stairway that led to the underground dungeons, where the most dangerous criminals were to be kept in absolute isolation.

Upon their entrance, the newly arrived inmates were supposed to be photographed and then brought to the reception cells, where they took a shower, registered their personal data, and dressed in their new uniforms. After this, each inmate was transported to his own cell in the proper department. In the interior, prisoners were supposed to follow a rigid daily schedule of prayer, work, and mealtimes. According to the *reglamento*, they were to be recognized by the number of their cells, so the inmates lost, from the very beginning, their identity.[89] Each inmate's number was inscribed on his uniform's collar and hat. Inmates were not permitted to talk, communicate with gestures, smoke, or use coca. If they wanted to say something to a guard or to the workshop master, they had to do so very quietly. While moving in groups inside the prison, they had to be formed in rows with their faces turned toward the guards. Hygienic routines were also scheduled with rigid precision, as were work schedules. Prisoners were supposed to wake up at 5:00 A.M. in summer and 5:30 A.M. in winter. Half an hour later they had to be in their workshops; at 9:00 A.M. they had a half hour for breakfast and at 3:00 P.M. another half hour for supper. At 5:30 P.M. in winter and 6:00 P.M. in summer the daily work schedule ended. Prisoners returned to their cells and stayed there until the next day. On Sundays and other holidays, the schedule was very similar, with attending Mass and praying taking the place of work.

A system of rewards was also established for stimulating good behavior among the inmates. Rewards included decreased workload, more leisure and reading time, permission to cultivate plants for sale, the chance to have extra instruction, consumption of tobacco and coca (but only in solitude), sending letters to relatives, and receiving visits.

Conversely, bad behavior led to different forms of punishment: personal services to the institution, reduced food provisions, privation of reading time and visits, isolation in the underground dungeons, suspension of earned wages, and the "rain shower."[90]

The government issued a special medal to commemorate the inauguration of the penitentiary, which took place on July 23, 1862. Decades, even centuries, of social disorder and prisoners' suffering were apparently coming to an end at the same time that progress and civilization were finally touching Peruvian soil. The dreams of a European-like society were beginning to be realized. Like railroads, the penitentiary summed up all the dreams of the civilizing elites. As the director of the penitentiary wrote years later, "if the institutions adopted by a country are the best thermometer for measuring its culture and degree of civilization, then Peru must be proud of being one of the most civilized peoples, because it has, among its institutions, the penitentiary system, as it is understood and practiced by the most developed nations on both continents."[91]

## The Penitentiary at Work

Reclusion in the penitentiary, considered to be the most severe sentence after the death penalty, was reserved for the most dangerous criminals from all over the country. It had four different degrees, each divided into three terms (minimum, middle, and maximum), ranging from four to fifteen years.[92] Convicts receiving a sentence to the penitentiary were also subject to the authorities' surveillance for a period of one to five years after completing their prison terms, according to the behavior the authorities observed in prison. There was a long list of crimes that were punished with incarceration in the penitentiary, including counterfeiting, murder, assault, rape, dueling, arson, and piracy, among others. The Lima penitentiary was designed to accommodate prisoners sent by judicial courts from all over the country, so its population became a sort of criminal "elite"; at least, that is the way the authorities and the public perceived the inmates. Stories, rumors, and all sorts of panics spread as a result of the way people imagined the prison and its population. There was a difference, however, between image and reality. Given the vices and inaccuracies of the judicial system, too many prisoners claiming innocence were sent to the penitentiary, especially poor people from the interior. Besides the murderers and serial killers there were always harmless criminals and, more commonly, people suffering from an unjust sentence. But perceptions were important in the shaping of prison life and relations. For the guards, it was generally imperative to exert brutality over such "dangerous" inmates, although this did not preclude the appearance of other types of interaction between inmates and guards.[93]

Paz Soldán was the first director of the penitentiary, but only a month later he resigned to become minister of public works. Prisoners gradually began to fill the cells of the penitentiary. In September 1862 there were only fifty-three inmates, thirty-five males and eighteen females. One month later, the number had increased to sixty-two.[94] Though their numbers were still low, inmates were already causing trouble to the administration. Prisoners being moved from other prisons would arrive completely drunk because the soldiers in charge of their custody allowed them to enter *pulperías* (taverns) to drink alcohol.[95] Some early external attacks also shook the initial security felt by the administration. In November 1862, a few months after its inauguration, the penitentiary became the target of armed groups trying to rescue prisoners.[96] At the same time, the strong discipline mandated inside the brand-new building began to crack. A detailed report by the new director stated that "there are some prisoners with a rebel spirit for whom the warnings and penalties established by the bylaws have become impotent."[97] Not even the rain shower, reclusion, or isolation—the most severe penalties included in the penitentiary bylaws—was sufficient to persuade the most reluctant prisoners. The director suggested the adoption of stocks for those inmates, but in spite of the favorable opinion of the prison's physician, Paz Soldán—who was still being consulted on these matters—considered it unnecessary to increase the catalog of penalties.

During these early years two things became clear: first, the way Paz Soldán imagined the penitentiary in operation and the way it actually functioned were remarkably different; second, the authorities of the prison were not really convinced about their role, did not really embrace the ideology of penal reform, and finally gave up the pursuit of humanity and reform in the treatment of criminals. Obviously not only criminals but especially authorities, guards, and employees needed to be reeducated under the principles of the new penitentiary science. In addition, the penitentiary soon became overcrowded. By June 1866, the director warned authorities that there were only eight empty cells, and a year later there were none.[98] The director demanded the construction of eighty new cells: the building was already overpopulated and the inmates' living conditions were worsening.[99] The director also reported the "pathetic condition of the inmates due to the lack of adequate clothing."[100] Sanitation was also a problem. Twenty-two deaths inside the prison brought to light the prisoners' unhealthful environment. Fourteen of them (65 percent) had died of tuberculosis.[101]

The rapid decay in living conditions inside the penitentiary and the prisoners' reluctance to easily accept their confinement resulted in insubordinate acts and attempted riots. On December 9, 1866, a riot that included a massive escape attempt was aborted. The detailed inspection that followed revealed ten cells with holes already opened, and, in almost all the cells, stolen tools from the workshops were found. As the whole prison was in turmoil, those inmates directly involved in the riot were sent to isolated cells in the underground dungeons. The current director, Francisco Valdizán, emphatically demanded urgent and severe corrective measures. In such a situation, he argued, slight penalties like rain showers and food deprivation were good only for schoolchildren, not for the corrupted and recidivist criminals sheltered at the penitentiary.[102]

As disillusionment with the penitentiary increased, a rhetoric of severity more attuned to the elites' mentality surfaced. The arguments for more severity and rigor showed an erosion of the confidence in Paz Soldán's methods. To Director Antonio Noya, not prison walls and persuasion but severe penalties were the main deterrent for criminals. For the kind of criminals he had to deal with, "incentives or whatever means other than true rigor [were] a chimera."[103] Noya lasted only two months in his position. In a setting in which prison authorities were changing one after another, nobody seemed willing to implement the reformist program. The next director, Juan Bautista Mariscal, wrote his own report to the minister of justice after another riot. Twenty-three inmates had revolted, taken hostages, and finally been subdued with the aid of external armed forces. On this occasion the director was authorized to flog the leaders. He defended his actions (against charges of cruelty) with a cynical logic: if, in spite of legal prohibition, whipping was used in the army, in the household, and at school, why couldn't he use it to punish those "obstinate criminals"?[104] The overwhelming and familiar presence of physical violence had shaped the common notion that whipping "worked." If this was true, it could—and must—be used against criminals. The humanitarian expectation of eliminating cruel punishment was displaced by the more pragmatic and widespread rhetoric of severe discipline and swift correction.

The conditions under which the penitentiary was operating led to disillusionment with the penitentiary model itself. The new director stated in August 1867 that the congregate regime was a failure, for it made it very difficult to restrict conversation among inmates, through which they became aware of external events that stimulated their plans to escape or revolt.[105] In a climax of impotence, after a new attempt to escape in December 1867, the director asked for the removal of the most dangerous prisoners from the penitentiary.[106] This entailed an admission of failure: the penitentiary was ineffective in reforming criminals.

The realities of the prison forced the authorities to put aside their rhetorical support for reform and to bluntly speak out their own convictions. Only the original model's repressive dimension and the emphasis on work remained. No doubt the new penitentiary was a more secure prison than the older jails, and in that sense it largely satisfied one of its goals. But the allegedly final purpose of reform and humanitarianism had failed. The failure of a project whose purpose was to optimize social control and domination speaks of the pervasiveness of traditional mental structures—of an authoritarian view of social relations and its corresponding theory of swift justice—in spite of the rhetoric about modernization.

Nevertheless, the penitentiary kept functioning, not really under Paz Soldán's utopian guidelines but following the pragmatic and authoritarian hand of the authorities. Prisoners worked at the workshops, the chaplain celebrated Masses on Sundays and confessed the criminals, and guards and employees did their job. The sense of failure applies to the general and ambitious aim of reform and humanitarianism, but this general statement shouldn't obscure the fact that the new prison was a reality. It had become a small community of people, with its own rules and practices and its own management problems. Equally important, changes took place over time: decades later the penitentiary was to become the site for novel experiments in the science of punishment.[107]

Later on, in 1890, the annual *memoria* of the minister of justice included a revealing report on the conditions of the penitentiary written by the president of the Junta Inspectora. Discipline had loosened to the extent that prisoners had physical contact with outside persons. Prisoners had no shoes or clothes, and food was insufficient. Demoralization among the prisoners had worsened. Alcohol consumption and gambling prevailed over industriousness and religious instruction. The official attributed this situation to the system of private contracts used to run the workshops. His assessment of the state of the penitentiary was clearly pessimistic: "It would be better to close the doors of this house of correction and reform; it would be preferable to go back to the old and hateful carceral regime than to tolerate disorder in this facility that once was unique in South America."[108]

In the late nineteenth and early twentieth centuries a new wave of reformist rhetoric professed by penologists and criminologists revived the emphasis on the redemptive nature of work. But the performance of the penitentiary workshops was rather poor and the living conditions inside the penitentiary did not improve.[109] By the 1920s the penitentiary had become the center of a new attempt to modernize Peruvian penal institutions, this time aided by "scientific" devices such as anthropometric laboratories and an Instituto de Criminología organized within the penitentiary. In spite of these and other changes, the *panóptico*—as the Lima penitentiary was commonly labeled—remained a place where people from lower-class origins and militants of reformist or radical political parties were subjected to rigor, violence, and affliction. The sinister edifice was finally demolished in the mid-1960s.

## Conclusion

The modernization of Peruvian penal justice, the core of which was the penitentiary, was an aborted process. What Peruvian legal historian Fernando de Trazegnies called "traditional modernization"—a modernizing project that circumvented social change, maintained traditional sources of power and privilege, and imitated foreign, Eurocentric social models[110]—is clearly reflected in penal reforms. Various factors help to explain this compromise between modernity and tradition: the permanence of typically colonial social and labor relations such as slavery (abolished in 1854 but with a long-lasting mental and cultural legacy), domestic servitude, and coerced labor in haciendas and other productive centers; the diffusion of racism and its supposed "scientific" basis; the Europeanization of elite manners, cultural values, and social practices, with the concomitant enlargement of the distance between them and the lower strata. All these factors influenced the outcome of penal reform, creating mental structures, attitudes, and forms of social interaction that undermined the reformatory project.

The adoption of the penitentiary can be used to illustrate the relations between state and society in nineteenth-century Peru. Once the age of *caudillismo* was over, Peruvian liberal elites perceived the importance of having a strong and centralized state. They were unwilling to tolerate social disorder and chaos. Modernization required order and discipline. The dream of building a European-like society was pursued by increasingly repressive policies and by centralizing the administration of justice.

Correctional punishment was part of a complex array of interventions whose function was to "rehabituate" the population.[111] Mutual associations of artisans were encouraged because their activities included the instilling of industry and honesty into their members. Strict labor regulations were issued for factories and artisan workshops. An Escuela de Artes y Oficios was founded based on the principles of instruction and industry. Continuous campaigns against drinking, gambling, and other popular customs were launched. At the same time, the seclusion of mentally ill people took a great step forward.[112] The creation of urban police regiments with more strict duties of control and vigilance paralleled the building of the penitentiary.[113] Penal reforms included the promulgation of the first republican penal code in 1862, whose main goal was to end dispersion and to simplify penal legislation.[114] Thus, the penitentiary was immersed in a wider attempt at refining and optimizing social control, a project closely related to state formation in nineteenth-century Peru and informed by the elites' sense of danger in the face of the rebellious and disrespectful "lower orders."

As many scholars have recently argued, state consolidation in mid-nineteenth-century Peru resulted in an apparent contradiction: a liberal trade policy coexisted with a centralized and repressive state.[115] In actuality, both were part of the same process. As Guardino and Walker state, "The struggles of the early independent period shaped the character of relations between the state and civil society created in the mid-nineteenth century." With political centralization came the search for order (after the period known as the age of *caudillismo*), which ultimately prevailed over the egalitarian content of political and social liberalism. More important, centralization reinforced established notions about how to achieve obedience and subordination—a knowledge shaped in the terrain of private, conflictive everyday relations and later carried over into state institutions.

This "bastardized" (Gootenberg) or "stillborn" (Mallon) liberalism was thus unable to carry on the challenge of building a reformed penal system. Traditional relations of power and mental settings, as well as current political and social tensions, impeded it. The final disillusionment with the penitentiary model shows the irresolvable contradiction between a liberal egalitarian discourse and its application in a profoundly hierarchical society. That brings us one step forward into the question of the reception and appropriation of liberal discourse in Latin America. Was liberalism just an ideological import from societies in a different stage of social development? Or was it a malleable set of propositions that was used for different purposes in the region as compared to Europe? As Florencia Mallon argues, "In contrast to Europe, where liberalism arose in the context of a bourgeois challenge to the centralism and economic monopolies of absolutist states, liberalism in Latin America was discussed in the context of state making and of stubbornly precapitalist social and economic relations."[116] The result was the subordination of liberalism to the needs of centralized political control and traditional elites. Its egalitarian and humanist dimensions were subsumed under the project of state building. It was those needs that prevailed in the pursuit of "modernization" in the penal system in nineteenth-century Peru. The failure of the penitentiary goal of reforming criminals is only one side of the story. The other side is its success in reinforcing the authoritarian nature of the Peruvian state and of the modernization project pursued by its elite.

## Notes

Part of the materials used in this chapter were collected during a year of dissertation research in Lima, funded by the MacArthur Interdisciplinary Program of the University of Minnesota. The final version was written while I held a Harry Frank Guggenheim dissertation grant. I want to express here my profound gratitude to both institutions. I would also like to thank Rainer Baehre, Robert Buffington, Ricardo Salvatore, and Charles Walker for their criticism and suggestions. All remaining errors and misconceptions are, of course, entirely mine.

1. This theme receives central attention in my forthcoming dissertation, "Crime, Punishment, and Modernization in Lima, Peru, 1860–1930," Department of History, University of Minnesota.

2. George Rusche and Otto Kirchheimer, *Punishment and Social Structure* (New York: Columbia University Press, 1939). For an attempt to salvage the Rusche-Kirchheimer thesis, see Dario Melossi and Massimo Pavarini, *The Prison and the Factory: Origins of the Penitentiary System* (Totowa, N.J.: Barnes & Noble, 1981).

3. Michael Ignatieff, *A Just Measure of Pain: The Penitentiary in the Industrial Revolution, 1750–1850* (New York: Pantheon Books, 1978).

4. Michel Foucault, *Discipline and Punish: The Birth of the Prison*, trans. Alan Sheridan (New York: Pantheon Books, 1977). According to David Rothman, "Foucault's analysis never enters into the everyday world of criminal justice. It is one thing to claim that the goal of surveillance dominated the *theory* of punishment, quite another to examine what actually happened when programs were translated into *practice*." Rothman, *Conscience and Convenience: The Asylum and Its Alternatives in Progressive America* (Boston: Little, Brown and Company, 1980), p. 11. See also David Garland, *Punishment and Modern Society: A Study in Social Theory* (Chicago: University of Chicago Press, 1990), chaps. 7 and 8, and Michael Ignatieff, "State, Civil Society, and Total Institutions: A Critique of Recent Social Histories of Punishment," in Stanley Cohen and Andrew Scull, eds., *Social Control and the State: Historical and Contemporary Essays* (Oxford: Basil Blackwell, 1985) for critical accounts of Foucault's interpretation of the birth of the prison.

5. Pieter Spierenburg, *The Spectacle of Suffering: Executions and the Evolution of Repression: From a Preindustrial Metropolis to the European Experience* (Cambridge: Cambridge University Press, 1984); Spierenburg, *The Prison Experience: Disciplinary Institutions and Their Inmates in Early Modern Europe* (New Brunswick, N.J.: Rutgers University Press, 1991).

6. The recent book by Adrian Howe, *Punish and Critique: Towards a Feminist Analysis of Penality* (London and New York: Routledge, 1994), offers a good summary and an intelligent criticism of these approaches. The author emphasizes the fact that all these histories of punishment—including the "revisionist" trend—deal exclusively with the Western experience, something that is not always stressed in the literature on this topic.

7. Erving Goffman, "On the Characteristics of Total Institutions," in Donald R. Cressy, ed., *The Prison: Studies in Institutional Organization and Change* (New York: Holt, Rinehart and Winston, 1961).

8. Patricia O'Brien, *The Promise of Punishment: Prisons in Nineteenth-Century France* (Princeton, N.J.: Princeton University Press, 1980), p. 4. See also Ignatieff, "State, Civil Society and Total Institutions."

9. José Hurtado Pozo, *La ley "importada": recepción del derecho penal en el Perú* (Lima: CEDYS, 1979), p. 38.

10. On colonial criminal legislation, see Miguel Bonifaz, *Derecho indiano* (Sucre: Universidad Mayor de San Francisco Xavier de Chuquisaca, 1961), pp. 342–348. On public executions, see Alberto Flores Galindo, *Aristocracia y plebe: estructura de clases y sociedad colonial, Lima 1760–1830* (Lima: Mosca Azul Editores, 1984), pp. 149–150. Sarah Chambers has noticed that although colonial penal legislation was severe and cruel, its application was rather lenient. Sarah Chambers, "The Many Faces of the White City: Urban Culture and Society in Arequipa, Peru, 1780–1854," Ph.D. diss., University of Wisconsin, 1992.

11. Juan Oviedo, *Colección de leyes, decretos y órdenes publicados en el Perú desde el año 1821 hasta el 31 de diciembre de 1859* (Lima: F. Bailey, 1861–1872), 12: 325.

12. Mariano Santos de Quirós, *Colección de leyes, decretos y órdenes publicados en el Perú desde su independencia en el año de 1821, hasta el 31 de diciembre de 1830* (Lima: Imprenta de J. Masías, 1831), decree no. 102.

13. Ibid., 3: 16.

14. Archivo General de la Nación (hereafter AGN), Prefecturas, Lima, Leg. 120, 1836/46.

15. Interestingly enough, this "colonial" institution never really functioned in Peru during the colonial period, in spite of several attempts and strong demands from authorities and elites, especially after the Tupac Amaru rebellion. It did work, however, during the republican period, which speaks of the contradictions and ambiguities of the republican leaders' intentions and needs. See Barbara V. Montgomery, "The Evolution of Rural Justice in New Spain, Culminating in the Acordada, and Attempts by the Spanish Crown to Institute the Tribunal in Peru," Ph.D. diss., Loyola University, 1973. The Acordada in Mexico has been studied by Colin MacLachlan, *Criminal Justice in Eighteenth Century Mexico: A Study of the Tribunal of the Acordada* (Berkeley and Los Angeles: University of California Press, 1974).

16. The debates around the death penalty are summarized by Carlos Valladares, "La pena de muerte," thesis, Universidad Nacional Mayor de San Marcos, Lima, 1946.

17. See *El Telégrafo de Lima*, December 20, 1829, for the case of the bandit Tomás, alias "Animita," executed in the same place where he was captured. See also Jacobo Von Tschudi, *Testimonio del Perú, 1838–1842* (Lima: Consejo Consultivo Suiza-Perú, 1966), p. 176, for details on the execution of bandits.

18. *El Telégrafo de Lima*, January 13, 1829, expressed eloquently the convictions about public executions: "three or four famous bandits will be executed next week. For making the lesson fruitful, it would be convenient to hang them after the execution in those places where they used to attack the travelers with more frequency. This is practiced in Europe and is an effective way to reform some and to avoid that others, encouraged by impunity, commit the same crimes."

19. Max Radiguet, *Lima y la sociedad peruana* (Lima: Biblioteca Nacional, 1971), pp. 114–118.

20. On the weaknesses and contradictions of nineteenth-century Peruvian liberalism, see Gonzalo Portocarrero, "Conservadurismo, liberalismo y democracia en el Perú del siglo XIX," in Alberto Adrianzén, ed., *Pensamiento político peruano* (Lima: Desco, 1987), and Paul Gootenberg, "Beleaguered Liberals: The Failed First Generation of Free Traders in Peru," in Joseph Love and Nils Jacobsen, eds., *Guiding the Invisible Hand: Economic Liberalism and the State in Latin American History* (New York: Praeger, 1988).

21. See Carlos Aguirre, "Disciplina, castigo y control social: estudio sobre conductas sociales y mecanismos punitivos, Lima, 1821–1868," Licenciatura thesis, Universidad Nacional Federico Villarreal, Lima, 1990, chap. 3, for a review of these informal forms of punishment in early republican Peru.

22. On racist discourse and attitudes in early republican Peru, see Alberto Flores Galindo, "República sin ciudadanos," in *Buscando un Inca: identidad y utopía en los Andes*, 3d ed. (Lima: Editorial Horizonte, 1988); Charles Walker, "Rhetorical Power: Early Republican Discourse on the Indians in Cusco," paper presented to the AHA Annual Conference, Chicago 1991; and Cecilia Méndez, *Incas sí, Indios no: apuntes para el estudio del nacionalismo criollo en el Perú* (Lima: Instituto de Estudios Peruanos, 1993).

23. "Hit her harshly, because she doesn't feel."

24. AGN, Causas Criminales, Leg. 78, 1844.

25. J. Carlos García Basalo, *San Martín y la reforma carcelaria: aporte a la historia del derecho penal argentino y americano* (Buenos Aires: Ediciones Arayú, 1954), p. 38.

26. *Gaceta de Gobierno de Lima*, 27-2-1822, p. 347. The practice of converting convents into prisons had become common in Europe by the late eighteenth century.

27. On the horrors of the Cárcel de Guadalupe, see, for instance, Carlos Aurelio León, *Nuestras cárceles* (Lima: Librería e Imprenta Gil, 1920), and the magazine *Variedades*, March 24, 1923, pp. 703–704.

28. See Portocarrero, "Conservadurismo, liberalismo y democracia"; Flores Galindo, "República sin ciudadanos"; Charles Walker, "Montoneros, bandoleros, malhechores: criminalidad y política en las primeras décadas republicanas," in Carlos Aguirre and Charles Walker, eds., *Bandoleros, abigeos y montoneros: criminalidad y violencia en el Perú, siglos XVIII–XX* (Lima: Instituto de Apoyo Agrario, 1990), pp. 105–136.

29. See Julio Altmann Smythe, *Reseña histórica de la evolución del derecho penal, con conclusiones sobre la futura política criminal del Perú* (Lima: Sanmartí y Cía., 1944), p. 264.

30. Ibid., p. 264.

31. For a crude description of early-nineteenth-century Peruvian jails, see Mariano Felipe Paz Soldán, "Estado actual de las cárceles y presidios en el Perú," in *Examen de las penitenciarías de los Estados Unidos* (New York: S. W. Benedict, 1853).

32. Ibid., p. 96.

33. Ibid., p. 101.

34. AGN, Prefecturas, Lima, Leg. 117, 1825/28, July 16, 1827.

35. Paz Soldán captured the feelings involved: "It is impossible to compute all the evils resulting from the flight of a prisoner; a fact that seems to be so simple and without consequences is a direct attack on morality, the law, and the improvement of customs; it helps to lose respect for judges, fear of penalties, and even the hope for reform." Paz Soldán, *Examen de las penitenciarías*, pp. 91–92.

36. Ibid., p. 91.

37. Ibid., p. 94.

38. To explain the apparent contradiction between this assertion and the fact that imprisonment was already the main form of punishment, we need to differentiate the operation of the judicial system from the overall strategy of control and repression used by the ruling elites and the state. The latter was much broader than the former, which speaks not only of the weakness of formal institutions but also of the difficulties of checking the private exercise of power. The permanence of slavery in republican Peru was certainly a factor behind the extended use of arbitrary and private forms of punishment.

39. On these issues, see Salvatore and Aguirre's essay, chapter 1, this volume.

40. On this, see Flores Galindo, "República sin ciudadanos," and Carlos Aguirre, "Patrones, esclavos, y sirvientes domésticos en Lima, siglo XIX," in Pilar Gonzalbo, ed., *Familia y vida privada en la historia de Iberoamérica* (Mexico City: El Colegio de México, 1995).

41. AGN, Prefecturas, Lima, Leg. 117, August 29, 1827.

42. *El Telégrafo de Lima*, July 24, 1832.

43. The workhouse was not, according to Melossi and Pavarini, "a true and proper place of production, it was a place for teaching the discipline of production." More references about these institutions are found in Spierenburg, *The Prison Experience*, and Joanna Innes, "Prisons for the Poor: English Bridewells, 1555–1800," in Francis Snyder and Douglas Hay, eds., *Labour, Law, and Crime: An Historical Perspective* (London: Tavistock Publications, 1987), pp. 42–122.

44. Altmann, *Reseña histórica*, p. 265.

45. Medina was a very active local authority, engaged in a comprehensive campaign of repression and "cleaning" in the city of Cusco. I thank Thomas Kruggeler for this information.

46. The use of convict slaves in bakeries is detailed in Aguirre, "Disciplina," chapter 3; the use of prisoners in mines during early republican Peru is mentioned in José Deustua, *La minería peruana y la iniciación de la República* (Lima: Instituto de Estudios Peruanos, 1987), and the use of prisoners in guano islands is referred to in Cecilia Méndez, *Los trabajadores guaneros del Perú, 1840–1879* (Lima: Seminario de Historia Rural Andina, 1987).

47. See Justo Serna Alonso, *Presos y pobres en la España del siglo XIX* (Barcelona: PPU, 1988), p. 13, for a similar situation in nineteenth-century Italy and Spain.

48. Lima: Imprenta del Gobierno por Eusebio Aranda, 1854.

49. Ibid., pp. 63–67, 80–86.

50. For a general overview of this period and the multiple efforts at modernizing Peruvian society, see Julio Cotler, *Clases, estado y nación en el Perú* (Lima:

Instituto de Estudios Peruanos, 1978); Heraclio Bonilla, *Guano y burguesía en el Perú*, 3d ed. (Quito: FLACSO, 1994); and Paul Gootenberg, *Between Silver and Guano: Commercial Policy and the State in Post-Independence Peru* (Princeton, N.J.: Princeton University Press, 1989).

51. Paz Soldán, *Examen de las penitenciarías*, p. 10.

52. The "criminal" was almost invariably presented as a male subject.

53. The developments to which we have made reference are summarized in Ignatieff, "State, Civil Society, and Total Institutions," and O'Brien, *The Promise of Punishment*. For different interpretive overviews of these changes, see Foucault, *Discipline and Punish*; Rusche and Kirchheimer, *Punishment and Social Structure*; and Melossi and Pavarini, *The Prison and the Factory*. An excellent and balanced assessment of these different approaches is Garland, *Punishment and Modern Society*.

54. Paz Soldán was one of the many foreign visitors who came to the United States to investigate its penitentiaries and prisons. People from all over the world did the same tour at different times during the nineteenth century. Most of them wrote reports, the most famous being Alexis de Tocqueville and Gustave de Beaumont's *On the Penitentiary System in the United States and Its Application in France* (Philadelphia: Carey, Lea & Blanchard, 1833).

55. "Day-association for maximum industrial production; night-separation and the silent system for maximum prevention of contamination." Melossi and Pavarini, *The Prison and the Factory*, p. 158.

56. Ibid., p. 154.

57. See Rothman, *The Discovery of the Asylum*, p. 81. For further insights on both penitentiary models, see Tocqueville and de Beaumont, *On the Penitentiary System in the United States*. See also Lawrence M. Friedman, *Crime and Punishment in American History* (New York: Basic Books, 1993), pp. 77–82.

58. On nineteenth-century Peruvian elite racism, see note 22. For related intellectual constructions of the Indian, see also Gustavo Buntinx, "Del 'Habitante de las cordilleras' al 'Indio alfarero': variaciones sobre un tema de Francisco Laso," *Márgenes* 10/-11 (1993). There is a growing literature on this topic in Latin America. A recent contribution is Blanca Muratorio, ed., *Imágenes e imagineros: representaciones de los indígenas ecuatorianos, siglos XIX y XX* (Quito: FLACSO, 1994).

59. Paz Soldán, *Examen de las penitenciarías*, p. 109.

60. Ibid., p. 110.

61. Ibid.

62. The penitentiary was envisioned to accommodate criminals from all over the country. Indians constituted roughly 55 percent of the Peruvian population, and it was assumed that they would also make up the majority of the criminal population. See Paul Gootenberg, "Population and Ethnicity in Early Republican Peru: Some Revisions," *Latin American Research Review* 26, no. 3 (1991) for a recent assessment of nineteenth-century population figures.

63. "Whites are friends of society, and even if they could live in the cell, their character would yield more easily in the company of people to whom they are generally superior; their self-esteem will inspire them to keep their primacy." In Mexico discussions about the "best" penitentiary model were also shaped by

racial stereotypes about Indians and mestizos. See Laurence Rohlfes, "Police and Penal Correction in Mexico City, 1876–1911: A Study of Order and Progress in Porfirian Mexico," Ph.D. diss., Tulane University, 1983, p. 297.

64. On liberal state formation and indigenous populations, see especially Florencia Mallon, *Peasant and Nation: The Making of Post-Colonial Mexico and Peru* (Berkeley and Los Angeles: University of California Press, 1995). On the way Peruvian criminology approached the "Indian question," see Deborah Poole, "Ciencia, peligrosidad y represión en la criminología indigenista peruana," in Aguirre and Walker, eds., *Bandoleros, abigeos y montoneros*, pp. 335–367.

65. See José Casimiro Ulloa, "Higiene de las prisiones," *Gaceta Médica de Lima* 67 (1859).

66. For information on guards and employees, see Aguirre, "The World They Made Together: Guards, Employees, and Inmates in the Lima penitentiary, 1860–1930," unpublished manuscript.

67. Ulloa, "Higiene de las prisiones," p. 51.

68. Two prominent lawyers, Manuel A. Fuentes and M. A. de la Lama, who published in 1877 the standard dictionary of criminal legislation in Peru, also expressed their preference for the Philadelphia regime: "This system not only contains and prevents prisoners' corruption, prohibiting any conversation among them, but in addition it easily achieves order and discipline and prepares the inmate for moral redemption." It is not clear whether this statement reflects true convictions or was induced by the poor performance of the Lima penitentiary during its early years. Fuentes and de la Lama, *Diccionario de jurisprudencia y de legislación peruana: parte criminal* (Lima: Imprenta del Estado, 1877), p. 509.

69. Paz Soldán, *Examen de las penitenciarías*, p. 120.

70. Mariano Felipe Paz Soldán, *Reglamento para el servicio interior de la prisión penitenciaria de Lima* (Lima: Imprenta de José Masías, 1863).

71. Paz Soldán, *Examen de las penitenciarías*, p. 124.

72. Ibid. Tocqueville and de Beaumont had described the regime in an American congregate prison using similar words: "their bodies are together, but their souls are separated, and it is not the solitude of the body which is important, but that of the mind." Quoted in Melossi and Pavarini, *The Prison and the Factory*, p. 161.

73. Paz Soldán, *Examen de las penitenciarías*, p. 124.

74. Melossi and Pavarini, *The Prison and the Factory*, p. 143.

75. See, for instance, Charles Walker, "Voces discordantes: discursos alternativos sobre el indio a fines de la colonia," in Walker, ed., *Entre la retórica y la insurgencia: ideas y movimientos sociales en los Andes en el siglo XVIII* (Cusco: Centro Las Casas, 1995).

76. See especially Paul Gootenberg, *Imagining Development: Economic Ideas in Peru's "Fictitious Prosperity" of Guano, 1840–1880* (Berkeley and Los Angeles: University of California Press, 1993), and Carmen McEvoy, *Un proyecto nacional en el siglo XIX: Manuel Pardo y su visión del Perú* (Lima: Pontificia Universidad Católica del Perú, 1994). Of course, this was a topic that had colonial antecedents. See Ignacio de Lequanda, "Discurso sobre el destino que debe darse a la gente vaga que tiene Lima," *Mercurio Peruano* (Lima) 10 (1794).

77. Paz Soldán, *Examen de las penitenciarías*, p. 132.

78. Ibid.

79. On the principles of the panopticon, see Foucault, *Discipline and Punish*; John Bender, *Imagining the Penitentiary: Fiction and the Architecture of Mind in Eighteenth Century England* (Chicago: University of Chicago Press, 1987); and Robin Evans, *The Fabrication of Virtue: English Prison Architecture, 1750–1840* (Cambridge: Cambridge University Press, 1983). A recent assessment is Janet Semple, *Bentham's Prison: A Study of the Panopticon Penitentiary* (New York: Oxford University Press, 1993).

80. "Revisionist" literature on the subject is abundant, but we can consider Foucault's *Discipline and Punish*, Rothman's *The Discovery of the Asylum*, and Ignatieff's *A Just Measure of Pain* as key works. See Ignatieff, "State, Civil Society, and Total Institutions" for a critical appraisal of this literature.

81. See Ignatieff, "State, Civil Society, and Total Institutions"; Garland, *Punishment and Modern Society*; and William J. Forsythe, *The Reform of Prisoners, 1830–1900* (New York: St. Martin's Press, 1987).

82. Forsythe, *The Reform of Prisoners*, p. 229.

83. Between 1840 and 1870 the Peruvian economy boomed thanks to revenues from the export of guano (bird droppings). The finest general interpretation on this period is Gootenberg, *Between Silver and Guano* (on the economic and social realities), and Gootenberg, *Imagining Development* (on the elites' modernization projects).

84. Rohlfes, "Police and Penal Correction," pp. 288–311.

85. For further information, see Carlos Moreyra Paz Soldán, *La obra de los Paz Soldán: bibliografía* (Lima: Talleres Gráficos P. L. Villanueva, 1974), pp. 37–40.

86. Paz Soldán calculated that 377,874 working days were used, of which only 16,333 were from prisoners. See the final report by Paz Soldán in *Memoria que el ministro de gobierno, policía y obras públicas presenta al Congreso Nacional de 1862* (Lima: Imprenta la Época, 1862), document no. 26.

87. As the city began to expand, however, especially after the demolition of the city walls in the late 1860s, the penitentiary actually became part of the city's main central area. See Juan Bromley and José Barbagelata, *Evolución urbana de Lima* (Lima: Editorial Lumen, ca. 1945), p. 82.

88. For the German visitor E. W. Middendorf, the penitentiary was "the biggest, most solid, and best constructed edifice in the city." Ernst W. Middendorf, *Perú: observaciones y estudios del país y sus habitantes durante una permanencia de 25 años* (Lima: Universidad Nacional Mayor de San Marcos, 1973), 1: 296.

89. The practice of calling each inmate by his number was legally abolished in the 1920s, although there is evidence that it continued to be used after that date.

90. Paz Soldán, *Reglamento*. The "rain shower," or *baño de lluvia*, was the uninterrupted exposure of the criminal to a heavy shower, causing him/her serious breathing difficulties. It is revealing that in his report on American prisons Paz Soldán expressed his horror with the rain shower, a penalty that, he thought, was even more horrendous than shooting. Later, he adapted it for the penitentiary in Lima as a way of lessening prisoners' punishment. Paz Soldán, *Examen de las penitenciarías*, p. 47.

91. "Memoria del director de la penitenciaría," June 30, 1870, AGN, Ministerio de Justicia, Legajo 3.20.3.3.1.4.1 (Libro Copiador), fol. 372.

92. The division was as follows:

| Grades | Minimum Term | Middle Term | Maximum Term |
|---|---|---|---|
| I | 4 years | 5 years | 6 years |
| II | 7 years | 8 years | 9 years |
| III | 10 years | 11 years | 12 years |
| IV | 13 years | 14 years | 15 years |

Source: M. A. Fuentes and M. A. de la Lama, *Diccionario de jurisprudencia y legislación peruana: parte criminal* (Lima: Imprenta del Estado, 1877), p. 523.

93. See Aguirre, "The World They Made Together."

94. AGN, Penitenciaría, Leg. 242, September 25, 1862.

95. Ibid., October 10, 1862.

96. Ibid., November 1, 1862.

97. Ibid., November 20, 1862.

98. Ibid., June 22, 1866.

99. Ibid., June 18, 1867.

100. Ibid., May 17, 1867.

101. A dramatic case was that of the inmate Luis Núñez, who, twenty-six days before his anticipated release, began to cough blood as a result of tuberculosis. The director himself believed that when the day of the inmate's release arrived the man would not be able to enjoy it. Ibid., July 30, 1868.

102. Ibid., September 6, 1866.

103. Ibid., September 10, 1866 (emphasis added).

104. Ibid., March 7, 1867.

105. Ibid., August 7, October 24, 1867.

106. Ibid., December 10, 1867.

107. See Aguirre, "Crime, Punishment, and Modernization."

108. "Memoria presentada por el presidente de la junta inspectora del panóptico, Dr. D. Augusto S. Albarracin al Ministerio de Justicia, Culto, Instrucción y Beneficencia," in *Memoria que presenta el ministro de justicia, culto, instrucción y beneficencia al Congreso Ordinario de 1890* (Lima: Imprenta de Torres Aguirre, 1890).

109. See Juan José Calle et al., "Informe que la comisión encargada de examinar el estado administrativo y técnico de la penitenciaría de Lima, ha presentado al Ministerio de Justicia" (1915), in *La Revista del Foro* 7, no. 12 (1920) and 8, no. 13 (1921). See also Víctor M. Villavicencio, *La reforma penitenciaria en el Perú* (Lima: Imprenta A. J. Rivas Berrio, 1927).

110. Fernando de Trazegnies, *La idea de derecho en el Perú republicano del siglo XIX* (Lima: Pontificia Universidad Católica del Perú, 1980).

111. It would be useful to introduce here the distinction that Adam J. Hirsch makes between "rehabilitation" and what he calls "rehabituation." The first seeks a deep change in the criminal's morality essentially through noncoercive means, while the second is "an inherently superficial form of rehabilitation. It addresse[s] outward routines and abilities rather than inner moral values. [It is also] inherently coercive, acting quite against the inmate's will." The way the Lima penitentiary operated tended more to "rehabituate" the criminal than to "rehabilitate" him or her. Adam J. Hirsch, *The Rise of the Penitentiary: Prisons and Punishment in Early America* (New Haven, Conn.: Yale University Press, 1992), pp. 14–15.

112. See Augusto Ruiz, *Psiquiatras y locos* (Lima: Instituto Pasado & Presente, 1994).

113. In 1855 a Cuerpo de Gendarmería was created (*El Comercio*, August 22, 1855), while in 1860 another body, the Compañía de Seguridad Pública de la Capital, was added (*El Peruano*, March 6, 1860). One of the first activities of the latter was to gather precise information about residents, their "nations," and their occupations.

114. A committee for the elaboration of this code was formed in 1853, the draft was ready in 1859, and it was finally approved in 1862. See Jorge Basadre, *Historia de la República del Perú* (Lima: Editorial Universitaria, 1983), 4: 253–254, and Hurtado Pozo, *La ley 'importada,'* p. 46.

115. Florencia Mallon, "Economic Liberalism: Where We Are and Where We Need to Go," in Joseph Love and Nils Jacobsen, eds., *Guiding the Invisible Hand: Economic Liberalism and the State in Latin American History* (New York: Praeger, 1988); Gootenberg, *Between Silver and Guano*; and Peter Guardino and Charles Walker, "The State, Society and Politics in Peru and Mexico and the Late Colonial and the Early Republican Period," *Latin American Perspectives* 19, no. 2 (1992).

116. Mallon, "Economic Liberalism," p. 184.

# 3. Vicious Women, Virtuous Women: The Female Delinquent and the Santiago de Chile Correctional House, 1860–1900

*María Soledad Zárate Campos*

> On a throne, above which is a crucifix, a sister is sitting; before her, arranged in two rows, the prisoners are carrying out the task imposed on them, and, as needlework accounts for almost all the work, the strictest silence is constantly maintained . . . It seems that, in these halls, the very air breathes penitence and expiation.[1]

This essay examines the experience of the Casa Correccional de Santiago, a facility hosting women that elites considered "aggressive," "bad-living," "vicious," or "lost," during the second half of the nineteenth century.[2] It looks at what kind of women the inmates were, what kind of felonies they committed, and how they were perceived by society. The essay focuses on the disciplinary system that Chilean elites devised for these women and its transition from a civil to a religious administration around the 1860s. Confinement, a pillar of the disciplinary system in male penitentiaries, also served to discipline "vicious" women, but their treatment in other respects was different. The Correctional House, under the administration of the Sisters of the Good Shepherd, aimed not at reform or rehabilitation from a criminal past but at reparation and rectification of vice. Female delinquents were construed as having lost their "virtue" and "modesty"; consequently, their reincorporation into society demanded treatment different from that accorded to men. A review of disciplinary discourses and practices at the Santiago Correctional House serves to illustrate key connections between gender and crime that guided the methods of punishing and correcting women in late-nineteenth-century Chile.

This subject is linked to the renewed interest in lower-class women and their history produced by historiographical trends like the history of mentalities, the history of social movements, oral history, and women's history.[3] The latter discipline in particular attempts to reverse the traditional male-centered approach to history, opening up for research areas such as the family, interpersonal relations, marriage, and other related institutions.[4] At the same time, the "new women's history" uses the concept of gender to establish a closer collaboration and exchange with social history and to emphasize the diverse ways of "being a woman"—the profound differences encountered when we consider class, race, ethnic, and generational factors.[5] The notion of diversity allows us more flexibility in approaching women's history, avoiding stereotypes and abusive generalizations. In addition, the concept of gender helps us uncover the (masculine) ideologies that underlie the policies, practices, and social constructions that affect women's lives.

Within this conceptual framework, this essay suggests that the dichotomy vicious woman/virtuous woman helps explain the practices of the Correctional House and connects its institutional history to larger processes of class formation and the construction of women's place in Chilean society. As the Correctional House's main objective was to rectify the "offenses against virtue" committed by female delinquents, its disciplinary regime centered on religious instruction, domestic work, and literacy with an emphasis on the production of self-respect and "virtue." Portraying the inmates as weak and the outside world as dangerous, the sisters endeavored to retain some of the inmates after they had served their time. The Correctional House's superior asserted her role as mother of the inmates, favoring personal relations in the context of rigid, conventual rules.

The main sources used for this investigation are reports on the Correctional House written by the mother superior to the minister of justice from 1864 through 1889. These periodic reports provide considerable information on the organization and administration of the new facility, the methods of discipline used, and the lives of prisoners and nuns. As the Correctional housed only women of little education and meager income, many of them rural migrants, these documents give us an insight into the lives of lower-class women as perceived by their religious guardians. The main limitations of this source—the sisters' prejudice against lower-class women and their unquestioned confidence in their own methods of rehabilitation—are also its strength, for it allows us to gauge the location of the female inmate's place (between virtue and vice) at the very moment of its production or construction. Other reports and essays written by members of Chile's intellectual and political elite are also used to describe the situation (and the potential threat) produced by female delinquents. The absence of writings or other types of evidence expressing the voice of the inmates prevents us from examining alternative perceptions of discipline, religious instruction, and reformation.

In the first section of the essay I briefly review the living conditions of Chile's popular sectors and the way they were viewed by elites. I then analyze the way authorities viewed lower-class women and their criminal behavior. In the third section I examine the operation of the Correctional House as reflected in the correspondence of the mother superior with government officials. Finally, I analyze the discourse of these reports and its connections to modern disciplinary forms (Foucault's carceral system) and Chilean elites' perception of gender roles.

## Fin de Siècle Santiago (the Two Cities)

By the second half of the nineteenth century, Chile had begun to experience a dramatic and complex social transformation. Increased population and urbanization, especially in Santiago, created a critical situation for the lower classes. Urban expansion accelerated between the 1860s and 1880s. The 1874 to 1876 world economic crisis was followed by the War of the Pacific and the 1891 Civil War, which further encouraged migration from the countryside and exacerbated social tensions in the larger cities. The population of the capital, Santiago, increased from 115,000 in 1865 to 150,000 in 1875 to 260,000 in 1891.[6] The new arrivals, who contributed to the formation of a proletariat class in the city, worked in public works, the incipient manufacturing industry, commerce, and domestic service (especially women) or simply increased the ranks of the unemployed.[7]

The transition from traditional to preindustrial society contributed to social divisions within the urban population. The presence of two highly differentiated social groups soon became evident: an affluent sector of social elites and the popular sectors. In their search for a more comfortable and modern lifestyle, members of the upper class occupied the center of the city, the "proper city," with elegant buildings and adequate services.[8] The lower classes—the *rotos*—occupied the outlying areas and suffered a gradual deterioration of their living standards.[9]

Faced with a disintegration of the old social order, the upper class took measures, pushing for protection against the *rotos* with whom they shared the city. Minor problems in the past, such as vagrancy, prostitution, crime, and disease, now became serious conditions that had to be addressed or at least concealed. By the 1870s the Santiago elite perceived the decline in lower-class living standards as a dangerous "demoralization" of Chilean society. The elite expressed disgust with "pestilent odors," the "city's nastiness" around the *rancheríos* and *conventillos* (types of lower-class housing), the spread of contagious diseases like smallpox and syphilis, and high rates of infant mortality.[10] Elites also expressed shock at increased violence and illicit acts that disturbed order and good behavior. Beginning in the 1870s, the issues of marginality and delinquency became conflated in a debate between different sectors of

Chilean society: central and local governments, Congress, and the Catholic Church. Crime began to be perceived as the most evident manifestation of the corruption of the lower classes.

The elites found it difficult to accept a popular presence in public spaces: street, plaza, market, neighborhood, liquor store (*chingana*). As María Angélica Illanes has stated, the lower classes were a presence "poor and miserable as a body, unpredictable and threatening as a mass." She adds that elite "displeasure was thus discharged with scorn and fear, a double sentiment that enhanced social distance and produced retreat and social separation."[11] Public spaces, the site for the interaction of different social groups, became the locus of disciplinary projects. For the disciplining of popular groups, the ruling elites chose the path of "progress" and "morality." These groups were to be "civilized" by inclusion in a modernizing Chilean society through the educational efforts of both church and state.

### Scandalous and Vicious Women

During the second half of the nineteenth century in Chile, we encounter an ideology that defined "the woman's mission in this world." This ideology asserted that a woman was subject to God, husband, and children; that she was a second-class citizen unable to control the direction of her life. Others guaranteed her welfare and regulated her wishes and aspirations. Nineteenth-century Chilean society saw women as an extension of their biological, and especially of their reproductive, characteristics. Society committed itself to policing female sexuality. A woman's value came from virginity, sexual honor, and maternity. Her sphere of action was reduced to the family, where she performed domestic roles consisting mainly of child rearing.

This ideal role contrasted with the actual conditions of nineteenth-century lower-class women. Women constituted more than half the peasant migrants to Santiago until the 1870s. Some of them sold food—bread, beverages, liquors, *empanadas*, fruits, vegetables, fritters—on the street. They were called *vivanderas* because they promoted *ramadas*, popular festivities with music, dance, food, and drink. Generally located on the outskirts of the city, these festivities were attended by upper-class men, *labradores*, peons, and other passersby in search of diversion and sexual commerce. Historian Gabriel Salazar provides a suggestive interpretation of these women's character:

> The *ramadas* constituted only the visible, bubbling, and somehow touristic manifestation of both a peon's peasant culture and the subsistence economy of independent lower-class women. In their

essence, they summed up or epitomized a new type of popular sociability that differentiated itself from that of conventional peasant families. While in peasant society the dominant figure was the *labrador* working the land and raising livestock (in spite of female peasants' artisanal production), in urban popular society the figure of the independent woman prevailed. She promoted, through subsistence trade, the development of open social relations and a public, unconstrained cultural expression.[12]

Because of their perceived extroversion, elites characterized these women as immoral, prostitutes, and "abettors of thieves." They received all the blame for illegal cohabitation, "natural children," love triangles, and adulteries. These *vivanderas*, together with laundresses, cooks, domestic servants, and seamstresses, constituted the principal target of church and state disciplinary efforts. Living their lives at the margins of acceptable society, these women became the focus of concern for the maintenance of public order. Among them, female criminals (those that actually broke the law), in spite of their scant visibility and statistical irrelevance, symbolized the flagrant transgression of female "duty."[13]

What do we know about these female criminals? They were generally poor, marginal women; only rarely were upper-class women arrested. The judicial system tried and arrested very few women in general. In 1864 authorities prosecuted 2,380 persons, but only 150 of them were women, a ratio of 1 woman for every 16 men.[14] Net entries from the penitentiary, the prison, and the Santiago Correctional House for 1865 recorded 1,300, 1,421, and 487 prisoners, respectively. The first two were male facilities. In a study of "public morality" initiated by Vicuña Mackenna, 3,735 male and 553 female criminals were consigned between June 1872 and March 1873: 1 woman for every 7 men.[15] According to these statistics, female criminality was growing faster than male criminality, a process that continued to the end of the nineteenth century.[16] However, female criminality figures, although inflated by many cases in which women were accomplices or abettors, reflect only those cases brought to the court and effectively tried, certainly only a portion of the total number of offenses.

Statistical sources also note the occupations of female criminals. By 1873 the proportions were four seamstresses, two domestic servants, one cook, and one laundress out of every ten incarcerated women.[17] Toward the end of the century the proportion of laundresses would increase. Significant numbers of female inmates were registered as not having an occupation or as being engaged in illegal activities like prostitution and gambling. *Vivanderas*, often imprisoned for crimes committed by men (frequently drunken brawls), were deported to the South to serve as domestics even after 1850.[18] Vagrant or jobless women, like all the women that crowded the nation's jails, were used to produce candle snuffs and flannels.[19]

According to statistics, vagrancy increased in alarming proportions. One source noted that "while the population increased in the last decade (1885–1895) by 11 percent, the number of people without trade or occupation increased . . . by the enormous proportion of 471 percent."[20] The increased ratio of female to male criminals was even more alarming. Whereas in 1870 as many unemployed males as females were imprisoned, in 1898 the inclusion of female prostitutes and gamblers among unemployed women changed that ratio to two women to one man.[21]

The most common female crimes were petty thefts and insults. Theft usually involved domestic servants stealing small domestic goods like clothes, sewing machines, or kitchen and laundry implements.[22] Laundresses were the most likely to be accused of illicit acts and apparently had the most opportunities. Their work involved transporting clothes to their own neighborhoods, and customers accused many of not returning garments. Even though these crimes were relatively trivial, the high frequency of the denunciations greatly disturbed the authorities.[23] The cases involving insults came mostly from minor disputes among women, generally neighbors in the *rancheríos* or *conventillos*, who accused each other of being "whores," "evil women," or "man-hunters." Verbal aggression typified this particular crime, as accusations of prostitution or adultery seriously affected a woman's reputation, a fact often noted in plaintiffs' complaints. Adultery was another common female crime, since fidelity was a woman's rather than a man's obligation. Women were also frequently accused of aiding and abetting crimes committed by their husbands or lovers, an accusation most denied.

### The Santiago Correctional House

Imprisoning criminals is a relatively modern practice. The birth of the prison is linked to the disappearance of the scaffold and the spectacle of corporal punishment which occurred near the beginning of the nineteenth century. Physical punishment was not totally suppressed but generally replaced by other punishments like forced labor and imprisonment, the latter often accompanied by food rationing, sexual deprivation, confinement, and beatings.[24] Since it punished all alike, penal reformers considered imprisonment the quintessential egalitarian punishment. Imprisonment also quantified punishment, establishing a direct relationship between the crime, the duration of the punishment, and the reparation owed society. Thus imprisonment recognized in concrete terms that the offense had injured not only the victim but society as a whole.[25] The establishment of incarceration as punishment and its later perfection in the penitentiary system developed through a series of reforms, projects, reorganizations, theoretical discourses, and research. Recurrent themes in this process were the efficacy of confinement, the prisoner's acceptance of penitentiary rules, the reform of the delinquent, and his or her reintegration into society. The prison gradually became the center of the penitentiary system. In the prison, penalties were executed, penalized individuals were observed, and "clinical knowledge" about the prison population was gathered.[26] Surveillance became widespread. The prisoner's behavior, work, physical well-being, and moral attitude were under constant observation.[27]

Inside the prison, the condemned was both cause and object of a disciplinary apparatus carefully designed to "straighten out" his or her behavior. According to Foucault, this is one of the effects sought by carceral disciplining. "The chief function of disciplinary power," he argues, "is to 'train,' rather than to select and levy." He adds that "discipline makes individuals; it is the specific technique of power that regards individuals both as subjects and as instruments of its exercise."[28] The prison provides the physical location for a protracted process of experimentation with and refinement of the correctional endeavor. By the end of the nineteenth century, this process culminated in a penitentiary system with its own juridical principles and goals.

Three of the seven penitentiary principles highlighted by Foucault are important for our analysis of the contrast between the penitentiary model and the discourses and practices of the Santiago Correctional House: correction, work, and classification. According to Foucault, these principles are integrated into "three great schemata: the politico-moral schema of individual isolation and hierarchy; the economic model of force applied to compulsory work; the technico-medical model of cure and normalization."[29] These features were part of ongoing discussions about the positive effect of the "penitentiary technique" on prisoners. They were also the target of repeated political and juridical criticism: does the prison correct, or does it, in attempting to correct, lose its rigor and punitive strength?

Foucault never specifically studied women's prisons. Nevertheless, his propositions can be applied to women's correctional houses as long as their singular characteristics are taken into account. In the Santiago Correctional House the terms "reform" and "correction," commonly used in masculine penology, were replaced by the terms "reparation" and "rectification." In an institution driven by social and religious goals, the disciplinary rigor appears to have been somehow softened, weakened. The Correctional House was to lead a process of rectification from "offenses against virtue" committed by poor, vicious women. The institution had to provide these women with an opportunity to enter the "path of virtue." Confinement, work, and classification were part of the disciplinary system, but religious instruction and the inculcation of respect for the mother superior and for the women themselves became central elements of the rectification process.

Until the 1860s civil authorities administered the Correctional House. A superintendent oversaw the allocation of funds, the maintenance of facilities, and the feeding and treatment of prisoners.[30] The *reglamento* of 1853 also stipulated that an administrator be charged with the Correctional's security. Religious and moral instruction were entrusted to a chaplain, whose functions, according to the *reglamento*, included "celebrating mass in the facility on the prescribed days, giving the prisoners a doctrinal speech on Thursday evenings and a moral one on Saturday, confessing them, and providing every service the House might require of him."[31] The municipal council covered the expense of feeding prisoners, but the Correctional used its own funds for basic necessities such as uniforms, beds, lighting, and special diets for sick prisoners.

"Moralization" of the prisoners consisted of the application of an intense work regimen based on sewing. The scanty revenue this work produced went for the most part to the prisoners themselves. By the end of the nineteenth century an increase in the number of free seamstresses in Santiago (pushing down wages and piece rates) reduced the demand for prisoners' work, thus lowering profits for them and the Correctional. The superintendent, in a letter to the minister of justice, complained that the prisoners languished in "punishable idleness," adding, "I hope you can get the government to commission the House to produce army uniforms, thus providing work for the prisoners."[32] During this period, "moralization" of prisoners depended to a great extent on the outside world.

House bylaws also prescribed thorough surveillance of prisoners. Even in the solitude of the cell, the inmates' behavior was under observation in order to detect any violation of the reform ideal. The *reglamento* prescribed "composure" and "restraint." Life inside the Correctional House developed slowly around daily rituals of inspection and the compliance with house rules. For prisoners, the routine of work, prayer, and meals was only occasionally disturbed by visits to the hospital or an attempted escape.

The Santiago Correctional House also functioned as a jail: in addition to long-term inmates, it also hosted women awaiting trial and those with short sentences (terms of the sentences varied from eight days to fifteen years). This was cause for considerable concern. The superintendent noted that daily entrances and exits, which resulted in the mingling of long-term and short-term inmates, disrupted the teaching of "habits of moralization and order" and encouraged disorder and escapes. In addition, as the Correctional House statistics revealed, a significant proportion of the inmates came from the provinces, adding a new difficulty to the problem of imposing discipline.[33]

In the mid-1860s, the recently arrived Sisters of the Good Shepherd took over the administration of the Correctional House from civil authorities.[34] The arrival of the first cohort of nuns in Chile was closely associated with the activities of the Sociedad de Beneficencia de Santiago (the Beneficent Society) under the direction of Antonia Salas de Errázuriz.[35] The Beneficent Society was made up of elite women, usually the wives, sisters, or mothers of prominent male public figures. Like its sister societies throughout nineteenth-century Latin America, it concentrated its activities in hospitals, orphanages, asylums, and prisons.[36] In lieu of government sponsorship, the society organized boards of directors to oversee the operation of these institutions. The principal goal was to protect the interests and needs of poor women, "to exert a sort of guardianship or patronage over the activities of the Beneficencia oriented toward women; to supervise existing projects and to create new ones; to get government permission to operate in public institutions; and to obtain licenses for fund-raising activities."[37]

The magnitude of the task (the growing number of destitute women in Santiago) soon overwhelmed the society's resources and membership. The society then turned to female religious communities for help. Sisters from the Order of Saint Vincent de Paul were invited to take charge of hospitals, Sisters of the Providence to administer and staff orphanages, and Sisters of the Good Shepherd to run the asylum for fallen women and the Correctional House.[38]

Charity and the responsibility for protecting the needy were delicate matters. Social problems and "social work" were not considered areas of state concern. Preoccupation with social problems and attempts to deal with them were assumed by private individuals working through civil organizations like the Beneficent Society or by donations to religious charitable institutions. Given these circumstances, the society appealed to Bishop Santiago Valdivieso to recruit Sisters of the Good Shepherd to help "the poor girls, more or less abandoned and helpless and in danger of perdition . . . those that having lost themselves need to be regenerated and encouraged to direct their lives along the path of virtue."[39]

Concern with the destiny of "helpless girls" and "those that need to be regenerated" was widespread. This concern was shared by the Catholic Church, which in spite of its preoccupation with fallen women had previously neglected the special needs of poor women.[40] The sisters' function was specifically outlined before their arrival in Chile.[41] They were to focus attention on poor women, especially those in danger of committing or who had already committed crimes. Their principal concern was to elevate the morality of confined women. The work of this religious order had no parallel for male criminals; no specific religious order attended male criminals. In the men's penitentiary, religious influence was limited to the presence of the chaplain, who had no general supervisory or administrative responsibilities.

The presence of the sisters, who arrived in February 1847, was supplemented by the foundation of the Santiago Correctional House.[42] The establishment of the Correctional House required some repairs to the old building housing the female prisoners in order to incorporate a chapel, visiting rooms, and bedrooms for the nuns. The facility included sections for "Magdalenes," as well as for "repentant," deaf-mute, "preserved," and "external" women. The official inauguration took place on April 24, 1864. In his inaugural speech, Father Mariano Casanova reflected on the reformatory mission of the prison:

> Prison, though thought of as harsh, will be used to satisfy public
> vengeance and especially to correct and to sanctify the guilty. . . .
> By entrusting this House to the Congregation of the Good Shepherd
> we are seeking not only to foment Christian piety among its
> inhabitants; it is necessary that industriousness accompany piety
> . . . . This House testifies to the evils of idleness. Its history tells us
> that honest and industrious women never arrive here. . . . We must
> force the love for work upon those that already know the meaning
> of crime, those that do not preserve the innocence proper to their
> sex.[43]

The decree regulating the Correctional House gave the nuns ample freedom to organize and administer the facility and the prisoners. That process—the gradual construction of the Correctional House's disciplinary system—is evident in the mother superior's correspondence with the minister of justice. These reports, though reflecting a one-sided perspective (that of the sisters) of the lives of inmates, allow us to understand the evolving strategies and reasons used by the sisters in "correcting" lower-class women.

### The Prison as a Home

Condemned and accused women entered the prison with few belongings, which were withheld until the women were discharged. Their children, however, presented a more difficult problem since they were generally considered each woman's exclusive responsibility. This was a crucial dilemma: due to lack of space and child care, children could not be admitted into the Correctional House even though many of them depended exclusively on their mother's care. In cases like these, the mother superior sent the children to the orphanage "with the request that once the prisoner finishes her sentence, she comes by to get her child." This situation reflects the prisoners' degree of abandonment and distance from family support systems either because they were newly arrived immigrants to Santiago or because their disgrace severed family ties.

The first Correctional House proved inadequate. The mother superior reported in June 1865 that cramped quarters and cold and unhygienic facilities threatened the prisoners' health.[44] Consequently, after some searching by the Congregation of the Good Shepherd, the government purchased a larger site, the Casa de Ejercicios, or Casa de Santa Rosa, which had several patios, a large garden, and abundant water.[45] The building was renovated to divide the religious community from the penal area and to accommodate the sectioning of inmates. A dining room, workshops, laundry room, and bathrooms were added as well.

Security was a constant concern even though soldiers guarded the Correctional House and the inmates were not really dangerous. The deteriorating conditions of the house and walls led to incursions by thieves, and the unstable walls posed a safety hazard.[46] Although reports make no mention of violent episodes, vigilance over even passive prisoners was ongoing. This was the main reason for the great attention paid to house repairs.[47]

Until the nuns took charge of the Correctional House, feeding the inmates had been in the hands of a private concessionaire. For the mother superior, this had proved inadequate. "Almost all the inmates need better food," she advised. "Many of them are so weak that, unable to get the food they need from outside, they eat just bread, a situation that eventually leads to serious illnesses."[48] Food and clothing were recurrent topics in her subsequent reports. The typical menu included "soup for lunch, abundant meat at noon except on Fridays, and beans for supper; they also get fruit two or three times a week." The Correctional House supplied inmates with a uniform, underwear, a mattress, bed sheets, and blankets. Only occasionally did they get shoes.[49]

According to the mother superior, the inmates occupied themselves with "all those tasks proper to their sex," which included sewing, embroidering, washing, spinning wool, and cleaning. These tasks reflected the disciplinary goals of the nuns as well as the limited education of the inmates. Most entered the prison without skills. Half of the profits from the sale of the inmates' products and services went to the inmates; the Correctional House collected the remainder to cover maintenance and other expenses. Revenue from the inmates' work was essential to the Correctional House's finances, and any shortfall seriously affected its budget. It was important for inmates, too, who not surprisingly preferred the most profitable activities.[50]

Laundering was the most lucrative source of revenue for the Correctional House. According to the national census, laundering and sewing were the most frequent occupations for poor women in the nineteenth century. Thus there were many laundresses among the inmates "able to take a lot of orders from outside, which will yield good revenues for those devoted to this hard, burdensome occupation."[51] Inmates also cultivated the prison garden and worked in the binding shop that had been established around 1870 or 1871. Prisoners went through successive training periods because "when they first come here they are unable to perform even the less skilled tasks." It was "through the teaching they receive here and the care with which they are made to work," the mother superior concluded, that the inmates "grow fond of their work and learn how to make a living."[52]

For the nuns the prisoners were mostly "lazy" (*flojas*). It was necessary not only to teach them a trade but also to instill an "affection" for work, one of the penitentiary principles highlighted by Foucault. The mother superior noted that "the worst penalty the inmates had to bear was to be constantly subjected to the House's work and regimen."[53] Thus they had to be kept busy. In the 1874 economic crisis, work was scarce and the demand for sewing declined. The nuns sought alternatives. They began to manufacture mattresses and shoes and experimented with manufacturing matches for a Rancagua firm.[54]

Apart from productive labor, all inmates were obliged to attend a school established in 1867. There they learned reading, writing, arithmetic, and catechism. Attendance was mandatory, despite excuses by those "who are naturally lazy and lack diligence in their studies." The mother superior evaluated the school's performance, remarking that although attendance was high only a few inmates could read acceptably well.[55] But education's value transcended literacy. School had relevance because it dignified the inmates. The Correctional House was "frequented by the most ignorant segment of our society, this usually being the reason these unfortunate women enter into the criminal profession from which we, with our counsel, try to discourage them in order to return to society a useful member, earlier excluded with horror."[56] Education and work seemed the proper means to combat crime.

Religious instruction was the concern of the chaplain and the nuns. They conducted the daily routine of praying and ritual, modified according to the distinct nature of each religious celebration. The nuns appreciated the importance and power of prayer, convinced that it was the most powerful means "to contain one of God's creatures within the limits of reason and justice." The nuns themselves were astonished by the extraordinary effect the Jesuit spiritual exercises had on the prisoners' behavior, leaving "a great impression on those souls devoted to vice and corruption, in which we can detect a true reform." Vigilance over the religious practices of inmates "of tough character" was even greater since "only through great effort can they finally be subdued."[57]

Once the nuns took charge of the Correctional House, segregation of inmates became a principal concern. Following the move to the Casa de Santa Rosa, the building was divided into four sections. The first section housed thieves; the second, serious offenders; the third, petty offenders; and the last, prostitutes. The purpose was to avoid contact between prisoners sentenced for serious crimes and those convicted of minor offenses, who stayed only eight to fifteen days. Various financial difficulties, however, prevented the completion of new buildings, which made the segregation policy impractical, at least during the second half of the nineteenth century. The only segregated groups were those sentenced to eight to fifteen days, women raising children, and "contagious" prostitutes. According to the nuns, the latter group got "themselves imprisoned with the sole objective of coming to the house to conquer young women that once free will become prostitutes."[58]

The nuns eagerly awaited the creation of a separate section for inmates who wished to remain after their sentences expired. This section, known as de las preservadas, provided inmates "all they need to obtain religious instruction and perfection of their skills, thus preserving them from the dangers awaiting them outside the House."[59] The image constructed around these regenerated women was highly suggestive. The outside world was portrayed as dangerous, turbulent, and risky. These abandoned women, many of them rural migrants who lacked contacts in the city, were forced to ask for shelter in their former prison. The "preserved" section thus became a protected space within the prison for the care and defense of former inmates.

Establishing this section, however, was a difficult endeavor. The Correctional House's financial resources were designated only for sentenced prisoners and the religious community. A shortage of resources prevented the nuns from administering to former inmates, as well as young female vagrants and beggars turned over to the Correctional House by the courts. These young women, generally without parents or adult guardians, were not included in the municipal council's food budget.[60]

Inmates' lives were taken up with work, study, and religious instruction. What was most unbearable for the inmates, according to the nuns, were not the inconveniences and shortcomings of the Correctional

House but "the regime and strict dependency which they must submit to once they enter the House, which is extremely painful for people of untamed character and accustomed to freedom like those that normally come here." Obedience to the rules was a central objective of the disciplinary experiment. According to the mother superior, the nuns' responsibility was "to deal with these kinds of people and domesticate them," to regenerate their spirit and lead them firmly to the "good way." Reform was considered a spiritual transformation. In most cases, the religious character of reclusion prevented situations of disobedience or lack of discipline. Authority, cloaked in religious attire, infused respect. "The mere presence of the sisters is imposing," the mother superior noted. "They are generally respected so their word is enough to command obedience, thus the need for the House's guardians is extremely rare." She added that the "conservation of order in an institution like this, however, results only from the most rigid and constant vigilance."[61]

In the 1840s the number of inmates fluctuated between forty and fifty. By the 1860s this number had gradually increased to between eighty and one hundred inmates. This increase caused serious problems due to limited space and the institution's inability to separate out different criminal types. By 1872 the building was deemed inadequate to prevent "contagion" provoked by the daily contact among prisoners with varied sentences: "Those condemned for serious crimes and sentenced to long periods of imprisonment are now together with those there for short periods to purge minor offenses. This is neither just nor moral, for the latter, who perhaps acted only through weakness, are exposed to the pernicious influence of those condemned through a perverse inclination to crime."[62] Implemented in 1874, separation of inmates by type of crime and personality facilitated, according to the nuns, the moralization of inmates and the observance of rules. Thus, in spite of the importance of religious authority and its ordering of daily life, inmate discipline still required a modern ordering based on classification and segregation.

By the mid-1870s the number of inmates had declined, due, in the nuns' view, to the lack of police vigilance; while "evil grows every day" in Santiago, the number of inmates decreased. The "valuable" service performed by the sisters seemed underappreciated and underused. To fill up space, the nuns suggested the creation of a section that would "pick up vagrant girls with the authorities' consent, condemning them to some period of reclusion in the House, to learn to work, to avoid idleness, and thus vice, which is its most immediate consequence."[63] This section would capture and reform those whose only crime was vagrancy and who, being abandoned in the streets, were exposed to serious danger. It would also gather prostitutes, who were normally imprisoned only when involved in public scandals or the corruption of minors.

There were also concurrent attempts to encourage the transfer of female delinquents from the provinces. Nuns complained that provincial criminals were not sent to the Correctional House but fulfilled their sentences in inadequate provincial facilities. They argued that this "does not seem convenient at all, but rather harmful to public morality, for the guilty cannot be reformed as effectively as in a well-regimented establishment like this one, designed to receive prisoners from all over the country."[64] The mother superior thus requested that the government authorities transfer the sentenced to the capital, as they had done before. Subsequently, she asked that prisoners staying at the public jail during their trial be transferred to the Correctional House. This request was granted in 1878.[65]

The nuns' reasoning emphasized the difference in and specificity of their disciplinary model. The extremely disordered public jail failed to correct women's behavior, and they left even more corrupted than when they had entered. The material and especially the moral advantages enjoyed by the Correctional House's inmates were the most compelling reasons for transferring them. The nuns also insisted on the profound differences between the disciplinary regimen of the penitentiary and the Correctional House. The mother superior's reports suggest that the contact between nuns and inmates was more humane and familiar than in the penitentiary.

The nuns' statements about inmate behavior were always positive. The moral influence that nuns had over the inmates excused them from using "harsh punishment, and even less, armed force for achieving respect." According to the sisters, the inmates, motivated by gratitude, commonly obeyed promptly and even made "heroic sacrifices in overcoming their bad habits as a demonstration of submission and love."[66] Discipline was thus constructed not so much from modern penal techniques—confinement, regulation, work, separation, schooling—as from personal relationships of respect, gratitude, love, and submission.

## Conclusion

Review of the mother superior's correspondence with the justice minister reveals the Santiago Correctional House's institutional procedures and especially its unique institutional discourse. At first glance, the language appears formal and firm; it underscores the hierarchical relationship between civil and religious authorities. The main purpose of the correspondence was to inform the government about conditions in the Correctional House and to lobby for additional resources. The tone of these texts, however, is discordant. The mother superior's comments on the inmates bore little resemblance to those of a bureaucrat's routine, impersonal report. Descriptions of material conditions were sometimes profoundly dramatic. By interweaving scattered information on the institution, the mother superior conveyed the impression not of a prison but of a house inhabited by an extended family. The inmates performed domestic duties just as "free" women did in their homes. Just as in any other Chilean home, at the prison-house, the mother, incarnated in the mother superior and the nuns, imposed a daily persuasive order. The institutional discourse has become familial and domestic.

The importance of the mother figure was therefore determinant in the construction of female identity. Femaleness was inextricably linked to maternity, to the power of giving life, a status that defined women. Anthropologist Sonia Montecino illustrates the symbolism of the maternal, arguing that

> consecration to the family, to child-rearing, and to domestic
> reproduction defines the content of being a mother. Her domain
> will be anchored in the private sphere, in the territory of the house,
> along with her children. The mother's daily life develops at home:
> preparation of food and clothing, socialization of children, and
> religious practices. There, the woman will realize her existence as
> wife and protector.[67]

The mother superior assumed the role of the inmates' mother. She took care of them, she sheltered them, and when necessary she reprimanded them. Her reports thus produced a hybrid discourse of institutional authority, on the one hand, and motherhood, on the other. In her first role, the "paternal" mother superior insured the observance of conventual rules, Christian regeneration, and the conversion of inmates. In her second role, she assumed her maternal function as the mother of these wayward and abandoned children. In her own description, she displayed a reasonable and affectionate attitude with those inmates who broke discipline, acting more as a mother than a jailer.

Like any other mother, the mother superior did not like to be separated from her children. Accordingly, she invented the "preserved" section for those prisoners who had no place to go after completing their sentences. This section fulfilled her aspiration that her children not be part of the world.[68] The nuns tried to attract the inmates to the female option of a religious life. Not to be part of the world has in this case two meanings. It represents first a mystic or sublime inclination; second, a distancing from an external world that the nuns considered dangerous. The "preserved" section was a stimulus for the inmates to stay under the protection of the Correctional House, to choose shelter and sustenance over uncertain freedom. The religious option offered inmates a protected space besides the male-dominated household and the public street.

A popular poem represents the criminal woman's reclusion as an appropriately harsh solution to her perverse nature and her challenge to the institution of the family:

> It says in the declaration,
> I killed him for pure enjoyment
> and now I am scared,
> thinking of prison.
> Keep her in the Correctional House,
> in a very narrow dungeon.
> The crime is outrageous,
> committed by this tyrant;
> with a pagan intention,
> she murdered her loyal husband.[69]

In fact, the disciplinary solution implemented in the Correctional House with its persuasive and intimate methods was far removed from confinement in a dungeon. The Correctional House put into practice correctional techniques oriented more toward the conversion of the wayward woman than toward vengeance and social retribution for an "insulting" and perverse crime.

This situation forces a reconsideration of the penitentiary rigor of the Correctional House. The rigor mentioned by Foucault was considerably diminished by the Sisters of the Good Shepherd. Here, rigor was not asphyxiating because of the way the nuns constructed the female criminal. The mother superior's statements on the inmates involve a certain contradiction: these criminals were "women of untamed character" and of such a "vicious nature" that they must be regenerated and "domesticated." But there was also the recognition that they were unlucky, abandoned, and mistreated; that they stole to feed themselves and their children; that they killed to liberate themselves from overwhelming oppression. We have here two interpretations of the motivations for female crime. In the first, a woman's peculiar nature favored delinquency. Female criminality was a normal outcome of women's "immoral," "pernicious," and even "diabolic" nature. In this interpretation, a paternalistic authoritarianism is intertwined with the biological explanations developed by nineteenth-century criminological science. The second interpretation establishes a relationship between female criminality and poverty and lack of education that reflects the influence of French sociological criminologists like Tarde. Both perceptions of crime permeated the discourse of the mother superior.

Some additional remarks on other important connections between the discourse of the nuns, penology, and the dominant ideology in Chile need to be emphasized. Correction and work, crucial disciplinary features in the nineteenth-century penitentiary, were also important to the Correctional House. The value ascribed to work within the Correctional House reflects the profoundly negative connotations of idleness for the Santiago elite. Idleness was thought to be the source of all vice, and for that reason ruling groups tried to instill "affection for work" among the lower classes in an effort to neutralize the danger of the "other Santiago." Elites sought to moralize the poor in order to mitigate the horror they felt toward the "nastiness of the city," disorder in the markets, and rising crime among the lower classes. Like the Santiago elite, the nuns endorsed this moralization of the poor but within the context of the female virtues of domesticity and religiosity.

For the nuns, the transformative power of religious discipline was also necessary to reform female delinquents. Praying and the imposition of Catholic sacraments were the principal instruments of reform and repentance. This feature reveals the difference between the treatment of male and female criminals in Chile. Intellectual elites and the church ascribed religion a greater influence over women than men. The nuns had authority over inmates not just because they were jailers but also because their religious status exalted them and projected a beneficial effect. According to the mother superior, the mere presence of a nun generated respect and rendered soldiers unnecessary.

The nuns' image of the female delinquent was that of a vicious, almost possessed woman. Poor women were just one step away from crime and perversion, exposed to the dangers of a barbarous and amoral world. The nuns by contrast were virtuous women, exemplary models of prudence and sanctity. The Correctional House's mission was thus to reverse the sinful nature of the criminal woman, to repress her deviant instincts and libertine sexual behavior, and to instill repentance. In the Congregation of the Good Shepherd's diagnosis, women who entered the Correctional House came from a violent and shocking environment where socioeconomic conditions led them to criminal practices like theft, violence, and infanticide.

The institutional discourse of the Correctional House exhibits a Manichaean dichotomy between vicious and virtuous women that corresponds to the idealized image of a nineteenth-century woman. The virtuous woman—in this case the nun-guardian but also the charitable upper-class woman and the self-sacrificing schoolteacher—became the paradigm of womanhood. This image was reinforced by the presence of its opposite, the vicious woman, a product of her environment (lower-class, popular culture) and her biological nature. Models of womanhood were constructed in relation to an antimodel, an antagonistic being, an alter ego: woman-angel/woman-devil; resigned woman/rebel woman; balanced woman/lost woman; working woman/lazy woman. These models rigidly framed roles and conduct.

Popular women were obviously not a compact homogeneous mass with a common behavior; their unquestionable diversity and complexity are lost in the institutional discourse of the mother superior. This discourse is not alien to the nineteenth-century science of punishment (aimed primarily at men) or the elites' moralizing view of the lower classes. But there is something more. Models of womanhood from within the Correctional House reflect a sometimes explicit, sometimes implicit ideology of the feminine, accepted and transmitted by men and women both inside and outside the correctional space, that is probably of masculine origin given the institutions—the state apparatus, the church—that promote it. Female criminals appear as a transcendent violation of the normative female condition, their correction thus acquiring a special significance that produced distinct institutional practices.

*(This chapter was translated by Carlos Aguirre and revised by Robert Buffington.)*

## Notes

1. Michel Foucault, *Discipline and Punish: The Birth of the Prison,* trans. Alan Sheridan (New York: Pantheon Books, 1977), p. 243.

2. Research for this article was conducted under the direction of Professor Armando de Ramón and is part of a larger work that was presented as a licenciatura thesis at the Pontificia Universidad Católica de Chile in 1993. I would like to thank historian Ma. Angélica Illanes and my friend and colleague Lorena Godoy C. for their comments and criticism.

3. One of the motivations for this research was the scant attention to and discussion of the issues concerning the female penitentiary population generated at the governmental level. The way female criminal behavior was conceptualized is at the root of this situation. Women were generally considered less violent than men. This explains the lack of state interest in this issue. Putting the administration of the female prison in the hands of a religious congregation—something that would not have been done if it was considered risky for the sisters—confirms this view of women as less dangerous than men.

4. In an interesting article about new trends in women's history, historian Mary Nash writes: "Traditionally, prevailing history has focused on the public

sphere, and the processes of social transformation have been analyzed from a political and economic perspective, embracing both short-term and long-term changes. Usually, social change is located in the public sphere, while the processes, institutions, and organisms related more directly with the individual, that is, the family, marriage, and interpersonal social relations, are ignored." Mary Nash, ed., *Presencia y protagonismo: aspectos de la historia de la mujer* (Barcelona: Serbal, 1984), p. 18.

5. Nash identifies two previous stages, the first one consisting of studies about outstanding women, and the second—which she calls "contributing history"—focusing on the contribution, status, and oppression of women in a male-dominated society.

6. Luis Alberto Romero, "Condiciones de vida de los sectores populares en Santiago de Chile (1840–1895)," *Nueva Historia* 3, no. 9 (1984): 4.

7. See Gabriel Salazar, *Labradores, peones y proletarios* (Santiago: Editorial Sur, 1985).

8. During his tenure as intendent of Santiago, Benjamín Vicuña Mackenna designed a roadway that would divide the city into two sectors, the "proper city" for the residence of the elites and the outskirts for the lower classes.

9. See Romero, "Condiciones de vida."

10. But they also recognized the possibility for profit in the poverty of others through speculation on valuable urban real estate.

11. María Angélica Illanes, "Entre-muros: una expresión de cultura autoritaria en Chile post-colonial," *Contribuciones* (FLACSO, Santiago) 39 (1986): 3.

12. Salazar, *Labradores*, p. 274.

13. Women represented a small portion of the criminal population in Chile, although by the end of the nineteenth century their numbers experienced a relative increase. This was partly due to the gradual deterioration of living conditions of poor women but also to remarkable improvements in statistical sampling.

14. *Anuario estadístico de la República de Chile: 1864* (Santiago: Sociedad Imprenta y Litografía Universo, 1864).

15. "Single women constitute the largest population with 60.52 percent, married make up 28.33 percent, and widows 11.15 percent. The contrast between men and women shows that there is 1 single woman for every 6.9 single men; for every 8 married men there is 1 married woman; and for every 3.2 widowers there is 1 widow." Benjamín Vicuña Mackenna, *Un año en la intendencia de Santiago: lo que es la capital y lo que debería ser* (Santiago: Imprenta de la Librería del Mercurio, 1873), 2: 251.

16. Luis Galdamés, *La lucha contra el crimen* (Santiago: Imprenta de E. Blanchard, 1903), p. 27.

17. Vicuña Mackenna, *Un año en la intendencia*, p. 252.

18. Gabriel Salazar, "Ser niño huacho en Chile (siglo XIX)," *Proposiciones* 9 (1990): 65.

19. Salazar, *Labradores*, p. 310.

20. Félix Escudero, "Vagancia y mendicidad," Memoria de Prueba, Facultad de Leyes y Ciencias Políticas, Universidad de Chile, Santiago, 1899.

21. The following are the figures for the prison population unemployed or

without trade:

| Year | Total | Men | Women |
|------|-------|-----|-------|
| 1870 | 418 | 209 | 209 |
| 1880 | 319 | 111 | 208 |
| Year | Total | Men | Women |
| 1890 | 2,321 | 1,901 | 420 |
| 1895 | 2,183 | 1,240 | 943 |
| 1898 | 2,989 | 941 | 2,048 |

Source: Ibid., pp. 26–27.

22. There was a general feeling of insecurity regarding the employment of female domestic servants and coachmen: "All the houses of the capital are entirely open to the abuses and even atrocious crimes of the first one looking for 'service,' who received immediate accommodation because the neighbors have no choice: to accept his service or have no service at all." Vicuña Mackenna, *Un año en la intendencia*, pp. 203–204.

23. "Those that do not know that, just read the newspaper's daily police report, attend the intendent hearings, or go back to your own houses to interrogate your housewives; and if there is just one, at least one, of the 5,000 families of Santiago that is satisfied with their servants, we will retract all our assertions in this respect." Ibid., p. 205.

24. Foucault, *Discipline and Punish*.

25. Ibid., p. 232.

26. Ibid., p. 249.

27. Ibid., p. 236.

28. Ibid., p. 170.

29. Ibid., p. 248.

30. *Boletín de las leyes y de las órdenes y decretos del gobierno* (Santiago: Imprenta La Independencia, 1810–1922), 21 (1853): 185.

31. Ibid., p. 338.

32. Archivo Ministerio de Justicia de Santiago, vol. 304, Casa de Corrección de Mujeres (hereafter referred to as AMJS-CCM, followed by the volume number), May 1862.

33. They came to Santiago either sent by other cities' *juzgados* or through migration.

34. The congregation began in the early nineteenth century in France. A house for "penitent" women under the direction of Mother Saint Eufrasia Pelletier, who belonged at that time to the Congregation of Our Lady of the Charity of the Refuge, was established in the city of Angers. The achievements of this house spread to other French dioceses, forcing the creation of a generalship to provide central direction to the new houses. Subsequently, this congregation adopted the name of Our Lady of the Good Shepherd of Angers to distinguish itself from the old Institute of Our Lady of the Charity of the Refuge.

35. Antonia Salas de Errázuriz was the daughter of Manuel de Salas who took over the charity and relief duties traditionally performed by the wives of the oligarchs.

36. These organizations proliferated in Latin America during the second half of the nineteenth century. Asunción Lavrin notes their importance not just to understand the ideals of service and sacrifice that motivated elite women but

also to recognize how the state used them for social control and for their role in reinforcing women's traditional roles even as they encouraged them to step into the public sphere. See Asunción Lavrin, ed., *Latin American Women: Historical Perspectives* (Westport, Conn.: Greenwood Press, 1978).

37. Juan Isern, *El buen pastor en las naciones del sud de América (Argentina, Brasil, Chile, Paraguay y Uruguay): estudio histórico documentado* (Buenos Aires: S. de Amorrortu, 1923), 1: 29.

38. Amalia Errázuriz de Subercauseux, *El ángel de caridad: doña Antonia de Salas de Errázuriz, 1788–1867* (Santiago: Imprenta Lagunas y Co., 1922), p. 17.

39. Isern, *El buen pastor,* p. 31.

40. Father Blas Cañas, a secular clergyman distinguished by his compassion toward abandoned children and founder of the House of Mary and the Patrocinio San José, pointed out the impact of the Congregation of the Good Shepherd on its charges: "Poor creatures! Candor shines on their foreheads, the air of innocence highlights their juvenile beauty, they are hungry; at their feet they see the tempting gold; the dilemma is to succumb or suffer. You, then, by promoting the foundation of the Sisters of the Good Shepherd, are going to provide them with education and a future; later, they will be able to get an honorable profession or to be virtuous and loyal domestics. You will find in your enterprise thousands of obstacles and contradictions; but the God that you have just invoked will provide you with all the means to help you fulfill your wishes." Ibid.

41. "They are in charge of the Correctional House for Women, substituting the dungeons—that reform the criminal only by the fear of entering there again—for workshops that teach the prisoners a trade and create the habit of making their living from honest work. . . . They have founded schools for the complete instruction of poor girls and single women, either as boarding or outside students; and schools for the deaf-mute and for those children whose mothers cannot provide them with appropriate instruction. They, in their infinite charity, in their will for regenerating and saving women, have defeated obstacles that usually break the strongest characters." Joaquín Fernández Blanco, *La congregación del Buen Pastor* (Santiago: N.p., 1884), p. 7.

42. The correctional experience of the Congregation of the Good Shepherd was later extended to many other South American countries.

43. Quoted in Isern, *El buen pastor,* pp. 204–208.

44. AMJS-CCM, vol. 304, June 20, 1865.

45. Isern, *El buen pastor,* p. 213.

46. The surrounding wall was partially repaired in 1874. According to the mother superior, this would "protect us from the serious inconvenience that we have been suffering, produced by the continuous invasion of thieves that at night alarm the whole house." AMJS-CCM, vol. 407, April 30, 1874.

47. Ibid., vol. 304, May 14, 1870.

48. Ibid., June 20, 1865.

49. Ibid., March 20, 1868.

50. It was impossible in 1870 to continue with the "outside laundry" because the new buildings were not yet completed. This had important consequences. The mother superior noted that the loss of these revenues was "deeply felt." Ibid., May 14, 1870.

51. Ibid.

52. Ibid., vol. 407, March 9, 1871.

53. Ibid., April 30, 1874.

54. Ibid., April 13, 1877.

55. In 1868 the mother superior reported that only nine students could read "correctly" and seventeen could do it acceptably well (*regular*). In 1870 daily attendance was "forty to fifty students." Ibid., vol. 304, May 14, 1870, March 20, 1868.

56. Ibid., May 14, 1870.

57. Ibid., vol. 407, March 9, 1871.

58. Ibid., vol. 304, March 20, 1868.

59. Ibid.

60. After being brought to court for vagrancy or begging, they were sent to the Correctional House by the judge. There was no other way to protect these girls, and their numbers were on the rise on the outskirts of Santiago. The mother superior reported "with great regret" that "in the future I will be forced not to accept these young women because the municipality has informed me that it will provide food only for the inmates that are fulfilling their sentences." Ibid., May 14, 1870.

61. Ibid., vol. 407, April 30, 1872.

62. Ibid., n.d., 1872.

63. Ibid., April 17, 1875.

64. Ibid., May 1, 1876.

65. Ibid., May 15, 1878.

66. Ibid., vol. 559, April 29, 1882.

67. Sonia Montecino et al., "Identidad femenina y modelo mariano en Chile," in *Mundo de mujer: continuidad y cambio* (Santiago: Centro de Estudios de la Mujer, 1988), p. 514.

68. Ibid., p. 513.

69. Poem by Daniel Meneses, found in the section on "Literatura de cordel chilena del siglo XIX y comienzos del XX," Amunátegui Collection, Biblioteca Central de la Universidad de Chile.

# 4. What the Eyes Can't See: Stories from Rio de Janeiro's Prisons

*Marcos Luiz Bretas*

Prison: the variety of thoughts and emotions awakened by this simple word is enormous. Long before the epistemic changes brought about by the Enlightenment and the French Revolution (i.e., long before the idea of the penitentiary inspired reformers to fight for the elimination of cruel, debasing, and arbitrary punishment), there existed a public avid for stories of misfortunes involving dungeons and jails. Judging by the popularity of prison novels in the nineteenth and twentieth centuries, this public maintained its aesthetic preferences well after the fall of the Bastille. What attracted readers to the hidden space of the prison must be of interest to researchers investigating the construction of modernity, particularly in its connection with popular culture.

Put at the center of the historiographical debate about the meaning of modernity by the remarkable work of Michel Foucault, *Discipline and Punish*, the prison remains today an attractive subject of research. Prisons have been examined as disciplinary regimes associated with the emergence of capitalism, in relation to society's evolving sensibilities about punishment, as an expression of the anguish of emerging bourgeoisies, or simply as branches of an ever more complex state. Comparatively less effort, however, has been devoted to the sphere of representation. One overlooked aspect that deserves greater attention is the meaning of the prison in the imagination of societies. In this connection, the examination of different narratives of prison life can offer some answers to the question of the reception of punitive innovations by the "public."

Punishment and publicity had a central meaning for royal justice in the absolutist world—turned into a spectacle, punishment functioned to preserve the monarch's authority. Brutal executions intently followed by avid crowds reaffirmed the monarch's right to intervene on any subject's body to restore hierarchy, order, and legality. In this context, confinement created ambiguity and distrust. By hiding the prisoner and depriving the public of the exercise of justice, the royal justice failed to assert the offender's guilt and introduced the possibility of arbitrariness into the mind of the public. Even when a strong presumption of guilt existed, there was still the chance that the crime was more serious than supposed and that the state, acting arbitrarily, preferred to hide the offender rather than punish him.

Denying the spectacle of punishment, the state restricted the public imagination to guessing what was happening behind the walls of prisons and fortresses. This vacuum was to be filled with written and oral representations which gave content and meaning to the public's anguish and distrust. Eighteenth- and nineteenth-century literature constructed prisons as places of terrible punishment and sites of unjust suffering. The prison, even after the Revolution, continued to be seen as a hidden place with the power to transform individuals in a direction different from that envisioned by enlightened reformers.

The Bastille was not just a prison, it was a monument to the hidden, to events beyond general knowledge. Testimonies to the horrors of this prison proliferated, making the unknown terribly familiar to Parisians. Those who escaped from prison and lived to tell the story ceased to be criminals and became popular heroes. Guessing who might be the mysterious "man in the iron mask" turned into a national pastime, a matter of intense debate. This fictitious character represented a double imprisonment: the secret inside the secret. Real or not, Parisians believed in the existence of this strange figure; inside the walls everything seemed possible.

According to Foucault, the construction of a carceral society proceeded out of the destruction of the hidden: modern methods of punishment as well as new ways of seeing and new subjectivities emerged after the fall of the Bastille.[1] This metaphor, however, should not be extended so easily to the sphere of popular imagination. The Revolution brought down the walls of this ancien régime prison but not the myth which surrounded it. Rather than consolidating Bentham and his panopticon (codification, confinement, and impersonal justice), the nineteenth century signaled the triumph of Dumas and his prison novels. The saga of Edmond Dantès, left fourteen years in the dungeons of the Fortress of If, a victim of conspiracy and the abuse of state power, irrevocably condemned to be forgotten, is still very familiar. When the Count of Monte Cristo emerged from prison, he had changed so much that nobody could recognize him.[2]

Though they have undertaken a very ambitious and difficult project, some historians have tried to reconstruct the feelings produced by reading.[3] When we know that a large number of readers voraciously consumed Dumas's books or Eugène Sue's *Les Mystères de Paris*, it becomes legitimate for us to wonder about the effects of these readings on the public's imagination. What were readers seeking in the adventures and misadventures of Dantès, and, more important, what did they find? For some popular publications, we can obtain explicit responses by readers: "It seems to my simple mind [wrote a Parisian concierge to Eugène Sue] that an author's merit is to come as close as possible to the truth."[4] Or: "Those who had the mere power to read perused only the narratives of banditti, of swindlers, of thieves; they filled their minds with that species of information that only polluted," remarked an English lord in the same period.[5]

The concierge's truth and Lord Brougham's pollution were to be found in the same works, adding ambiguity to the investigation of readership. Still today, the amount of truth or falsehood present in narratives can produce lively arguments among historians. Thus, true and false turns into "evidence" in portraying epochs or ideologies. What sometimes is harder to apprehend is that reading can contribute to the organization and construction of worldviews. *Les Mystères de Paris* helped the concierge to confer meaning to the events of her world.[6]

The emergence of carceral institutions can be used as a good example of this process. According to Bender, the idea of reform through confinement elaborated in British literature in the eighteenth century was essential to the success of the penitentiary as a punitive form by the end of the century. But the problems of the carceral system were just beginning. A comprehensive history of prisons must also deal with the failure of the rehabilitation model in the nineteenth century, made evident by the rising rates of crime. If, in spite of the advancements in the science of punishment, prisons were unable to reform their inmates and recuperate them for society, new explanations had to be found in the innate differences separating the criminals from the good citizens. Thus, in literary and scientific representations of the nineteenth century criminals ceased to be considered misguided persons and became special creatures—remains of barbarian tribes, savages living in the civilized city.[7]

The question of prisons acquired a remarkable dimension during the nineteenth century. Many penitentiary congresses were held at which the different carceral techniques were shown and their success stories were reported and admired. As noted by a contemporary observer, these events looked like the fashionable world exhibitions.[8] In them, a huge corpus of knowledge built around the prisons was presented as the raw material for a comprehensive penitentiary science. Details of script and setting were thoroughly examined; even prison architecture provided clues about the potential for reformation.[9]

But the main search was to focus on a protagonist: the inmate. Without the inmate construed as a special creature, the carceral apparatus risked losing its meaning. Incarcerating the common man would have given back to the prison its unbearable association with torture. All this made the early-nineteenth-century prisoner an object of exhibition to the public. More than trying to enlighten the public, there was an attempt to stress the differences between those within and those outside the prison. The scene must have been anything but edifying, for exhibiting the prisoner also meant exhibiting the conditions of imprisonment. Certainly this was not something of which nineteenth-century philanthropists were proud. Modern prisons (confinement, rehabilitation, and differentiation) emerged almost at the same time as the campaigns for the reform of prisons.

The convicts themselves and their life in prison are issues that challenge the historian. Prison records from Brazil, now under scrutiny, offer useful data on the age, race, and profession of prisoners, but we still lack more detailed descriptions of what was happening inside the prison walls.[10] To fill the gap we must resort to a different type of writing. Stories about prison life occupy a place in the public mind very similar to that of the narratives of travelers. Prison administrators, political prisoners, reporters, and reformers who wrote about prisons guided the reading public into the inner, unknown world of the prison, providing some understanding of this strange land, so far from and yet so close to the reader.

Prison reform in Brazil left much to be desired, creating disillusion among prison administrators and filling the public with a desire to know the world of the prisoner. Brazilian prisons in the nineteenth century were places of death. The statistics from the Casa de Correção do Rio de Janeiro are impressive: 245 inmates died in prison out of the 1,099 who entered between June 1850 and December 1869. If we exclude those sentenced to less than 2 years, we have 236 deaths in relation to 656 inmates (36 percent). For those sentenced to more than 10 years, mortality rates exceeded 50 percent, and out of the 32 inmates sentenced to more than 20 years, 27 died, 2 were transferred, and 2 were pardoned. The only survivor had entered the prison one year before; we can guess how long he would survive.[11]

This prison was an ironic embodiment of the reformers' dreams. Planned in the 1830s by the Sociedade Defensora da Liberdade e Independência Nacional (Society for the Defense of National Freedom and Independence) and based on the panoptical model, it was never finished. The first wing was inaugurated in 1850, becoming the Casa de Correção; the second, built some years later, was reorganized into another prison, the Casa de Detenção; the other wings were never built.[12] From the beginning, many critics condemned its architectural design, and men who worked there were especially critical of the terrain in which the buildings were erected.[13]

The main discussion about prison reform focused on the best system to regulate the inmates' lives, a debate which reproduced those of prison reformers elsewhere in the world.[14] By 1890 a consensus had been reached. "The Republic's Penal Code [from 1890] established the bases of the penitentiary system which seemed to the government more appropriate to adopt. It is the Philadelphia system, combined with the Auburn system, modified by Crofton's Irish method."[15] Several studies made by jurists and physicians such as Pádua Fleury, Souza Bandeira, and Moraes Júnior served to inform the decisions of government. In the next few years, many others appeared, all incorporating the best knowledge of international penitentiary science. These studies and reports, however, were almost ignorant of the conditions of inmates. Until the beginning of the twentieth century, the inmate remained hidden to the public. Built in the middle of the town, the Casa de Correção was a world apart, a distant land that very few had visited.

The contact between the prisoner and the public was established in the first decades of the twentieth century through different types of narratives. I shall try to reconstruct a history of these narratives and their constructions. Like the studies written by reformers, the reports of prison managers did not reach wide audiences; they remained largely unread in dusty public offices. They encouraged, however, visits from reporters and journalists, whose reports created a public interest in the issue of prison reform.[16] The emergence of the Republic brought about a new type of writer: political prisoners wrote long and often dramatic accounts of their tribulations in prison. Except for the work of journalists, the other accounts were not concerned with the common inmate. Thus, the construction of the criminal as an "urban savage" was based on the writings of popular reporters like Ernesto Senna, João do Rio, and Orestes Barbosa or, more rarely, on the accounts left by common criminals or criminologists turned writers. All these narrations were guided by different purposes and reached different readers. Though all tried to report "real conditions" at the prison, each of the authors went a step farther on the path from document to fiction. When fictional works claimed to be authentic, the argument of the narrative became stronger and the readership wider.

By the late 1920s, there was already a public avid for stories about prisons and prisoners, and, more important, readers had acquired some familiarity with and understanding of the strange land behind the prison walls. The success of these stories permitted a recovery of the penitentiary project, a project whose "success" as an institutional practice was at best doubtful. Urban readers must have found in these stories the necessary elements to create or reaffirm their belief in the existence of creatures fitted only for prisons. The stories I examine here did not restore the belief in rehabilitation, that is, the prisons imagined by nineteenth-century reformers. On the contrary, prisons were presented as places where innocence was lost. The stories (re)established only the belief about the existence of difference, that is, about subjects irredeemable for society, warped either by biological or social factors and destined to fill the prisons. The traditional myth of prisons as secret places in which to hide offenders was confirmed, but the narratives made the criminal savage and familiar at the same time. The reading public had now transformed the penitentiary project into its opposite: had made it hidden and alien by desire.

## The Memories of the Colonizers

The prison builders, its managers, and all the technicians who worked in the penal system wrote largely about how to maintain prison discipline and almost nothing about the inmates themselves. Curiously, the scientific methodology familiar to contemporary positivists was seldom used in describing life in the prison. The director of São Paulo's prison portrayed its daily activities as an amorphous peace which presented no problems but also showed no improvement from the point of view of rehabilitation:

> What constant observation has suggested to me is the tenderness of character, the good mood, the resignation and the patience with which those unfortunates—especially the Brazilian ones—suffer their punishment. But this is not and never will be the same as regeneration. It is not surrendering a life in crime to enter the path of reason and justice. It is not abandoning perverse inclinations to pursue virtuous aspirations. It might be calculation, hypocrisy, or at best the conviction that patience diminishes pain.[17]

The prisoners appear as uninspiring figures, especially Brazilian "natives," in the director's opinion, neither rebellious nor reformed. Penitentiary science had been developed by physicians and jurists to accomplish a reform about which prison administrators remained skeptical. The latter seemed interested only in maintaining discipline and order among the inmates. To prison administrators prisoners were dangerous creatures who, by calculation or hypocrisy, rarely showed their true traits. Under the mask of conformity, criminals remained unchanged.

In Rio de Janeiro, the manager who paid the greatest attention to the behavior of prisoners was the director of the Casa de Correção, Luiz Vianna de Almeida Vale. He was appointed in 1868, "leaving an advantageous medical practice to dedicate all his efforts to the improvement of the Casa de Correção da Corte."[18] In an 1870 report, Almeida Vale discusses the inmates. Once again emphasis is placed on the impossibility of reform, due to the vile origins of most of the convicts.[19] In this assertion, biological and social valuations are mixed: signs of evil are physically perceptible, and social origins prevent the proper moral and religious upbringing required for the good citizen. Education, considered by liberal discourse as a major instrument in crime prevention, is lacking among convicts. Of the forty-nine inmates who left the prison in 1869, only four had had a regular education. Those educated convicts seemed to have better chances of reform: one of them was sentenced for bankruptcy and, ashamed, refused his wife's visits and payment for his work in prison. The second was an old man, sentenced for murder, calm, always alleging self-defense. The third was a foreigner, an Englishman. Almeida Vale had no confidence in the regeneration of the fourth, "an adventurer without restraints" sentenced for embezzlement—even a good education could not prevent certain cases from being accounted on the side of degeneration.[20]

According to Almeida Vale, the common uneducated criminal usually landed in prison because of his "lust for gold, [of his] desire to live as a rich man without contenting himself with an honest job."[21] The criminals Almeida Vale chooses to describe, however, are the most cruel, like "the murderer with an irresistible tendency to bloodshed" who killed a prostitute with an axe in order to steal a pair of earrings without even having sex with her, or the female poisoner who, having used treachery and torture to kill, now worked in the infirmary.

Once arrested, the criminal was subject to a new education, the adaptation to confinement. Vale's description of an inmate's entrance into the Correção for the first time deserves careful reading:

[The new prisoner], with an expression of foolishness, idiocy, looks like a child to whom all must be taught; he has to be shown how to change his clothes, piece by piece, his eyes staring at the floor with an air of imbecility while his hair and beard are cut; the barber must turn his head all the time in order to do his job. . . . Entering into his cell, all impresses him. . . . at the strident and loud noise of the closing door a convulsive shaking possesses his body. Some minutes later he will notice the iron wicket, at the end, through which he is watched. He looks, meditates for a long time, seated all the time close to the door. He misses his hair, if he had it long, and the beard now shaved, passing his hand over his head and face, always in deep meditation. He checks with suspicion the bed sheets and other objects in the cell, sometimes moaning, baffled. He seems to be in an electrically laden atmosphere, all his move-

ments seem more agitated than normal. He takes a long time to
sleep . . . uttering monosyllables which refer to persons of his
family. . . . In his first meal, he eats little, not before mechanically
examining the different compartments of his tray. His favorite
place is close to the door, where he remains seated until the curfew
bell.[22]

After these initial sufferings, the learning process starts, which is not
described by Almeida Vale. When the prisoner returns to the Correção
for a second time, he begins to act in a different way; his relationship with
prison has changed: "He looks as if he has come to his home, he changes
his clothes as if preparing to dine, familiar with everything, he packs the
clothes, which he will use someday to leave, with remarkable care and
caprice."[23] Through some mysterious process he has grown into a
habitué of prisons, as a frequently quoted book called this type of
inmate.[24] The world of prisons is now split between the poor devils who
suffer their fate and these creatures for whom prison is a natural habitat.

The carceral taxonomy contributes to the constitution of the modern
punitive instrument, dividing the individuals into those unfit for confinement, for whom the prison is a terrible punishment, and those born
to prison, members of a recently identified species. The values of reason
and humanity that oriented the emergence of imprisonment become an
attribute of only part of society, with a group, looking much like all the
others, not sharing these values. Freedom, the deprivation of which is
the basis of modern punitive sanction, does not seem so important to the
typical prisoner. The example chosen by Almeida Vale is a forty-two-
year-old man, a five-time recidivist, with a criminal career that started
when he was eighteen: "He is so accustomed to the monotonous habits
of prison that I think it would be the same for him to be jailed or not!
Man's most precious possession, freedom, does not move his soul, and
this is something which escapes our comprehension."[25]

The signs by which criminals can be recognized begin to be noted;
describing this same inmate, Almeida Vale stresses the feminine shape
of his body and the traits of his face. Even his disposition appears "serene
as a woman." The physical characteristics of the criminals, soon to
blossom with Lombroso, are shown already to be a valuable object of
analysis; the temper of criminals is more difficult to perceive but
becomes visible on more unexpected occasions.[26] An example is the
exemplary inmate who "in a moment of anxiety" answered aggressively
to another inmate. Reprimanded, he apologized, crying, his face con-
vulsed.

As a prison administrator, Almeida Vale builds an image of the
criminal to suit his needs. The prisoner must remain quiet, maintaining

the system's stability. The main discussion is still the duration of the sentence. To Almeida Vale, it should be at least two years and never more than twenty. Less than two would not have any effect on the inmate's behavior and more than twenty would destroy the person. His distinction between those criminals "born to the prison" and those who suffer the institution as a torture and his notion that men learn to be inmates both privilege an administrative perspective which separates itself from the rehabilitation project. Almeida Vale's narrative appears more concerned with maintaining internal peace and with preserving harmonious power relations within the penitentiary than with seriously "looking" at the inmate. It would be the task of other narrators to tell the prisoners' story to the public.

## The Internal Exile

The next group to narrate the world of the prison appeared with the newborn Brazilian Republic: the political prisoners.[27] Such offenders were almost unknown during most of the liberal monarchy but were soon noticeable in the republican prisons. Enemies of the new regime, monarchists, or defenders of a different republic, their numbers grew steadily during the early years of military rule. Their narrations had a common concern: when the political prisoner wrote about a prison, the subject was basically his own confinement. It was not a critique of the place but of being there. Naturally, views of the prison varied with the prison and with the treatment the prisoner received. In the exceptional case of Gerson Macedo Soares, a navy officer, the conditions in prison did not seem so bad:

> The description of the prisons [of the Romans in the time of Nero] makes us shiver. There, dark, fetid, almost without light, damp, big rats stroll, bed is a bunch of straw, and food is scant and bad. This to a hero, a brave, a true patriot! . . . Today there is a sensible difference; men did not improve, but prisons did. Men are the same, but under more restraints. . . . Prisons have changed: instead of rats, they only have mosquitoes; instead of a crack, a big window with a lovely view; instead of straw, a hygienic iron bed with a spring mattress; instead of a jar of water and a slice of bread, we receive lunch and dinner, every day a different and delicate meal, besides coffee all the time.[28]

This is not irony. In another passage, the author suggests that every young man should spend a season in prison to contemplate the meaning of life. Certainly, this navy officer was an exception. The most common reaction was the shock of being treated "like a common criminal" or "carried to the Casa de Correção in the cars the police used to carry thieves."[29] Like the prison administrator, the political prisoner calls the reader's attention to look at the prison while, at the same time, concealing its traditional occupants. Prisons appear, once again, as an infamous place of injustice, but there is not a debate about whether they contribute to either justice or reformation.[30] The confinement of the political prisoner may produce a critique of prison hygiene as effective as that of any commission; the critique may also become a publishing success (though this was only to happen many years later). But it presents the prison without its main character: the prisoner.

The prison terms for the enemies of government during the administrations of Floriano Peixoto (1891–1894) and later Arthur Bernardes (1922–1926) were always different from those for common criminals. Sometimes common prisoners appear working in services such as cleaning or serving meals, tasks probably given by the administration to prisoners with good behavior.[31] In this type of narrative, the political/common division of the carceral would appear upside down. Olavo Bilac, who spent some time in the Detenção during the rule of Floriano, commented on the "privileges" of common prisoners, stating that they were able to escape through the sewers, while political prisoners suffered endlessly the unavoidable harshness of the prison: "They escaped through the sewers. It isn't clean . . . but who gives a shit? Better dirty than arrested, better pig than slave! . . . From the Detenção thieves, murderers, rapists, embezzlers, all kinds of crooks can escape . . . political prisoners never!"[32] Political prisoners distinguished themselves from an undifferentiated mass of "others"—common prisoners—whose stories are not worth the reader's attention.

The use of prisons for political ends brings back part of the cultural universe of the eighteenth century, when prisons were subjected to public curiosity and experienced as a place of injustice. Here the prison narratives replicate the motifs of personal suffering, unjustified punishment, and oppression. There are, however, two important differences. Now the main source of injustice consists of sharing a space with the common criminal, an aberration in terms of class which bears no relation to the question of the penitentiary project. Now the penitentiary does not transform the prisoner into someone different—unlike the Count of Monte Cristo, political prisoners return to society unscathed, uncontaminated. At a time when the republican government regularly sent "marginals" and laborers to prison under charges of vagrancy, disorderly conduct, or theft, political prisoners had the opportunity to describe the common criminals and their experiences. They missed it. They came back from their visit to this inner world without any interesting account of the "savages"—they did not bother to look around them. They also paid no attention to the prison as a modern institution of social control and behavior modification. Other writers would have the task of showing prisons as a good invention of modern science, thus generating their own readership.

## One Day in a Prison

At the end of the nineteenth century, several articles appeared in the press with such headings as "One Day in a Prison." Prisons began to receive a new variety of visitor, different from lawyers and philanthropists. The reporters found in the convicts good subjects for their daily articles. The first treatment was similar to that of the official commissions, describing material conditions. To visit a prison was considered a public service:

> In order to serve our readers and inform them of matters of interest, the *Jornal* yesterday sent a man to visit the Casa de Detenção of our city. Our reporter arrived without warning and went through the whole building, visiting all places, questioning and listening to many inmates. He is able to give our readers, with full knowledge, precise details of the prison.[33]

Ernesto Senna was the first reporter to publish his remarks about the prisons. The prison appeared to him as "generally pleasant"; the institution provided good food and a healthful treatment to inmates. Sometimes the ambience he describes is bucolic: "There is a small chalet in the garden, with two marble tables, used as a deposit for corpses." The representation of the carceral space is more benign than that presented by lawyers. The report made by the commission sent by the Bar Association to inspect the same facility declared in 1899: "The Casa de Detenção is an unpleasant testimony against public administration and shows how careless we have been with the important subject of our prisons."[34]

Both Senna and the Bar Association had to discuss the inmates in order to denounce injustices. The members of the bar told the story of a famous prisoner, José Antonio de Almeida, known as the Estudante (Student), locked in his cell for five years, deprived of both walks and bath facilities. The director of the prison justified this procedure because of the bad behavior of the prisoner. Ernesto Senna criticized the large number of prisoners who remained at the Detenção waiting for trials that sometimes never happened.

But there is also a new element in Senna's stories; he spoke with "many criminals well known to the public for their notoriety and the repercussion of their crimes." He showed well-behaved inmates who did not repent of their crimes. Women criminals were popular with him, like the nurse Januária Medeiros, who murdered the midwife Asty with a knife. Dressed "cleanly, a blue skirt and a white suit, with a blue scarf around the neck and golden glasses," she showed some timid remorse. "She is calm, doesn't cry, and speaks moderately about her crime as something irreparable she now regrets." But this was not the case with the Paraguayan woman who killed a man in the Ladeira do Barroso: "She doesn't seem to attribute any great importance to her crime. She killed, she tells us, for protecting her honor. Nothing more. She doesn't tell the story or answer questions: she just looks at us and laughs disdainfully."

The inmates with artistic qualities are also described; convict number 1979, Manoel Ramos, a specialist in mosaics, was finishing a work showing the coat of arms of the Republic the same day that his sentence ended. The function of photographer of the prison belonged to the only French prisoner, René Baltzinger, robber and graduate in literature, who filled his empty hours translating from English a book called *Cast-ways* (*sic*).

At the end of the article another famous prisoner appears, the above-mentioned Estudante. We meet him eight years before he testified to the Bar Association. Here is the journalist's description:

> Our representative met many of the large number of convicts. One of them was the Estudante, who killed a police sergeant years ago. He had been sentenced to the galleys, and men in such a position constitute the lowest class in this sad hierarchy; they perform the more painful tasks and don't have many privileges.[35] The present director, obeying the decree that changed his life sentence to twenty years, had removed his irons. The Estudante appeared dressed in the house uniform, blue lenses in yellow glasses, shoes, and a humble air. He is inmate number 3139. He greeted our reporter by name. He has been in prison for three years. . . . Speaking about his crime, he was excited. "They said I was a bad man and persecuted me like a beast. I had no peace; they were always after me. It would drive a saint mad. One day I was calmly walking in Campo de Santanna when the military police arrested me; swords in hand, they seized my umbrella. I had a gun and lost my mind: I committed my crime. . . ." Are your parents alive? What are their names? He hesitated for a moment, then spoke dramatically: "No, I don't! I don't have honor, I'm a wretch! I made myself this way and don't have the right to set the name of my parents in the same mire that I've placed myself!" And he cried.[36]

In this first visit to the prisons, Ernesto Senna still presented a story of reform and repentance. His interest concentrated mainly on the crimes the inmates had committed in the outside world rather than on prison life. The inmates were, fairly or not, paying their debts. He came back ten years later to write a book on the Detenção that focused on the experience of ordinary prisoners.[37] What mattered this time was what went on inside the prison, not outside. There were no more names quoted; it was the prisoners' activities and habits that were described.

Senna's *Através do cárcere* (Through the prison) can be read as the most neutral description of prison life. The author describes—with many illustrations—the games of the inmates, their craftsmanship, the weapons they produce, their press, and their poetry. Without the exaggerated refinement of many of his contemporaries, Senna starts to build an image of this world apart. Now readers can look into prison and find out "how the criminals make their hours pass more quickly."

To this world João do Rio and Orestes Barbosa were to give the passion that makes a drama successful. João do Rio is certainly the most famous of the urban reporters in Rio de Janeiro. His work, articles as well as books, made him a celebrity in his own time and a favorite source for historians.[38] The prison has a very special place in his work, providing an end to his travel through the streets of the city. "Where the streets sometimes end" is an appropriate title for the part of his book *A alma encantadora das ruas* (The charming soul of the streets) in which he describes his visits to the Detenção.[39] Here the prisons lose their character of special places where we meet special creatures and become instead part of the city. The universe of crime and its monstrosity is not circumscribed by the walls of the prison, it exists in every street of the city for those who can see it. The bourgeois is surrounded, and perhaps he should find a prison for himself, out of this mad world. In prison we find instead a kind of museum, where specimens of the urban fauna can be observed and preserved.

The similarity between prisoners and urban inhabitants can be perceived on visiting days. The chronicler begins by depicting the crowd, in its "strange and uniform aspect, like a picture violently painted, all by the same delirious hand," slowly mixing the images of the inside and the outside worlds: "There is swearing, violent words, hands clutching someone else's clothes, furious deprecation; and from inside, from the mystery of the prison court, comes an undistinguished and appalling noise, which excites and increases the wish to go in and see."[40]

From the mass come the individual cases, showed in a quick movement, "all feelings pouring, burbling into a vortex of disgrace." We cannot get any closer, for the chronicle is short. The story ends with a bit of hope: "Sister Paula, the only visitor to comfort the prisoners," changes this "painful corner in the gardens of crime . . . into the rose garden that St. Thomas de Kempis speaks of."[41]

When João do Rio leaves the exterior, the structure of his narrative obeys the same pattern. The depiction of the Upper Gallery in the Detenção also begins with a crowd: "The crowding makes them hostile. There are conferences of hate, angry murmurs, laughs as sharp as razors." Then we come close to the individual stories, finishing with the flower in the mud, little José Bento, longing for a knife to protect himself from all these evil men.

The representation of the prisoner is partly generic to humanity and partly specific to each criminal. In the same paragraph, João do Rio can state that "the criminal is a man like all the others" and assert that "there are two men inside each inmate: one committed the crime, the other is the prisoner. This latter is perfectly (totally) human."

The ambiguous character of the prisoner appears both in his inner spirit as well as in his outer appearance. Even our guide is confused; he thinks he is able to distinguish the "good" from the "evil" inmates, but he must sometimes acknowledge his mistakes. It is terrible, the mixing that places together "fearful murderers, known thieves, the regrettable troop of recidivists, ingenuous children, tradesmen, newspaper sellers, so many people that careless judges make into criminals. . . . Victims of chance, humble workers enter the Detenção for less well founded reasons."

But we must not forget that we can be deceived by appearances. Maria José Correia, the schoolteacher, presents a painful vision. Why should she be in such a place? The experienced eyes of a warden solve the mystery: "Stop talking rubbish, Maria. Everybody knows you. You must know sir, that she is well known in the bars around the railway station. She arrives at five in the morning and only stops drinking when they close. . . . She is a worse drunk than any other." But, of course, Maria was not known to everybody; not all knew the surroundings of the railway station and its bars. Now we are more aware that a human exterior can hide a mysterious life where our common values are blurred. Even religion is not a sufficient sign, for criminals used to have a strong faith. "There is not a disorderly murderer who does not present tattooed in his right hand the five ulcers of Christ." Who can survive a blow from these tattooed hands? In the prison ideas are confused. What looks similar is absurdly different and what seems different could be the same. To the common man, prison "is the school of all vices and degeneracy," but to the criminal it appears as natural and routinized. Criminals are branded with an invisible mark.

The inmate as the center of a narrative to interest readers was taken up again some years later in the works of Orestes Barbosa. A good journalist, condemned for slander, Orestes was at the same time inmate and reporter. Even without the prestige of João do Rio, Orestes's book *Na prisão* (In prison, 1922) became very successful, rapidly selling out its first edition and stimulating Orestes to write two other books in the same vein: *Ban ban ban* (1923) and *O pato preto* (The black duck, 1927).[42]

*Na prisão* cannot be considered a book written by an inmate.[43] The reporter prevails, writing about his fellow prisoners as an outsider. Perhaps because of the forced intimacy, perhaps because of the extension of his work, Orestes produces a large inventory of criminals, some famous, some not, whom he met in the Detenção. He even resurrects an old memory of the prison, telling the story of—who else—the Estudante, whom we now find freed in 1912, having been supervisor of the prisoners' uniforms in the correctional colony and "leaving many admirers among the sentenced."[44] Accompanying Orestes through the prison wards, we meet some familiar names such as Manso de Paiva, murderer of Senator Pinheiro Machado, "ferocious, ignorant, and cowardly." Others are unknown outside of the criminal pages of the press or the chronicles of prison, like Maria Margarida, "prison's *encarapinhada* Sappho,"[45] or João Agi, who refused to confess his crime even when he was beaten by Major Bandeira de Mello.[46]

The inmate is clearly different from the common citizen, even when he or she looks similar. Felix Gerard, accused of smuggling, looked innocent, but he was later identified as Batistin Marius Anatole Travail, a dangerous murderer. The innocents in prison, still present in João do Rio's work, disappear in Orestes's: "The inmate does not want tenderness. He is bad, possessed of a latent evil. Sister Paula finally gave up attending them and a Protestant priest had serious troubles in the Detenção." There is no reform for these criminals, and the death penalty would be the only solution, but unfortunately it is not permitted: "The general trend in this remarkable country is to leave everything to chance."

These images receive their definite shape in Orestes's second book: *Ban ban ban.* The prison is not part of the city; it is another city, "the city of the knife and the jack." The description here is wonderful:

> The Casa de Detenção is a city administered by Colonel Meira
> Lima. It has its trades, its authorities, its politics, its elegant clubs
> and the not so elegant ones—it has love and books of love. Built to
> hold eight hundred inmates, it holds an average of more than one
> thousand—of both sexes and various ages and social classes. It
> wakes up with the sun. The cells are family homes. There are
> noble palaces—halls number one and two, named Flamengo and
> Botafogo. There are smaller houses, also with important occupants:

notably the first and third galleries, where only two inmates are placed in each cell. The first and third galleries are like Tijuca and Vila Isabel. In one side of the second gallery is Mangue, Catumby, and Ponta do Cajú; in the other Saúde, Madureira, and Favela. Tough guys.[47]

Daily life in prison is portrayed as in any city, with bakers, newspaper sellers, and the milkman (the milkman is just for the higher classes— "those in the Favela don't drink milk"), with families and family life and visits to doctors and dentists. At night, "men of the sinister city return home early. Dinner and rest. The elegant neighborhoods have the looks provided by money. Catumby tries to make its sambas. The wardens watch. The noise diminishes, but doesn't end. At 7:00 Officer Campos arrives, in charge of power, and there is light." It is time then to start the activity in the casinos and prostitution houses.

The prison clearly has its own subculture, quite unlike that where the readers live. It is not the only place where this life lurks but part of a generally unattainable world. Few get to know it: "certainly, there are two towns in Rio. The mysterious is the one that charms me. . . . People in these strange places are special. They are as they are, natural, in its mixture, with its surprises, and its horror. For all this they are remarkable. I love the Favela."[48]

## Closing the Doors

We end by drawing attention to the emergence of two new figures in the portrayal of crime. The first to appear is the writer criminologist, moving from fiction to science, fascinated by the possibilities of real life. Elysio de Carvalho, a former anarchist, became head of the Department of Identification of the police and a writer on high-society life.[49] He also made a visit to the prison but did not receive as much public recognition. Armed with experience and learning, he was able to declare that readers didn't really know the prison. The prison is not, as readers might think, an "endless rosary of tortures, provocations, and punishment" but a space "sought out and wished for as one of the best places in the world."[50] To be arrested is like getting a holiday in the mountains (the author mentions Petrópolis); the inmate is not a sufferer. This can be seen on visiting days, when the inmates are not as sad as the visitors.

Elysio introduces us to a man who probably was the most famous criminal in early-twentieth-century Rio: Carleto. Responsible for a jewelry store robbery during which two persons were murdered, Carleto is the symbol of the criminal and, according to Elysio, might well illustrate Lombroso's criminal gallery. Each visitor to the Detenção goes to see him, the jailed beast, surrounded by awful stories about a criminal career which began with stealing from his own mother. He was not mad, insisted the police doctors in a very interesting report; he was just bad, the visitors were assured. To observe him was a way to understand with Elysio de Carvalho that "the world of wrongdoers is a colony of savages, moving inside civilization."

Only a minor role in the elaboration of this image can be credited to the prisoner himself. He almost never speaks by himself; rather, he is exhibited. An exceptional case is Dr. Antonio, a criminal who published his memoirs, the *Memórias de um rato de hotel* (Memoirs of a hotel thief).[51] According to this story, Dr. Antonio is not a common criminal but a deviant youngster from a wealthy family in the south of Brazil. He treats his fellow criminals very spitefully. In a certain sense, his story repeats what we have already heard: prisons are the school of crime, destroying those who enter, making them irredeemable. The new aspect is the clash between prison and prisoner, narrated with a violence not found in the other writers:

We must behave well in the Correção. All are mean. They are
mean because it is impossible not to be. Against rage, rage. Against
violence, violence. A man given a large sentence, who enters young
to leave old (if he leaves!), unable to see the streets, unable to feel
the freedom, loses his love for life and becomes a jackal. To restrain
him one must be the tamer with a hot iron stick.[52]

The clash between inmate and prison makes Dr. Antonio doubt the validity of any evidence from prisoners, even when collected in prison, "because criminals have two faces, one for the public and another for their partners and fellows in crime. Unfortunately, both are lies. To the public, just one worry: show innocence. To the fellows, just one wish: show their great abilities and their hard luck."[53]

Dr. Antonio, disguised as a criminologist, went to visit the penitentiary in São Paulo: "I decided to make the *tournée* of the grand dukes into the dungeons. . . . How many visits like that have I seen, in many different cities, from the other side! The impression is very diverse. When you are a prisoner, a visitor upsets or provokes hatred. When you visit, you do it as an afternoon walk. It's curious."[54]

A closer look at the penitentiary replicates the doubt and ambiguity felt by popular reporters, now extended into the terrain of the narrative itself. The view of "outsiders" is questioned, imposing over the duality in the behavior of the prisoner a duality in perspective and interpretation. The prison, like its residents, becomes more inscrutable. At the same time, these writings turn back the clock to prereform times, when criminals were exposed as curiosities and punishment was a spectacle. The prison is now open to the public eye, but the knowledge gained by this perusal is at best ambiguous and often confusing. The prison is a world of its own; its residents have fallen into apathy and hypocrisy and understand only the language of power.

All those visitors, while writing their stories, provided the eyes for many others. Though we can hardly speak of moral panics, in the same sense that Jennifer Davis does, some kind of internal fear was fed by these stories. In a society experiencing rapid change due to the demise of slavery and the increase in immigration, the prisons seemed a good place to put the unfit, to displace society's anguish, and to distinguish those accustomed to the prison regime from those who suffered the rigors of the new scientific, institutional torture. The literature here described raised strong doubts about the penitentiary project of identifying and reforming criminals. The double nature of criminals, the deceptive nature of appearances and confessions, turned the project of deciphering criminal behavior back to its starting point: to estrangement and indetermination. The prisoner became a "savage" living within a modern, civilized "city."

Gradually, the prison stories have naturalized these "savages" and their world into the eyes of the public. Now, the idea of the coexistence of two cities populated by two different but apparently similar species, one of citizens, the other of criminals, seems a commonplace. In a sense, the description of the criminal has replaced that of the slave, sharing his docility and his incapacity to learn or change his uncivilized behavior. If the task of controlling the slave was mainly in the hands of the owner, now the task of controlling the criminal was given to the state.

Building a carceral system never had been a priority to state administrators, who did not trust the reformatory promises of the penitentiary, but now they were confronted by a strong urban group that demanded new prisons. The development of prisons, so slow during the nineteenth century, would now find fertile soil in which to grow. The public is already familiar with this world apart. It is not by chance that most of the prisons in Rio are named after reformers of the first quarter of the century. Lemos de Brito, Esmeraldino Bandeira, Evaristo de Moraes, Heitor Carrilho, and others found the inmates ready to fill their new prisons.

### Notes

1. The vision of prisons before the nineteenth century, especially about the Bastille, can be found in Monique Cottret, *La Bastille à prendre* (Paris: Presses Universitaires de France, 1986).

2. The choice of Dumas and his Count might look arbitrary. We could use, for the same purposes, Hugo and Valjean or Balzac and Vautrin, also fascinating. But Monte Cristo has a stronger attraction given what we may call an archetypal image; see, for example, the uses of Monte Cristo in Umberto Eco, *Sobre os espelhos* (Rio de Janeiro: Nova Fronteira, 1989) and in Roberto Da Matta, *Carnavais, malandros e heróis* (Rio de Janeiro: Zahar, 1981), translated into English by John Drury and published as *Carnivals, Rogues, and Heroes: An Interpretation of the Brazilian Dilemma* (Notre Dame, Ind.: University of Notre Dame Press, 1991).

3. See, for example, Robert Darnton, *The Kiss of Lamourette: Reflections in Cultural History* (New York: Norton, 1990), chap. 9.

4. Quoted in Louis Chevalier, *Laboring Classes and Dangerous Classes in Paris during the First Half of the Nineteenth Century* (New York: Howard Fertig, 1973), p. 491, n. 13.

5. Quoted in Clive Emsley, *Crime and Society in England 1750–1900* (London: Longman, 1987), p. 74, n. 42.

6. "Subjectivity does not properly exist until it is . . . organized, art forms generate and regenerate the very subjectivity they pretend only to display. Quartets, still lifes and cockfights are not merely reflections of a pre-existing sensibility analogically represented; they are positive agents in the creation and maintenance of such a sensibility." Clifford Geertz, *The Interpretation of Cultures* (New York: Basic Books, 1973), p. 451; quoted in John Bender, *Imagining the Penitentiary: Fiction and the Architecture of Mind in Eighteenth Century England* (Chicago: University of Chicago Press, 1987).

7. The choice of Dumas against Bentham casts some doubt over the success of the penitentiary model, even if not over the idea of penitentiary. Many of the myths about prisons resisted the utilitarian—and even the Foucauldian—approach. Comparisons between criminals and savages had a scientific expression through Lombroso and the criminal anthropologists but persisted also as a more general view, expressed in diverse representations. Examples can be found in the work of Chevalier, *Laboring Classes*, Emsley, *Crime and Society*, and Michelle Perrot, *Os excluídos da história* (São Paulo: Paz e Terra, 1989).

8. Antonio H. Souza Bandeira Filho, "A questão penitenciária no Brasil," *O Direito* (May 1881): 229.

9. This is how a civil engineer and an architect described their visit to the Casa de Detenção of Recife in northeastern Brazil: "Every element in that building has a meaning; every line can awake a feeling which can help to attain the ends expected with the general disposition. The Casa de Detenção . . . is then an enormous book that one can read." Pereira Simões and Herculano Ramos, *Uma visita a Casa de Detenção por um arquiteto e um engenheiro civil* (Pernambuco: Tipografia do Jornal do Recife, 1882), p. 9.

10. There exist two main studies on prison records in Brazil. On Rio de Janeiro, Samuel Adamo, "The Broken Promise: Race, Health and Justice in Rio de Janeiro 1890–1940," Ph.D. diss., University of New Mexico, 1983; and on Recife, Martha Huggins, *From Slavery to Vagrancy in Brazil: Crime and Social Control in the Third World* (New Brunswick, N.J.: Rutgers University Press, 1985). A very interesting essay that gives an ethnographical account of prison life in Britain is that of Philip Priestley, *Victorian Prison Lives: English Prison*

*Biography 1830–1914* (London: Methuen, 1985). For our purposes, unfortunately, Priestley overlooks the differences which might exist, according to the place of the author in the system, among the various narratives of prison life.

11. *Relatório da Comissão Inspetora da Casa de Correção da Corte* (Rio de Janeiro: Imprensa Nacional, 1874). According to the reports of the minister of justice, at the end of the century the conditions were far better. The Casa de Correção registered only one or two deaths of inmates each year in the 1890s.

12. The Casa de Detenção was created to receive persons waiting for trial (like a remand prison in modern Britain); the Casa de Correção would receive those already sentenced. The plan never actually worked in reality.

13. See, for example, the report presented by its physician and later director, João Pires Farinha (annex to the report from the minister of justice), in 1895. Curiously, nowadays the prison is in an extremely valuable zone of downtown Rio, and politicians cherish the idea of transferring it and selling the lot to building societies.

14. See, for example, Joaquim de Almeida Leite Moraes, Jr., "Qual o melhor dos sistemas penitenciários conhecidos?," *O Direito* 11, no. 32 (December 1883).

15. *Exposição apresentada ao chefe do governo provisório da República dos Estados Unidos do Brasil pelo General Dr. Manoel Ferraz de Campos Salles*, January 1981, p. 89. The Irish system, from Walter Crofton, mixed, progressively, the different methods then in use, starting with isolation and ending with parole. See Antonio Ferreira de Souza Pitanga, *Organização penitenciária nos países latino-americanos: memória jurídica* (Rio de Janeiro: Imprensa Nacional, 1907), pp. 35–37.

16. We must not forget that we are dealing with a society with a large amount of illiteracy. The impact of books was probably stronger among the growing urban middle classes. These groups would become a very important source of opinions.

17. Quoted by Souza Bandeira Filho, "A questão penitenciária no Brasil," p. 42.

18. Ibid., p. 71.

19. Luís Viana de Almeida Vale, *Relatório do diretor da Casa de Correção da Corte* (Rio de Janeiro: Imprensa Nacional, 1870).

20. Sérgio Luís Carrara, "Crime e loucura: o aparecimento do manicômio judiciário na passagem do século," M.A. thesis, Universidade Federal do Rio de Janeiro, 1987.

21. Almeida Vale, *Relatório*, p. 14.

22. Ibid., pp. 9–11.

23. Ibid., p. 10.

24. Emile Laurent, *Les Habitués des prisons de Paris* (Lyon: A. Storck, 1890).

25. Ibid., p. 9.

26. We can find the same trend almost everywhere. For Britain, see Jennifer Davis, "The London Garrotting Panic of 1862: A Moral Panic and the Creation of a Criminal Class in Mid-Victorian England," in V. A. C. Gatrell et al., *Crime and the Law: The Social History of Crime in Western History since 1500* (London: Europa, 1980), p. 201. Davis shows the process of creating the London criminal in London, not as a general process but as a spin-off of the garrotting

panic of 1862. The construction of Rio de Janeiro's criminals cannot be traced back to any such collective fear.

27. For purposes of exposition, I present the different groups as a chronological sequence. In reality, the different writings overlap; the emergence of a new type of narrative does not imply the disappearance of the former ones.

28. Gerson Macedo Soares, *Quinze dias nas prisões do estado* (Rio de Janeiro: Benjamin Costallat & Miccolis, 1924), pp. 81–82.

29. Alfredo de Barros, *Notas e apontamentos sobre minha prisão na fortaleza da conceição, na Casa de Correção e em minha residência (sob palavra) desde 4 de novembro de 1893 até 14 de agosto de 1894* (Rio de Janeiro: Oficina de Obras do Jornal do Brasil, 1895), p. 20; and Lourenço Augusto de Sá e Albuquerque, quoted by Dunshee de Abranches, *Governos e congressos da República dos Estados Unidos do Brasil, 1889 a 1917* (São Paulo: N.p., 1918), p. 416. In Recife another prisoner offers a quite different view in an autobiographical account presented as a novel: "Batista [the author's alter ego] could have avoided imprisonment. He had been warned. Someone saw his name in the list of men to be caught. He thought of hiding as many others did. But, at the same time, he really longed to be arrested. It was quite nice to be a political prisoner. Imprisoned with José Mariano! Political prisoners were nice and exalted individuals. It would be a sacrifice for an idea. It was nice to suffer, or even die for an idea. Through his young mind passed the names of many famous prisoners. Glorious figures of history had been arrested or hanged. . . . And the women? They admire those who suffer bravely. Many family relationships were influencing his life, instigating him from afar. All his future would depend on this prison, which wasn't happening. Had he been forgotten? Was he considered unharmful?" Quoted from José Gonçalves Maia, *Horas de prisão* (Recife: Imprensa Universitária, 1967), p. 69.

30. This is true even in the case of political prisoners from the Left such as Evaristo de Moraes. See his *Minhas prisões e outros assuntos contemporâneos* (Rio de Janeiro: Edição do Autor, 1924). More critical was the anarchist Everardo Dias, in his *Bastilhas modernas* (São Paulo: Edit. de Obras Sociais e Literárias, 1926).

31. "At five o'clock we had dinner, having as servant an Arab convict, sentenced for murdering another Arab for religious reasons. The meal was broad, with soup, three dishes, mineral water, fruits, sweets, and coffee. . . . At ten o'clock, after coffee and toasts, we went to bed." Israel Ribeiro, *As minhas prisões: episódios de 34 dias de exílio* (Bahia: N.p., 1926), pp. 51–52.

32. Olavo Bilac, "O carrilho da bruxa," *A Bruxa*, March 13, 1896. In the same review there is a poem by Bilac that suggests that the prison is not the same without the political prisoners.

33. Ernesto Senna, *Notas de um repórter* (Rio de Janeiro: Tipografia do Jornal do Commercio, 1895), p. 7.

34. "Prisões do Distrito Federal: relatório da comissão incumbida de visitar as prisões do Distrito Federal," *Revista de Jurisprudência* 4, no. 28 (February 1900): 139.

35. Article 44 of the penal code of 1830 established the penalty of the galley: convicts were chained, together or separated, and used in public works, as in building the Casa de Correção. This type of punishment was abolished in 1890.

36. Senna, *Notas*, p. 46.

37. Ernesto Senna, *Através do cárcere* (Rio de Janeiro: Imprensa Nacional, 1907).

38. There are many studies on João do Rio and his work. See, as an example, Marcos Guedes Veneu, "O flaneur e a vertigem," *Estudos Históricos* 5 (1991).

39. João do Rio, *A alma encantadora das ruas* (Rio de Janeiro: Prefeitura da Cidade do Rio de Janeiro, 1987).

40. Ibid., pp. 149–150.

41. Ibid., p. 152.

42. Orestes Barbosa, *Ban ban ban* (Rio de Janeiro: Benjamin Costallat & Miccolis, 1923); idem, *O pato preto: crônicas da rua, da cadeia e de Paris* (Rio de Janeiro: Brasil Contemporâneo, 1927).

43. Orestes Barbosa, *Na prisão* (Rio de Janeiro: Jacintho Ribeiro dos Santos, 1922).

44. The Colônia Correcional de Dois Rios was an agricultural prison, mainly for vagrants, on an island near Rio de Janeiro.

45. The kind of hair characteristic of blacks. Dictionaries offer "crisp, curled hair."

46. The sensationalism of Orestes Barbosa makes him the only author in this study to write about police violence without trying to reproach it. In a different part of the book it is a forger, Isidoro Von Altenberg, who behaves inconveniently with the director and is beaten.

47. Barbosa, *Ban ban ban*, pp. 77–78.

48. Ibid., pp. 276–278.

49. Another criminologist who left an account of his own experiences in prison is Evaristo de Moraes.

50. Elysio de Carvalho, *Sherlock Holmes no Brasil* (Rio de Janeiro: Casa A. Moura, n.d.).

51. I would like to thank Professor Plinio Doyle for the valuable reference to this book. Like our other sources, it was published originally in a newspaper, the *Gazeta de Notícias*, in 1912. The memoirs are attributed by Francisco Prisco to João do Rio. See João Carlos Rodrigues, "Memórias de um rato de hotel: um inédito de João do Rio?," *Letras & Artes* (September 1990): 22.

52. Dr. Antonio, *Memórias de um rato de hotel: a vida do Dr Antonio narrada por ele mesmo* (Rio de Janeiro: N.p., 1912), p. 103.

53. Ibid., p. 95.

54. Ibid., p. 160.

# 5. "Forcing Them to Work and Punishing Whoever Resisted": Servile Labor and Penal Servitude under Colonialism in Nineteenth-Century Puerto Rico

## Kelvin A. Santiago-Valles

If punishment as a form of legal control is one visible symbol of the inner nature of social organization, then the study of punishment should tell us a great deal about how societies are coordinated, regulated, and stabilized (i.e., how social order is achieved), and how and why societies undergo certain types of basic social change.

—Steven Spitzer[1]

Whenever the colonizer adds, in order not to fall prey to anxiety, that the colonized is a wicked, backward person with evil, thievish, somewhat sadistic instincts, he [sic] thus justifies his police and his legitimate authority . . . Since the colonized is presumed a thief, he must in fact be guarded against (being suspect by definition, why should he not be guilty?).

—Albert Memmi[2]

In adopting the name of *jíbaro*, the Spaniards used it to describe the Indians and later the mestizos and the blacks who escaped to the mountains, fleeing servitude, don Pedro said. Later, it came to identify the *criollos* [Creoles] or Puertorriqueños in the rural zones "who kept the rustic way of life and who were free of assimilation." . . . In the *Nuevo Diccionario Velázquez* the word *jíbaro* is said to be of Cuban Indian origin, meaning to "run wild." . . . And the historian Salvador Brau . . . writes that the Spaniards used the word fearfully to describe "the country folk of Puerto Rico," because of "their rough and wild habits." . . . There is no Spanish equivalent for *jíbaro*.

—Stan Steiner[3]

To what extent did Spain's late-eighteenth- and nineteenth-century forms of punishment become "visible symbols of the inner nature" of Puerto Rican society—perceived and lived—as well as "visible symbols" of the limits of "social organization" on the island? Were Spanish carceral forms and regulatory patterns in this case in any way related, not just to the economic needs, but also to the anxieties and fears of the colonizers (and of the propertied Creoles) regarding "mestizos," "blacks," and/or "the country folk of Puerto Rico," who still "escaped to the mountains, fleeing servitude," between 1788 and 1898? How did "[colonial] punishment as a form of legal control" intersect the "rustic way of life" and the "rough and wild habits" of these heterogeneous subaltern subjects?

I do not pretend to have unlocked here the mythical and essential(ist) politico-economic secret of punitive structures on the island during the nineteenth century. On the contrary, and in the case of Puerto Rico, I tend to share Gayatri Chakravorty Spivak's apprehension when she distinguishes between the traditional/Marxist political economies of colonialism in India and the research of the Subaltern Studies group. In her essay "Subaltern Studies: Deconstructing Historiography," Spivak characterizes the traditional approach as defining "the insertion of India into colonialism . . . as a change from semi-feudalism into capitalism. Such a definition theorizes the change within the great narrative of the modes of production and, by uneasy implication, within the narrative of the transition from feudalism to capitalism."[4] To this paradigm she counterposes the work of the Subaltern Studies group that instead focuses on

revising this general definition and its theorization by proposing at least two things: first, that the moment(s) of change be pluralized and plotted as confrontations rather than as transition . . . and, secondly, that such changes are signalled or marked by a functional change in sign systems . . .

A functional change in a sign system is a violent event. Even when it is perceived as "gradual," or "failed," or yet "reversing itself," the change itself can only be operated by the force of a crisis.[5]

These are the concepts that direct my present research. These are also the concepts that inform what might initially seem like a detour leading away from the principal object of study: namely, penal institutions in Puerto Rico. Here I suggest alternative ways of understanding a number of processes, starting with the links among colonialism, economic transformation, punitive structures, and discourse production. Deciphering these links should involve a corollary understanding of how such processes violently constituted, refashioned, and depicted Puerto Rican society and most of its members. But it is equally necessary that the reader understand how the island's majorities contested and partially set limits to the social changes that unfolded between 1788 and 1898.

Consequently, this chapter does not immediately scrutinize the Spanish prison system in Puerto Rico. I did not set out to simply describe colonial penal institutions in Puerto Rico or to examine such issues and their broader context in conventional or self-explanatory ways. Instead, I found it more useful to begin by analytically situating the structural and cultural forces grounding this prison system, as well as by characterizing the specific Caribbean social reality that both authorized and restricted the way these forces materialized on the island. I trust the reader will soon see the wisdom of what, at first glance, might otherwise seem like a needlessly circuitous approach.

The chapter starts with a brief examination of the "force of a crisis" that brought about a shift in (1) the needs of the Spanish state for colonized labor and (2) how such labor was obtained in late-eighteenth- and early-nineteenth-century Puerto Rico, vis-à-vis how such measures were partially undermined by the continuing abundance of land. The following two sections examine the proliferation of nineteenth-century sign systems of "native" waywardness and of social prejudice among the propertied classes in Puerto Rico (Creole, Spaniard, and others) in terms of how the signifiers of "poverty," "vice," and "race" were being conflated in the West. The third and fourth sections explore the variations of punitive institutions across the island in general, particularly San Juan's carceral network. The final three sections critically analyze the case of the Casa de Beneficencia de San Juan, along with the inherently brutal (yet failed) functional changes in the second sign system of colonial punishment that emerged by midcentury (namely, utilitarian correctionalism), ending with some preliminary conclusions. Such an analysis could tell us a great deal about how the Spanish colony of Puerto Rico was coordinated, regulated, and stabilized and about how social order was achieved—and disrupted—throughout the nineteenth century.[6]

### Reining in Those Who "Escaped to the Mountains, Fleeing Servitude"

Given the problems within its colonial empire that eventually culminated in the South American Wars of Independence, Spain attempted to overcome the force of these crises and to augment its colonial surplus by, among other things, transforming Puerto Rico during the 1788 to 1873 period from an isolated outpost and military enclave into a commercially profitable agro-exporting colony. This maneuver radically reoriented the island's position within the international market, particularly in how nonwage mechanisms of exploitation in Puerto Rico (and Cuba) were being used to launch wage-based production in Spain and fuel capitalist accumulation on a world scale.[7]

Similar to other European colonial ventures during the eighteenth and nineteenth centuries, the Spanish regime violently reconstructed the existing relations of production in its remaining colonies by expanding the latter's commercial linkages (internally and externally) and by extracting surplus value mostly outside salary-based systems, for example, debt peonage, sharecropping, slavery and/or the slave trade, heavy fiscal burdens on imports and exports, usury, merchant capital, and so on. Such nonwage forms of surplus extraction on an islandwide scale were a relatively recent phenomenon and were imposed in a moderately piecemeal and extremely uneven manner compared to the rest of the Caribbean and Latin America.[8]

In retrospect, the years spanning the abolition of slavery (1873) and the Spanish-American War (1898) can be understood as an extremely asymmetrical and partial confrontation between the Puerto Rican social formation and the emergent elements of a capitalist production grounded on the wage system. But before 1898 this confrontation never actually materialized via the generalization of monetary-wage labor on the island. This entire process, rather, was caught up within the stagnation, brutality, and protracted crisis of the persistent nonsalaried forms of exploitation and their disputed sign systems. As we shall see below, this was not historically foreordained; neither was it the simple expression of the global political economy.[9]

Compared to the remainder of the West, Spain did not emulate the handful of European and U.S. interests that had begun expanding and transforming their colonies and spheres of influence. I am referring to the exportation of capitalist social relations of production in the wake of burgeoning industrialization and the rise of monopoly capital in these other European and Euramerican countries during the final decades of the nineteenth century. The Spanish state, on the contrary, did not significantly realign or transform its Caribbean, Philippine, and African colonial enterprises at this time.[10]

During much of the 1800s, Spain's Caribbean enterprise extracted surplus through two overlapping mechanisms. For part of Spain's budding capitalists, a rapid and ruthless "primitive accumulation" occurred, on the one hand, via the vast and omnivorous machinery of colonial taxes and unequal commercial exchange. On the other hand, such an accumulation was enabled by the intensive commercial exploitation of a colonial agricultural production built on the backs of "primitives" (local and imported).[11] None of this denies the constraints such mechanisms placed not only on propertied Creoles in Puerto Rico (as well as in Cuba) but even on significant sectors of the propertied classes in Spain.

The restricted circulation among metropolis and colonies of capitalists and commodities (and . . . labor power) thus reflected opposing economic and political strategies of a regionally divided metropolitan bourgeoisie that had not fully consolidated its control over the emergent class of free workers within the national territory [of Spain] itself. . . . The protectionist policy of the metropolitan state that issued from this fractious constellation of social forces led not only to the regional disarticulation of important sectors of the economy; high tariffs and burdensome taxation also blocked the development of colonial productive forces, especially as these measures were compounded by the large contingents of bureaucrats, clerics, and military required to maintain some semblance of unity for this shaky edifice.[12]

First, let us examine the general features of the colonial enterprise and the internal contradictions it experienced at this time. As a business venture the socioeconomic transformation of Puerto Rico presented certain inherent problems during the late eighteenth and early nineteenth centuries. Foremost among them was the small labor pool available to these large landowners and to the colonial government's public works efforts, a difficulty not due to general demographic limitations per se. Rather, such complications were based on the simple fact that few laborers were willing to work on fields they effectively did not own (or on roads and fortifications they had no use for). In other words, these laborers were not inclined to voluntarily perform agricultural and road labor merely for the benefit of the large landowners, or hacendados (Creole, Spaniard, and foreign), and/or for the colonial administration.

In the early nineteenth century, most of the available acreage in Puerto Rico had not been alienated in practice by any person or institution, despite the vast tracts of territory that nominally belonged to the Crown, the Church, and others.[13] Because land was so abundant on the island, it became extremely difficult to "persuade" the local free peasants (i.e., most of Puerto Rico's population) of the "virtues" of working for the hacendados or for the government. The role of the Spanish state in Puerto Rico at this time was to decisively alter this situation through direct coercion coupled with a shift in colonial juridical-political sign systems. According to historian Labor Gómez Acevedo,

if the government could not transform the reality of a fertile soil and a warm climate, allowing men [sic] to live without any great worries, it could promote laws forcing them to work and punishing whoever resisted; and if investing a person with a sense of responsibility and with the value of labor was the task of educators and a

long-lasting enterprise, so too could an authoritarian government
come up with an immediate solution to this: imposing statutes
forcing an individual to accept something which he did not understand and placing outside the law whoever did not abide by norms
whose benefits excluded him.[14]

The Crown simultaneously began encouraging the immigration of
propertied settlers (fleeing Haiti and the rest of the new American
republics, as well as Spain and other European countries) to stimulate
commercial agriculture, making estates readily available to them along
with the corresponding punitive and legal support (the Real cédula de
gracias of 1815 being the principal example of such laws).[15] These
measures had considerable demographic consequences: official census
figures indicated that the island's population more than doubled between 1815 and 1846 (from 220,051 to 447,914).[16] Free peasants who
were living on soil their family had occupied for generations and/or on
fields de jure not registered in anybody's name, suddenly found themselves within the confines of the new hacendados' legitimate property.
This amounted to a profound metamorphosis in the official sign systems
marking these rural independent producers as imperial subjects.
     None of this would have been possible, to the extent that it was, if the
new property rights had not been extensively policed (morally,
semiotically, and literally) by forcing peasant "natives" (those born in
Puerto Rico, the Canaries, or Africa) to work for the new landowners
and/or for the colonial government if they wanted to remain living on
what was now, legally, somebody else's property. Such coercive and
discursive transformations were both authorized by and embodied in the
antivagrancy laws (Leyes de corrección de vagos), in particular, the 1832,
1833, and 1844 statutes, as well as by and in the day-laborer codes (Leyes
de reglamentación del trabajo) of 1839 and 1847 to 1876. These laws and
their corollary penal structures, along with the practices of usury and
debt peonage, compelled the former free-peasant family to render labor
in exchange for wages in kind and/or for the right to farm a subsistence
plot of land.[17] Failure to comply would often condemn these peasants
(and artisans) to hard-labor sentences in colonial prisons.
     Although these rural direct producers went on having effective pos-
session of the principal means of production (concretely, the land), the
peasants were now toiling in order to generate a surplus directly appropriated by the new legal landowners. For most of this century, there was
a total absence of banking institutions and an extreme dearth of liquid
capital on the island.[18] Therefore, what the rural laborers obtained (in
return for their work) was a "wage" completely or mostly in kind and/
or a plot of land with which to replenish the physical energy they spent.

In other words, their labor power did not circulate freely because it was not being effectively bought and sold by the highest bidder (or employer) in the open (labor) market: the latter was, for the most part, nonexistent. Instead, "native" peasants were locked into servile labor contracts with particular hacendados.

Rural laborers who worked regularly under such contracts for an hacendado were not the only ones positioned within these basically nonwage social relations. The latter also socially inscribed those peasants laboring for an hacendado without having formally registered any such written agreement, as well as those who cultivated the hacienda's fields as sharecroppers.[19] It seems that even the relatively small number of farmers (i.e., independent peasants with rightful land titles) were unevenly and seasonally bound by such relations to the hacendado, particularly when the weather was unfavorable and/or when these small farmers had difficulties with subsistence production or in marketing their marginal produce.

Even in the few isolated cases in which the direct producers depended totally on some form of wages in kind for their subsistence (because they were completely dispossessed with respect to the soil), this dispossession process continued to be fundamentally structured *outside market relations*. Landless peasants and artisans worked for the hacendados, for urban property owners, and/or for the colonial government because they were forced to do so by the rural guards, the village vice-mayors, the overseers, the antivagrancy laws, the courts, the prisons, the Church, ritual kinship relations, custom, superstitious influences, and so on, but hardly by any vital economic need such as hunger. Had it not been for these nineteenth-century politico-practical and discursive technologies, many more landless peasants and artisans would have—literally—headed for the hills or at least for those more remote mountain tracts still not yet legally alienated by an hacendado as late as the 1890s. This was one of the fundamental differences between the nineteenth and the twentieth centuries in Puerto Rico.

Granted, social conditions such as malnutrition and particularly starvation had also existed in the nineteenth century but not as commonplace features—or at least not with enough frequency to compel the colonized majorities to perform this type of surplus labor on a regular basis. This may be seen in the writings of a whole series of North American travelers and entrepreneurs who visited the new Caribbean possession in 1898 and 1899 to survey the island's economic potential. For instance, upon visiting the island during the U.S. invasion, Alfred G. Robinson observed that the "tones of the mandate which implies man's starvation if he will not work were but feebly heard in Porto Rico [*sic*]," this being a place where "nature weakens the force of even so much of it as may be heard, by a lavish bounty which reduces the necessity for work to its minimum."[20]

From 1788 to 1873, hacendados and the colonial government complemented the servile labor of the former free peasants with the use of slaves, particularly during the rise of sugar production between 1820 and 1854. This was one of the other crucial mechanisms that linked Puerto Rico to capitalist circulation on a world scale. The expansion of slavery entailed a series of new slave codes aimed at ensuring the orderly regulation and ideological representation of this socioeconomic regime, including penal sentences for unruly slaves. At times, "black codes" even included provisions that restricted the local movements and travel of free people of color (both black and mulatto) on the island.[21] Such legislation operated in similar ways to the antivagrancy laws and day-laborer statutes. They were all attempts to guarantee and socially construct an adequately numerous, diverse, and subordinated labor force to meet the economic and semiotic needs of the growing export-oriented agricultural interests across the island and the public-works needs of the Crown.

However, surplus-extractive and labor-intensive systems in Puerto Rico operated under severe constraints that, in turn, defined just how much the island could be transformed into a profit-based and export-oriented colonial economy. Even during the last quarter of the nineteenth century, hacendados (European-born and Creole, liberals and conservatives alike) still had difficulties in securing an "adequate" labor supply. For example, in 1874 one hacendado in the municipality of San Germán protested to the local authorities that his ex-slaves, "instead of working more earnestly," "abandon[ed] their labor completely, preferring to obtain a smaller income and work only half the week than to secure a good wage and work continuously [i.e., full time]."[22] Such statements clearly echoed hacendado complaints earlier in this century.[23] Even by the 1890s, fallow fields remained both within and outside of coffee haciendas and sugar plantations. These untilled stretches were one of the factors still placing limits on all agricultural exploitation at this time.[24] Therefore, most of the island's population continued to have direct access to small plots of land, as well as to the fruits of overseas commerce—legal and, often, illegal—and other mostly prohibited sources of sustenance.

## Contending with "Depositories of Idleness and Vice"

Once in place, these coercive-discursive measures sought to limit the independent income-gaining and subsistence activities of the heterogeneously stratified and free laboring natives—among them, numerous ex-slaves and people formerly convicted as vagrants.[25] Additionally, such labor-control mechanisms tried to restrict the way these subaltern laborers disrupted the expansion of exploitation-based export activities.

Given the particularly dense foliage of the island's mountainous interior and rural hillsides, one of the most common forms of social resistance was flight. Running away was not typical just of slaves but also of many poor peasants and ruined artisans seeking to escape from mounting debts and involuntary labor contracts. Once situated (permanently, intermittently, or briefly) beyond the immediate reach of governmental sanction, most of these subaltern sectors reconstituted themselves as free peasants or independent artisans.[26] This transformation not only included a return to the subsistence economy which had prevailed during the previous three centuries, it also meant periodic involvement in a very broad spectrum of social practices then being extensively criminalized such as smuggling, bootleg rum manufacture, gambling, nomadism, cockfights, consensual marriages, settling in urban areas without a government permit, participating in "profane" dances and music, rustling, and petty theft. So vast was this obstreperous universe within the emergent culture of the "natives" that it necessarily overlapped with the lived experience of the few remaining legitimately independent peasants, as well as with the everyday practices of slaves, debt-bound peons, and landless urban laborers.[27]

These labile working majorities (peasant, artisan, and/or slave) enacted a number of additional social resistances, among them slowing down the general pace of work while it was being performed; feigning ignorance or incompetence with respect to how particular aspects of official hacienda or town life should operate; emphasizing subsistence crops over the export cash crops being appropriated by the large landowners; and indulging in drunkenness, festivities, and/or any other Luddite activity that would halt or stall the labor process.[28] During the entire nineteenth century, such proclivities led the propertied classes in Puerto Rico (Creole, Spaniard, or foreign) and their politico-intellectual agents to ideologically represent the majority of the population in the island—particularly the poor peasantry—as being both lazy and depraved.

For example, in a report prepared in 1809, the mayor of San Juan, don Pedro Yrisarri, indicated that peasants "hardly ever . . . grow the coffee, the plantains, the sugarcane, the cotton, or any other crop that will bring perpetual profit," preferring instead to grow subsistence crops and to

find [a temporary haven] in everyone that owns uncultivated lands which they [later] easily abandon to resettle in others, something which they do with such frequency that it is rare to find one [peasant family] that lives a full year in one place, and some only a

month. Always vagrant, errant, and without a fixed residence, they
neither know nor follow the habits of a rural laborer who is settled
and is tenacious.[29]

According to this colonial officer, such characteristically peasant/"native" conduct could only lead to ruin—both economic and moral.

> This is what they are partial to, they camouflage and hide their
> own behavior and, by a continuous series of underhanded and
> painful dealings, many of them have been given to the sad experi-
> ence of being harmful to promoting the increase and the develop-
> ment of the general population and of abundant harvests, . . . being
> also a depository of idleness and vice, proof of which one need only
> point to their general reputation as being uncouth men, ungrateful,
> inconstant and indolent authors of the destruction of the Mother-
> land.[30]

The 1765 report of military governor O'Reilly was the immediate
predecessor of these racist narratives decrying the "native" barbarism
and perversity allegedly plaguing Puerto Rico.[31]
   In 1834 another European colonial functionary on the island, G. D.
Flinter (an English officer in the Spanish army), made analogous observations about the deceptive and cunning "nature" of the island's peasants.

> The Xivaros [sic], a name which is applied to these people who
> reside in the country (I do not allude to the better classes), are very
> civil in their manners. But though they seem all simplicity and
> humility, they are so acute in their dealings that they are sure to
> deceive a person who is not very guarded. Although they would
> scorn to commit robbery,[32] yet they think it only fair to deceive or
> overreach in a bargain.[33]

For Flinter, the textual referent went from Britain's most immediate
ward and "lesser peoples" (the Irish) to the United Kingdom's recent
colonial domains in Africa and India. Like Puerto Rico, these last two
continents were also exotic lands, similarly populated with cavorting
monkeys, jumping from limb to limb, as well as with simian/infantile
natives and other unusual tropical creatures.

> Like the peasantry of Ireland, they are proverbial in their hospital-
> ity; and, like them, they are ready to fight on the slightest provoca-
> tion. They swing to and fro in their hammocks all day long, smok-

ing cigars and twanging their guitars. The plantain groves which surround their houses, and the coffee trees which grow almost without cultivation, afford them a frugal subsistence. If in addition they have a cow and a horse, they consider themselves rich and happy.[34]

## "Wicked, Backward Persons with Evil, Thievish, Somewhat Sadistic Instincts"

Racist and class-based correlations of this sort had proliferated in the West before the 1800s. During the seventeenth and eighteenth centuries, the propertied and educated classes of Europe and European America were already conflating the laziness, poverty, and vice of Western laboring classes with objective threats to—if not actual disruptions of—the established order.[35] As Foucault has remarked,

idleness is rebellion—the worst of them all, in a sense: it waits for nature to be generous as in the innocence of Eden, and seeks to constrain a Goodness to which a man cannot lay claim since Adam. Pride was the sin of man before the Fall; but the sin of idleness is the supreme pride of man once he has fallen, the absurd pride of poverty. . . . All of the seventeenth-century texts . . . announced the infernal triumph of Sloth: it was Sloth which led the round of the vices and swept them on.[36]

By the mid– to late nineteenth century, scientific discourses in the West (particularly the ones introduced by Lombroso, Ferri, and Garofalo) canonized this fusion of class perversity and racial depravity by fashioning the "dangerous classes" as a breed apart: literally, as evolutionary throwbacks. Pasquale Pasquino summarizes these views in the following manner:

Within the same social organism there can coexist different stages of the evolution of the species; in this sense, society is a mixture of different natures. At the very heart of social evolution and by virtue of that process itself, one can recognize as archaic residues those individuals or groups which, unable to keep up with the proper pace of evolution and left behind it, endanger by their existence the proper functioning of the whole.[37]

At the time, Western culture in general was replete with narratives of socio-biological-cultural regression: from Zola's Lombrosian *La Bête humaine* to Renan's recuperation of the Shakespearian colonialist imaginary and racist bestiaries when, in *Caliban: suite de "La Tempête,"* Renan recast the Paris Commune as the work of "bloodthirsty savages" and "menacing barbarians." In Spain, too, this scientifically authenticated vernacular became a universal grammar among the propertied and educated classes, facilitating the reading and decoding of social disorder.[38] As we shall see below, distinguished Puerto Rican Creole intellectuals (liberals, mostly) also shared this same Europocentric and custodial-punitive grammar.

However, the groundwork for all these arguments had already been laid from the sixteenth to the eighteenth centuries when the dregs of Europe and of Spain's mid-Atlantic and North African colonies were sent to the Caribbean to colonize these new territories and/or to suffer penal servitude. There, this disreputable rabble supposedly degenerated even further due to the allegedly debilitating effects of the tropical sun and to the miscegenation between these commoners, sub-Saharan Africans, and the aboriginal populations of the Caribbean.[39] The subaltern social condition and the "natural" immoralities of these motley laboring classes (European, Taino/Carib, Arab/Moor, Canarian, West and Central African, and Creole) were all collapsed together over this long gestation period. It was perhaps only logical that by the 1800s their colonized progeny would all be ideologically represented as being innately disrespectful of property and of the prevailing social order. Hence, the subordinate racialization of the European and/or white criminal in the West had its concurrent and necessary analogue in the criminalization of the "subject races" from and in the Americas and the Caribbean, as well as Africa and Asia, during the nineteenth and early twentieth centuries.[40]

The Yrisarri and Flinter passages cited above clearly illustrate such discourses of "vice," "class," and "race." Similar cultural cartographies continued to inform much of the textual mapping in Puerto Rico until the 1890s, as may be seen in the following excerpts from the writings of two prominent Creole intellectuals, both of them liberal political leaders and critics of Spanish colonialism. For example, in his acclaimed 1887 sociographic essay on the Puerto Rican peasant, the physician Francisco del Valle Atiles remarks that

> a *jíbaro* does not prove to be very scrupulous when it comes to duties originating in the love for others; we believe that he [*sic*] does not have a clear idea of the value of certain acts as demonstrated by the little respect he seems to profess for other people's property in the case of low-priced goods. . . . [A] *jíbaro* does not believe he is violating any right when [he] takes farm fowl, a bunch of plantains, or any other small item that nevertheless and no

matter how insignificant does not stop being somebody else's property and that therefore we are forbidden to use without the permission of its owner, or if he believes this it is not because he is convinced that he is practicing a proscribed act, but because he knows that if caught he will be punished.[41]

This time the semiotic template is labor radicalism in Europe, although the signs of savagery remain the same.

Surely not all *jíbaros* profess this type of communism, but there are definitely many of them who do not have any compunction in practicing [these sorts of activities], be it in this type of form, be it borrowing money when they have no intention of repaying the debt, or be it purchasing something without paying for it. Let us mention in passing that these moral defects, mainly regarding the lack of formality in everyday exchanges, are not the exclusive traits of the peasant but are profusely generalized throughout the entire country [namely, Puerto Rico].[42]

Another late-century example of this viewpoint is the 1882 essay on the working classes in Puerto Rico written by the eminent sociologist and historian Salvador Brau. Albeit not as blunt or as overburdened with the social prejudice of his fellow party member del Valle Atiles, Brau still reached very similar conclusions. In one instance, Brau registers "a certain lack of respect for property that makes itself felt most particularly among the rural farms."[43]

### ... and "Their Rough and Wild Habits"

As independent production and subsistence activities linked to petty property were being progressively encroached upon on the island, property itself increasingly emerged as an arena of social contention and legal demarcation. The rise in the number of social practices officially characterized as property crimes throughout this century is a clear indication of this conflict. For example, the official number of thefts between 1837 and 1864 increased more than four times, subsequently more than doubling between 1864 and 1880. This was not due to a demographic explosion, because the island's population only increased by 55.6 percent during 1832 to 1860, in the first case, and by 71.4 percent during 1860 to 1887, in the second case, that is, from 330,051 (in 1832) to 583,308 (in 1860) to 798,565 (in 1887).[44]

True, this rise in property crimes was a partial response to the expansion of the criminal justice system in the colony and to the corresponding growth in the number and scope of interventions. But the criminalization of growing areas of everyday life among the island's laboring classes—gambling, cockfights, and consensual marriages being cases in point—illustrates just how wide the punitive/discursive net was being cast.[45] As early as 1855, for instance, colonial governor García Camba applied vagrancy penalties to couples found "living in sin."[46] Twenty-five years later colonial governor Despujols still described the Puerto Rican peasantry as

> being entirely scattered in isolated huts, lacking every kind of religious instruction and of moral restraint, without more or less durable unions being legitimated by the efficacy of the sacrament or the sanction of the law, unions created only upon the feeble basis of the sensual appetite, it may be truly stated that the family in the rural regions of Puerto Rico is not morally constituted, being perhaps the principal obstacle for its progress.[47]

The social resistance of the laboring classes in Puerto Rico had an additional component, namely, social violence, the latter not being limited to slave uprisings and the banditry of isolated debt-bound peons and landless peasants.[48] This rubric also included the vandalism, riots, and physical attacks of slaves, peasants, and artisans against hacendados, overseers, usurer-merchants, government officials, and/or their family members.[49] The subsequent liberal anticolonialist reinscription of some of this "political brigandage" and social violence should not blind us to alternative, sociohistorically more complicated readings of these practices. The same is true for the occasional hacendado and/or petty-urban professional hegemony found in some of these resistances.[50]

In addition to social violence, the laboring classes on the island constantly invented new ways of standing punitive laws on their heads: from changing the dates on which they would sign up for labor and signing bogus work contracts with their own relatives, in the case of the poor peasantry, to even taking their master to court and using this eminently property-based forum to denounce the brutality they were being subjected to, in the case of the slaves.[51] In the short run, these and other subaltern counterpractices provoked continuous amendments within the existing labor codes and in some cases led to the creation of new codes altogether. By the last quarter of this century, however, all these resistances (legal, extralegal, but mostly illegal) had also contributed decisively to the breakdown of the existing ways of organizing the labor process and everyday life in the haciendas: the abolition of slavery and of the forced day-laborer contracts by the mid-1870s clearly illustrates the deterioration of some of the predominant labor-control mechanisms.

The social fabric of nineteenth-century Puerto Rico was rethreaded through this uninterrupted interplay between socioeconomic and juridical-political coercion and textual practices, on the one hand, and the "weapons of the weak," on the other. This process unfolded in rural areas, where the overwhelming majority of the island's population resided in relatively modest-sized and export-oriented haciendas that oscillated between 100 and 300 *cuerdas* (97 to 291.3 acres) and in very small farms that generated a meager surplus not absorbed by land rents and state taxes, barely providing a minimum of rural family subsistence. The handful of urban centers accommodated the local agents of Spanish merchant capital (exporters, importers, and/or usurers), juridical-political officialdom, and the Church hierarchy. These few towns and cities also included equally limited spaces of artisan activity and the services of the liberal professions.[52] But what were the penal institutions that operated within—and for—the new direction taken by the Spanish colonial enterprise in Puerto Rico during this century?

### Carceral Way Stations, Hard Labor, and Penal Torture

Throughout the nineteenth century, the development of punitive structures in the island should be seen within the context of the emergent export-based, profit-oriented requirements and semiotic needs of the colonial regime. But since penal institutions in Puerto Rico predate the nineteenth century, their development can best be clarified by subdividing the chronology of this punishment into two overlapping periods. At first, the carceral institutions and quasi-penitentiary signifying practices that predominated in Spain during the medieval and early modern periods (until the late eighteenth century) were transplanted to the island. Second, and already by the mid–nineteenth century, the discourse of utilitarian correctionalism was introduced in Puerto Rico and formal attempts were made in this respect, despite their glaring lack of success. Benthamist narratives are clearly present in the formal intent of some of the labor-control legislation mentioned above, as well as in the corollary penal measures promoted at this time. However, these new carceral mechanisms and sign systems crystallized in extremely complex, stillborn, and paradoxical ways, accordingly reflecting the tensions and limits of the Spanish colonial regime in Puerto Rico.

During much of the nineteenth century nonutilitarian punitive structures and carceral ideological representations on the island assumed two concurrent forms. One of the most common uses of lockup was to detain a person to secure his or her appearance before a magistrate. The person was usually held under military guard in the nearest detention unit, which often resembled the municipal jails that had been established by the late eighteenth century. Mirroring the modalities prevalent in the West from the Middle Ages to the Enlightenment, this form of confinement employed jails and prisons primarily as way stations.[53] Under such circumstances, imprisonment did not tend to be in and of itself a form of punishment. In Puerto Rico, socially constructing, regulating, and textually marking the Empire's criminal subject in this manner did not signify depriving the confined person of his or her useful and valuable labor time simply because such calculus could not fully materialize on the island.

These way stations were the bureaucratic and financial responsibility of the town governments, a condition that remained unaltered until the 1898 U.S. invasion.[54] Between 1800 and the 1830s this type of detention began taking place within the larger district prisons then being erected, one for every judicial district so authorized. As early as 1802, Puerto Rico was subdivided into five such districts, increasing to seven in 1825. By the last quarter of the nineteenth century district prisons, now numbering eleven, came under the administrative responsibility of the islandwide governing council (the Diputación Provincial).[55]

The second penal structure that prevailed during much of this century was the use of hard labor and/or prolonged torture, both of which unevenly corresponded to several needs and social rationales of the existing regime. Let us first examine hard labor as penal servitude. Spanish colonialism saw the condemning of prisoners to hard labor as functional because it mobilized considerable numbers of laborers as cheaply as possible. Given the scarcity of laborers and the reluctance of the "natives" to enlist in the hacienda's and in the colonial administration's labor reserves, this punishment was congruent with the regime's economic and textual logic. It was a brutal response to a colonized population imagined as "naturally" recalcitrant because they did not willingly supply the labor needed to fulfill Puerto Rico's new role within the Empire. When combined with torture, hard labor also served the vindictive purpose of expiating (through suffering) whatever crimes had been committed against the Crown's authority—direct or indirect.[56] As we have already seen, in Puerto Rico the immense juridical-political universe designated as "crimes against the Crown" comprised indeed most of "native" everyday life. This is the type of punishment that Pashukanis described as "an equivalent which compensates the damage sustained by the injured party."[57]

Especially in sugar cultivation, the hacendados (both European-born and Creole) needed to secure unskilled laborers already disciplined in performing extended hours of grueling work for somebody else.[58] This convict labor was not directly rented or placed at the disposal of the hacendados. Rather, such penal mechanisms were deployed to capture, subdue, and train free peasant and artisan "natives" by socially inscribing them as vagrant and/or as involved in illegal subsistence activities and outlawed customs.

Confinement to hard labor in Puerto Rico had two immediate precedents, the first one being forced labor in the naval arsenals. This form of penal servitude prevailed in Spain after the suppression of the galleys in 1748 and persisted on the Iberian peninsula until the early nineteenth century.[59] From 1760 to 1809 those condemned by the Crown to hard labor in the overseas fortifications were forced, among other things, to rebuild and expand San Juan's principal bulwarks. This prison population usually consisted of people accused of being deserters, vagrants, smugglers, buccaneers, and filibusters. During the final third of the eighteenth century, for instance, between seven hundred and eight hundred prisoners—including common criminals as well as political and religious prisoners from Spain, Venezuela, and Colombia—arrived in San Juan to perform this kind of hard labor. The first *presidio* built in the capital city (Cuartel de Presidiarios or Cuartel de los Desterrados) was established at this time to shelter and control the felons working on these fortresses. It was only in 1837 that this institution was supplanted by the Cárcel de la Princesa (Presidio de San Juan).[60]

There were other antecedents of confinement to hard labor in Puerto Rico, among them the public works *presidios* organized in Spain between the 1770s and the mid–nineteenth century for the expansion and upkeep of roads, canals, public sanitation, and so on. By 1837, prisoners so sentenced amounted to about a third of the island's penal population. By 1842, this proportion had risen to approximately two-thirds of all prisoners in Puerto Rico.[61] One of the most ambitious deployments of convict labor was the construction of the military road, weaving through the island's central mountain range, that connected San Juan with Ponce. The latter, located on the southern coast, was the island's second-largest city and a major site of sugar production and export. Between 1874 and 1889 the entire prison population of the *presidio* at La Puntilla arsenal in San Juan was mobilized for this purpose, along with many common detainees from other institutions, including those legally identified as vagrants, idle poor, slaves, and former slaves.[62]

Torture was the second form of legal punishment adopted in nineteenth-century Puerto Rico. Penal torture entailed shackling the prisoner with heavy chains for an extended period of time. After the penal code of the 1870s, this meant twelve to twenty years in the case of *cadena temporal* and the remainder of the convict's life in the case of *cadena perpetua*.[63] Flogging, with or without imprisonment, was also a common legal punishment at least until the 1860s. Punitive torment could also be meted out via the use of various devices such as the *palillos*

and the *cordeles*. Here was yet another early modern European tradition
overlapping with the aims of colonialism; namely, exerting physical
pain on the colonized body so that the latter could achieve penance and
in this manner personify Truth and the Right of the Empire. Although
formally abolished in Spain in 1814, official torture continued to be
extensively utilized by the colonial regime in Puerto Rico against those
accused of sedition—the infamous Año Terrible del 1887 is a case in
point.[64]

Of course, the ultimate penal sanction was capital punishment.
Although death by hanging was abolished in 1832, strangulation with an
iron collar, or garrote, took its place.[65] As Coll y Toste observes, the
ceremony and details of this type of punishment were hierarchically
differentiated to indicate the social position of the condemned and the
enormity of his or her crime.[66] Many of these executions were public,
and once in a while an exceptionally notorious convict would be
executed not by garrote but by a firing squad. Such was the case of the
well-known "native" bandit Ignacio Ávila (a.k.a. El Águila), whose
robberies, daring escapes, and other exploits spanned the 1838–1848
period. After being captured for the last time, Ávila was formally shot by
a firing squad from the Fourth Asturias Battalion in the presence of over
eight hundred spectators.[67]

### San Juan's *Presidios, Cárceles,* and *Penitenciaría*

The *presidio* at La Puntilla arsenal in the capital district was one of the
principal institutions confining those sentenced to hard labor. La Puntilla
was built and organized between 1809 and 1820 as a house of correction
(*presidio correccional, presidio menor,* or *cárcel correccional para vagos*)
modeled on the institutions established in Spain under the *Reglamento
de prisiones* of 1807.[68] However, similar to what historian Ruth Pike
found for the entire Iberian peninsula, in La Puntilla, "despite the intent,
the idea of rehabilitation did not become fully operative until much
later."[69]

La Puntilla fundamentally operated as a public-works and prolonged-
detention *presidio*. Part of the convict labor thus mobilized worked in
the naval yard, munitions depot, and docks located next to the *presidio*.
The felons were directly supervised and guarded by the soldiers stationed
in the nearby artillery post and barracks. Although I have not been able
to ascertain the exact date when it ceased operations, La Puntilla was
still being used during the last quarter of the nineteenth century.[70]

By midcentury, San Juan already had the highest concentration (per
square mile and per capita) of carceral institutions on the island, all of
which operated primarily as temporary detention way stations as well as

centers of prolonged detention and/or penal torture. Besides La Puntilla, there was the Real Cárcel de San Juan, or Cárcel Pública. Built between 1811 and 1813 in the Calle Luna sector of the capital (behind city hall), the Real Cárcel de San Juan continued operations for most of the century. Additionally, there was the Cárcel de la Princesa or Presidio de San Juan, erected in 1837 outside the city walls and functioning through 1898. This penal archipelago was completed in 1887 when a building originally destined to be a general hospital (Hospital Civil) in the Puerta de Tierra sector of San Juan was turned into a large-scale prison for felons from all over the island (Cárcel Provincial, or Penitenciaría Insular y Presidio).[71]

Generally speaking, though, Bentham's famous principle of inmate classification and compartmentalization tended to be absent within carceral institutions in the Spanish colony of Puerto Rico. At first glance, this is peculiar given the early introduction of Bentham's ideas in Spain. In 1819 the social philosopher Villanueva y Jordá had already published in Spain a work about panopticism and prison organization, while Universidad de Salamanca professor Toribio Núñez had translated Bentham's "Principles of Civil and Penal Legislation" in 1820. Núñez was also the author of *Ciencia social según los principios de Jeremías Bentham*, published by the Royal Press in 1835 by order of the Spanish government.[72] Benthamist elements were present in Spanish prison codes during the remainder of the century, particularly the *Ordenanza general de presidios del reino* of 1834 and the *Código Narváez* of 1848. These principles also infused the work of renowned utilitarian prison reformers such as Luis Silvela from the 1870s to the 1890s. However, Bentham's precepts of prison organization only began to materialize in Spain several decades later with the *Real decreto* of 1913.[73] This distance between scholastic debate, academic publishing, and the letter of the law, on the one hand, and the concrete application of juridical-punitive doctrine, on the other, partially explains the reality of nineteenth-century prisons in Puerto Rico, specifically those in San Juan.

These institutions were primarily characterized by the random accumulation of inmates within large open halls, or *galeras*. According to Colonel Flinter's firsthand observations during the 1830s, in these very dimly lit and squalid *galeras* the convicts were all huddled together, sleeping on the bare floor.[74] Under military guard and while dragging their heavy and noisy chains, the prisoners periodically left the *galeras* to march to and from the public works, where they performed hard labor. At the turn of the century, U.S. Commissioner Henry K. Carroll described the *galeras* at the Cárcel Provincial in San Juan as being "on the upper floor" and lacking "hygienic conditions, on account of the lack of windows for ventilation and because of the fact that the prisoners are constantly in their departments, where they eat, sleep, wash their clothes, and have their closets."[75]

Flinter mentions that the principal form of prisoner segregation was between the *galeras* of those condemned for greater offenses—murder, robbery, and violations of military law, including desertion, insubordination, neglect of duty, drunkenness, and quarreling—and the *galeras* confining those sentenced for lesser offenses—petty theft, disorderly conduct, vagrancy, public immorality, and so on. The former were subject to long years in jail or to life imprisonment, whereas the latter served only months or a few years.[76]

The bodies of the condemned were at times regulated/fragmented, both institutionally and semiotically, along lines of gender but especially along lines of property ownership. The badge of class may be clearly seen in the existence of the "preference room" in San Juan's carceral detention units.[77] But these special quarters were not limited to capital city jails, as may be seen in the declarations of the mayor of the district of Humacao, who, immediately after the 1898 U.S. invasion, described these unique rooms to Commissioner Carroll as "devoted to prisoners who do not wish to be in the same quarters with the rest and for which prisoners have to pay."[78] Other island prisons, such as the one in the district of San Germán, also had these private rooms.[79] Being poor, most prisoners were herded into *galeras*: making do with whatever their relatives provided for them and with whatever their jailers left them after prison officials had skimmed off the paltry government funds assigned to feed the inmates.[80]

For Flinter, 1830s prisons in Puerto Rico and primarily San Juan's institutions needed to be "new-modelled, newly organized, and their inmates classified with scrupulous exactness," this being a fundamental component of administering the inmates along "more humane, more honest, and philanthropic principles."[81] Flinter proposed that Spain emulate in Puerto Rico "those countries where a well-regulated system of prison discipline had been established."

> The uniform experience, for a series of years, of the prisons of England and the United States, where sanguinary penal codes, after having been for ages in operation, have yielded in practice to the more rational and humane substitution of hard labour, restricted diet, solitary confinement, and judicious classification, furnishes unquestionable practical evidence that the energies of the law in the suppression of crime, are most potent and efficient when directed with a constant view to the moral faculties of our nature, in order that it may safely forgive.[82]

Prisons in England and the United States at this time were hardly the models of clemency that Flinter imagined.[83] Moreover, San Juan prisons were not above proclaiming their commitment to merciful and humanitarian aims. The Cárcel Pública de San Juan had the following inscription emblazoned on its broad portals: "Hate the Crime / feel compassion for the Criminal / year of 1813" [Odia al Delito / compadece al Delincuente / año de 1813].[84] Nevertheless, this institution and its counterparts in San Juan and on the rest of the island were the furthest thing from charitable treatment or even utilitarian discipline. As a whole, carceral sites in Puerto Rico did not incarnate the Benthamist discourse of classification, prisoner separation, central inspection, and panopticism in general. Attempts and recommendations were made in this regard, but they bore no fruit during this century.

La Princesa *presidio* clearly illustrates these limitations. Although expanded in 1879, La Princesa enclosed all of its 672 inmates within a single *galera* three meters long by twelve meters wide, in addition to being notoriously filthy and dark.[85] As late as 1895, the chief of the *presidio* and an architect both submitted a report advising the colonial governor to authorize the construction of separate quarters for women convicts, as well as restructure the central building along panoptic or radial lines. Notwithstanding similar suggestions made for the Real Cárcel de San Juan at this time, neither was fully implemented.[86] Commissioner Carroll observed in 1899 that "with the exception of the separation of sexes, no division whatever is attempted."[87] He found similar conditions in the prisons of Humacao, Vega Baja, Utuado, Mayagüez, and San Germán.[88]

## The Case of the Casa de Beneficencia de San Juan

The use of prison labor for commercial profit did not completely materialize within the structuring of penal discipline in the colony of Puerto Rico, particularly in the capital city. Institutions that combined the poorhouse, the workhouse, and the prison (i.e., genuine houses of correction) had appeared in various parts of Europe since the sixteenth century and in Spain as of the last quarter of the eighteenth century.[89] Despite the explicit title of La Puntilla *presidio*, the latter did not actually fit the bill. The closest an island-based institution ever came to fulfilling such goals was the Casa de Reclusión y Asilo de Beneficencia, or simply Casa de Beneficencia during the second half of the nineteenth century. A more detailed examination of this institution, however, shows that the Casa de Beneficencia did not fulfill these aims either.

Plans for the Casa de Beneficencia had been drawn up in 1838, when colonial governor López Baños decided to put into effect an already sixteen-year-old law providing for public charities, poorhouses, and corrections (*Reglamento nacional de la beneficencia pública*) established in Spain. López Baños originally intended this institution to be a gender-segregated detention center for wayward women in San Juan's other jails because the latter also housed male prisoners.[90] These aims changed when the succeeding colonial governor, Santiago Méndez Vigo, did not limit the Casa de Beneficencia (built between 1841 and 1844) to confining and disciplining "vice-ridden" women. He was also interested in having this institution contain the rising numbers of "[male] delinquents," "invalids, orphans, paupers, abandoned old people," "the demented," "deserters," "patricides and infanticides," and "unruly slaves [until 1873]" of both sexes who populated as well as wandered throughout the urban centers of the island, particularly San Juan.[91] From 1844 to 1898 the Casa de Beneficencia's inmate population tended to oscillate between four hundred and six hundred, two hundred to three hundred of which were usually children. The holding capacity of the Casa de Beneficencia should not be underestimated, because by century's end it contained a little over half as many inmates as there were in the colony's entire penal system—municipal jails, district prisons, and *presidios* included.[92]

After searching for a proper place to erect the Casa de Beneficencia, the colonial government finally decided on the Barrio Ballajá, located in one of the highest elevations of the islet of San Juan, near the army barracks (Cuartel de Milicias) on the Calle San Sebastián. It was hardly coincidental that "a neighborhood populated by a very large number of indigent families" already stood in this site, characterized by "rows of huts distributed into streets that, given their primitive use, constituted one of the poorest shantytowns."[93] In 1854 colonial governor Fernando de Norzagaray proudly declared to the Council of Ministers that the Casa de Beneficencia "contributed to public embellishment and demonstrated to whatever traveler should visit us that although no riches or luxuries" were bestowed upon the inmates, the institution's modesty could proclaim with satisfaction: "here the suffering soul is comforted and the helpless orphan is succored."[94]

This institution went through two more or less distinct periods. Between 1844 and 1863 it was predominantly a space for confining those socially constructed as mentally deficient (deranged or retarded), and it operated concurrently as an orphan asylum. In the Casa de Beneficencia at this time there was practically no gender and age segregation and very limited vocational instruction and moralization through labor. From 1863 to 1898 nuns administered the Casa de Beneficencia and attempted to introduce partial inmate separation, dividing those confined according to the more stringent dictates of piety and prudence, that is, by gender, age, and condition. This second period saw the expansion of the workshops devoted to craft education and labor discipline.[95]

The broad heterogeneity of the Casa de Beneficencia's confined population had its immediate antecedent in the Casa de Corrección de San Fernando established in Spain in 1776.[96] As Rusche and Kirchheimer have observed, in the houses of correction of the West

> every effort was made to draw upon all the available labor reserves, not only to absorb them into economic activity but, further, to "resocialize" them in such a way that in the future they would enter the labor market freely. . . . Its main aim was to make the labor power of the unwilling socially useful. By being forced to work within the institution, the prisoners would form industrious habits and would receive a vocational training at the same time. When released, it was hoped, they would voluntarily swell the labor market.[97]

In order to further such aims, inmates in Europe and North America were mobilized into work gangs under the direct supervision of the institution or by the lease system, that is, contracting out this cheap—and captive—labor to private entrepreneurs.[98]

On paper, the Casa de Beneficencia of San Juan had similar goals insofar as its official principles stipulated that the institution was "a public establishment [organized] for the purpose of shelter, care, occupation, instruction, and moralization."[99] Shoe repair, tailoring, and blacksmith workshops were established in 1856; bookbinding and carpentry were added between 1871 and 1873; a printing shop and a vocational school were organized during the 1889–1894 period.[100]

I have not found any evidence linking these workshops with anything resembling a lease system and/or profitable employment of inmates within the Casa de Beneficencia itself. True, whatever labor instruction occurred there must have contributed to the overall aim of disciplining dispossessed "natives" to toiling extended hours for the large property owners and/or in public works. In this sense, the Casa de Beneficencia partially operated in tandem with the forced labor regime functioning within the formal penal system. But the existing differences should also be borne in mind: work gangs collectively mobilized to perform unskilled hard labor were the hallmark of explicitly carceral institutions, whereas the workshops of the Casa de Beneficencia positioned inmates to carry out very individualized and partially skilled craft work. Although similar utilitarian attempts at instruction surfaced within the written law structuring the colony's penal system during the final decades of the nineteenth century, such efforts never became generalized, remaining a moot formality or being abandoned very quickly.[101]

### Utilitarian Reforms and Other Late-Century Colonial Fictions

The socioeconomic crisis of the 1880s and 1890s advanced the pauperization and partial disintegration of artisan labor in Puerto Rico. This crisis contributed to the rise of a handful of protocapitalist manufactures, as well as to an increase in urban riots, theft, panhandling, prostitution, and child nomadism during the last decades of this century.[102] The Casa de Beneficencia could have played an important role in disciplining this emergent urban labor supply, perhaps even more than the general penal system. The evidence in this regard, however, is still forthcoming.

On the whole, the Casa de Beneficencia seems to have primarily acted as a depot for the growing number of cases of urban nomadism and sociomoral disruption being identified, intervened, and confined in a largely undifferentiated manner by the local authorities. During the 1844–1898 period, what tended to prevail was the generalized idleness of its inmates.[103]

The Casa de Beneficencia was not unique in terms of jointly restricting the movements both of common criminals and of people classified as insane in nineteenth-century Puerto Rico. Carroll, for instance, found in 1899 that in the northern district of Arecibo "they imprison[ed] the insane . . . with criminal offenders."[104] Discussing the situation of the demented on the island, another group of U.S. commissioners related that same year that "many of them are in prisons, and when not dangerous, are not necessarily separated from the prisoners confined therein."[105] One famous seventeenth-century French precedent immediately comes to mind, as documented by Foucault:

> For a long time, the house of correction or the premises of the
> Hôpital Général would serve to contain the unemployed, the idle,
> and the vagabonds. Each time a crisis occurred and the number of
> the poor sharply increased, the houses of confinement regained, at
> least for a time, their initial economic significance. . . . One-tenth
> of all arrests made in Paris for the Hôpital Général concern "the
> insane," "demented" men, individuals of "wandering mind," and
> "persons who have become completely mad." Between these and
> the others, no sign of differentiation.[106]

The Casa de Beneficencia also resembled other carceral institutions in Puerto Rico in its extremely harsh methods of physical restraint and/or punishment. Manacles, iron fetters, and similar forms of chained restriction were commonplace in the Casa de Beneficencia, as were whips for flogging and booths provided with streams of high-pressure water at extreme temperatures. All of these punitive technologies were deployed to physically discipline and morally refashion the inmates, on whose colonized bodies the Truth of medical cures and Christian repentance were being inscribed in the vernacular of pain. The disorder and the social crisis embodied by these subaltern subjects (who, in turn, personified the "rough and wild habits" of the "native" majorities) would be finally domesticated on the very flesh of the Casa de Beneficencia's inmates. Envisioned as therapeutic treatment and moralization, the Spanish colonialist imaginary continued to unfold as torture within this institution until the 1890s. The same held true for the scarce differentiation between those identified as mental patients, the poor in general, and criminals of all ages and both sexes.[107]

Some Creole social philosophers subsequently took note of the similarities between a supposedly nonpenal institution like the Casa de Beneficencia and the formal carceral system in the colony. In 1904, for instance, Salvador Brau commented that "don Santiago Méndez Vigo created in 1841 . . . a Casa de Beneficencia where orphans and the demented would be housed while, in 1846, his successors turned the charitable asylum into a General House of Confinement (Casa de Reclusión General): it became necessary to wait until the new governors detached the jail from the haven."[108]

The Casa de Beneficencia's most prominent director, Francisco de Goenaga, expressed himself along similar lines when in the 1930s he candidly admitted: "In time, the Asilo de Beneficencia became a *presidio* and for long years it was not a house of public charity but a den of abominations and of incredible horrors."[109] According to de Goenaga, toward the end of the nineteenth century several reforms were long overdue. This meant recognizing "the radical difference of objectives within society between the criminal and the madman" by distinguishing between "the life and treatment of carceral and clinical institutions": it was the absence of such a contrast that had made the "regime of the Asilo de Beneficencia" one where the "idea of punishment seemed to prevail."[110]

## Conclusion

The question then arises: why did the formal penal system on the island and even in the Casa de Beneficencia not materialize into bona fide houses of correction as these were then formally understood? Perhaps the answer is related, partially, to the character of the socioeconomic transformations taking place in Puerto Rico (as well as in Spain) and in the changes of the corresponding sign systems during this century. To some extent, the constraints and incongruities of the forms of economic organization appear to be linked to the contradictions within the forms of punitive organization and the discourses of colonialist regulation. The structure of the "primitive accumulation" of capital that prevailed on the island at this time seems to have meant that, to paraphrase Foucault, "the methods for administering the accumulation of people," in the case of Puerto Rico, would not supersede the "traditional, ritual, costly, violent forms of power."[111]

However, such forms of power and accumulation were violently imposed on people being culturally inscribed as "primitive" and "disreputable" even before they began defying the nineteenth-century expressions of such exploitation and punishment. In turn, phenomena such as subaltern nomadism, flight, smuggling, theft, hacienda vandalism, and so on tended to justify among the propertied and educated classes (Creole and European-born, both liberal and conservative) the expansion of penal servitude and the attempts at moral engineering by the colonial authorities. Since the late eighteenth century the island had been forcibly reinserted within the world capitalist market by transforming subsistence agriculture into export-oriented, exploitation-based agriculture. But by limiting the course, extension, and profitability of extracting surplus value within overwhelmingly nonwage forms of labor, the waywardness of the natives also ended up confining the development of the modes of confinement.

These resistances were one of the factors impeding the fruition of debt peonage, slavery, merchant capital, and so on and their eventual transformation into and confrontation with wage-based forms of surplus-value production. Even by century's end, therefore, the primitive accumulation of capital never delivered the material conditions for generalizing monetary-wage labor on the island. Without the crystallization/extension of such production, prison time could not be socially calculated in terms of labor value—a process that we saw in passing was barely and unevenly beginning in Spain itself. Only by translating penal confinement into the loss of labor time/value could carceral utilitarianism be constructed, both literally, socially, and semiotically. According to Pashukanis,

> for it to be possible for the idea to emerge that one could make recompense with a piece of abstract freedom determined in advance, it was necessary for all concrete forms of social wealth to be reduced to the most abstract and simple form, to human labour measured in time. . . . Industrial capitalism, the declaration of

human rights, the political economy of Ricardo, and the system of imprisonment for a stipulated term are phenomena peculiar to one and the same historical epoch.[112]

Without wage-based relations of production, there was no socioeconomic basis for the abstract equality and individuality of all citizens and no need to distribute and classify them according to their function and social position. What practical use could there be, then, for the extended division and classification of inmates, as well as for their panoptic regulation? As María Jesús Miranda has observed,

> The distribution of space is going to be one of the great concerns of the nineteenth [century] because it is one of the apprehensions of a bourgeoisie obliged to reinstall—and to do so "conveniently"—an enormous mass of people, expelled from a rural society or, simply, the product of the enormous demographic advances of the century. . . . The transparency of the panoptic is the ideal image of one of the dreams of the social sciences: society as a group of individuals perfectly accounted for, weighed, and measured . . . [This is] an equality that, to be believed, has to be created, [one] that, as a matter of fact, capitalist society has been creating and continues to create every day.[113]

By effectively imposing a phantasmic parody of European "feudalism" on nineteenth-century Puerto Rico, Spain's colonial enterprise remained hostage to the disruptions of the subaltern subjects it had originally created yet still needed. The even more spectral pretensions of instituting bourgeois-utilitarian penal structures (via the introduction of Benthamist sign systems, among other things) in the island could only remain a world on paper. In this sense, the corresponding institutions of punishment and labor moralization ultimately could not transcend the limits of the prevailing social structure and of "native" disorder.

## Notes

1. Steven Spitzer, "Notes toward a Theory of Punishment and Social Change," *Research in Law and Sociology* 2 (1979): 207.

2. Albert Memmi, *The Colonizer and the Colonized* (Boston: Beacon Press, 1970), pp. 82, 90.

3. Stan Steiner, *The Islands: The Worlds of Puerto Ricans* (New York: Harper and Row, 1975), pp. 93–94.

4. My own previous work is often reduced to such "great narrative of the modes of production" and its corollary "narrative of the transition from feudalism to capitalism." See, for example, K. Antonio Santiago, "El Puerto Rico del

siglo XIX: apuntes para su análisis," *Hómines* 5, nos. 1-2 (January–December 1981): 7–23; Kelvin Santiago, "Algunos aspectos de la integración de Puerto Rico al interior del estado metropolitano," *Revista de Ciencias Sociales* 23, nos. 3–4 (July–December 1981): 297–347.

5. Gayatri Chakravorty Spivak, "Subaltern Studies: Deconstructing Historiography," in Gayatri Chakravorty Spivak, ed., *Other Worlds: Essays in Cultural Politics* (New York: Routledge, 1988), p. 197.

6. Spitzer, "Notes," p. 207.

7. Eugenio Fernández Méndez, *Historia cultural de Puerto Rico, 1493–1968* (San Juan: Ediciones "El Cemí," 1970), pp. 161, 164, 213; Darío de Ormaechea, "Memoria acerca de la agricultura, el comercio y las rentas internas," in Eugenio Fernández Méndez, ed., *Crónicas de Puerto Rico* (Río Piedras: Editorial Universitaria, 1976), pp. 398–399, 418; Jordi Maluquer de Motes, "El mercado colonial antillano en el siglo XIX," in Jordi Nadal and Gabriel Tortella, eds., *Agricultura, comercio colonial y crecimiento económico en la España contemporánea* (Barcelona: Editorial Ariel, 1974), pp. 342–344; Miguel Izard, "Comercio libre, guerras coloniales y mercado americano," in Nadal and Tortella, eds., *Agricultura, comercio colonial*, pp. 295–321.

8. See Carlos Assadourian et al., *Modos de producción en América Latina* (Córdoba, Argentina: Cuadernos de Pasado y Presente no. 40, 1973); Roger Bartra et al., *Modos de Producción en América Latina: Historia y Sociedad* 5 (spring 1975); Ángel Quintero Rivera, "Background to the Emergence of Imperialist Capitalism in Puerto Rico," *Caribbean Studies* 13, no. 3 (October 1973); History Task Force, *Labor Migration under Capitalism: The Puerto Rican Experience* (New York: Monthly Review Press, 1979), pp. 67–86; Santiago, "El Puerto Rico del siglo XIX," pp. 7–23.

9. Here I try not to fall into the trap of whether nineteenth-century Puerto Rico (or, for that matter, any other part of the so-called Third World) was or was not "feudal" and "precapitalist" because it would amount to exhuming "the great narrative of the modes of production," that is, reproducing the Europocentric and teleological vision of the West as the measure of all things. Alternative viewpoints have tended instead to equate capitalism per se with the existence of commodity circulation, particularly with a system of commodity circulation linked to the world capitalist market. See Fernández Méndez, *Historia cultural*, pp. 213–216; Arturo Morales Carrión, *Albores históricos del capitalismo en Puerto Rico* (Río Piedras: Editorial Universitaria, 1972); Laird Bergard, *Coffee and the Growth of Agrarian Capitalism* (Princeton, N.J.: Princeton University Press, 1983). A few other scholars have characterized nineteenth-century Puerto Rican social formation as indeterminately precapitalist production with some capitalist elements. See Manuel Maldonado Denis, *Hacia una interpretación marxista de la historia de Puerto Rico* (Río Piedras: Editorial Antillana, 1977), pp. 21–24, 41–42, 132–135; James Dietz, *Economic History of Puerto Rico* (Princeton, N.J.: Princeton University Press, 1986), pp. 31–34.

10. Maluquer de Motes, "El mercado colonial antillano"; Jordi Nadal, *El fracaso de la revolución industrial en España, 1814–1913* (Barcelona: Editorial Ariel, 1975); Manuel Tuñón de Lara, *La España del siglo XIX*, vol. 2 (Barcelona: Editorial Laia, 1977), pp. 56–66.

11. Lidio Cruz Monclova, *Historia de Puerto Rico (siglo XIX)*, tomo II,

*primera parte* (Río Piedras: Editorial Universitaria, Universidad de Puerto Rico, 1957), pp. 57, 88, 115, 225, 229–231; Lidio Cruz Monclova, *Historia de Puerto Rico (siglo XIX), tomo I (1808–1868)* (Río Piedras: Editorial Universitaria, Universidad de Puerto Rico, 1958), pp. 420, 583, 594–595, 641–642, 693; Maluquer de Motes, "El mercado colonial," pp. 323, 335–336, 345–353; Rosa Marazzi, "El impacto de la inmigración a Puerto Rico, 1800 a 1830: análisis estadístico," *Revista de Ciencias Sociales* 18, nos. 1–2 (March–June 1974): 8, 10, 16, 20–21, 25–26; Gervasio García, *Primeros fermentos de organización obrera en Puerto Rico, 1873–1898* (Río Piedras: Cuadernos de CEREP, no. 1, 1974), p. 4; Manuel Tuñón de Lara, *Estudios sobre el siglo XIX español* (Madrid: Siglo XXI Editores, 1974), pp. 213, 247–248, 256–257, 269; Tuñón de Lara, *La España del siglo XIX*, vol. 1 (Barcelona: Editorial Laia, 1977), pp. 142, 151, 166, 187, 226–228. In other words, these were investments carried out by Spanish capitalists, or by elements in the process of becoming such capitalists, within colonialist enterprises that structurally were not grounded in the wage system such as usury, merchant capital, sharecropping, debt peonage, slavery, the slave trade, and so on.

12. Frank Bonilla and Ricardo Campos, "Imperialist Initiatives and the Puerto Rican Worker: From Foraker to Reagan," *Contemporary Marxism* 5 (summer 1982): 4.

13. Fernández Méndez, *Historia cultural*, pp. 161, 164; Labor Gómez Acevedo, *Organización y reglamentación del trabajo en el Puerto Rico del siglo XIX (propietarios y jornaleros)* (San Juan: Instituto de Cultura Puertorriqueña, 1970), pp. 52–53; Marazzi, "El impacto de la inmigración," pp. 5, 18.

14. Gómez Acevedo, *Organización y reglamentación*, p. 88; all translations are mine.

15. Cruz Monclova, *Tomo I (1808–1868)*, pp. 106–114; Félix Mejías, *Más apuntes para la historia económica de Puerto Rico* (Río Piedras: Ediciones Edil, 1978), pp. 31–36; María García Ochoa, *La política española en Puerto Rico durante el siglo XIX* (Río Piedras: Editorial de la Universidad de Puerto Rico, 1982), pp. 252–256.

16. U.S. War Department, *Report on the Census of Porto Rico—1899* (Washington, D.C.: Government Printing Office, 1900), p. 40. This increase partially resulted both from the rising number of propertied migrants settling on the island and from the growing importance of slavery and debt peonage.

17. Gómez Acevedo, *Organización y reglamentación*; Salvador Brau, *Ensayos (disquisiciones sociológicas)* (Río Piedras: Editorial Edil, 1972), pp. 49–50; Sidney Mintz, "The Cultural History of a Puerto Rican Sugar Cane Plantation: 1876–1949," in Fernández Méndez, ed., *Portrait of a Society: Readings in Puerto Rican Sociology* (Río Piedras: University of Puerto Rico Press, 1972), p. 144; Igualdad Iglesias de Pagán, *El obrerismo en Puerto Rico, época de Santiago Iglesias (1895–1905)* (Palencia de Castilla: Ediciones Juan Ponce de León, 1973), p. 15; García, *Primeros fermentos*, pp. 3, 4; Ángel Quintero Rivera, "La clase obrera y el proceso político en Puerto Rico—I," *Revista de Ciencias Sociales* 18, nos. 1–2 (March–June 1974): 164, 188; Fernando Picó, *Libertad y servidumbre en el Puerto Rico del siglo XIX* (Río Piedras: Ediciones Huracán, 1979); Fernando Picó, *Amargo café* (Río Piedras: Ediciones Huracán, 1981).

18. García, *Primeros fermentos*, pp. 1–2; Cruz Monclova, *Historia, (1808–1868)*, pp. 207–208, 255–256. The first three genuine banks on the island were

established between 1890 and 1895. See Cruz Monclova, *Historia, tomo III (tercera parte)*, p. 338.

19. Gómez Acevedo, *Organización y reglamentación*, pp. 107–109, 111–114; Fernández Méndez, *Historia cultural*, p. 221; Quintero Rivera, "La clase obrera—I," pp. 164, 168.

20. Albert G. Robinson, *The Porto Rico of Today* (New York: Charles Scribner's Sons, 1899), p. 161. See also Robert T. Hill, *Cuba and Porto Rico with Other Islands of the West Indies* (New York: Century Co., 1898), p. 167.

21. Colonel G. D. Flinter, *An Account of the Present State of the Island of Puerto Rico* (London: Rees, Orne, Brown, Greene and Longman, 1834), pp. 208–211; Cayetano Coll y Toste, ed., *Boletín histórico de Puerto Rico* (San Juan: Tipografía Cantero Fernández, 1921), 8: 366; Coll y Toste, ed., *Boletín* (1926), 13: 50–52; Coll y Toste, ed., *Boletín* (1915), 2: 124–126; Luis Díaz Soler, *Historia de la esclavitud negra en Puerto Rico* (Río Piedras: Editorial Universitaria, Universidad de Puerto Rico, 1970), pp. 214–223; Guillermo Baralt, *Esclavos y rebeldes: conspiraciones y sublevaciones de esclavos en Puerto Rico (1795–1873)* (Río Piedras: Ediciones Huracán, 1981), pp. 74–83, 129–131; Fernando Picó, *Al filo del poder: subalternos y dominantes en Puerto Rico, 1739–1910* (Río Piedras: Editorial de la Universidad de Puerto Rico, 1993), pp. 115–132.

22. Quoted in García, *Primeros fermentos*, p. 9.

23. See Marazzi, "El impacto," pp. 5–6, 18.

24. Lidio Cruz Monclova, *Historia de Puerto Rico (siglo XIX), tomo III—tercera parte (1885–1898)* (Río Piedras: Editorial Universitaria, Universidad de Puerto Rico, 1964), pp. 286–287; Ramón de Armas, "El otro pasado de Puerto Rico," *Revista Casa de las Américas* 70 (January–February 1972): 150–151; Francisco del Valle Atiles, *El campesino puertorriqueño* (San Juan: Tipografía J. González Font, 1887), p. 131; Brau, *Ensayos*, pp. 33–38; Picó, *Libertad y servidumbre*, pp. 104–105, 119; Fernando Picó, *Vivir en Caimito* (Río Piedras: Ediciones Huracán, 1988), pp. 31–32, 155.

25. See, for example, Ruth Pike, *Penal Servitude in Early Modern Spain* (Madison: University of Wisconsin Press, 1983), pp. 141–142; Gilberto Aponte, *San Mateo de Cangrejos (comunidad cimarrona en Puerto Rico): notas para su historia* (San Juan: N.p., 1985).

26. Picó, *Libertad y servidumbre*, pp. 109, 111; Baralt, *Esclavos y rebeldes*, pp. 42–45; Francisco Scarano, *Sugar and Slavery in Puerto Rico: The Plantation Economy of Ponce, 1800–1850* (Madison: University of Wisconsin Press, 1984), pp. 32–33; Fray Íñigo Abbad y Lasierra, *Historia geográfica, civil y natural de la Isla de San Juan de Puerto Rico: nueva edición anotada en la parte histórica y continuada en la estadística y económica por José Julián Acosta y Calbo* (San Juan: Imprenta y Librería de Acosta, 1866), p. 417; Coll y Toste, ed., *Boletín* (1921), 8: 21–23; José C. Rosario, *The Development of the Puerto Rican Jíbaro and His Present Attitude towards Society* (Río Piedras: University of Puerto Rico, 1935), p. 29; Brau, *Ensayos*, pp. 29–30; Picó, *Al filo del poder*, pp. 105–114, 133–160.

27. Brau, *Ensayos*, pp. 33–38; Picó, *Libertad y servidumbre*, pp. 104–105, 119; Picó, *Vivir en Caimito*, pp. 31–32, 69–72, 87–94; Benjamín Nistal Moret, *Esclavos prófugos y cimarrones: Puerto Rico, 1770–1870* (Río Piedras: Editorial de la Universidad de Puerto Rico, 1984); Guillermo Baralt, "Los últimos días de

esclavitud en la Hacienda La Esperanza (1850–1873)," in *La tercera raíz: presencia africana en Puerto Rico* (San Juan: Centro de Estudios de la Realidad Puertorriqueña e Instituto de Cultura Puertorriqueña, 1992), pp. 6–13; Ángel Quintero Rivera, "El tambor en el cuatro: la melodización de ritmos y la etnicidad cimarroneada," in *La tercera raíz*, pp. 42–53.

28. Henry K. Carroll, *Report on the Island of Porto Rico* (Washington, D.C.: Government Printing Office, 1899), pp. 712–754; Manuel Meléndez Muñoz, "El jíbaro en el siglo XIX," in *Obras completas de Manuel Meléndez Muñoz* (San Juan: Instituto de Cultura Puertorriqueña, 1963), 3: 509–518; Brau, *Ensayos*, pp. 27–29, 44–45, 47; Picó, *Libertad y servidumbre*, p. 120; Andrés Ramos Mattei, "La importación de trabajadores contratados para la industria azucarera puertorriqueña, 1860–1880," in Francisco Scarano, ed., *Inmigración y clases sociales en el Puerto Rico del siglo XIX* (Río Piedras: Ediciones Huracán, 1981), p. 129; Nistal y Moret, *Esclavos prófugos*, p. 22; Fernando Picó, *1898: la guerra después de la guerra* (Río Piedras: Ediciones Huracán, 1987), p. 40.

29. Rafael Ramírez de Arellano, "Instrucciones al diputado don Ramón Power y Giralt [1809]," *Boletín de la Universidad de Puerto Rico* 7, no. 2 (December 1936): 13–14. Some documents spell don Pedro Yrisarri's last name as "Irizarri."

30. Ibid.

31. *Boletín* (1920), 7: 109–110.

32. Interestingly enough, this same author had already noted that "for the Xivaro [sic], be his horse ever so lean, or the burthen [sic] ever so heavy, seats himself on the top of it, and thus guides the animal. *He will sooner steal a horse for a day, and ride him, than walk a league.*" *An Account*, p. 71, my emphasis.

33. Ibid., p. 76.

34. Ibid.

35. For the case of Spain, see William Callahan, "The Problem of Confinement: An Aspect of Poor Relief in Eighteenth-Century Spain," *Hispanic American Historical Review* 51, no. 1 (February 1971): 1–23; Rosa María Pérez Estévez, *El problema de los vagos en la España del siglo XVIII* (Madrid: Confederación Española de Cajas de Ahorro, 1976); Michael Weisser, "Crime and Punishment in Early Modern Spain," in V. A. C. Gatrell et al., eds., *Crime and the Law: The Social History of Crime in Western Europe since 1500* (London: Europa Publications Ltd., 1980), pp. 76–96.

36. Michel Foucault, *Madness and Civilization* (New York: Vintage Books, 1971), pp. 56–57.

37. Pasquale Pasquino, "Criminology: The Birth of a Special Savoir," *Ideology and Consciousness* 7 (autumn 1980): 24–25.

38. Luis Maristany, *El gabinete del Doctor Lombroso (delincuencia y fin de siglo en España)* (Barcelona: Editorial Anagrama, 1973).

39. See, for instance, Winthrop Jordan, *White over Black: American Attitudes toward the Negro, 1550–1812* (Chapel Hill: University of North Carolina Press, 1968), pp. 3–65; Christopher Miller, *Blank Darkness: Africanist Discourse in French* (Chicago: University of Chicago Press, 1985); Ronald Sanders, *Lost Tribes and Promised Lands: The Origins of American Racism* (New York: Harper Collins, 1992), pp. 3–210; Peter Hulme, *Colonial Encounters: Europe and the Native Caribbean, 1492–1797* (New York: Routledge, 1992); Jack D. Forbes,

*Africans and Native Americans: The Language of Race and the Evolution of Red-Black Peoples* (Urbana: University of Illinois Press, 1993); Philip P. Boucher, *Cannibal Encounters: Europeans and Island Caribs, 1492–1763* (Baltimore: Johns Hopkins University Press, 1992).

40. Some of my own recent research addresses this very question in the case of early-twentieth-century Puerto Rico: Kelvin Santiago-Valles, *"Subject People" and Colonial Discourses: Economic Transformation and Social Disorder in Puerto Rico, 1898–1947* (Albany: State University of New York Press, 1994). There is copious research on such issues concerning other geographical areas. See, for example, Stephen Jay Gould, *The Mismeasure of Man* (New York: W. W. Norton, 1981), pp. 30–145; José Luis Peset, *Ciencia y marginación: sobre negros, locos y criminales* (Barcelona: Editorial Crítica, Grupo Editorial Grijalbo, 1983); Louis Chevalier, *Laboring Classes and Dangerous Classes in Paris during the First Half of the Nineteenth Century* (Princeton: Princeton University Press, 1973); Martha K. Huggins, *From Slavery to Vagrancy in Brazil: Crime and Social Control in the Third World* (New Brunswick, N.J.: Rutgers University Press, 1985); David Trotman, *Crime in Trinidad: Conflict and Control in a Plantation Society, 1838–1900* (Knoxville: University of Tennessee Press, 1986); Edward Said, *Orientalism* (New York: Vintage Books, 1979), pp. 39–42, 206–208; Jenny Sharpe, *Allegories of Empire: The Figure of Woman in the Colonial Text* (Minneapolis: University of Minnesota Press, 1993); Fredrick Pike, *The United States and Latin America: Myths and Stereotypes of Civilization and Nature* (Austin: University of Texas Press, 1992), pp. 44–257; Donald Crummey, ed., *Banditry, Rebellion, and Social Protest in Africa* (London: James Currey, 1986), pp. 1–192; Ranajit Guha, "The Prose of Counter-Insurgency," in Ranajit Guha and Gayatri Chakravorty Spivak, eds., *Selected Subaltern Studies* (Delhi: Oxford University Press, 1988), pp. 45–88; Thomas Boyle, *Black Swine in the Sewers of Hampstead: Beneath the Surface of Victorian Sensationalism* (New York: Viking, 1989); Sander Gilman, *Difference and Pathology: Stereotypes of Sexuality, Race, and Madness* (Ithaca, N.Y.: Cornell University Press, 1985); Richard Drinnon, *Facing West: The Metaphysics of Indian-Hating and Empire-Building* (New York: Schocken Books, 1980), pp. 119–351.

41. Del Valle Atiles, *El campesino puertorriqueño* , p. 131.

42. Ibid.

43. *Ensayos*, p. 46.

44. U.S. War Department, *Census*, p. 40.

45. Jesús Lalinde Abadía, *La administración española en el siglo XIX puertorriqueño (pervivencia de la variante indiana del decisionismo castellano en Puerto Rico)* (Seville: Escuela de Estudios Hispano-Americanos de Sevilla, Secretariado de Publicaciones de la Universidad de Sevilla, 1980), pp. 42–49, 144–166; Coll y Toste, ed., *Boletín* (1915), 2: 32–44; Coll y Toste, ed., *Boletín* (1917), 4: 223–225; Coll y Toste, ed., *Boletín* (1918), 5: 22–23, 146–147; Coll y Toste, ed., *Boletín* (1919), 6: 242–248; Coll y Toste, ed., *Boletín* (1925), 12: 87–93; Picó, *Libertad y servidumbre*, pp. 107, 114–115.

46. De Hostos, *San Juan*, pp. 506–507.

47. Quoted in José C. Rosario, *A Study of Illegitimacy and Dependent Children in Puerto Rico* (San Juan: Imprenta Venezuela, 1933), p. 11.

48. Díaz Soler, *La esclavitud negra*, pp. 207–224; Brau, *Ensayos*, p. 56;

Ramos Mattei, "La importación de trabajadores," pp. 135–139; Baralt, *Esclavos y rebeldes*; Picó, *Vivir en Caimito*, pp. 69–72. The category of social violence is used here as synonymous with those individual or group expressions of physical force, or the implied threats of such force, that emanate from or arise within the dispossessed masses that make up the majority of the population. This is to distinguish such violence from the use/threat of physical coercion or harm that emanates from the state apparatuses and/or from the institutional mechanisms of large property in general and from capital in particular.

49. Carlos Buitrago, *Los orígenes históricos de la sociedad precapitalista en Puerto Rico* (Río Piedras: Ediciones Huracán, 1976), pp. 39–40; Alejandro Tapia y Rivera, *Mis memorias (1826–1882)* (New York: Laisne y Rossboro, 1928), p. 82; Baralt, *Esclavos y rebeldes*, pp. 176–177; Carlos Buitrago, *Haciendas cafetaleras y clases terratenientes en el Puerto Rico decimonónico* (Río Piedras: Editorial de la Universidad de Puerto Rico, 1982), pp. 140–145; Ángel Quintero Rivera, "Socialista y tabaquero: la proletarización de los artesanos," *Revista Sin Nombre* 8, no. 4 (January–March 1978): 110; Cruz Monclova, *Tomo II, primera parte*, pp. 70–76; Lidio Cruz Monclova, *Historia de Puerto Rico (siglo XIX), tomo II, segunda parte* (Río Piedras: Editorial Universitaria, Universidad de Puerto Rico, 1957), pp. 611–615; Manuel Meléndez Muñoz, "Artesanía, industrialismo y maquinismo," in *Obras completas*, p. 593; Juan Ángel Silén, *Historia de la nación puertorriqueña* (Río Piedras: Editorial Edil, 1973), pp. 117–118.

50. See, for instance, Loida Figueroa, *Breve historia de Puerto Rico* (Río Piedras: Editorial Edil, 1969), 2: 282; Antonio Pedreira, *Un hombre del pueblo: José Celso Barbosa* (San Juan: Imprenta Venezuela, 1937), pp. 59–62; Fernández Méndez, *Historia cultural*, pp. 283–284; Lidio Cruz Monclova, *Historia del año 1887* (Río Piedras: Editorial Universitaria, Universidad de Puerto Rico, 1970), pp. 188–195; Félix Mejías, *De la crisis económica del '86 al año terrible del '87* (Río Piedras: Ediciones Edil, 1972), pp. 72–73. As Fernando Picó, Mariano Negrón Portillo, and Ramón López have recently illustrated for the late 1890s, the Creole scholarship of today too often oversimplifies the enormously rich and complex character of this social violence. Picó, *1898*; Mariano Negrón Portillo, *Cuadrillas anexionistas y revueltas campesinas en Puerto Rico, 1898–1899* (Río Piedras: Centro de Investigaciones Sociales, Universidad de Puerto Rico, 1987); Ramón López, "Águila Blanca: notas sobre la imaginación histórica," *Suplemento en Rojo de Claridad* (July 27–August 2, 1990): 19–22.

51. See Gómez Acevedo, *Organización y reglamentación*, p. 91; Ramos Mattei, "La importación de trabajadores," pp. 128–129; Nistal Moret, *Esclavos prófugos*, pp. 22–24.

52. Fernández Méndez, *Historia cultural*, pp. 217–222; Quintero Rivera, "La clase obrera—I," pp. 164–168; Ángel Quintero Rivera, *Conflictos de clase y política en Puerto Rico* (Río Piedras: Ediciones Huracán, 1976), pp. 114–116; Buitrago, *Haciendas cafetaleras*; Bergard, *Coffee and the Growth of Agrarian Capitalism*.

53. George Rusche and Otto Kirchheimer, *Punishment and Social Structure* [1939] (New York: Russell and Russell, 1968), p. 62; Michel Foucault, *Discipline and Punish: The Birth of the Prison*, trans. Alan Sheridan (New York: Pantheon, 1977), pp. 117–119; Dario Melossi and Massimo Pavarini, *The Prison and the Factory: The Origins of the Penitentiary System* (Totowa, N.J.: Barnes

and Noble Books, 1981), pp. 2–3; Michael Ignatieff, "State, Civil Society, and Total Institutions: A Critique of Recent Social Histories of Punishment," in Stephen Cohen and Andrew Scull, eds., *Social Control and the State: Historical and Contemporary Essays* (Oxford: Basil Blackwell, 1985), p. 79; Pike, *Penal Servitude*, p. 153; Carlos García Valdés, *Régimen penitenciario de España (investigación histórica y sistemática)* (Madrid: Publicaciones del Instituto de Criminología, Universidad de Madrid, 1975), pp. 23, 24; Steven Spitzer and Andrew Scull, "Social Control in Historical Perspective: From Private to Public Responses to Crime," in David F. Greenberg, ed., *Corrections and Punishment* (Beverly Hills, Calif.: Sage Publications, 1977), p. 272.

54.  Coll y Toste, ed., *Boletín* (1925), 12: 165; Carroll, *Report*, p. 19.

55.  Coll y Toste, ed., *Boletín* (1926), 13: 177; Carroll, *Report*, p. 34; George W. Davis, *Report of Brig. Gen. Geor. W. Davis, U.S.V. on Civil Affairs in Porto Rico—1899* (Washington, D.C.: Government Printing Office, 1900), p. 11; José Trías Monge, *El sistema judicial de Puerto Rico* (Río Piedras: Editorial Universitaria, Universidad de Puerto Rico, 1978), p. 15.

56.  Pike, *Penal Servitude*, pp. 49–110.

57.  Evgeny B. Pashukanis, *Law and Marxism: A General Theory* (London: Ink Links, 1978), p. 169.

58.  Ramos Mattei, "La importación de trabajadores," pp. 127–128; Scarano, *Sugar and Slavery*, pp. 33–34.

59.  Félix Sevilla y Solanas, *Historia penitenciaria española (la galera), apuntes de archivo* (Segovia: Tipográfico de "El Adelantado de Segovia," 1917), p. 35; Gregorio Lasala Navarro, *Galeotes y presidiarios al servicio de la Marina de Guerra de España* (Madrid: Editorial Naval, 1979), pp. 114–115.

60.  Adolfo de Hostos, *Historia de San Juan, ciudad murada: ensayo acerca del proceso de la civilización en la ciudad española de San Juan Bautista de Puerto Rico, 1521–1898* (San Juan: Instituto de Cultura Puertorriqueña, 1966), pp. 193–194, 212–213, 475; Abbad y Lasierra, *Historia geográfica*, p. 213; Nicolás Cabrillana, "Las fortificaciones militares en Puerto Rico," *Revista de Indias* 107 (1967): 157–188.

61.  Carlos Cambronero, "El Prado de Madrid," *Revista Contemporánea* 129 (1904): 9–21; Rafael Salillas, *Evolución penitenciaria en España* (Madrid: Imprenta Clásica Española, Biblioteca Criminológica y Penitenciaria, 1918), 2: 28–30, 80–84; Francisco Tomás y Valiente, *El derecho penal de la monarquía absoluta (siglos XVI–XVII–XVIII)* (Madrid: Editorial Técnos, 1969), pp. 366–368; Coll y Toste, ed., *Boletín* (1924), 11: 273; Coll y Toste, ed., *Boletín* (1922), 9: 16; de Hostos, *San Juan*, p. 486; Picó, *Vivir en Caimito*, pp. 67–68.

62.  Coll y Toste, ed., *Boletín* (1918), 5: 229–230; María de los Ángeles Castro Arroyo, "La construcción de la carretera central en Puerto Rico," M.A. thesis, University of Puerto Rico, Río Piedras Campus, 1969, pp. 94, 98; Picó, *Vivir en Caimito*, pp. 68–70, 95; Picó, *Al filo del poder*, pp. 126–127.

63.  *Código penal para las provincias de Cuba y Puerto-Rico y ley provisional de enjuiciamiento criminal mandados a observar por real decreto de 23 de mayo de 1879* (Madrid: Imprenta Nacional, 1879); Lloyd McKin Garrison, "The Penal Code of Cuba and Porto Rico," *Harvard Law Review* 13 (1898–1900): 124–136.

64. Pike, *Penal Servitude,* pp. 60–61; Carroll, *Report,* p. 605; Cruz Monclova, *1887,* pp. 260–262, 278–280, 312–317.

65. Coll y Toste, ed., *Boletín* (1916), 3: 14.

66. Ibid.

67. Coll y Toste, ed., *Boletín* (1921), 8: 21–23.

68. Coll y Toste, ed., *Boletín* (1917), 4: 254; *Boletín* (1922), 9: 21.

69. Pike, *Penal Servitude,* p. 109.

70. Coll y Toste, ed., *Boletín* (1917), 4: 254; de Hostos, *San Juan,* p. 474.

71. Coll y Toste, ed., *Boletín* (1919), 6: 316; *Boletín* (1922), 9: 21; *Boletín* (1926), 13: 284; Roberto H. Todd, "La antigua cárcel," in *El Mundo* (August 6, 1939): 12; Francisco J. García, "El edificio de la Real Cárcel de San Juan (1800–1898)," *Plural 3,* no. 2 (1984): 171–178; *Lealtad y heroísmo de la Isla de Puerto Rico, 1797–1897* (San Juan: Imprenta de Lynn e Hijos de Pérez Moris, 1897), pp. 327, 328–329; de Hostos, *San Juan,* p. 474.

72. María Jesús Miranda, "Bentham en España," in J. Bentham, *El panóptico* (Madrid: Ediciones de La Piqueta, n.d.), p. 141.

73. García Valdés, *Régimen penitenciario,* p. 37; Miranda, "Bentham," pp. 140, 142–144.

74. *An Account,* pp. 284–286.

75. *Report,* p. 606.

76. *An Account,* pp. 283–285, 300–302.

77. García, "Real Cárcel de San Juan," pp. 180–181.

78. *Report,* p. 594.

79. Ibid., pp. 609–610.

80. De Hostos, *San Juan,* p. 473; Flinter, *An Account,* pp. 301–302; Insular Commission, *Report of the U.S. Insular Commission to the Secretary of War upon Investigations Made into the Civil Affairs of the Island of Porto Rico with Recommendations* (Washington, D.C.: U.S. War Department, 1899), pp. 48–49.

81. *An Account,* p. 287.

82. Ibid., pp. 290–292.

83. In the case of Britain, several descriptions of the day have been reprinted, as in the case of Flora Tristan, *The London Journal of Flora Tristan* (London: Virago Press, 1982), pp. 111–154; Arthur Griffiths, *The Chronicles of Highgate* (New York: Dorset Press, 1987), pp. 303–555. See also Louis P. Masur, *Rites of Execution: Capital Punishment and the Transformation of American Culture, 1776–1865* (New York: Oxford University Press, 1989), pp. 71–92; Russell Hogg, "Imprisonment and Society under Early British Capitalism," in Anthony Platt and Paul Takagi, eds., *Punishment and Penal Discipline: Essays on the Prison and the Prisoners' Movement* (Berkeley, Calif.: Crime and Social Justice Associates, 1980), pp. 57–70; Martin B. Miller, "At Hard Labor: Rediscovering the 19th Century Prison," in *Punishment and Penal Discipline,* pp. 79–87; Melossi and Pavarini, *The Prison and the Factory.*

84. Coll y Toste, ed., *Boletín* (1922), 9: 21; Todd, "La antigua cárcel," p. 12; de Hostos, *San Juan,* p. 474.

85. María de los Ángeles Castro, *La arquitectura en San Juan de Puerto Rico (siglo XIX)* (Río Piedras: Editorial Universitaria, Universidad de Puerto Rico, 1980), p. 308.

86. García, "Real Cárcel," pp. 179–181; Castro, *La arquitectura*, pp. 308–309.

87. *Report*, p. 34.

88. Ibid., pp. 594, 606–610.

89. Rusche and Kirchheimer, *Punishment*, pp. 41–52; Pike, *Penal Servitude*, p. 55; Manuel de Rivacoba y Rivacoba, "La fundación de la Casa de Corrección de San Fernando," in Agustín Calabró, ed., *Estudios en homenaje al profesor Luis Jiménez de Asúa* (Buenos Aires: Abeledo Perrot, 1964), pp. 204–217; Callahan, "The Problem of Confinement," pp. 6–7; U. R. Q. Henriques, "The Rise and Decline of the Separate System of Prison Discipline," *Past and Present* 54 (1972): 61–62; Thorsten Sellin, *Pioneering in Penology: The Amsterdam Houses of Correction in the Sixteenth and Seventeenth Centuries* (Philadelphia: University of Pennsylvania Press, 1944).

90. De Hostos, *San Juan*, p. 469.

91. Coll y Toste, ed., *Boletín* (1922), 9: 54, 57, 58; Manuel Ubeda y Delgado, *Isla de Puerto Rico (estudio histórico, geográfico y estadístico)* (San Juan: Tipografía del Boletín Mercantil, 1878), pp. 123, 127; Federico Asenjo, *Efemérides de la Isla de Puerto Rico* (San Juan: Imprenta de J. González Font, 1886), p. 86; de Hostos, *San Juan*, pp. 469, 471; Cayetano Coll y Toste, *Historia de la instrucción pública en Puerto Rico hasta 1898* (San Juan: Imprenta del Boletín Mercantil, 1910), p. 165. Soon after it opened, the Casa de Beneficencia also began disciplining and housing, under special conditions, the willful children of the propertied classes (Creole and Peninsular), although they were hardly this institution's traditional inmates.

92. Francisco R. de Goenaga, *Desarrollo histórico del Asilo de Beneficencia y Manicomio de Puerto Rico* (San Juan: N.p., 1929), pp. 25–26, 34, 36, 38; de Hostos, *San Juan*, p. 472; Carroll, *Report*, p. 612.

93. Francisco de Goenaga, *Antropología médica y jurídica* (San Juan: Imprenta Venezuela, 1934), p. 226.

94. Castro, *La arquitectura*, p. 222.

95. De Goenaga, *Antropología*, pp. 227–231.

96. John Howard, *The State of the Prisons in England and Wales with Preliminary Observations and an Account of Some Foreign Prisons and Hospitals*, 3d ed. (Warrington, England: William Eyres Publisher, 1784), pp. 156–157; Salillas, *Evolución penitenciaria—I*, pp. 74–86.

97. Rusche and Kirchheimer, *Punishment and Social Structure*, p. 42.

98. Frances Fox-Piven and Richard Cloward, *Regulating the Poor* (New York: Vintage Books, 1971), pp. 27–29.

99. Coll y Toste, ed., *Boletín* (1922), 9: 54.

100. Paul G. Miller, *Historia de Puerto Rico* (Chicago: Rand McNally & Co., 1939), p. 368; Armando Morales Rildow, *Report Relating to the Ownership of Land and Buildings on the Island which Constitutes the Principal Part of the City of San Juan, Puerto Rico, Document 2, 1st Part—List of Military and Other Buildings* (Santurce, Puerto Rico: Bureau of Public Works, Department of the Interior, n.d.), p. 9; de Hostos, *San Juan*, p. 471.

101. Lidio Cruz Monclova, *Historia de Puerto Rico, tomo II, segunda parte (1875–1885)* (Rio Piedras: Editorial Universitaria, Universidad de Puerto Rico,

1970), p. 729; Carroll, *Report*, pp. 606–607; García, "Real Cárcel de San Juan," pp. 178–181.

102. García, *Primeros fermentos*; Cayetano Coll y Toste, *Reseña: el estado social, económico e industrial de la isla de Puerto Rico al tomar posesión de ella los Estados Unidos* (San Juan: Imprenta de La Correspondencia, 1899), pp. 372–375; Silvia Álvarez Curbelo, "El Motín de los Faroles y otras luminosas protestas: disturbios populares en Puerto Rico, 1894," *Historia y Sociedad* 2 (1989): 120–146; Cruz Monclova, *Tomo III (segunda parte)*, pp. 223–225; Cruz Monclova, *Tomo III (tercera parte)*, pp. 252–253.

103. De Goenaga, *Asilo de Beneficencia*, p. 15.

104. *Report*, p. 599.

105. *Insular Commission*, pp. 70–71.

106. Foucault, *Madness and Civilization*, pp. 50, 65.

107. De Goenaga, *Antropología*, pp. 228–229, 231.

108. Salvador Brau, *Historia de Puerto Rico* (New York: Appleton, 1904), p. 251, emphasis in the original.

109. *Antropología*, p. 228.

110. Ibid., p. 231.

111. *Discipline and Punish*, pp. 220–221.

112. *Law and Marxism*, pp. 180–181.

113. "Bentham," pp. 134, 135.

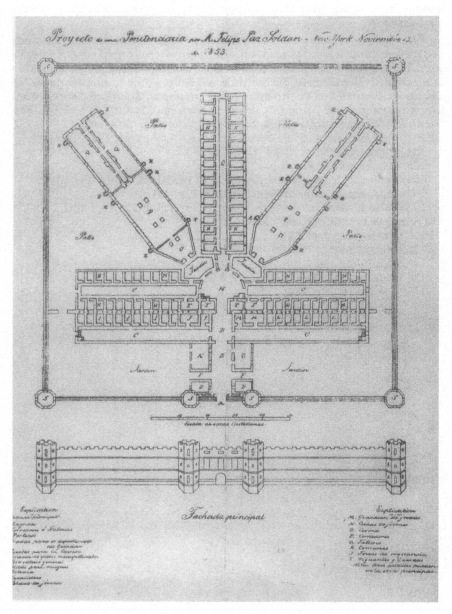

Original 1853 plan for the Lima penitentiary by Mariano Felipe Paz
Soldán. Source: Mariano Felipe Paz Soldán, *Examen de las penitenciarías
de los Estados Unidos* (New York: S. W. Benedict, 1853).

Chilean prisoners in the laundry room of the Casa Correccional in Valparaíso, Chile (n.d.). Source: Juan Isern, *El buen pastor en las naciones del sud de América* (Buenos Aires: S. de Amorrortu, 1923).

Anonymous *corrido* showing popular concern with the inauguration of the Mexico penitentiary. The accompanying engraving is from José Guadalupe Posada (c. 1900). Source: Taylor Museum for Southwestern Studies of the Colorado Springs Fine Arts Center.

Aerial view of the Buenos Aires penitentiary (1925). Source: Archivo General de la Nación, Buenos Aires.

Guards at the observation center of the Buenos Aires penitentiary (1915). Source: Archivo General de la Nación, Buenos Aires.

Internal view of pavilions at the Buenos Aires penitentiary (c. 1923).
Source: Archivo General de la Nación, Buenos Aires.

External view of the Penitenciaría Insular of Río Piedras, Puerto Rico (1939). Source: Antonio Monteagudo, ed., *Álbum de oro de Puerto Rico* (Havana: Artes Gráficas, 1939).

Inmates of the Penitenciaría Insular of Rio Piedras assembled in its main yard (1939). Source: Antonio Monteagudo, ed., *Álbum de oro de Puerto Rico* (Havana: Artes Gráficas, 1939).

Inmates of the São Paulo, Brazil, penitentiary displaying emblems to salute Chilean visitors (1939). Source: Israel Drapkin, *Actualidades penales y penitenciarias del Brasil* (Santiago de Chile: Instituto Chileno-Brasileño de Cultura, 1939).

# 6. Revolutionary Reform: Capitalist Development, Prison Reform, and Executive Power in Mexico

*Robert Buffington*

> *Todo cambiará en el futuro.*
> —PLM program, 1906[1]

On Christmas afternoon, 1916, José Natividad Macías, still angry over the bitter credentials fight of three weeks earlier, addressed the Constitutional Convention at Querétaro for the first time. A prominent lawyer, national deputy under the three previous presidents, and coauthor of President Carranza's proposed constitution, Macías had declined for twenty-two long December afternoons to participate in a convention dominated by radical young "Jacobins" who had vehemently denounced him as a "neo-Porfirian" and a *"huertista."*[2]

When the Committee on the Constitution presented its revision of proposed article 18 on prison reform, however, Macías's stoic detachment quickly evaporated.[3] The committee's mutilation of the original article, Macías insisted, betrayed an appalling ignorance of recent advances in modern penology and threatened to undo sixty years of progress by Mexican penal reformers. As the self-appointed spokesman for this distinguished tradition, he demanded that the new constitution demonstrate a firm commitment to the nation's moral advancement. A comprehensive national prison system, he declared, was crucial to a modern, "civilized" Mexico and thus merited a constitutional mandate.[4]

The Mexican Revolution was ultimately a struggle to control political discourse, a process that culminated in the 1916–1917 Constitutional Convention debates.[5] Having achieved nominal political control, Venustiano Carranza's Constitutionalist regime faced the unavoidable and difficult task of establishing its legitimacy in the face of a militant, mobilized populace led by actual or potential adversaries purporting to represent different but seldom clearly defined political agendas. Under these circumstances, control of political discourse was a matter of survival. But in order to control the revolution, the Constitutionalists had first to define it, to produce a revolutionary agenda that co-opted, defused, or discredited that of their opponents.[6] Carranza responded by calling a constitutional convention.

Defining the terms and formulating the parameters of "legitimate" discourse, even within the Constitutionalist coalition, was far from easy. The nature of revolutionary reform, the issue that prompted Macías's outburst, occupied the central place in these debates. The presence of two distinct reform traditions complicated matters considerably. Delegates to the Mexican Constitutional Convention sought both to reclaim a nineteenth-century liberal reform agenda that included education, prison reform, and temperance and to introduce new social reforms like workers' rights and agrarian reform.[7] Both reform agendas served to ensure the legitimacy and thus the political authority of the revolutionary regime by publicizing its concern for the "people" and excusing its many transgressions. Only the promise of social reform could justify the tremendous sacrifices of the Revolution, and only a broad spectrum of reforms could hold together a heterogeneous revolutionary coalition.

In spite of this link between nineteenth- and twentieth-century reform agendas, constitutional scholars have ignored the debate over prison reform, focusing instead on innovative constitutional commitments to agrarian reform and workers' rights. In *Ideología de la Revolución Mexicana*, Arnaldo Córdova argues that, by insisting on a strong executive to carry out the constitution's more radical provisions, convention delegates effectively undermined the traditional reform agenda of liberal precursors. The Mexican presidency, he concludes, was stronger after the Revolution than before. Revolutionary regimes were just as committed to capitalist development as either Díaz or Madero, regardless of their radical constitutional mandate.[8] Later political and economic developments in Mexico, Córdova's conclusions seem self-evident.

The prison reform debate, however, sheds new light on the 1917 constitution and especially the revolutionary vision of executive power. Revisionists like Córdova have long noted continuities, especially in the developmentalist agenda of Mexican elites.[9] Closely linked to nineteenth-century liberal economic development, the prison reform discourse logically reflects these continuities. Along with their positive counterpart, modern schools, reformed prisons were to inculcate liberal values like hard work and respect for authority and provide an institutional model for the reform of Mexican society. They would also preserve social order by punishing and isolating dangerous criminals. As an essential component of liberal ideology, prison reform helped mitigate and legitimize the dislocations caused by liberal social engineering. Although specific goals shifted occasionally, reflecting the incidental concerns of individuals or generations of reformers, most reformers continued to accept the fundamental tenets of liberal prison reform shaped during the Porfiriato, even after the Revolution itself.

In spite of these continuities, prerevolutionary prison reformers never resolved the crucial issue of jurisdiction. Most accepted government's role in prison reform. But while some reformers favored local or state control, others insisted that only a national prison system guaranteed comprehensive reform. Porfirian prison reformers, in particular, favored centralized administration as a necessary corrective to an overly hetero-geneous society that undermined the development of a Mexican na-tional identity. Abuses perpetuated by the Díaz regime, however, re-vived concerns about control of the prison system. This debate carried over into the Constitutional Convention. Thus, convention delegates hotly contested jurisdictional aspects of prison reform even while reaching a general consensus on its underlying assumptions.

Explaining these continuities and contestations in the prison reform discourse is essential to an understanding of Mexican liberalism and its contribution to Mexico's discursive revolution.[10] While the 1917 consti-tution created a political system that favored a strong executive, it also retained many of the checks and balances of traditional liberalism, including a decentralized prison system. Convention delegates con-tested prison reform not because they disputed its underlying principles but because they disagreed about who should administer it. The convention's rejection of a centrally controlled prison system, the issue which so angered Macías, suggests that most delegates recognized the inherent dangers of a strong executive and sought to restrict its access to the means of repression. The prison represented a sort of political mirror; through its reform delegates aspired to decentralize and thus diffuse the locus of power.

## Liberal Prison Reform

In Mexico the language of prison reform throughout most of the nine-teenth century was closely associated with liberalism and the progres-sive ideas of English philosopher and systems-maker Jeremy Bentham.[11] Bentham's utilitarian doctrine with its emphasis on efficient manage-ment systems appealed to a broad spectrum of elite liberal reformers who sought to replace "feudal" colonial institutions with "rational" modern ones. This included the prison system, which, along with modern schools, served as a paradigm for the reform of Mexican society. Secular public schools would teach the requirements of citizenship, and modern penitentiaries would isolate and (ideally) rehabilitate transgressors.

The first Enlightenment-inspired prison reform proposals surfaced in

the late eighteenth century under the reform-minded Bourbon monarchs. In his 1782 *Discurso sobre las penas*, Mexican-born penologist
Manuel Lardizábal y Uribe remarked that the punishments typically
inflicted on late-eighteenth-century criminals (confinement to *presidios*,
shipyards [*arsenales*], and jails), by refusing to discriminate between
incidental and hardened criminals, corrupted the relatively innocuous
victim of unfortunate circumstance without reforming the dangerous
habitual offender. He thus advised the Crown of the "indispensable
necessity of creating correctional facilities [*casas de corrección*] in
which work and punishment were proportional to the crime and the
criminal."[12] The emphasis on work as a corrective to "the continual and
forced idleness" of jail inmates coincided nicely with Bourbon
developmentalists' concerns about the productivity of the colonial
workforce.[13]

Their post-Independence Creole counterparts shared these concerns.
Drawing on his extensive personal observation of modern prisons in the
United States, Britain, and France, Ecuadoran diplomat and advisor to
the Anastacio Bustamante government Vicente Rocafuerte formulated
specific proposals for the reform of Mexico's notorious prisons. In his
*Nuevo sistema de cárceles*, he argued that inmates had "the right to be
treated humanely and encouraged in the exercise of their physical and
moral faculties . . . because their correction is the object of the punishment imposed upon them." To facilitate rehabilitation, his modernized
prisons would reflect concern about "the conservation of [the inmate's]
health, the purity of the air that he breathes, the cleanliness of his room,
productive work, religious instruction, silence, reflection, and order in
everything he does."[14] To this end, he recommended the adoption of the
internationally renowned Philadelphia system, which isolated inmates
to prevent them from corrupting each other and to provide them a quiet
cell in which to contemplate their mistakes. As early as 1824 he had
offered Mexico City officials the use of a "treading mill" acquired during
his tour to the United States which was designed to accustom inmates
to regular (and meaningless) work.[15]

In the 1840s Rocafuerte's recommendations received further endorsement from Interior Minister Mariano Otero and official foreign corre-
spondent José María Luis Mora. Otero condemned the Federal District's
three principal facilities—La Diputación, La Acordada, and the old
convent of Santiago Tlatelolco—as "dens of iniquity [*sentinas de
corrupción*], where the innocent man encounters a school of crime."[16]
These colonial institutions, by encouraging rather than discouraging
crime, represented yet another obstacle to liberal modernization efforts.
He proposed instead the adaptation of a modern "penitentiary system"
based on "solitude that forces reflection, work that dominates evil

tendencies, isolation that protects, instruction that elevates, religion that moralizes, and repentance that regenerates."[17]

Mora, in his report on English prisons, generally concurred but with the caveat that the "silent" Philadelphia system favored by Rocafuerte and Otero, although effective, was too expensive and unnecessarily oppressive. He recommended instead a "system of individual isolation" that allowed inmates contact with moralizing influences, especially the prison chaplain.[18] Not surprisingly, given their concerns about corrupting prisons and their underlying faith in uncorrupted human potential, both Mora and Otero also stressed the need for separate facilities and even distinct punishments for juvenile offenders, who as fledgling criminals stood the best chance of rehabilitation.[19]

According to Mexican utilitarians, rationally ordered penal institutions would ultimately rid society of crime. Specifically, utilitarian prison reforms stressed the regenerative power of supervised work in a suitable environment, the penitentiary. The salutary effect of enforced productivity and a wholesome environment would remove the criminal from evil influences, inculcate respect for authority, and teach the value of remunerated work. Isolation of delinquents also protected society from their disruptive influence. These two principal themes of isolation and rehabilitation, directly linked to the larger developmentalist agenda of modernizing elites, dominated nineteenth-century Mexican prison reform efforts.[20]

In keeping with liberalism's egalitarian pretensions, Mexican prison reformers generally ignored issues of race, gender, and age. This ignorance was both selective and self-serving. Reformers recognized that Indians would react differently from mestizos and whites to certain prison regimes, especially solitary confinement, which penologists believed harmful only to gregarious mestizos and whites.[21] But since Mexican prison reformers sought to discipline a largely mestizo urban workforce, they expressed little interest in recognizing or accommodating racial differences.[22] The presence of prominent liberal presidents of Indian ancestry like Benito Juárez and Porfirio Díaz probably discouraged an overtly racist discourse.[23]

Prison reformers also paid scant attention to the needs of female inmates, in part because female criminality also posed little threat to the liberal disciplinary project. They noted that male criminals far outnumbered their female counterparts, represented a far greater danger to society, and therefore warranted greater attention. The same rationale justified the neglect of juvenile offenders. Thus, although prison reformers occasionally discussed the special needs of women and children, they made no serious efforts to reform penal facilities for either group.[24]

Although concern about prison conditions in Mexico had surfaced

even before Independence, the prison reform movement's first noteworthy act was to establish workshops in Mexico City's Cárcel Nacional in
1833. These workshops served two practical purposes, forcing indigent
inmates to work to cover expenses while permitting those with resources to earn extra money during incarceration, presumably to help
support their families. Typically, the workshops had a moralistic purpose as well, keeping the inmates from "excessive leisure," an acknowledged cause of crime, especially among the "marginal" classes.[25]

Concern, especially over the inmates' moral state, continued to grow.
In 1840 Mexico City passed a prison reform law which sought to separate
convicted criminals and simple detainees previously endangered by
exposure to hardened criminals.[26] Early prison reform efforts culminated in October 1848, when the national congress passed a law obliging
the government to develop a penitentiary system. The newly established
Junta Directiva submitted plans for a Federal District penitentiary with
over five hundred cells and suggested an internal regimen, the Philadelphia system, which isolated inmates to prevent them from corrupting
each other and provided them a quiet cell in which to contemplate their
mistakes.[27] Political turmoil and perennial lack of funds, however,
undermined these early efforts. Article 23 of the 1857 constitution again
enjoined the central government to establish a penitentiary system "as
soon as possible."[28]

Frustrated during the Second Empire, liberal prison reformers re-
doubled their efforts with the coming of the new Republic. In 1868 the
Juárez administration approved plans for a Federal District penitentiary
to house fourteen hundred inmates. In deference to recent advances in
penology, Antonio Martínez de Castro proposed a mixed regimen that
isolated prisoners from each other but permitted contact with prison
personnel and "persons capable of providing moral guidance."[29] A new
penal code, written by Martínez de Castro, went into effect in 1871, and
that same year the interior minister allocated 200,000 pesos to construct
the penitentiary.[30] The prologue to the 1871 penal code eloquently
expressed the pride and optimism of Mexican penal reformers during the
first years of the Republic, noting that "today, with scientific spirit and
resolute will, immeasurable distances have been suddenly crossed and
monuments of science and culture have emerged unexpectedly from
chaos."[31] After years of debilitating civil war, Mexico had suddenly
emerged as a "civilized" nation with an innovative new penal code and
plans for a modern penitentiary that symbolized its commitment to the
future.

As part of this commitment, Juárez appointed prominent American
penal reformer Enoch C. Wines to represent Mexico at the First Interna-

tional Penitentiary Congress held in London in 1872.[32] These international congresses, held regularly during the last quarter of the nineteenth century, provided a forum for the discussion and dissemination of the latest advances in penology. They also demonstrated, according to Wines, "the comparative condition of nations as regards intellectual and social development."[33]

For self-conscious Mexican prison reformers, the lack of modern penal institutions reflected badly on Mexico, and they continued to lobby vigorously for a penitentiary. Wines's critical *Report on Penitentiary Systems Presented to the Supreme Government of the Mexican Republic*, published in 1873, followed two years later by Francisco J. Peña's damning exposé of Mexican prison conditions, reinforced their demands.[34] Peña noted that most Mexican prisons "benefited from changes imposed by civilization yet still exhibited the traces of barbarism."[35] Just like earlier English, French, and North American humanitarian prison reformers, prerevolutionary Mexican reformers justified the need for change, and their own interventions, in the language of the Enlightenment.

Unfortunately for prison reformers, political unrest continued, and hard-pressed national governments again postponed action on the proposed penitentiary. Wines reported that

> though all Mexican statesmen and philanthropists have of late
> become aware of the importance and utility to the public of the
> establishment of a penitentiary system, the financial difficulties,
> the instability of the Governments, and the constant necessity in
> which the State has been placed to defend its existence . . . have
> until now prevented the realization of this great social reform.[36]

Mexican prison reformers realized that without an extended period of political stability significant prison reform remained a frustrating chimera.

## Porfirian Prison Reform

The ascension of Porfirio Díaz in 1876 marked a watershed in Mexican prison reform. During the next thirty-five years the discourse of prison reform underwent various changes as supporters and opponents of the regime manipulated it to suit their respective ends. The Porfiriato also saw the construction of the long-awaited Federal District penitentiary and a new penal colony off the Pacific coast, the culmination of a fifty-year struggle to bring modern penal institutions to Mexico. These changes in the discourse and the institutions in turn laid the foundation for the 1917 Constitutional Convention debate and the resulting dispute over prison reform.

The most significant change in the Mexican discourse about prison reform came with the widespread dissemination of European positivism among liberal intellectuals during the Reforma. Although most positivists accepted liberal critiques of colonial institutions as inefficient and irrational, they took issue with earlier liberals' reliance on abstract, ideal solutions which ignored reality.[37] Institutions, they insisted, should reflect scientifically determined needs, not metaphysically constructed ideals. Rationality still figured prominently in the positivist prison reform discourse, but its meaning had shifted considerably.

The positivist emphasis on practical, scientific solutions found an especially sympathetic audience among Porfirian *científico* intellectuals eager to create the effective disciplinary system necessary to economic and social development. Traditional liberalism had failed, they declared, precisely because it ignored Mexican reality, attempting to impose inappropriate institutions and thereby encouraging disorder. Justo Sierra, a prominent *científico*, noted in an 1889 essay that "the moral and social state of human societies depends on their economic state."[38] For Mexico to achieve "liberty" and "individual rights" the country had first to advance economically. Economic development, *científicos* agreed, was impossible without long-term political stability. In a revealing twist on French positivist Auguste Comte's original motto "Love, Order, and Progress," the Díaz administration chose to replace "Love" with the less ambitious "Peace."[39] Enforced peace ensured social stability, which in turn encouraged economic growth, the only practical solution, *científicos* insisted, to Mexican "backwardness."

This increased focus on social order reflected not only the fear of continued political chaos but also growing concern about a perceived crime wave, especially in the capital. In his 1901 study *La génesis del crimen en México*, Julio Guerrero, a respected Mexican lawyer, thoroughly examined all possible causes of crime in Mexico, including geography, climate, class structure, and social development, but singled out overpopulation as especially pernicious.[40] The urban poor, he warned, were alcoholic, promiscuous, uneducated, and potentially criminal. Only positivist education, industrial development (which fostered the "morality of the workshop"), and Porfirio Díaz "with his exemplary behavior" had kept Mexico from "degenerating" into chaos.[41] In a study of Mexican criminals published three years later, criminologist Carlos Roumagnac noted three principal "social causes" for the rise in crime: "abandoned children, begging, and drunkenness."[42] These perceived problems, generally associated with rapid urbanization, reinforced efforts to promote social order.

Some observers considered inadequate, overcrowded prisons among the principal causes of crime. Justo Sierra, in an 1875 article in *El Federalista*, denounced conditions in Belem, the national jail. He remarked sardonically that "the state prison system actually encourages crime, providing the criminal with everything he needs to complete his education [in crime]."[43] That same year, Francisco Peña published the following vivid description of Belem's notorious "galleries": "The principal dormitories are high-ceilinged, badly ventilated with an open latrine in one corner, and furnished with sleeping mats for approximately six hundred inmates. Here they pass the time lying around, smoking marijuana and tobacco."[44]

Under these circumstances, minor offenders quickly became experienced criminals. According to an 1882 account, even the establishment of workshops had failed to "dislodge idleness, that inexhaustible source of vice and prostitution exacerbated by the presence of so many individuals advanced in crime."[45] Miguel S. Macedo, the Porfiriato's leading penologist, remarked that first-time, minor offenders "are not properly criminals but draftees in the army of crime, who, without proper direction will . . . become teachers and veterans."[46] For these observers, existing penal institutions not only failed to rehabilitate inmates but actually served as schools for criminal behavior and thereby contributed directly to rising crime.

A penitentiary, reformers insisted, was an indispensable weapon in a modern society's war on crime. The 1882 report on conditions in Belem observed that "a penitentiary system is one of our society's greatest needs."[47] Macedo concurred, noting somewhat pedantically that "the punitive function of the state which can do so much for social morality when directed with knowledge, conscience, and rectitude and which causes so many and such profound evils when badly or immorally administered . . . is surely one of the principal elements of social order."[48] With General Díaz guaranteeing peace, prison reformers believed, the time had come to restore order to Mexican society.

Spurred by growing public concern, in 1881 Federal District governor Ramón Fernández appointed a blue-ribbon commission, which included Miguel Macedo and future finance minister José Limantour, to formulate plans for a penitentiary. The following year the commission presented an elaborate proposal which boasted an innovative French-inspired radial design, an up-to-date internal regimen, and corresponding modifications of the 1871 penal code. Construction began in the plains of San Lázaro, northeast of Mexico City, three years later in 1885.

Delayed by unstable soil and forced to await the completion of the Great
Drainage Canal in 1897, the new Penitenciaría de México finally opened
on September 29, 1900.[49]

Attended by the cream of the Porfirian elite, including General Díaz
himself, the inaugural ceremonies were both social event and celebration of Mexico's long-awaited arrival as a civilized nation. In his opening
remarks, Macedo paid homage to his predecessors. He noted that the
penitentiary "was not just a building but a social institution, crowning
the efforts of more than half a century and many generations."[50] It was
also, Macedo continued, a symbol of successful government, "of the
already fecund fields of our efforts and ingenuity, whose fruits . . . mark
a new era in the annals of national progress."[51] Delegates to future
International Penitentiary Congresses could point with pride to Mexico's
model penal facility.

For the Porfirian elite, however, the penitentiary represented more
than just progress. Along with related efforts to reorganize federal
prisons, professionalize Mexico City police, and control the notorious
*rurales*, the new facility symbolized the Díaz administration's commitment to maintain order and rationalize national institutions. In his
inaugural speech, Federal District governor Rafael Rebollar noted por-
tentously that the opening of the penitentiary heralded "a new era in the
evolution of repressive systems in Mexico."[52] These symbols of order
served a less obvious function as well, demonstrating the administration's
vigor and control to political opponents and anxious investors in Mexico's
expanding economy.[53]

The penitentiary's avowed purpose, however, was rehabilitation and
social defense—in the words of Carlos Roumagnac, "to correct those
capable of correction and isolate those who, incapable of correction,
endanger others through their pernicious contact."[54] Rebollar agreed,
noting pessimistically that "even if it proves worthless as a means of
rehabilitation, the [penitentiary] will still segregate criminals from the
medium in which they have exercised their abnormal and pernicious
activity."[55] Macedo, equally gloomy, observed that "experience, coldly
and serenely analyzed, demonstrates the impotence as well as the
necessity of penal institutions." Nevertheless, he added, "this penitentiary, even if it fails to return virtuous men to the bosom of society, shall
never be a source of moral corruption . . . nor a chamber of pain, misery,
infamy, and horror."[56] In spite of their reservations, commission members recommended an elaborate internal regimen, based on the innovative Irish or Crofton system, which had received the endorsement of
recent International Penitentiary Congresses.[57] This regimen comprised
an intricate system of rewards and punishments designed to modify and
direct an inmate's behavior, firmly but without violence. Every facet of

prison life played a role, including access to food, clothing, furnishings, exercise, remunerated work, education, fellow prisoners, and medical care.[58] The regimen allowed inmates to accumulate points for good behavior, work, and school attendance that decreased the severity of their internment and led, in some cases, to early release on parole.[59] Conversely, inmates who failed to cooperate were increasingly isolated to prevent them from "contaminating" their more cooperative fellows. The commission report noted contentedly that "a system based on these principles forces the delinquent to choose between pleasure and pain, inspiring both terror and hope . . . and it is hardly surprising that they are controlled like docile sheep."[60] Macedo announced proudly that "here for the first time, a complete regimen has been established, directed toward moral correction and encompassing all facets of an inmate's life."[61] Imbued with a positivist intent (internalized "moral" change and total institutional control), the language of the report still betrayed the Benthamite origins of Mexican prison reform.

Like its liberal predecessor, the Porfirian penitentiary regimen became a paradigm for the reformation of Mexican society. The system worked, supporters observed, because, unlike earlier "unnatural" systems, it utilized existing social mechanisms like reward and punishment which provided inmates with incentives for self-improvement. The commission report noted the penitentiary's resemblance to an idealized version of society, remarking that this similarity "should teach the prisoner that . . . the means of obtaining health and happiness is honesty and that vice always leads to pain and ends in misfortune."[62] The lesson for Mexico City proletarians was clear.

As good Porfirians, commission members also emphasized the role of the director. Without the proper director, they concluded, "the penitentiary will be completely useless."[63] In this sense, too, the new facility and its internal regimen reflected an idealized Mexican society and symbolized Porfirian intentions. A benevolent but authoritarian administrator and his resident technocrats presided over both penitentiary and country. In *científico* social engineering, reform invariably came from above.

The Islas Marías penal colony off the coast of Tepic represented a further refinement of the Porfirian prison reform discourse. Acquired by the national government in 1905 and opened three years later, the penal colony, like the penitentiary, resulted from more than sixty years of lobbying by determined prison reformers.[64] As with the penitentiary, great pains were taken to define its function and determine the proper internal regimen.

Islas Marías was destined to play a distinct role in the new federal penal system. A prominent political journalist and Porfirian national deputy who would later serve under Madero and Huerta, Querido Moheno, wrote the initial proposal and enabling legislation.[65] His instructions from Interior Minister and Vice-President Ramón Corral were to "find a practical method, both scientific and legitimate, to end delinquency . . . in our cultured capital."[66] Moheno noted that while the penitentiary isolated serious offenders, the overcrowded jails continued to breed petty criminals: habitual alcoholics, vagrants, pimps, prostitutes, beggars, thieves. Repeat offenders were a particular problem. The Islas Marías penal colony, Moheno declared, would "free us of the habitual criminals . . . who comprise the daily clientele of our jails."[67] Appealing astutely to the Díaz administration's obsession with national image, he insisted that removing recidivists would relieve overcrowded jails, remove a potent source of social contamination, improve police efficiency, and ultimately reduce crime in the cultured capital. It would also reduce criminality among the working classes, thus promoting economic development.

Moheno's regimen, like that of the penitentiary, sought to reproduce a controlled version of Mexican society within which the inmates could learn to function normally. To improve the inmates' social instincts, Moheno even suggested that the government transport their families to the penal colony at state expense. "It is to be hoped," he noted, that "penal colonies will one day be organized along accepted social lines, and the most effective way of achieving this is through the colonist's family."[68] Moheno's system also provided considerable "executive" latitude, allowing the president or his proxy to double an incorrigible inmate's sentence at his own discretion.[69] Thus, although designed to serve different functions within the federal penal system, both model Porfirian penal institutions exhibited two essential characteristics: strong executive control and scientific management techniques that relied heavily on behavior modification.

## The Political Opposition on Prison Reform

Drawing on the same liberal reform tradition, Díaz's political opponents generally supported both the *científicos'* social diagnosis and their proposed solutions.[70] Like their *científico* opponents, the editors of the liberal journal *El Monitor Republicano* attributed Mexico City's crime wave to alcoholism, gambling, prostitution, "habitual idleness," lack of respect for the police, and "bloody spectacles" like bullfighting that incited the lower classes to violence.[71] Enrique Chávarri, writing as "Juvenal," lobbied persistently for a larger, better-trained police force to protect the capital.[72] His editorial counterpart, Enrique M. de los Ríos, went still further, calling for enforcement of the penal code regulations against the sale of alcohol and gambling as well as a prohibition of "bloody spectacles."[73] Both editors also insisted on the need to complete the penitentiary. In a series of articles exposing unsanitary, overcrowded conditions at Belem, Chávarri noted that "it is evident that these conditions will never improve until the establishment of the penitentiary." An "adequate penal system," he insisted, was a fundamental corrective to rising crime.[74]

Although the Porfiriato's liberal opponents participated unreservedly in the prison reform discourse, they nevertheless vigorously protested the Díaz administration's misuse of its penal institutions. In 1885, angry over the exposure of a crony, Díaz imprisoned a number of opposition journalists, including Chávarri and de los Ríos.[75] This group, the Club de Periodistas Encarcelados, bitterly attacked the administration for its hypocritical approach to prison reform. De los Ríos, commenting on Díaz's 1889 presidential address, noted an inherent contradiction in his advocacy of "rehabilitation which transforms the delinquent into a useful member of society." The president's theory was unassailable, de los Ríos sarcastically conceded, adding that "it is regrettable that journalists are to be made the exception."[76]

A product of his time, de los Ríos never questioned Díaz's right to imprison his opposition, insisting only on separate facilities. In his influential *State of Prisons and of Child-Saving Institutions*, North American penologist Enoch Wines, who had earlier advised the Juárez administration, had observed that "as to political offenders, it has been taken into account that, if in some cases they proceed from unruly passions, they may in others be the result of errors of opinion, yet of good intentions. For this reason the offenders of this class are not placed on the same level as ordinary criminals but are simply confined in a special prison used for this object alone."[77] De los Ríos concurred, noting the importance of "avoiding the mixing of prisoners that is so repugnant to those incarcerated only for political reasons."[78] In fact, the penitentiary commission's reforms of the penal code recognized the special status of political prisoners by allowing them to keep all prison wages and permitting them relative freedom within the institution.[79]

Their experience as political prisoners strongly affected the attitude of other Díaz opponents toward prison reform as well. Some years later, Mexican Liberal Party (PLM) leader Ricardo Flores Magón dramatically described an early experience in Díaz's prisons:

The jail lacked a proper floor . . . and the walls oozed a thick fluid that prevented the spittle of countless, careless occupants from ever drying. Huge webs hung from the ceiling, covered with enormous, black, horrible spiders . . . my pallet was wet, as were my clothes, and from time to time I heard the sound of spiders falling on the pallet or floor, or in the early morning on my body.[80]

Not surprisingly, the revised draft of the 1906 PLM program included an article on prison reform.[81] The manifesto to the program noted that "existing prisons serve only to punish men, not to better them."[82] As a solution, article 44 of the program itself recommended "the establishment, whenever possible, of penal colonies based on regeneration in place of the jails and penitentiaries in which delinquents currently suffer punishment."[83]

Like the liberal editors of *El Monitor Republicano*, PLM leaders endorsed prison reform while denouncing Díaz's abuse of the penal system. A 1903 article in *El Hijo del Ahuizote* remarked that Díaz "treated the jails like his personal property, which he used to remove his opposition when he could not justify having them killed."[84] This systematic abuse of public institutions indicated, according to opposition leaders, the larger criminality of the Díaz government itself.

As opposition to Díaz intensified, increasingly radical PLM leaders refined their position on prison reform. They identified structural inequalities within the capitalist economic system, rather than the moral failings of the marginal classes, as the true cause of crime. A 1911 PLM manifesto observed that systematic exploitation of the laboring classes generated "antisocial behavior, crime, prostitution, and disloyalty . . . the natural fruits of an old and hated system."[85] That same year, Ricardo Flores Magón noted optimistically that "with the disappearance of the greed and falsity necessary to survival under existing circumstances, there will be no reason for crime."[86] Implicit in this explanation for delinquency was the need to restructure Mexican society. Prison reform, while a necessary corrective within an exploitive system, would prove unnecessary in a truly equitable society. This radical position was, however, the exception that proved the rule.

**Revolutionary Prison Reform**

After Díaz's fall, less radical revolutionaries like Carranza took up the call for social justice. In his 1913 Hermosillo speech, Carranza scorned the Porfiriato as a time of "hopeless calm . . . without material or social progress in which the people found themselves for thirty years without schools, hygiene, food, and, worst of all, liberty."[87] Two years later, in San Luis Potosí, Carranza identified the Revolution with a "general systemic transformation" that would bring real progress to Mexico.[88] From prohibitionist governor of Coahuila under Madero, Carranza had become, at least rhetorically, a social reformer.

On December 1, 1916, President Carranza convened a Constitutional Convention at Querétaro to "reform" the 1857 constitution. In his inaugural speech, he proudly noted that his proposed constitution, drafted by lawyers José Natividad Macías and Luis Manuel Rojas, reflected "all the political reforms which years of experience and careful observation have suggested to me are indispensable."[89] Félix Palavicini, a Carranza delegate, observed that Macías and Rojas, "following the president's inspiration, have given the revolution a program that would make it a true Social Revolution."[90]

That Christmas, Macías made similar claims for the proposed prison reform article. The president, he noted, "after pondering prison organization in the United States, England, and Germany, realized the need for far-reaching reform in Mexico."[91] Recent advances in penology rendered existing legislation obsolete. For Macías, the "classical penal system" which had inspired the 1857 constitutional article on prison reform was based on abstractions that punished the crime but ignored the intent and background of the criminal.[92] He proposed instead a modern penal system, based on penal colonies controlled by the national government, that would not just punish crime but also address the moral, biological, and environmental factors that affected each criminal's behavior. According to Macías, this new system would "provide all Mexican criminals, the majority delinquent because of poverty, heredity, training, and the lack of available education, the means to satisfy the demands of life."[93]

Delegates generally agreed with Macías on the multiple causes of crime. Prohibitionists, including nominal opponents like General Múgica and Macías, linked the adverse effects of alcohol, drug abuse, gambling, and bullfighting to lower-class criminality and recommended severe sanctions. Dr. José María Rodríguez, head of Mexico City's Consejo Superior de Salud Pública (Superior Council of Public Health), attributed 80 percent of Mexico City's violent crimes to drinking, estimating that nine-tenths of the lower classes were alcoholics. Other delegates noted structural causes for crime, especially "lack of education and general ignorance."[94]

Nor was there debate on the need for prison reform. Macías observed that "many delegates present today were imprisoned with me in the penitentiary." One of those delegates, Félix Palavicini, incarcerated by Huerta along with Macías and Rojas, recalled his month in solitary confinement as "the only time I ever contemplated suicide." He confessed that "from that moment I saw prison in a new light."[95] Many convention delegates shared Palavicini's reaction to Porfirian prisons and his desire for reform.

Macías attacked the Díaz administration's blatant misuse of existing penal facilities on practical grounds as well. He noted that the penitentiary, designed to hold only fifteen hundred inmates, now contained more than four thousand.[96] He condemned the Porfiriato's model penal institution as "fatal, infernal, detestable," adding that it "warrants destruction even at the loss of millions spent on its construction."[97] Under such conditions, rehabilitation of inmates was clearly impossible.

Although delegates frequently cited Italian positivist criminologists Lombroso, Ferri, and Garofalo to support their respective cases, they sometimes differed on the penal system's fundamental purpose. Querétaro lawyer José María Truchuelo credited positivist criminologists with developing a modern penal system "based on the theory of the correctability of man" and insisted that workshops and schools be integrated into future penal facilities.[98] Enrique Colunga, speaking for the Committee on the Constitution, took a less humanitarian approach. "The committee," he declared, "does not believe that the penal system should be based on public vendetta, but neither does it believe in readaptation. For committee members, the penal system is based on the principle of social defense."[99] These were differences of focus rather than substance, representing the extremes of prison reformers' concern for both rehabilitation and isolation.

In fact, the influence of the liberal-Porfirian discourse about prison reform on convention delegates was profound. Delegates agreed that Díaz had grossly abused the penal system, but most never questioned the fundamental tenets of Porfirian prison reform: rehabilitation, social defense, and top-down reform. In spite of some concern about the structural causes of crime, many delegates continued the Porfirian focus on the moral state of the lower classes.

The controversy centered not on prison reform itself but on the issue of national government control—what Luis Manuel Rojas called the "old and much debated question of 'federalism' and 'centralism.'"[100] The Committee on the Constitution refused to consider Carranza's proposed article 18 principally because it called for national government control of the proposed penal colonies. Committee president General Francisco Múgica noted that "the one thing the committee could not accept was that they [penal colonies] be established exclusively by the federal government."[101] Rebutting Macías's argument that centralized control meant better prisons, the committee insisted on each state's right to punish its own criminals. Enrique Colunga, the committee's secretary, warned that the penal colonies "would become a terrible political weapon . . . should a ferocious, cruel man occupy the presidency." He added that "if we accept this penal system, tomorrow we will have in Islas Marías and Quintana Roo a sinister reflection of the deportations to Siberia."[102]

Given the recent experience of many of the delegates, Colunga's argument seemed quite sensible. Although Macías promised that future penal colonies would be run by doctors and professors rather than the executive, pragmatic General Heriberto Jara expressed serious reservations. Representing Veracruz, with its notorious San Juan de Ulúa military prison, Jara insisted that penal colonies, because of their isolation and resultant lack of proper supervision, "lent themselves only to abuses." The Díaz administration's recent misuse of Islas Marías and Quintana Roo, he observed, was typical.[103]

Pragmatists objected to penal colonies for other reasons. One delegate cited the obvious expense and construction time involved. Another, responding to Macías's argument that isolation from contaminating environments was crucial to rehabilitation, retorted that isolating prisoners in penal colonies cut "civilizing" family ties and discriminated against the "poorer classes" who could not afford transportation.[104] These practical arguments won the day for states' rights advocates. Although national penal colony supporters insisted that poorer states lacked funds to build proper penal facilities, most delegates agreed that the potential for abuse and considerable expense involved represented too great a risk. Logistical problems and the need to curb the national government's power far outweighed the less tangible benefits of nationally directed penal reform.

After its initial rejection on a technicality, the convention finally approved article 18 on January 3, 1917, by a vote of 155 to 37. The article's first paragraph required separate facilities for detainees and convicted criminals. The second instructed the state and national governments "to organize their respective penal systems—colonies, penitentiaries, or military prisons—on the basis of work as the means of regeneration."[105]

For Macías, the approved article, "instead of advancing our humanitarian and republican institutions, drags us back to . . . 1857."[106] The delegates' misunderstanding of modern advances in penal reform and their oversensitivity to past abuses, he implied, had set Mexican prison reform back sixty years. Lack of centralized administration, he argued, precluded national standards and thus the effective administration of Mexican prisons, especially in the poorer states.

The discursive struggle over prison reform, however, had little actual impact on Mexican prisons, national or otherwise. The national government showed little interest in building any new model penal institutions, and the penitentiary and Islas Marías continued to function as inefficiently as before. Typically, General Múgica, who had so adamantly opposed federal penal colonies during convention debates, became director of the Islas Marías penal colony in 1928. Having reclaimed the prison reform discourse of the liberal and Porfirian eras, financially strapped revolutionary governments failed to follow through with expensive reforms until the relatively flush 1960s.[107]

Aside from the issue of jurisdiction, the Constitutional Convention debate had little effect on the prison reform discourse. In 1922, an article in the prestigious *Boletín de la Sociedad Mexicana de Geografía y Estadística* lamented the ongoing Mexico City crime wave in typically liberal-Porfirian terms. The study cited alcoholism, abandoned children, consensual relations outside marriage, and lax enforcement of existing laws as the principal causes of rising crime.[108] Penal solutions likewise followed Porfirian guidelines, stressing scientific management by trained administrators. Significantly, Miguel Macedo, the Porfiriato's leading penologist and godfather of the penitentiary, continued to influence Mexican penology, first as professor of penal law at the Escuela Nacional de Jurisprudencia from 1883 to 1904 and later at the Escuela Libre de Derecho from 1912 to 1920. Mexico's leading postrevolutionary penologists, including the editors of *Criminalia*, the professional journal for Mexican criminologists and penologists, proudly admitted Macedo's ongoing influence on Mexican penology.[109]

In *Judas at the Jockey Club*, William Beezley explores Porfirian efforts to replace public spectacles like Judas burnings, which excited the "dangerous classes," with more controlled bicycle parades in the latest European fashion.[110] Perceived danger from a growing urban underclass and obsession with international image also affected prison reform. In fact, prison reform came of age during the Porfiriato as modernizing elites like Miguel Macedo oversaw the construction of model penal facilities and the consolidation of a liberal-positivist prison reform discourse. Prison reform thus served as an essential element in Porfirian plans to develop a disciplinary Mexican carceral system that included everything from public education to bicycle races.[111]

The revolutionary prison reform discourse, as demonstrated by the 1917 Constitutional Convention debate, was in many ways an extension of its predecessors. Most convention delegates recognized an established prison reform tradition closely linked to nineteenth-century liberal efforts to modernize Mexico. Institutional reform, including prisons and schools, played a key role in the liberal project. Liberal prison reformers advocated a prison system that would isolate criminals, provide for their rehabilitation, and permit their eventual reintegration as productive members of society. But, caught between contradictory ideological commitments to individual freedom and a rationally ordered society, liberal reformers never resolved the vital questions of agency and jurisdiction.

Porfirian *científicos* saw centralized control as the solution to this liberal dilemma. Drawing on the insights of European positivists, the *científicos* insisted that only specifically Mexican solutions could solve Mexico's problems. Since social disorder and economic underdevelopment precluded private initiative, a strong centralized administration seemed the logical answer. Porfirian prison reformers thus favored disciplinary prison regimens based on behavior modification that inculcated liberal values like hard work, honesty, and respect for authority under the administration of a powerful director and his team of scientifically trained experts who supervised reform and guaranteed order. They also insisted that, given Mexico's heterogeneous nature, only centralized control by the national government could guarantee comprehensive prison reform. Accepting the basic tenets of liberal prison reform, *científicos* sought to devise effective means for their realization.

At the Constitutional Convention debates, delegates acknowledged the *científicos'* contribution to penal reform but insisted that abuses perpetuated by the Porfirian prison system far outweighed its accomplishments. Many spoke from firsthand experiences in Díaz's prisons. But in spite of this consensus on the accomplishments and failures of Porfirian prison reform, delegates hotly contested the nature of the constitutional mandate, focusing especially on the issue of state versus national control. Taking their cue from *científico* social engineering, Carrancista delegates like Macías argued that only a network of nationally controlled penal colonies could ensure effective administration and reform of all Mexican prisons. The majority disagreed, noting the tremendous potential for abuse inherent in a nationally controlled system and contesting Macías's assertion that centralized administration was necessarily more efficient or humane.

The resulting constitutional article represented a defeat for Macías's centrally administered prison system. While the accepted article acknowledged the need for different kinds of penal institutions and their general reformative purpose, it rejected national government control as too risky. For most delegates, a decentralized prison system limited a strong president's ability to dominate the Mexican penal system, as Díaz had attempted to do. The greater means available to postrevolutionary presidents made the need for checks and balances that much greater. Thus, although the 1917 constitution created a strong president capable of imposing broad social reforms, it also sought to check potential abuse of executive power in traditional liberal fashion by decentralizing the means of repression. The images of the past autocracy lingered deep in the positions and rhetoric of convention delegates, weaving into the positivist model of the penitentiary a preoccupation alien to its European and American origins. More than providing a discursive space for the construction of a politically and socially functional subject representing "modernity," the penitentiary became a field of force for the discussion of the future Mexican state.

## Notes

A version of this chapter was published by *Mexican Studies/Estudios Mexicanos 9*, no. 1 (winter 1993). Comments and suggestions on earlier drafts of this chapter by Michael C. Meyer, Donna Guy, Kevin Gosner, Robert Dean, Ricardo Salvatore, Carlos Aguirre, and the readers for *Mexican Studies/Estudios Mexicanos* were invaluable and much appreciated.

1. Manuel González Ramírez, *Fuentes para la historia de la Revolución Mexicana*, vol. 1: *Planes políticos y otros documentos* (Mexico City: Fondo de Cultura Económica, 1954), p. 24.

2. For an account of the credentials fight, see E. V. Niemeyer, Jr., *Revolution at Querétaro: The Mexican Constitutional Convention of 1916–1917* (Austin: University of Texas Press, 1974), pp. 44–59. A transcription of the proceedings by a participant can be found in Félix F. Palavicini, *Historia de la constitución de 1917* (Mexico City: Consejo Editorial del Gobierno del Estado de Tabasco, 1980), pp. 57–143.

3. México, XLVI Legislatura de la Cámara de Diputados, *Derechos del pueblo mexicano: México a través de sus constituciones*, vol. 4: *Antecedentes y evolución de los artículos 16 a 27 constitucionales* (Mexico City: XLVI Legislatura de la Cámara de Diputados, 1967), pp. 86–143. The legislative debates without commentary and antecedents can also be found in *Diario de los debates del Congreso Constituyente, 1916–1917*, 2 vols. (Mexico City: Talleres Gráficos de la Nación, 1960).

4. *Derechos del pueblo mexicano*, 4: 91.

5. For another example of a discursive revolution, see Keith Michael Baker, *Inventing the French Revolution: Essays on French Political Culture in the Eighteenth Century* (New York: Cambridge University Press, 1990). Baker provides a useful definition of discourse as "a set of linguistic patterns and relationships that defined possible actions and utterances and gave them meaning" (p. 24).

6. Although he uses the term *ideology* rather than *discourse*, Arnaldo Córdova reaches a similar conclusion in *La ideología de la Revolución Mexicana: la formación del nuevo régimen* (Mexico City: Ediciones Era, 1973).

7. On the temperance debate, see Niemeyer, *Revolution at Querétaro*, pp. 181–197.

8. Córdova, *Ideología de la Revolución Mexicana*, p. 28.

9. For an analysis of revisionist historiography, see David C. Bailey, "Revisionism and the Recent Historiography of the Mexican Revolution," *Hispanic American Historical Review* 58, no. 1 (February 1978): 62–79; and William Dirk Raat, "Recent Trends in the Historiography of the Mexican

Revolution," in *The Mexican Revolution: An Annotated Guide to Recent Scholarship* (Boston: G. K. Hall and Co., 1982), pp. xxiii–xxxvii.

10. Charles Hale, for example, ignores prison reform even though most liberals saw modern penitentiaries as an essential disciplinary component of economic and social development. See his *Mexican Liberalism in the Age of Mora, 1821–1853* (New Haven, Conn.: Yale University Press, 1968) and *The Transformation of Liberalism in Late Nineteenth-Century Mexico* (Princeton, N.J.: Princeton University Press, 1989).

11. See, for example, Vicente Rocafuerte's "Ensayo sobre el nuevo sistema de cárceles," in Neptalí Zúñiga, ed., *Colección Rocafuerte*, vol. 9: *Rocafuerte y las doctrinas penales* (Quito: Gobierno de Ecuador, 1947). Liberal prison reform first surfaced in Mexico under the Bourbons. See Francisco Blasco y Fernández de Moreda, *Lardizábal, el primer penalista de América española* (Mexico City: Imprenta Universitaria, 1957).

12. Manuel Lardizábal y Uribe, *Discurso sobre las penas* (Mexico City: Editorial Porrúa, 1982), p. 197. Concern about rationalizing punishment was typical of enlightened absolutist monarchs. Lardizábal, for example, cites a 1781 memorandum on the subject by Louis XVI's controversial finance minister, Jacques Necker. Ibid., pp. 215–218.

13. Ibid., p. 214.

14. Rocafuerte, *Nuevo sistema de cárceles*, p. 8.

15. Ibid., pp. ii, 14. The "treading mill" (treadwheel) and its relation to incipient industrialization is discussed in Michael Ignatieff, *A Just Measure of Pain: The Penitentiary and the Industrial Revolution, 1750–1850* (New York: Pantheon Books, 1978), pp. 177–187. Ignatieff includes illustrations. On the links between capitalist development and prison reform, see also Dario Melossi and Massimo Pavarini, *The Prison and the Factory: Origins of the Penitentiary System* (Totowa, N.J.: Barnes & Noble, 1981).

16. Mariano Otero, "Iniciativa dirigida a la Cámara de Diputados, por el Ministerio de Relaciones sobre la adopción y establecimiento del régimen penitenciario en el Distrito y territorios (1848)," in *Obras* (Mexico City: Editorial Porrúa, 1967), 2: 665.

17. Mariano Otero, "Indicaciones sobre la importancia y necesidad de la reforma de las leyes penales (1844)," in ibid., 2: 657.

18. José María Luis Mora, "Memoria sobre cárceles inglesas," in *Obras completas*, vol. 7: *Obra diplomática* (Mexico City: Secretaría de Educación Pública, 1988), pp. 102–103. Interestingly, liberals like Rocafuerte, Otero, and Mora accepted the Church's moralizing role in Mexican society even as they denounced its political and economic influence. The prominent role of religion in North American and English prison reform and a belief that the superstitious lower classes could still benefit from a depoliticized Catholicism probably encouraged tolerance.

19. Ibid., pp. 66–67, and Mariano Otero, "Mejora del pueblo (1859)," in *Obras*, 2: 685–693.

20. For additional details on liberal and Porfirian prison reform efforts, see Laurence J. Rohlfes, "Police and Penal Correction in Mexico City, 1876–1911: A Study of Order and Progress in Porfirian Mexico," Ph.D. diss., Tulane University, 1983. On prison reform efforts in the state of Puebla, see Nydia E. Cruz Barrera,

"Confines: el desarrollo del sistema penitenciario poblano en el siglo XIX," Tesis de maestría en Ciencias Sociales, Universidad Autónoma de Puebla, 1989.

21. Rohlfes, "Police and Penal Correction in Mexico City," p. 292.

22. Peruvian penologists directly concerned with disciplining Native Americans took a different approach. See Aguirre's essay, chapter 2, this volume; and Deborah A. Poole, "Ciencia, peligrosidad y represión en la criminología indigenista peruana," in C. Aguirre and C. Walker, eds., *Bandoleros, abigeos y montoneros* (Lima: Instituto de Apoyo Agrario, 1990), pp. 335–367. For the influence of race in the language of criminology in Argentina and Brazil, see Salvatore's essay, chapter 7, this volume.

23. Henry C. Schmidt provides a detailed history of racial consciousness in Mexico in *The Root of Lo Mexicano: Self and Society in Mexican Thought, 1900–1934* (College Station: Texas A&M Press, 1978).

24. Typically, separate buildings for female and juvenile inmates at the federal penitentiary in Mexico City were planned but never constructed. See Rohlfes, "Police and Penal Correction in Mexico City," p. 14.

25. Gregorio Cárdenas Hernández, *Adiós, Lecumberri* (Mexico City: Editorial Diana, 1979), p. 22.

26. Sergio García Ramírez, *El artículo 18 constitucional: prisión preventiva, sistema penitenciario, menores infractores* (Mexico City: UNAM, 1967), p. 63.

27. José Enrique Ampudia, ed., *Boletín del Archivo General de la Nación* 5, no. 4 (October–December 1981) and 6, no. 1 (January–March 1982): 15.

28. Felipe Teña Ramírez, *Leyes fundamentales de México, 1808–1964*, 2d ed. (Mexico City: Editorial Porrúa, 1964), p. 610.

29. Miguel S. Macedo, "Los establecimientos penales," *Criminalia* 20, no. 7 (July 1954): 429.

30. Ibid.

31. *Código penal para el distrito de la Baja California y Méjico y para toda la república* (Madrid: Establecimiento Tipográfico de Pedro Núñez, 1890), p. 5.

32. Antonio Sánchez Galindo, "Mexico," in Elmer H. Johnson, ed., *International Handbook of Contemporary Developments in Criminology: General Issues* (Westport, Conn.: Greenwood Press, 1983), p. 263.

33. Enoch C. Wines, *The State of Prisons and of Child-Saving Institutions in the Civilized World* (Cambridge: University Press, John Wilson and Son, 1880), p. 42.

34. Sánchez, "Mexico," p. 263; Francisco Javier Peña, "Cárceles en México en 1875," *Criminalia* 25, no. 5 (August 1959): 468–503.

35. Peña, "Cárceles en México en 1875," p. 469.

36. Wines, *The State of Prisons and of Child-Saving Institutions*, p. 538.

37. Leopoldo Zea makes this point in a number of works, including *El positivismo en México* (Mexico City: El Colegio de México, 1943) and *Apogeo y decadencia del positivismo en México* (Mexico City: El Colegio de México, 1944).

38. Quoted in Jesús Silva Herzog, *El pensamiento económico, social y político de México, 1810–1964* (Mexico City: Fondo de Cultura Económica, 1974), p. 281.

39. William Dirk Raat, *El positivismo durante el Porfiriato* (Mexico City:

Secretaría de Educación Pública, 1975), p. 21. Raat also notes that during the Reforma liberal positivist Gabino Barreda replaced "Love" with "Liberty."

40. Julio Guerrero, La génesis del crimen en México: estudio de psiquiatría social (Mexico City: Librería de la Viuda de Ch. Bouret, 1901), p. 310.

41. Ibid., p. 390.

42. Carlos Roumagnac, Los criminales en México: ensayo de psicología criminal (Mexico City: Tipografía "El Fénix," 1904), p. 54. Note the similarity with Argentine positivist criminologists; see Ricardo D. Salvatore, "Criminology, Prison Reform, and the Buenos Aires Working Class," Journal of Interdisciplinary History 23, no. 2 (autumn 1992): 279–299.

43. Justo Sierra, Obras completas del maestro Justo Sierra, vol. 4: Periodismo político (Mexico City: UNAM, 1948), p. 308.

44. Peña, "Cárceles en México en 1875," p. 497.

45. "Estado de la Cárcel Nacional conocida como Cárcel de Belén en el año de 1882" (from Manuel Riviera Cambas, México pintoresco), Criminalia 25, no. 8 (August 1959): 398.

46. Miguel S. Macedo, "La condena condicional," Criminalia 20, no. 7 (July 1954): 387.

47. "Estado de la Cárcel Nacional," p. 401.

48. Macedo, "Los establecimientos penales," p. 437.

49. Ampudia, ed., Boletín del Archivo General de la Nación, pp. 46–50.

50. Ibid., p. 12.

51. Ibid., p. 13.

52. Ibid., p. 16.

53. See Rohlfes, "Police and Penal Correction in Mexico City," and Paul J. Vanderwood, Disorder and Progress: Bandits, Police, and Mexican Development, 2d ed. (Wilmington, Del.: Scholarly Resources, 1992).

54. Roumagnac, Los criminales en México, p. 40.

55. Ampudia, ed., Boletín del Archivo General de la Nación, p. 17.

56. Ibid., p. 12.

57. Ibid., pp. 23–25.

58. Ibid., pp. 102–120.

59. Ibid., pp. 24–25.

60. Ibid., p. 26.

61. Ibid., p. 13.

62. Ibid., p. 26.

63. Ibid., p. 28.

64. García Ramírez, El artículo 18 constitucional, pp. 45–46.

65. Javier Piña y Palacios, ed., "Las Islas Marías a principios de este Siglo," Criminalia 36, no. 5 (May 1970): 211–227.

66. Ibid., p. 216.

67. Ibid., p. 223.

68. Ibid., p. 224.

69. Ibid., p. 222.

70. On the continuity of "scientific politics" see Hale, The Transformation of Liberalism in Late Nineteenth-Century Mexico.

71. El Monitor Republicano (Mexico City), November 22, 1889.

72. Ibid., May 29, 1889, December 27, 1889.
73. Ibid., December 10, 1889.
74. Ibid., February 15, 1889, December 10, 1889.
75. Daniel Cosío Villegas, *Historia moderna de México*, vol. 9: *El Porfiriato: la vida política interior* (Mexico City: Editorial Hermes, 1972), part 2: 221.
76. *El Monitor Republicano*, March 9, 1889.
77. Wines, *The State of Prisons and of Child-Saving Institutions*, p. 534.
78. *El Monitor Republicano*, January 12, 1889.
79. Ampudia, ed., *Boletín del Archivo General de la Nación*, p. 84.
80. Quoted in Silva Herzog, *El pensamiento económico, social y político de México*, p. 22.
81. The first draft, published in April 1906, made no mention of prison reform. See *El programa del Partido Liberal Mexicano de 1906 y sus antecedentes* (Mexico City: Ediciones Antorcha, 1985), pp. 219–225.
82. Comisión de Investigaciones Históricas de la Revolución Mexicana, ed., *Documentos históricos de la Revolución Mexicana*, vol. 10: *Actividades políticas y revolucionarias de los hermanos Flores Magón* (Mexico City: Editorial Jus, 1966), p. 57.
83. Ibid., p. 62.
84. Armando Bartra, ed., *Regeneración, 1900–1918* (Mexico City: Ediciones Era, 1977), p. 150.
85. Silva Herzog, *El pensamiento económico, social y político de México*, pp. 555–556.
86. Bartra, ed., *Regeneración*, p. 270.
87. Fabela, *Documentos históricos de la Revolución Mexicana*, 4: 86–87.
88. Ibid.
89. Ibid., pp. 161–180.
90. Palavicini, *Historia de la constitución de 1917*, pp. 119–120.
91. *Derechos del pueblo mexicano*, 4: 95.
92. Ibid., p. 93.
93. Ibid., p. 118.
94. Ibid., pp. 138 and 113.
95. Félix F. Palavicini, *Mi vida revolucionaria* (Mexico City: Ediciones Bota, 1937), pp. 183–184.
96. *Derechos del pueblo mexicano*, 4: 116.
97. Quoted in García Ramírez, *El artículo 18 constitucional*, p. 68.
98. *Derechos del pueblo mexicano*, 4: 127.
99. Ibid., p. 107.
100. Palavicini, *Historia de la constitución de 1917*, p. 203.
101. *Derechos del pueblo mexicano*, 4: 134.
102. Ibid., pp. 141–143.
103. Ibid., pp. 141–142.
104. Ibid., p. 106.
105. Ibid., p. 143.
106. Ibid., p. 91.
107. Sánchez Galindo, "México," p. 254.
108. Casimiro Cueto, "Consideraciones generales y apuntes para la crítica estadística de la criminalidad habida en el Distrito Federal durante el año de

1922," *Boletín de la Sociedad Mexicana de Geografía y Estadística* 37, nos. 1–6 (1928): 40–41.

109. Germán Fernández del Castillo, "La obra histórica de don Miguel S. Macedo," *Criminalia* 11, no. 8 (August 1945): 460–461.

110. William Beezley, *Judas at the Jockey Club and Other Episodes of Porfirian Mexico* (Lincoln: University of Nebraska Press, 1987).

111. For the role of education in the Mexican carceral system, see Mary Kay Vaughn, *The State, Education, and Social Class in Mexico, 1880–1928* (Dekalb: Northern Illinois University Press, 1982).

# 7. Penitentiaries, Visions of Class, and Export Economies: Brazil and Argentina Compared

## Ricardo D. Salvatore

During the period 1890 to 1910, prison reform in Argentina and Brazil paralleled new developments in criminology. Positivist criminology, introduced in the region by the late nineteenth century and almost hegemonic among intellectual circles by the 1910s, provided the needed impetus. It contributed new conceptions about the determinants of criminal behavior (inheritance, social environment, psychopathologies) and about the relation between law and punishment (the independence between legal retribution and institutional reformation). It also made possible the extension of state supervision and intervention into a wider territory of working-class life, hidden under the innocuous rhetoric of "social defense." Transplanted to Brazil and Argentina, the doctrine suffered minor but significant changes: influenced initially by Lombroso's "anthropological criminology," local practitioners added sociological and psychological dimensions to the interpretations of criminal behavior, starting a movement toward the "medicalization" of criminology.

The new criminology aided the project of prison reform, favoring a particular type of reformation based on individual treatment, work, education, and moral suasion. It advocated the transformation of prisons into "clinics" for the treatment of delinquents and also into "factories," because work and industrial discipline were considered essential instruments of reformation. Opposed to existing prisons (dark, unhealthful, and undifferentiated) and to prevailing methods of punishment (brutal and cruel, aimed chiefly at retribution), criminologists struggled for prisons that would be the symbols of modernity, prisons where medical science combined with the accumulated knowledge of penology could produce the reformation of inmates, or at least prevent those "irreformable" from contaminating the rest. In the imaginary of reformers, the penitentiary would in turn help science, providing the "evidence" that could serve to validate or reject theories of criminal behavior.

This model penitentiary (clinic-factory-laboratory) found a real expression in Argentina in the Penitenciaría Nacional at Buenos Aires

(1904–1915) and in Brazil in the Instituto de Regeneração at São Paulo (1925–1940). These institutions were exceptional in the region, emblems of modernity built at lavish expense, the embodiment of the combined apparatuses of "rehabilitation." They marked the culmination (hence the possibilities and also the limitations) of a reformist trend that had started much earlier (in the 1830s in Brazil, in the 1870s in Argentina) under a quite different set of circumstances and motivations. The location of these two institutions in the most dynamic areas of each country's export economy (São Paulo and Buenos Aires) points to the relationship between economic modernization and the establishment of institutionalized discipline. More significantly, these two penitentiaries denoted a synthesis of conceptions about crime, criminals, and the working classes incorporated into state projects of social regeneration.

This chapter tries to assess the achievement of these two pioneering efforts in prison reform in terms of their contributions to the construction of criminality, the "social question," and the obstacles facing Brazil and Argentina in their path toward "progress." The language of positivist criminology is presented here as an interpretive system about the social tensions of two export economies, Brazil and Argentina, during the period 1890 to 1920.[1] The penitentiary project, I argue, established a discourse about crime and punishment that provided the frame for interpreting each country's ambivalent modernity: its social tensions, its regional uneven development, and its obstacles in the road to "civilization" and "progress." Rather than passively providing disciplinary solutions to a given labor regime associated with a certain cycle of the export economy, criminology provided a way of interpreting the complex social problematic created by these social arrangements. Though both institutions embodied the same disciplinary technology, each project was inscribed in a distinct interpretive context and nurtured a somewhat different vision of class—ways of perceiving and representing "social problems" that carried into policy class, gender, and racial prejudice cloaked as science. The influence of these distinct interpretations of the social on the project of prison reform can be assessed in terms of the degree of optimism or pessimism that reformers invested in "rehabilitation." In this also, the contrast between Brazil and Argentina is noticeable. While informed by similar research premises and endowed with equivalent institutional power, Brazilian reformers saw their "criminal classes" as more recalcitrant to reformation than their Argentine counterparts.

The discussion of the Argentine case draws on a previous article,[2] elaborating further the relationship between export economies, visions of class, and the penitentiary project; that of Brazil is based on a new reading of the most important criminological works of the period. The analysis of the language of professional criminology focuses on the period 1890 to 1920; the review of penitentiary reform, a background to the issues dealt with by positivist criminologists during this period, goes back as far as the 1830s. The separation of the two spheres of disciplinary knowledge, penology and criminology, serves to emphasize the distinction between the institutional and the interpretive contributions of reformers.

## Prison Reform and Positivist Criminology in Argentina

Until the late 1870s, Argentina experienced little progress in the area of prison reform. The first penitentiary, built by the province of Buenos Aires in 1876, followed the plan of Pentonville and the disciplinary idea of the Auburn penitentiary: solitary confinement at night, work in common during the day.[3] Due to the lack of other facilities, the penitentiary served for a long time as both a detention center and an institution of confinement. By 1893, it hosted all sorts of prisoners: the young and the old, the processed and the condemned. Women were held in a separate pavilion.[4] Run by military officers, overtly concerned with prison finances, the project of rehabilitation received a low priority.

In the late 1880s the Association for Juridical Anthropology introduced the ideas of Italian positivism to the study of criminality in Argentina. Following the teachings of Lombroso, the members of the association began collecting criminal statistics, debating about the existence of atavism in Argentine culture, and mapping the contours of the "criminal world" within the city of Buenos Aires. The next generation of criminologists, most notably José Ingenieros and his followers, presented a modified version of positivism. Influenced by the youngest of the medical sciences, psychology, Ingenieros suggested a more complex view of criminal behavior. Rejecting "atavism," his approach emphasized the combined influenced of biological, psychological, and social factors in the formation of the delinquent's character. Delinquents combined different degrees of volitional, intellectual, and moral anomalies; it was the task of criminologists to identify these anomalies and suggest the appropriate therapy.[5]

Ingenieros's plan for "social defense" consisted of three parts: the prevention of crime, the reformation of delinquents, and the reinsertion of ex-convicts into society. For the second stage, he favored penitentiaries and reformatories based on the American model (the Elmira reformatory and the recommendations of the Cincinnati congress) as the most advanced form of treatment. Within a penitentiary, prisoners could internalize norms of conduct accepted by free and honest members of society, if only they could benefit from the therapy of work, elementary education, and religious instruction. Reformation depended on the effectiveness of individualized treatment. Due in large part to Ingenieros's efforts and to those of Antonio Ballvé, the Penitenciaría Nacional de Buenos Aires became by the 1910s an exceptional institution; it embodied the best practices of American penitentiaries and the theories of reformation pioneered by Italian positivists. Within the penitentiary's walls, inmates manufactured a variety of goods in twenty-five workshops which, due to their cleanliness and incessant labor, resembled a modern factory. Wages combined with other nonmonetary stimuli kept production lines busy. Unlike the Auburn system, the penitentiary allowed inmates to converse while working; at night all returned to cell isolation. In the penitentiary's chapel, a chaplain offered Masses every Sunday and "moral conferences" every afternoon. A school of twelve classrooms served to teach inmates basic reading and writing skills, math, and history. A professional corps of wardens, a group of doctors, the chaplain, the teachers, and the master artisans all shared the responsibility of reforming prisoners "from inside" based on case-by-case analyses of their tendencies and potentialities.[6]

Outside of the penitentiary's walls, criminologists had been mapping the "criminal class." Since the introduction of positivist anthropology, their ideas, images, and propositions served to describe the population at risk of becoming prison inmates, the criminal class. These depictions, despite claims of objectivity and scientificity, served to define social frontiers, to identify groups threatening order and progress, and to reinforce ideological elements central to the elite's project. Argentine criminologists concentrated on the study of urban crime, focusing on the case of Buenos Aires. Their essays typically dealt with abandoned children, street vagrants, and recidivist delinquents; only occasionally did prostitution engage their attention.[7] Portraits of the *mala vida*, a subculture with particular forms of social interaction and communication separated from, but at the same time dangerously close to, the world of working-class families, served to bring criminology closer to the public's interests.[8] The study of immigrants and their criminal tendencies also preoccupied positivists. Moyano Gacitúa, for example, assembled some defective criminal statistics to show that the influx of European immigration brought increasing crime rates instead of civilization and higher productivity. Similar remarks could be found in L. M. Drago's *Los hombres de presa.*[9]

The writings of Francisco de Veyga illustrate the centrality of work in positivist constructions about crime and criminals. Veyga portrayed "professional delinquents" as skilled workers lacking both moral qualities and a work ethic; he presented the "auxiliaries of crime" as an incipient entrepreneurial class, very diligent and productive but devoid of morality; and he associated vagrants with the unskilled and demoralized members of the working class.[10] The "world of crime" confronted the "world of work" as an appealing possibility. The passage from the latter to the former by means of apprenticeship and demoralization constituted a central theme in positivist studies. Pernicious circuits turning abandoned children and unemployed casual laborers into occasional and later professional delinquents concerned Veyga and other criminologists. José Ingenieros, in his *Criminología*, presented two cases of immigrants who, after changing so many casual jobs, ended up losing the "love of labor" and embracing criminal activities. Here, the theme of "the fall" from labor to crime combined nicely with the threat posed by an immigrant working class.

In this literature the dangers to the social order of the *república conservadora*[11] were clear: immigrants, children, vagrants, and professional thieves. The threat came chiefly from the "modern" class composition of the city; race, a constitutive signifier of Brazilian discourse about crime, had a minor role to play in Argentine criminological discourse. Concerns about the association between immigration and rising rates of crime, though present in Moyano Gacitúa, Lancelloti, and other criminologists, did not hinge upon a clearly racial ideology—the disillusionment with European immigration did not stem from its racial composition but from the "discovery" of its low social origins and its unacceptable work ethic.[12]

The female delinquent received less attention than other members of the criminal class. This was due in part to two reasons. First, the institutions for reforming women were under the control of *higienistas*, or quasi-religious institutions.[13] Second, prostitution, the most visible form of female criminality, was at the time legalized and, hence, not a felony.[14] Whether dealing with abandoned children, recidivist delinquents, street vagrants and thieves, or *caftans* (pimps), positivist criminologists' discourse emphasized the labor/crime duality over other signifiers. Their texts served to displace the problem of the social, previously defined in relation to an exterior "frontier," to the interior of the city. Positivists replaced the old polarity between civilization/city and barbarism/country with one more relevant to modern urban society: the formation within the city limits of a subculture of delinquents and their auxiliaries in opposition to the life of honest workers. Civilization could no longer consist of carrying to the exterior frontier the light of reason but of distinguishing the boundaries between the working class and the criminal class in the interior of city and selecting from the latter those worthy of reformation. This required institutional facilities, professional expertise, and a new scientific foundation.

Challenged by a new working class, predominantly immigrant and urban, with novel forms of expression and increasing demands, criminologists tried to readjust elite visions of class to the new realities. The years 1890 to 1910 witnessed the emergence of a militant labor movement, mobilized by anarchists and socialists; a movement that spoke many languages, had modern forms of association and struggle, and did not seem willing to join any national project.[15] Simultaneously, the export economy (exporting beef and cereals) created a structure of labor demand that was highly fluctuating and required few skills. The economy favored migration and mobility and typically produced seasonal or temporary "desertions" from the army of the employed. This reinforced the effectiveness of methods of direct action; at peak times in export demand, a few well-organized trade unions (stevedores, cart drivers, railroad workers, meat packers) were able to paralyze export production. Criminologists' intellectual challenge was to present these tensions (unemployment, poverty, vagrancy, trade unions, marches, radical politics) as the result of individual "anomalies," to imagine social problems as part of a more general phenomenon—criminality—reducible to systematic analysis, experimentation, and therapy.[16]

To this extent, positivist criminologists contributed to the remapping of class relations in early-twentieth-century Argentina. Their insights about the connection between labor discipline, economic cycles, and immigration pointed to the importance of questions insufficiently examined, much less debated, among the Argentine elite. Landowners connected to export business as well as the incipient immigrant industrial class did not consider labor discipline a problem. Criminologists showed a greater awareness of the problems posed by the export economy to the project of modernization and the building of the *república conservadora*. Reformers' interest in abandoned children, drinking, prostitution, theft, and vagrancy provided new information about immigrants' difficult assimilation into the elite's project of export-led development and added new sources of prejudice. Their descriptions of the criminal class reinforced existing beliefs in the threat of unchecked immigration to the peace and stability of the nation.

On the other hand, criminologists' gender-biased views prevented the visualization of the incorporation of women into industry and the problem that this implied for the patriarchal family. Criminologists' limited attention to this question contrasted with their obsessive interest in work and leisure among immigrant men. In fact, the "female challenge" is absent not only in relation to female criminality and work—even prostitution was presented as an anomaly that impeded normal work—but also in connection with the problem of abandoned children. Criminologists typically attributed this problem to environmental factors (the street, the gang, bad influences) or to the avarice of immigrant parents, not to the peculiar activities or propensities of women.

## Prison Reform in Brazil

Brazil's prison reform proceeded through waves of enthusiasm and disillusion. In the 1830s, the Regency made the first attempt to modernize prisons. A general plan, approved by Congress in 1832, called for the establishment of "houses of correction" in each and every province of the empire. In practice, however, the reform proved difficult to implement. The provinces lacked sufficient resources to replace their *cadeias* (jails) with more appropriate buildings. In Rio de Janeiro, the only place where a modern house of correction was built before 1860, errors in design and overcrowding defeated the purpose of reformation. The three "penitentiaries" built in the 1860s and 1870s (in São Paulo, Bahia, and Recife) were fraught with difficulties; none of them, critics agreed, could count as a modern penitentiary. In 1879 the goal of the reformation ideal remained unrealized. The grading system and a limited number of workshops in the prisons could not compensate for the extensive use of outmoded forms of punishment (deportation, the galleys, perpetual imprisonment, and death) or for the absence of separation among inmates.

Though the failure of penitentiary reform during the Empire (before abolition) could be attributed to a variety of factors (financial limitations, discontinuity of policy, and regionalism, among others), slavery proved the most important obstacle.[17] The penitentiary idea—the embodiment of a modern, bureaucratic, and formally egalitarian vision of society—clashed with the distinction between free and slave basic to the fabric of Brazilian society under the Empire. Even abolitionists, while abhorring slavery, shared the notion of a racially segmented society.[18] Men of darker skin received longer and harsher penalties than whites and light-skinned mulattoes. Brutality and public spectacle, eliminated for free men, continued to apply to slaves. As part of their galleys penalty, slaves walked along the streets and roads chained in gangs, and many of their offenses remained punishable within the confines of the plantation. The prison, used as an extension of the masters' power, could not be presented as an instrument of modernity.[19]

Two legal statutes and ways of punishment, one for free men, another for slaves, and a will to defend class difference conspired against the principles of penal reform.[20] The existence of human beings whose capacity for rehabilitation was denied by their very condition (black and slave) undermined the proposition that penitentiaries were supposed to validate. Since many whites attributed to free, dark-skinned men the propensities and traits of slaves, the reformation of other offenders was also in doubt. In the 1860s and 1870s a second group of reformers attempted to modernize Brazil's prisons, an effort that by 1900 again resulted in disappointment. The Casa de Correção in Rio de Janeiro, one of the targets of reformers, made some advances in the medicalization of treatment, in the classification of inmates, and in the eradication of corporal punishment. The reforms, however, foundered in the 1880s, when overcrowding, diseases, and internal disorder defeated the best efforts of the administrators.

This situation continued until a new administration from 1916 to 1918 began to introduce reforms similar to those enacted at the Buenos Aires penitentiary.[21] The medicalization of treatment, begun under Almeida Vale in the 1860s, became a reality only in the second decade of the twentieth century. The São Paulo penitentiary experienced a similar process of decay and revival. Criticized as an unhealthy and crowded facility at the turn of the century, the prison became an example of the reformatory ideal only in the second half of the 1920s. An Argentine observer writing in the mid-1930s was convinced that this facility—which had changed its name to Instituto de Regeneração—was the first of its type in South America.[22] Huge pavilions hosting a thousand inmates, twenty workshops, gardens, a school run by fifteen teachers, an eight thousand–volume library, careful follow-up of the inmates' progress, trained guardians, and the practice of individualized treatment produced the lowest rates of recidivism so far attainable.[23]

## Brazilian Criminological Discourse

In the 1890s a set of changes in legislation, labor regimes, and the economy prepared the terrain for a second wave of prison reform. The Republic brought about changes in legislation that imposed new requirements on the penal administration. The new penal code of 1890 incorporated important innovations in methods of punishment: the Irish system, the cellular prison, the unicity of penalty, and long terms of confinement.[24] The abolition of slavery in 1888 ended the division between slave and free in the penal system, making possible the extension of the penitentiary idea to all delinquents.[25] The sugar plantation crisis in the Northeast and the coffee economy boom in the south-central region favored a gradual transfer of black laborers from north to south, accelerating the transition to free labor.[26] In the coffee regions, restructuring the plantation-export economy demanded new forms of social relations, the *colonato* (contracted colonists) and sharecropping, and, above all, the replacement of slaves by European immigrants in the *lavouras* (small coffee plantations).[27] The incipient industrialization of Sao Paulo engendered in turn new imperatives: freedom of work and equality of treatment appeared as basic requirements for maintaining the immigrant flow.[28]

But the institutions that were to reform prisoners remained unchanged until the second decade of the new century. More important, the "experts" who could transform the punitive structure of the nation were pessimistic about the very possibility of reforming inmates. This was closely connected with the use made by local criminologists of the new positivist doctrine in the interpretation of the racial and class composition of the Brazilian poor.[29] After 1890 the pressure for reforming Brazilian prisons in accordance with European and North American standards of reformation came from a small cadre of positivist penologists and physicians working in Bahia, Rio de Janeiro, and Recife.[30] As in the Argentine case, these intellectuals gradually adapted the ideas of the Italian School to the interpretive needs posed by the Brazilian social structure. Initial followers of Lombroso were rapidly superseded by more critical practitioners who incorporated insights from sociology and medical science.[31] Tobias Barreto, the first to introduce Lombroso's *L'uomo delinquente* to Brazilian intellectual circles, rejected the concept of atavism and found the idea of a generic "madness" unacceptable.[32] His main follower, Clovis Bevilaqua, also resisted the idea that criminal propensities could be inferred from a person's appearance.[33]

Between 1900 and 1920, as the findings of psychology took hold of positivists' conceptions of criminal behavior, Brazilian criminology entered a process of medicalization. Members of the medical profession, psychiatrists in particular, took a greater interest in the reformation of delinquents. To them the psychological traits of the delinquent reflected both biological anomalies and the influence of the social milieu.[34] Crime was thought of as a disease (specialists spoke of "pathologies," "contagion," "diagnosis"), and its treatment became individualized and diverse. Psychological profiles of delinquents complemented the anthropometrical measurements recommended by the Lombrosian school. This process replicated with some delay the development of criminology in Argentina, where Ingenieros was leading a similar renovation.[35]

Typically, the writings of Brazilian criminologists summarized the history of penitentiaries from the Auburn and Philadelphia systems to the Crofton method and the Elmira reformatory, presenting the great distance that separated Brazilian prisons from the best European and North American institutions.[36] Their struggle, like that of reformers elsewhere, consisted of adapting existing penitentiaries to the reformatory ideal. Conceptions about Brazilian criminality, on the other hand, showed greater diversity. Understanding "national" crime required studying a variety of social interactions and cultural practices (work attitudes, race, gender, regionalism, and tradition) with a positivist perspective. In search of the meaning of what they believed constituted the peculiarity of the Brazilian nation, positivists constructed a vision of Brazilian civilization independent of the penitentiary idea, a vision which contributed to delineate the "social question" confronting the Republic.

Positivist discourse about crime served to construct the meaning of civilization in relation to race, social protest, and gender. One narrative strategy was to contrast Brazil's problems of social control with those of industrialized nations. In *Estudos de direito e economia política* (1902), Clovis Bevilaqua examined the combination of civilization and misery that existed at the very core of the world economy.[37] In Great Britain, he argued, the tremendous expansion of material wealth and productivity had given way to "pauperism," the illness of modern industrial societies. Behind the whistle of steam engines and the agitated animation of markets lay a gruesome reality: operatives and their families lived in misery, women surrendered their morality and health to the factory, and children were subject to unprecedented exploitation. In Brazil, on the other hand, the advancement of civilization confronted another obstacle: the legacy of slavery. The abolition of slavery had transformed a dependent work force into an ignorant, distrustful, and rebellious peasantry. Considering wage labor as a continuation of old forms of dependency, ex-slaves refused to work for their old masters, taking refuge instead in self-sufficient activities.[38] Slavery had engendered negative attitudes toward work among the Brazilian black masses.[39] Instead of the pauperism and trade unions proper to industrial societies, Brazil had to confront the problem of a black and mulatto peasantry insufficiently integrated into the market economy. For this reason, the disciplinary lessons drawn from the center's political economy had to be taken with care—institutional solutions adapted to Great Britain (charities, asylums, and prisons) did not seem to provide adequate answers to the problems Brazil faced in its march toward civilization.

In *Criminologia e direito* (1896) Bevilaqua explored another dimension of civilization: the taming of brutal passions concomitant with the progress of commerce. Whereas in industrialized nations, material progress corresponded with a decline in crimes against persons and an increase in crimes against property, northeastern Brazil—a region where the free *mestiço* peasantry outnumbered the black population—showed the opposite tendency: crimes against property remained remarkably low while interpersonal violence was on the rise.[40] Why were "criminal propensities" different in northeastern Brazil? To Bevilaqua ecology and economics explained the violent and cyclical nature of crime in the region. Constant and recurrent droughts broke down the rebellious spirit of peasants and made them more industrious, solidary, and provident; concerned exclusively with their own survival, peasants avoided the temptations of criminal activities. During the rainy season, on the other hand, as work at the *fazendas* (plantations) ceased almost completely, laborers were pushed into inactivity. This, together with torrid weather, tended to agitate men's passions, increasing the incidence of violent crimes.[41] Crimes against property remained low because of the beneficial influence of the export economy. Droughts pushed peasants to migrate to the Amazon, where the rubber boom provided employment and the possibility of a better life. Emigration represented a powerful factor "purifying" the social atmosphere of the region.[42] The passionate nature of the *sertanejos* (the inhabitants of the *sertão*) added another type of violence. Millenarian rebellions such as those led by Conselheiro and Joazeiro could easily arise when religious fanaticism fed upon regional migrations and climatic changes, threatening the very stability of the Republic.[43]

The question of race, so important to the social order and stability of the republic, infused many positivist texts about crime. Key in this regard was Raymundo Nina Rodrigues's *As raças humanas e a responsabilidade penal no Brasil* (1894), a book aimed at influencing public opinion in favor of reducing the penal responsibility of blacks, Indians, and *mestiços*. Blacks and Indians, argued Nina Rodrigues, shared an insufficient degree of civilization, the former due to biological traces inherited from their African ancestors, the latter as a result of centuries of Portuguese colonization.[44] Aided by traditional stereotypes, the author presented Afro-Brazilians as unstable, sexually violent, and given to drinking. Blacks' incomplete intellectual development made them unable to absorb but a small portion of reason and civilization. With similar preconceptions, Nina Rodrigues denied indigenous peoples the possibility of assimilating into Brazilian culture. Through centuries of colonial domination, they had degraded to the lowest denominator, becoming indolent, sexually promiscuous, and devoid of ambition. Marked by race, black and Indian "barbarism" could not be abated by the work of missionaries, educators, or the military. Consequently, concluded Nina Rodrigues, it was more convenient to declare blacks and Indians to be not responsible for their crimes than to attempt to integrate them into the social and political life of the Republic.[45]

*Mestiços* and mulattoes, the population that grew after centuries of miscegenation between blacks, Indians, and Portuguese, combined the worst features of the original races. The indolence, apathy, and improvidence characteristic of the *brasileiros* could be attributed to the effects of miscegenation.[46] If this was so, their penal treatment should be different from that of whites, for no degree of penalty could modify the inherited traces of *mestiços* and mulattoes. *Mestiços'* impulsiveness accounted for the prevalence of violent crimes in regions less affected by European immigration. Mulattoes' defective work energy served to explain the slack development of a labor market in areas recently liberated from slavery. How could the cellular prison with compulsory labor, asked Nina Rodrigues, change these inherited propensities?

In *As raças humanas*, race becomes the principal explication for the violent and uncivilized behavior of the lower classes. Consequently, the question of "social defense" hinges upon the selection of an appropriate racial policy.[47] Unchecked by a racially selective penal policy, crime would grow exponentially. To prevent this development, Nina Rodrigues recommended the enactment of distinct penal codes according to the racial composition of each region. Southern Brazil, with its white immigrant population, could not receive the same penal treatment as the Northeast, with its predominantly *mestiço* population. Penal responsibility should be lower among the latter and null in areas with a predominantly pure black or Indian population.[48] Without such an accentuated racism, Bevilaqua reached similar conclusions from his analysis of crime statistics in Ceará. He found *pardos* (mulattoes), *caboclos* and *cabras* (mixed black and Indian), and *pretos* (blacks) leading the ranking of all crimes. Quite naturally, he attributed this situation to the negative effects of miscegenation. Direct descendants of Europeans showed less tendency to criminal behavior than the descendants of blacks and Indians. This was not entirely due to biological causes. Besides inheritance, other factors contributed to the reproduction of criminal tendencies, most notably, ignorance, alcoholism, and the heritage of slavery.[49] Only a short step separated race from class; indeed, in postslavery society race became an important dimension of class. The same propensities that Nina Rodrigues attributed to the mixed races constituted for Afrânio Peixoto the "psychological features" proper to the lower classes: impulsiveness, improvidence, falsehood, vanity, and cowardice.[50]

The construction of criminality in northern Brazil showed the specificity of social control in a predominantly rural nation. Here the "struggle for life" centered on man's relationship to nature, not on economic competition or open social conflict. This explained why the Brazilian peasantry showed less propensity to criminal activity than the industrial proletariat of Europe. Occasionally, disaffection emerged in the form of rebellions and banditry, putting additional strain on the Republic's political order. These outbursts also revealed the peasants' dependence on meager natural resources and the vagaries of weather. In northeastern Brazil the social question had more to do with environmental conditions and the racial composition of the population than with the dual development of civilization and misery proper to industrial societies.

In the cities, the social question was of a different nature. While the crimes of the *mestiço* population and the peasantry of the *sertão*, the arid interior of the Brazilian Northeast, differentiated Brazil from the industrial nations in the question of social control, the issue of collective crime showed the common concern of Brazilian and European criminologists with modern forms of working-class protest. Collective crimes (*crimes das multidões*) presented criminologists with the problem of how to attribute penal responsibility. More important, they provided an open door into the question of urban social protest, the increasing power of workers' associations, and the influence of anarchism.

Nina Rodrigues in his work *La Folie des foules* (1901) studied the phenomenon of crowd suggestion, arguing that in conditions of collective exaltation individuals lost their discernment and consciousness and acted only on reflex. Being only *turbas neuróticas* (neurotic mobs), they required no special punitive theory. Evaristo de Moraes, a renowned criminologist, disagreed with this position. In his *Psicologia dos crimes coletivos* (1905), he recommended two solutions for collective crimes: either the crowd should be considered an extenuating circumstance during the trial, or a new category should be added to the penal code to consider this type of crime. Collective crimes, according to Moraes, deserved reduced penalties. As an expression of popular discontent and resistance to the illegitimate use of authority, they involved limited violence and no criminal intent.[51] Bevilaqua contributed a more sophisticated explanation of crowd behavior and penal responsibility. Group suggestion, he argued, affected differently the members of a crowd. Some impressionable individuals committed crimes as a response to the enticement of agitators; others, already in the world of crime, found in the crowd a stimulant to action and a refuge. In the former case, penal responsibility should be less than in the latter.[52]

Criminologists made explicit the problem of crowd behavior: the need to identify authors of crime and to separate individual pathologies from the modern social question, that is, urban riots, workers' marches, and the like. Criminologists were quite aware of the growing influence of a modern industrial proletariat in urban Brazilian society. Moraes, very critical of the conditions of work and rights in the incipient factory sector, embraced the new branch of law directly related to the subject, the Direito Operário.[53] Other criminologists were also sympathetic to the rising labor movement. Bevilaqua, for example, considered "association" a legitimate form of workers' defense against the depredations of industrial society. The interest in modern urban protest contrasts, however, with the scarce attention devoted to the issue of anarchism, the ideology that marked working-class organizations and protest in the first two decades of the century.

The question of female criminality also attracted the attention of Brazilian criminologists. In an initial egalitarian posture, Tobias Barreto protested the unequal treatment women received under Brazilian law. Considered as weak and incapable under civil law, women were given full penal responsibility by the penal code. This Barreto found "anomalous" and "absurd."[54] But instead of defending the enactment of civil rights for women, the author argued for the extension of the principle of female incapacity (*fraqueza*) to the penal realm.[55] Barreto justified this position with the argument that women's insufficient education rendered them incapable of understanding the law (a similar argument, we should recall, was employed in relation to people of color). He asked, consequently, that women be equated with children and declared not responsible for their crimes.[56]

Hygienist Afrânio Peixoto also tackled the issue of female criminality. Contesting the Lombrosian thesis about the subject, he argued, "women do not show fewer criminal propensities than men; in domestic crimes they are our equals; moreover, many of the crimes which are proper to women (infanticide, abortion, and poisoning), being ignored, remain unreported and in impunity; this compensates for the fact that, in the street, where female relations are less active, they commit fewer numbers of crimes."[57] Prostitution, the other form of female criminality, stemmed from two causes: one biological, namely, a congenital mental insufficiency which made prostitutes incapable of constant work and susceptible to erotic incitations; the other social and economic, that is, the greater responsibility women had in raising children put them at a disadvantage in the labor market, forcing them to choose illegal means of earning a living. Peixoto found a double explanation for the smaller number of female crimes. First, the leniency of male judges and police officers toward female delinquents decreased attention to the issue. Second, the limited exposure of women to the social sphere, the terrain where the great "struggle for life" took place, reduced the opportunities women had to commit crimes.[58] Like the peasants of northeastern Brazil, who were intimately related to the land, women remained attached to the private world of family. Not surprisingly, their crimes appeared less threatening to the social order of the Republic and as marginal as those of northeastern peasants.

To Bevilaqua, female criminality was not a problem. From the study of statistics in Ceará he found that women committed 2 to 3 percent of all reported crimes, and most of these consisted of wounds (*lesões corporais*). Female crime was rather exceptional and nothing but the expression of the passionate nature of Brazilians.[59] Female sexuality, however, could represent a social danger. The unbound eroticism of Brazilian mulatto women preoccupied Nina Rodrigues. The sex appeal of the *mulata*, celebrated in popular poetry, threatened to dissolve male physical and moral strength. The *povo amoroso* (loving people) were already infested with this disease, validating with their superstitious beliefs the myth of the magical power of *mulatas*.[60] Similar themes pervaded the literature about prostitution. *Higienista* doctors, for whom the control of prostitution constituted a major concern, presented prostitutes as "degenerates" who exacerbated the innate morbid sexuality of the lower classes.[61]

Positivist criminology located female criminality in a separate domain. Grouped with children and indigenous peoples, women appeared as irrational beings devoid of penal responsibility. To criminologists, crimes committed at home and prostitution put women in a special compartment, grouped with degenerates and those who commit crimes of passion, not with the modern professional criminal class. This mirrored common male understandings about gender roles; the distinction between private and public, the contrast between productive and reproductive, the polarity between the struggle for life and the empire of feelings. On the other hand, female delinquents came to embody traits considered inimical to the progress of the Brazilian nation: the indolence, impulsiveness, sexual promiscuity, and improvidence common to the "inferior races" and the peasantry. Like discussions about civilization, race, and slavery, propositions about women and crime betray a concern for the peculiarity of Brazilians. Women often assume the characteristics of the *povo baixo* (lower classes); indeed, they remain an abstract category representing something else. As Barreto acknowledged, positivist science had yet to capture the true nature of women and, in particular, that of female delinquents.[62]

Positivist criminology served as an interpretive moment for the discussion of important contemporary social problems. A clear example of this can be found in the debate around the extension or restriction of penal responsibility. While trying to recommend changes to the Brazilian penal code, criminologists had to deal with issues of crucial importance to the social and political stability of the Republic: social protest, racial tensions, regional diversity, and gender inequality. Tobias Barreto demanded raising the age of penal responsibility for minors and making women not responsible for crimes. Fewer opportunities for education and social norms that discouraged self-assertion prevented Brazilian children from understanding the implications of the law. At fifteen, French children had already acquired the knowledge and capacity to live under norms; this could not be expected of children the same age living in northeastern Brazil.[63] In this way, the degree of civilization of a country or region entered the determination of penal responsibility. Concerning women, Barreto supported the extension of female *minoridade* (childlike status or condition) to the penal sphere. To justify this position, he constructed women as beings dominated by emotions. Nina Rodrigues added race to the debate on penal responsibility. While suggesting a reduction in the penal responsibility of *mestiços*, he generously ascribed propensities and characteristics to the different races, finally suggesting that the order of the Republic required the fragmentation and regionalization of the law. Looking at the "modern" side of the criminal problem, Bevilaqua and Peixoto tried to alleviate the penal responsibility of delinquents influenced by crowd suggestion.

### Interpreting the Social Question

On the question of prison reform itself, Brazilian positivists did not differ from their Argentine colleagues. Like Ingenieros, Barreto presented the law as the source of social organization and discipline while, at the same time, demanding an enhanced role for medicine.[64] Physicians and psychiatrists, Brazilian and Argentine criminologists prescribed, should take a greater role in the rehabilitation of prisoners; doctors and only doctors understood the scientific foundations of human passions.[65] The medicalization of crime implied accepting the separation between the discipline of the law and the discipline of the prison. The universal validity of the law contrasted with the individual treatment of prisoners, precisely because criminal behavior could be reduced to an individual pathological dimension. Thus, the diagnosis and treatment of crime, of its social production, was reduced to the analysis of individual cases. The individual delinquent provided both a territory of professional intervention and a laboratory for social policy.

But if conceptions about crime, law, and medical power unified criminologists in Argentina and Brazil, attempts to adjust the theory to national characteristics introduced important variants in criminological discourse. Due to the "racial question," Brazil could not simply replicate methods of social control successfully applied in Europe and the United States. This was particularly true in relation to the penitentiary; the racial composition of the working classes made criminologists distrustful of the possibility of reforming delinquents through confinement and labor. Nina Rodrigues, for example, was convinced that the penitentiary was incapable of rehabilitating delinquents belonging to the "inferior race." Schools must first try to assimilate *mestiços* to white European culture before institutions of confinement could succeed.[66]

His Argentine colleagues, on the other hand, trusted that an adequate classification and diagnosis of inmates could produce true regeneration (of those who fitted the "reformable" types).

Even a staunch advocate of penitentiary reform like Souza Bandeira found that the passivity of the inmates at the penitentiary of São Paulo reflected more a superficial adaptation to rigid institutional rules than a true transformation of prisoners' attitudes and beliefs. Almeida Vale, an earlier reformer, expressed similar doubts about the Casa de Correção's ability to change prisoners of "vile origins" who lacked education. Those sentenced to short terms, mainly people without occupation, walked out of the prison without any change in their habits.[67] Other reformers resorted to environmental differences between Brazil and industrial Europe to justify the ineffectiveness of penitentiary discipline. Deputy Lobato's intervention is illustrative: "Here in Brazil, in this fertile land, in this pleasant climate, where nobody dies because of cold weather, where nobody dies of hunger, in this land where wild fruits supply enough food . . . I do not see the need to regulate our prisons by the same rules [as in Europe, with its paupers and its rigorous weather]."[68] A system of discipline, according to Lobato, should correspond to the nature of a country's laboring classes; in Brazil harshness and strictness would not yield modern work habits and submission to the law.

Doubts about the applicability of methods of punishment and discipline designed in racially homogeneous societies to a country like Brazil led positivists to betray some basic principles of positivist criminology. The legacy of slavery and the inherited traits of the "mixed races" added fuel to this skepticism. Before abolition, Souza Bandeira, while chastising the Brazilian penal code for its backwardness in the face of modern criminology, was ready to accept the continuity of the use of shackles and forced labor on the roads when the condemned were slaves. To slaves, he reasoned, the penitentiary must look like a place of relief. In some cases he even justified the use of capital punishment based on the argument that without that resource it would be very difficult to maintain order in a racially mixed society. He could quote Herbert Spencer in support of this argument: "for a civilized man, the fear of prolonged and monotonous discipline, like that reserved for delinquents, is enough; for those less civilized, it will be necessary to resort to corporal punishment and to death."[69]

Criminologists writing after abolition did not have to engage in this kind of defense, but they could resort to the "superstitious" nature of the northeastern peasantry, to the racial composition of the *povo baixo*, or to the sensual nature of its female component to throw into doubt the effectiveness of the reformatory model. In this regard, Peixoto was an exception; for him, modern methods of punishment were universal: "all progress lies in abolishing the death penalty, in regularizing work, in individualizing penalties, in allowing freedom within conditions of vigilance and commitment, and, finally, in replacing small penalties for fines paid through work and for suspended sentences." A hygienist, Peixoto combined the humanist argument against brutal punishment with the notion of hygiene characteristic of modernity: healthful prisons and healthy bodies were necessary requirements for individual reform.[70] Holding on to the universal principles of penology, Peixoto could not support a different treatment according to race. Closer than others to the workers' question, his conception anticipated a "modern" class vision of Brazilian society, less dependent on race: a disciplined and hygienic city reminiscent of Foucault's "carceral archipelago."

Drawing from the same resources (the theory of positivist criminology and the practice of North American and European penitentiaries), Brazilian and Argentine criminologists constructed different imaginaries about the dangers facing their societies. Argentine criminologists, concerned with problems of urban crime, contributed new understandings about the predominantly immigrant working class and its activities. Separating two ideal worlds, those of crime and labor, they called attention to the ease with which immigrants and their children could lose the "love of work." This was in itself an interesting interpretation of the social problems associated with Argentina's incorporation into the world market. The economic cycles of the beef and cereal economy expelled and attracted the labor force in an erratic fashion, increasing the problems of urban crime and the strength of working-class organizations. Traits inimical to a growing export economy—indolence, drinking, informality, and tolerance of theft—found an explanation in the "fall" from one world to the other. Immigrants represented a threat to the extent that they embodied attitudes and habits that prepared them insufficiently for the struggle for life, an exhausting struggle under a highly fluctuating labor market.

The conquest of the "frontier" (the extermination of Native Americans in the 1879 war) shifted the line demarcating civilization and barbarism to the interior of the city. Controlling the urban, mainly immigrant poor was similar to the problem of industrialized countries. Now that medical and criminological sciences provided the methods for distinguishing types of delinquent personalities from the mass of people, the social territory of the city could be made controllable with appropriate policies. The penitentiary, to be sure, was only a moment within an integral response to the problem of crime. Other solutions included child and female reformatories, *patronatos* (a type of halfway house) for ex-convicts, moral education, and the extension of state responsibilities toward the poor. The composition of the working class in Argentina, given the homogeneity of the immigrant flow, made the penitentiary idea feasible: those who had lost the love of work could be recycled into the world of wage labor; those who were already "professionals" of crime had to remain in confinement. The state, through its institutions, had to extend persuasion across society, particularly among those at risk of becoming criminals.

In Brazil, on the other hand, criminologists discovered a threatening reality in both cities and countryside. The possibility of peasant rebellions and banditry aided by droughts and adverse economic cycles represented a permanent danger to the stability of the Republic. In the cities, the *povo baixo*, composed of mixed races, showed both the premodern traits of indolence, apathy, and improvidence and the modern, collective forms of expressing discontent (riots and workers' protests). Race served to "explain" many of the "inherited" traits of the lower classes, but other factors, namely "crowd suggestion," intervened in the explication of modern urban protest. Women, a repository of the premodern attitudes of peasants and "inferior races," constituted no threat to the social order of the Republic. Immigrant labor, key to the renovation of the coffee economies of the south-central region, was also marginal to criminologists' discourse. Notably, criminologists failed to consider the crimes that concerned those in charge of enforcing order. Contemporary police reports constantly refer to the threat of *capoeiras* (street fighters) and *vagabundos* (vagrants), to the danger that abandoned children would join either of these two groups of outlaws, and to the demoralizing influence of prostitutes and gamblers.[71] In São Paulo, the "immigrant threat" constituted a central motif of police reports during this period.[72]

Regional differences in criminality—hence in economic and social development ("civilization") and in the possibilities for assimilation—referred immediately to the environment, race, and the economy. Brazilian positivists, more aware of the diversity of the working classes and their responses to "progress," presented a fragmented view of their country's criminality. The problems posed by the *mestiço* peasantry of the Northeast were different from those created by ex-slaves in the centers of coffee production. The cyclical growth of regional export economies—sugar, coffee, rubber—produced increasing income differentials between regions, creating the conditions for massive human migrations. The rubber industry, which attracted the population of neighboring states to Amazônia, was a clear example of the social costs of readjustment to conditions in the world market. The Northeast became a center of banditry and peasant revolts. In the 1890s the movement of coffee to new lands in the South also provoked tensions: abandoned plantations, idle hands, and racial violence. How to control peasant reactions to the cycles of export growth; how to assimilate those marked by slavery into the culture of work and thrift; how to reform the preindustrial habits and attitudes of a mixed-race, mobile proletariat became crucial challenges to the stability of the Republic.

Doubts and reservations about the effectiveness of individual reformation within the penitentiary show the work of race in Brazilian perceptions of the social question. Unlike Argentine reformers, who confronted a relatively homogeneous working class, Brazilian reformers found difficulties in imagining Amazonian Indians, northeastern *mestiços*, and black Paulista laborers subject to the same disciplinary system. Race colored positivists' perceptions of workers and influenced their ideas about social control. Some authors like Peixoto remained at the margins of the movement, precisely because they imagined a penitentiary based on universal rules provided by a capitalist work ethic.

To the practitioners of positivist criminology, police stations provided a mass of statistics essential for depicting the peculiarities of criminality and its connection with broader social issues (immigration, family and childhood, poverty and unemployment, workers' activism, property and distribution). For those interested in an in-depth look at social problems, the penitentiary represented an inestimable source of information, a kind of laboratory for the observation of the pathologies of the social body. The use of this information, however, was subject to the interpretive framework imposed by the researcher. Clinical reports of inmates could produce insightful comments about the social or could reproduce prejudice. Two clinical views of inmates, drawn from the files of Ingenieros and Nina Rodrigues, present us with the explanation of the problem posed at the beginning of the essay: the pessimism of Brazilian reformers versus the optimism of their Argentine counterparts in the context of quite similar influences (internationally circulated knowledge about modern technologies of punishment and the nature and treatment of delinquents).

In his *Criminología*, José Ingenieros reported a case he encountered at the Penitenciaría Nacional of an Italian immigrant who had served several terms in prison, the last time on charges of fraud: "EB, Italian, fifty years of age and thirty-two of residence in this country, Catholic, twice married." At age fifteen he dropped out of school and abandoned his home in order to follow a prostitute. Circumstances led him to robbery and swindling, and later, already related to *malvivientes* (criminal elements), he became a habitual delinquent. Then Ingenieros added to the file: "He has had numerous occupations that do not require any technical knowledge, has held them with less and less regularity as he entered the *mala vida* and professional criminality. He is barely educated. His means of living have been fortuitous and circumstantial.

Strong inclinations toward vagrancy and lack of love for work. Neuropathic temperament, unstable behavior, personality maladjusted to his social environment."[73] EB represented the tensions created by an export economy with a fluctuating labor market and an immigrant work force with an insufficiently developed work ethic. His rehabilitation within the penitentiary was simply a matter of time.

Nina Rodrigues visited the penitentiary of Bahia in the mid-1890s. There he interviewed a minor, José d'Araujo, interned in the Casa de Correção since age nine for parricide and later transported to the penitentiary. José grew up in poverty (his father cultivated a small plot of land) without education and at an early age was sent to the city to work under a shoemaker. This job initiated him into a life of vice and degradation. Later he became "homosexual, gambler, drunkard, a human being totally demoralized." He was also a liar: José used to recount a false story about his crime until Nina Rodrigues, using hypnosis, extracted from him the truth. At the penitentiary he added more crimes to the list, receiving repeated disciplinary actions; the administrator proved unable to reform him. According to the author, José was a *criminal nato* (born criminal). His lack of piety, his moral insensitivity, and his falseness were sufficient evidence. His passage to crime stemmed not from the vagaries of the labor market but from the inherited traits proper to his race. "He is a *pardo* in whom the features of mulatto and *mameluco* [a mixture of white and Indian] are perfectly combined."[74] The observer's apparent objectivity foundered in the face of racial stereotypes. As a result, individual treatment within the penitentiary promised few results. José was irreformable.

## Conclusions

In Brazil and Argentina at the turn of the century, the penitentiary project generated modern institutions of confinement that helped to present the "modernity" of both countries at a time when their economies were being more thoroughly integrated into the world economy. In both countries, initiatives for reforming prisons proceeded in various waves, each with phases of enthusiasm and disillusionment. The 1830s signaled the arrival of the penitentiary idea in Brazil, the 1860s and 1870s saw another reformist push, and the 1890s marked the beginning of a prolonged effort to modernize prison facilities, stimulated no doubt by abolition, the transition to a republican government, and the influence of the new criminology. In Argentina a late start fraught with difficulties was compensated for in the first decade of the century with the modernization of the national penitentiary. Considered a model among Latin American prisons, as well as one of the symbols of the country's progress during the era of export-led growth, this institution served as a center of activities and propaganda for the new criminology and its findings.

In this chapter I have examined the evolution of the two countries' reform efforts in the context of contending discourses about the social. The impetus of earlier reform efforts in both countries had dwindled under the obstacle of dominant conceptions of the social order: the distinction between slaves and freedmen in one case, that between civilization and barbarism in the other. After 1890, the success of the penitentiary project rested upon a reconstruction of these conceptions. While influenced by the same intellectual currents, positivists in Argentina and Brazil constructed different imaginaries about the threats facing their societies. Brazilian criminologists paid more attention to the backwardness of the Northeast and the Amazon frontier, to the racial origins of the country's producers, and to the "passionate" nature of the *povo baixo* in their explanation of criminal behavior. Argentine criminologists, on the other hand, produced multiple ethnographies of immigrants, urban laborers, abandoned children, prostitutes, and all sorts of occupationally and socially marginal people in their attempt to draw the boundaries between the world of labor and the world of crime within the port city.

Race, class, and gender, articulated in different fashion, resulted in the construction of two distinct criminalities, two different social questions. Changes in the location of export production and the composition of the working class as well as the emergence of obstacles to "progress" in the form of urban workers' protests, peasant rebellions, and preindustrial work habits filtered through criminologists' discussions of crime, providing the bases for their perceptions of the social. Their visions of class, then, incorporated and interpreted a diversity of "inputs": imported disciplinary knowledge, the readjustment of society to export development, and the reformers' own biases about and prejudices against people of different races, genders, and classes.

Ultimately, the perceived "success" and "failure" of institutional reform were measured within this set of constructs or visions of class. In Brazil, despite the precocity of its initial adoption[75] and despite the country's recurrent efforts to replicate North American models in various capitals (Recife, Bahia, Rio de Janeiro), reformers remained pessimistic, skeptical about the efficacy of the penitentiary model to reform delinquents. Not so in Argentina, where Ingenieros, Ballvé, Ramos Mejía, Veyga, and other reformers saw their interventions as key to the rehabilitation and treatment of those who had entered the world of crime.

The optimism or pessimism invested in the rehabilitative project reflected the distinct appropriation of positivist criminology for the construction of visions of class. Brazilian criminologists' reliance on race as a meaningful category to explain uneven regional development, criminality, and peasant protest nurtured a widespread skepticism about the potential of the penitentiary to reform the habits and customs of the lower classes. Argentine criminologists, preoccupied with redrawing the boundaries between crime and honest labor within an urban working class deceptively homogeneous (in terms of race), considered the penitentiary an appropriate instrument for endowing the fallen and the endangered with the attributes of modern, industrial, honest labor; hence their pioneer efforts to diagnose and individually treat the cases confided to their care. Thus, the distinction between Ingenieros's "psychopathology" of delinquency and Nina Rodrigues's "racial anthropology" depicted the difference—constructed at the interior of criminological discourse—between, on the one hand, the "propensities" of a *mestiço* peasantry marked by the heritage of slavery and Indian-white miscegenation and, on the other, an immigrant, urban working class. Not surprisingly, then, Brazil's Instituto de Regeneração, embodying the disciplinary model pioneered by Ingenieros, was established in an area of industrialization and European immigration at a time when the views of the more progressive criminologists (Peixoto, Moraes) replaced the racial determinism of Nina Rodrigues with the new utopia of racial democracy.

The analysis and narrative implied in this chapter is an illustration of what we have called an "interpretive social history" of prisons and disciplinary projects.[76] At stake is the question of interpretation, translation, and reception of disciplinary ideas, for the same punitive knowledge (the reformatory project embodied in the penitentiary and the clinical-taxonomical project of positivist criminology) served to derive quite distinct implications about social policy. As I have tried to show, studying the discourse of prison reformers and criminologists as an interpretive enterprise about the social (the constitution of class, race, gender) can provide additional answers to questions about the relationship between elite conceptions of punishment and discipline and those articulated by professionals or experts.[77] Professional language produces useful social constructions which, in the proper power context, can lead to the ideological reconstruction of class, gender, and race relations.

This investigation also raises questions about the functionality of prison reform as a class project of social control. European and North American historians have underscored the importance of modes of production, social structures, and labor markets for the rise of the penitentiary.[78] Similar associations have been found in the export economies of late-nineteenth-century South America. The view that a given social formation is consistent with certain forms of punishment and imprisonment is still dominant in the literature.[79] This view overlooks the process of adaptation and diffusion of disciplinary ideas as an important determinant of institutional changes. The penitentiary was after all the embodiment of a certain philosophy of punishment developed in Europe and the United States. Latin American reformers borrowed the idea wholesale, but in order to persuade state officials or congresses to devote funds to it, they had to connect it to perceived threats in the domestic social system. This required interpretation.

The same was true of scientific criminology. Rather than a universal recipe, it was a set of analytical tools to observe, classify, experiment with, and diagnose the problems of a given social reality. It provided a language within which criminologists could find new significations to old questions or reaffirm the validity of traditional conceptions and social practices. As a system of significations, positivist criminology resembled an ideology, a group of enunciations capable of transforming social fears and sentiments into more persuasive forms of meaning and social action. If this is so, reformers' contributions should be evaluated not so much for the degree to which their prisons replicated model institutions overseas but by the way they interpreted the social makeup and tensions of their own societies.

## Notes

1. The notion of an interpretive system is borrowed from Clifford Geertz, "Ideology as a Cultural System," in *The Interpretation of Cultures: Selected Essays* (New York: Basic Books, 1973).

2. "Criminology, Prison Reform, and the Buenos Aires Working-Class, 1900–1920," *Journal of Interdisciplinary History* 23, no. 2 (autumn 1992): 279–299.

3. J. Carlos García Basalo, *Historia de la Penitenciaría de Buenos Aires 1869–1880* (Buenos Aires: Servicio Penitenciario Federal, 1979), p. 43.

4. J. Carlos García Basalo, "Ballvé, Penitenciarista," *Revista Penal y Penitenciaria* 20 (1957): 48.

5. José Ingenieros, *Criminología* (Madrid: D. Jorro, 1913). For references to the general plan of social defense, see pp. 240–268.

6. While the penitentiary idea was extended to a few farm colonies, reformatories, and prisons in the country, most institutions remained untouched by the winds of reform before 1930.

7. Pedro Consiglio, "Los vagabundos," *Archivos de Psiquiatría y Criminología* 10 (1911); José Ingenieros, "Los niños vendedores de diarios y la delincuencia precoz," *Archivos de Psiquiatría, Criminología y Medicina Legal* 7 (1908); and Francisco de Veyga, *Los lunfardos: psicología de los delincuentes profesionales* (Buenos Aires: Talleres Gráficos de la Penitenciaría Nacional, 1910).

8. Eusebio Gómez, *La mala vida en Buenos Aires* (Buenos Aires: J. Roldán,

1908); and Antonio Dellepiani, *El idioma del delito* [1894] (Buenos Aires: Los Libros del Mirasol, 1967).

9. Luis M. Drago, *Los hombres de presa* (Buenos Aires: Félix Lajouane, 1886); and Carlos Moyano Gacitúa, *La delincuencia argentina ante algunas cifras y teorías* (Córdoba: F. Domeneci, 1905).

10. See Francisco de Veyga, *Los auxiliares de la delincuencia* (Buenos Aires: Talleres Gráficos de la Penitenciaría Nacional, 1910), and *Los lunfardos*.

11. The term is borrowed from Ezequiel Gallo and Roberto Cortés Conde, *La república conservadora* (Buenos Aires: Paidós, 1972).

12. See Carl Solberg, *Immigration and Nationalism: Argentina and Chile, 1890–1914* (Austin: University of Texas Press, 1970). For a different perspective, see Eduardo A. Zimmermann, "Racial Ideas and Social Reform: Argentina, 1890–1916," *Hispanic American Historical Review* 72, no. 1 (February 1992): 23–46. At a certain point, during the Semana Trágica of 1919, racial prejudices against Jews united with a new political myth to produce a hated character, the Russian maximalist agitator. It could be argued, however, that the fear of ideological "epidemic" in the context of a debilitated social body (and not race) provided the impetus for this construction. In fact, criminologists had been analyzing the "anarchist," not so much as a form of inherited characteristic but as a predominantly "moral anomaly."

13. Graciela Vivalda and Gabriela Dalla Corte, "La mujer y el asilo del Buen Pastor en Rosario, 1898–1911," paper presented to the "Jornadas sobre los Trabajadores en la Historia del Siglo XX," Fundación Simón Rodríguez, Buenos Aires, 1991.

14. In fact, both socialists and hygienists contributed to the legalization and regimentation of this profession, expanding the state's power of surveillance over prostitutes. See Donna Guy, "White Slavery, Public Health, and the Socialist Position on Legalized Prostitution in Argentina, 1913–1936," *Latin American Research Review* 23, no. 3 (1988): 60–80. See also by the same author, "Prostitution and Female Criminality in Buenos Aires, 1875–1937," in Lyman L. Johnson, ed., *The Problem of Order in Changing Societies: Essays on Crime and Policing in Argentina and Uruguay, 1750–1940* (Albuquerque: University of New Mexico Press, 1990), pp. 89–115.

15. See Roberto P. Korzeniewickz, "Labor Unrest in Argentina, 1887–1907," *Latin American Research Review* 24, no. 3 (1989): 71–92. Luis A. Romero suggests that during this period, workers, united by a common condition of job instability and crowded living conditions, assumed a "contestatory" identity vis-à-vis the state. See Romero, "Buenos Aires, 1880–1950: política y cultura de los sectores populares," *Cuadernos Americanos* 2, no. 14 (1989): 31–45. On the influence of "workerist" ideologies, see Hobart Spalding, *La clase trabajadora argentina* (Buenos Aires: Hachette, 1970); José Ratzer, *Los marxistas argentinos del 90* (Córdoba: Pasado y Presente, 1969); Jorge Solomonoff, *Ideologías del movimiento obrero y conflicto social* (Buenos Aires: Proyección, 1972); and Iaacov Oved, *El anarquismo y el movimiento obrero argentino* (Mexico City: Siglo XXI, 1978). On the connection between immigration and the labor movement, see Samuel S. Baily, "The Italians and Organized Labor in the United States and Argentina, 1880–1910," *International Migration Review* 1, no. 3

(summer 1967): 56–66. On elite responses to immigration and the "social question," see Solberg, *Immigration and Nationalism in Argentina and Chile*.

16. On criminologists' views of anarchist activity, see Patricio Geli, "Los anarquistas en el gabinete antropométrico: anarquismo y criminología en la sociedad argentina del 900," *Entrepasados* 2, no. 2 (1992): 7–24.

17. As Patricia Aufderheide has suggested, "the notion of individual rehabilitation was impractical in this seignorial society . . . The greatest difficulty surrounded the role of a penal institution that emphasized the value of work in a society where manual labor was the mark of poverty, racial discrimination, and enslavement." Aufderheide, "Order and Violence," pp. 310, 336.

18. Thomas E. Skidmore, "Racial Ideas and Social Policy in Brazil, 1870–1940," in Richard Graham, ed., *The Idea of Race in Latin America* (Austin: University of Texas Press, 1990), pp. 7–36.

19. Upon the masters' request, prisons accepted slaves for "correction" without the need of any judicial decision. Aufderheide, "Order and Violence," pp. 324–328, 330–331.

20. That is, confinement and work for all, rehabilitation based on work and isolation, individuation of treatment, and moral transformation.

21. Aufderheide, "Order and Violence," pp. 62–68.

22. Juan Silva Riestra, "La cárcel modelo de São Paulo," *Archivos de Medicina Legal e Identificação* 6, no. 13 (June 1936).

23. Earlier in the new century, reforms extended to the penitentiary of Fernando de Noronha, a facility that, having served as a center for political exiles, became the example of individualized treatment and persuasive discipline.

24. Moraes, *Prisões*, pp. 47–55.

25. For the impact of abolition on Brazilian society, see Rebecca J. Scott et al., *The Abolition of Slavery and the Aftermath of Emancipation in Brazil* (Durham and London: Duke University Press, 1988).

26. For the relationship between the coffee export economy and the industrialization waves in the south-central region, see João M. Cardoso de Mello and Maria da Conceição Tavares, "The Capitalist Export Economy in Brazil, 1884–1930," in Roberto Cortés Conde and Shane Hunt, eds., *The Latin American Economies: Growth and the Export Sector* (New York: Holmes and Meier, 1985), pp. 82–136. The effects of the crisis of the sugar economies were studied in Peter L. Eisenberg, *The Sugar Industry in Pernambuco, 1840–1910* (Berkeley and Los Angeles: University of California Press, 1974).

27. Faced with the abandonment of plantations and the refusal to work in them by many ex-slaves, planters' prejudices shifted to the freedmen: portrayed as ignorant, indolent, and habituated to tutelage, "indigenous workers" were considered unsuitable for the new economy. Stein, *Vassouras*, p. 266. See also George Reid Andrews's essay in Scott et al., *The Abolition of Slavery*.

28. The classic work in this regard is Warren Dean's *The Industrialization of São Paulo, 1880–1945* (Austin: University of Texas Press, 1969). For a more recent account of industrialization, see Nathaniel H. Leff, *Underdevelopment and Development in Brazil*, vol. 1 (London: Allen & Unwin, 1982); and Zélia Cardoso de Mello, *Metamorfoses de riqueza: São Paulo 1845–1895* (São Paulo: UCITEC, 1985). See also Flávio R. Versiani, "Industrial Development in an

'Export Economy': The Brazilian Experience before 1914," *Journal of Development Economics* 7, no. 3 (1980): 307–329. For a revisionist account, negating the connection between export-growth and industrialization, see João H. Lima, *Café e indústria em Minas Gerais (1870–1920)* (Petrópolis: Vozes, 1981).

29. Adjusting Brazilian penitentiaries to the standards established in the 1870 penitentiary congress at Cincinnati demanded the efforts of a new type of reformer and a context in which their visions of class could be shared by broad segments of the ruling class.

30. For a history of the reformatory model, see William J. Forsythe, *The Reform of Prisoners, 1830–1900* (New York: St. Martin's Press, 1987).

31. See Moacyr B. de Souza, *A influência da escola positiva no direito penal brasileiro* (São Paulo: Editorial Universitária de Direito, 1982); and Teodolindo Castiglione, *Lombroso perante a criminologia contemporânea* (São Paulo: Ed. Saraiva, 1962).

32. Tobias Barreto de Menezes, *Menores e loucos em direito criminal* (Rio de Janeiro: Laemert, 1884), pp. 117–119, 160.

33. The "Recife School," which had among its main exponents Barreto, Bevilaqua, Sílvio Romero, and Martins Júnior, was a reaction against crude positivism and spiritual eclecticism, two doctrines justifying the presence of a strong state. See Ricardo Vélez Rodríguez, "La historia del pensamiento filosófico brasileño (siglos XVII a XIX): problemas y corrientes," *Revista Interamericana de Bibliografía* 35, no. 3 (1985): 279–288.

34. Clovis Bevilaqua, *Criminologia e direito* [1896] (Rio de Janeiro: Ed. Rio, 1983), pp. 11–17.

35. Brazilian criminologists were aware of—and admired—both the reforms at the Buenos Aires penitentiary and Ingenieros's works. De Souza, *A Influência da escola positiva*, chap. 3; and Castiglione, *Lombroso perante a criminologia contemporânea*, chap. 23.

36. Antonio H. Souza Bandeira Filho, "A questão penitenciária no Brasil," *O Direito* 31 (May 1881); and Joaquim de Almeida Leite, Jr., "Qual o melhor dos sistemas penitenciários conhecidos?," *O Direito* 11, no. 32 (December 1883).

37. Clovis Bevilaqua, *Estudos de direito e economia política* [1901] (Rio de Janeiro and Paris: H. Garnier, 1902), pp. 1–53.

38. Ibid., pp. 40–41.

39. Evaristo de Moraes, another prominent positivist also concerned with the "social question," blamed slavery for the servility and indolence of agricultural labor. Evaristo de Moraes, *A campanha abolicionista 1879–1888* [1924] (Brasília: Ed. Universitária de Brasília, 1986), pp. 312–314.

40. Bevilaqua, *Criminologia e direito*, pp. 63–68.

41. A minority, however, followed the opposite logic. In years of drought, the penury of unemployment and lack of food forced them to join groups of bandits plundering the *sertão*. Ibid., p. 79.

42. Ibid., pp. 69, 74–77.

43. An alternative explanation of social conflict in the Northeast can be found in Hamilton de Mattos Monteiro, *Crise agrária e luta de classes (o nordeste brasileiro entre 1850 e 1889)* (Brasília: Horizonte, 1980). For an examination of the vision and organization of millenarian rebellions in the

Northeast, see Todd A. Diaccon, "Peasants, Prophets, and the Power of a Millenarian Vision in Twentieth-Century Brazil," *Comparative Studies in Society and History* 32, no. 3 (July 1990).

44. Raymundo Nina Rodrigues, *As raças humanas e a responsabilidade penal no Brasil* [1894] (Bahia: Liv. Progresso, 1957), pp. 105–124.

45. Ibid., p. 119.

46. Ibid., pp. 126–134.

47. Ibid., pp. 161–201.

48. Ibid., pp. 175–179. Like Bevilaqua, Nina Rodrigues was particularly intrigued by millenarian peasant rebellions. He devoted his analysis of "collective hysteria" to the study of Antônio Conselheiro and his followers at Canudos, and his study of the rebellion had a great influence on Euclides Da Cunha's *Rebellion in the Backlands*. Skidmore, "Racial Ideas and Racial Policy," p. 11.

49. Lack of elementary education increased inequalities among the races and prevented the understanding of legal norms. The experience of racial violence under slavery predisposed "people of color" to adopt violence as a natural form of expression. Alcoholism only exacerbated these tendencies. Bevilaqua, *Criminologia e direito*, pp. 91–98.

50. Afrânio Peixoto, *Psico-patologia forense* (São Paulo and Rio de Janeiro: Francisco Alves, 1916), p. 44.

51. Elias de Oliveira, *Criminologia das multidões*, 2d ed. (São Paulo: Ed. Saraiva, 1966), pp. 182–186.

52. Bevilaqua, *Criminologia e direito*, pp. 49–51. Afrânio Peixoto expressed the same need to allocate different penal responsibilities to leaders and followers. This could be done by contrasting each individual's degree of temerity with the interpsychological state of the crowd. Peixoto, *Psico-patologia forense*, pp. 151–156.

53. His writings about crowds were clearly influenced by the Vintem Riot of Rio de Janeiro, January 1880. Evaristo de Moraes, *Apontamentos de direito operário* [1905] (São Paulo: LTR, 1971).

54. Barreto, *Menores e loucos*, pp. 73–75.

55. Barreto wrote: "en quanto a mulher não tiver, como o homen, o direito de subir a tribuna, ella não debe ter igualmente com elles, nas mesmas proporcões que elles, o direito de subir ao cadafalso." Ibid., p. 94.

56. His defense of female *minoridade* was rooted in common stereotypes about the opposite sex. Women were less rational and more emotional than men. "A roupa de festa das grandes emoções, dos sentimentos elevados, ella não espera os momentos solemnes e dramáticos para vestir-la; viste-a diariamente. O homen, quando ama, ainda tem tempo de trabalhar, ou de dar o seu passeio, ou de fumar o seu cigarro; não assim, porem, a mulher, que nesse estado não tem tempo de pensar em outra cousa senão no seu amor." Ibid., p. 97. Their constant dedication to emotions hampered their ability to know and interpret the moral message embedded in the penal code. Men, on the contrary, were capable of separating reason from passion.

57. Peixoto, *Psico-patologia forense*, p. 99.

58. Ibid., p. 140.

59. Bevilaqua, *Criminologia e direito*, pp. 97–98.

60. Nina Rodrigues, *As raças humanas*, pp. 146–147.

61. Margareth Rago, *Do cabaré ao lar: a utopia da cidade disciplinar* (Rio de Janeiro: Paz e Terra, 1987), pp. 85–95.

62. Barreto acknowledged the lack of scientific studies about female psychology and suggested the foundation of a *gyneco-psychología* based on positivist principles. Barreto, *Menores e loucos*, p. 96.

63. "If a French youth of fifteen is not responsible [for a crime] how can a poor *matutinho* of the same age be, if his best education consists of extending his hand to ask the blessing of older persons, particularly the parish priest and the colonel owner of the land where his father cultivates manioc?" Ibid., p. 56.

64. "Law is the discipline of the social forces, an irresistible force in the sense of the romantic penal theory, an indispensable force. The social forces of which law is the discipline are precisely men and their passions." Ibid., p. 176.

65. Barreto recommended the establishment of medical courts with the power to evaluate penal questions related to their area of competence. "It is the physicians' competence, and only theirs, to evaluate the normal or abnormal state in the physical-psychic constitution of criminals." Ibid., p. 153.

66. Nina Rodrigues, *As raças humanas*, p. 199.

67. See Bretas's essay, chapter 4, this volume; and Moraes, *Prisões*, p. 20.

68. Brasil, Cámara dos Deputados, *Anaes 1856* (Rio de Janeiro, 1875), 3: 181.

69. Souza Bandeira, "A questão penitenciária," pp. 34–38.

70. Peixoto, *Psico-patologia forense*, pp. 71–75.

71. Relatório do Chefe da Polícia da Corte, Anexo do Relatório da Ministério da Justiça, 1880–1881, pp. 6–9.

72. Boris Fausto, *Crime e cotidiano: a criminalidade em São Paulo (1880–1924)* (São Paulo: Ed. Brasiliense, 1984); and Guido Fonseca, *Crimes, criminosos e a criminalidade em São Paulo (1870–1950)* (São Paulo: Ed. Resenha Tributária, 1988).

73. Ingenieros, *Criminología*, p. 134.

74. Nina Rodrigues, *As raças humanas*, pp. 189–193.

75. The Casa de Correção was the first example in Latin America of a penitentiarylike institution.

76. See Salvatore and Aguirre's essay, chapter 1, this volume.

77. Criminologists might have captured a multitude of elite propositions about the social and political order (fears of slave insurrection, preoccupation with labor shortages, or concerns about the lack of integration of immigrant workers) and simply translated them into a professional language. It is also possible that criminologists' discourse followed a process of reading, critique, and adaptation of foreign ideas in relation to interpretive clues gathered within their own societies. In the latter case, the focus and the content of new debates got displaced toward new questions, new patterns of organization, and new significations.

78. In their influential work, Dario Melossi and Massimo Pavarini rooted the emergence of the penitentiary in the development of generalized labor brought about by industrialization. See *The Prison and the Factory: Origins of the Penitentiary System* (Totowa, N.J.: Barnes and Noble, 1981). If the penitentiary came to resemble the factory it was because the latter created new problems of social control that made confinement and reformation necessary. Similarly,

in his study of Pentonville, Michael Ignatieff related the rise of a new philosophy of punishment to the breakdown of labor discipline in agricultural and industrial districts of Britain. Ignatieff, *A Just Measure of Pain: The Penitentiary in the Industrial Revolution* (New York: Pantheon, 1978). Different modes of production required different methods of punishment, according to M. Hindus, who contrasted the rapid progress of penitentiary reform in Massachusetts with the persistence of corporal punishment and traditional prisons in South Carolina. Michael S. Hindus, *Prison and Plantation* (Chapel Hill: University of North Carolina Press, 1980).

79. In her important study of criminality in Northeast Brazil, Martha Huggins argued for a close correspondence between the penal and prison reform of the late nineteenth century and the elite's need for labor. The justice and penal system began to systematically apprehend and deliver suspected vagrants at times of labor crises in the export (sugar) economy. Martha K. Huggins, *From Slavery to Vagrancy in Brazil: Crime and Social Control in the Third World* (New Brunswick, N.J.: Rutgers University Press, 1985).

# 8. Confinement, Policing, and the Emergence of Social Policy in Costa Rica, 1880–1935

*Steven Palmer*

> *El penalista da paso al psiquiatra. . . . Ya no estamos ante un tribunal, estamos en plena clínica social.*
> — Luis Castro Saborío, "Examinando el código penal"[1]

In November 1884 a young law student, Cleto González Víquez, secured his title with a precocious dissertation entitled "Criminal Irresponsibility." He declared as belonging to the past the "vengeful and despotic state" and promoted its replacement by the "educator state, which sees in the criminal nothing more than an unfortunate lack of moral education." Upon the remains of the former punitive system of revenge, violence, and mutilation he foresaw the raising of a "majestic and tranquil penitentiary that receives, like a profoundly loving [amorosísima] mother, the wretches who have strayed from the path of duty."[2] During the same examination period, his fellow student, Ricardo Jiménez, also chose to discourse on penal law. In stressing the inadequacies of Costa Rica's system of "collective prisons," he too advocated the adoption of the penitentiary model, which, with its "individualized cellular system," could not help but deter recidivism by "awakening the conscience of the criminal" and isolating him from "moral contagion."[3]

These two young luminaries were to become the brightest stars in a constellation of ideologue politicians known derisively as El Olimpo, due to the detached arrogance and self-assured elitism they displayed in implementing Costa Rica's program of liberal reform, a project begun in the 1880s with which both young law students had already been apprenticed by the time they reaped accolades for their learned discourses of 1884.[4] By decade's end, they had become important members of the College of Law, the braintrust of the reform, and had served in the cabinet. In the 1890s Jiménez became president of the Supreme Court; González Víquez would occupy the same post somewhat later. Both were influential members of Congress and championed urban reform at the helm of San José's Municipal Council. Finally, between 1906 and

1936, González Víquez and Jiménez between them occupied the presidency of the Republic for twenty years, presiding over the consolidation and transformation of the reforms begun in the late nineteenth century.[5]

The story of police, prison, and legal reform in Costa Rica has yet to be written. This silence, only recently beginning to be broken, is rather surprising, given the lawyerly rather than military caste of the majority of those responsible for the design and construction of Costa Rica's liberal state model. As Patricia Badilla has recently noted, these lawyer-statesmen, who dubbed themselves "los sacerdotes de la patria" (the priests of the fatherland), displayed a messianic zeal in advancing a comprehensive, and often unpopular, program designed to further capitalism, reason, secular morality, and order in the liberal era.[6] The absence of scholarship on prison and police reform is perhaps a product of certain peculiarly Costa Rican historiographical obsessions stemming from the consensus over the basic trajectory of Costa Rica's liberal period. The long dictatorship of General Tomás Guardia (1870–1882) brought to a close the period of incessant coups effected by one or another of the competing clans within the coffee oligarchy and laid the foundations of the modern state. In its wake the country would become an oasis of relative civil continuity in Central America. After 1884, presidential succession was decided by elections, which, though invariably fraudulent, cemented alliances and established symbolic appearances that were crucial to the transactions that followed. These postelectoral negotiations among the oligarchs might include some armed skirmishing, but the end result was usually a relatively orderly transition. After 1890, these regular political contests also included an increasing amount of popular, and eventually some popular democratic, participation.[7]

Costa Rica's political historians continue to be influenced by a tradition that understands the origins of Costa Rican democracy in terms of the oligarchy's allegedly moderate and humanistic brand of liberalism, different from the radical positivist and social Darwinist liberalism of Costa Rica's neighbors.[8] The themes of coercion, policing, and punishment have tended to be associated with the problem of military dictatorship and thus have been dismissed as a Latin American problem all but alien to the development of Costa Rica's democratic polity. Concomitantly, historians have emphasized the diminishing importance of the military in Costa Rica's political affairs, especially after the brief Tinoco dictatorship of 1917 to 1919, which in turn is seen as an aberration from the general trend observable since the 1880s.[9] The law and its attendant institutions are seen as part of a judicial power that, however politicized and occasionally unjust, gradually normalized its operation more or less in step with the evolving electoral system and the extension of male suffrage.[10]

A second obstacle to serious consideration of policing and punishment has been built by a left-oriented historiography that has criticized the liberal state as a purely noninterventionist, classic model of laissez-faire, its directors unable and unwilling to confront the rising "social question" forced upon them, especially after 1920, by increasingly organized and militant working-class unions and political parties. In this conception, such issues were left effectively unaddressed until the great social reforms of 1940 to 1943 initiated by the government of Calderón Guardia, first pressured by, then in alliance with, the Costa Rican Communist Party.[11] The successful reform of primary education, begun in 1886, is seen to have been the only "positive" social intervention of the liberal state.

The presidency of Alfredo González Flores (1914–1917) is understood to have been an extremely premature, indeed perhaps stillborn, precursor of the Costa Rican welfare state. For the first time, the executive strongly criticized the laissez-faire ideal and proposed a series of economic reforms to try to alleviate, through "nationalist" development initiatives, the social misery brought on by the wartime recession. This effort ended in the notorious Tinoco dictatorship, supported by the major actors in the political class (including González Víquez and Jiménez). Although overthrown in 1919, *tinoquismo* is seen to have set the classical liberal ship of state firmly back on course during the 1920s and 1930s, though with the captains now looking nervously over their shoulders for signs of a possible mutiny among the petty officers and crew. As Mark Rosenberg summarizes the argument, prior to the social reforms of the 1940s, the leaders of the liberal state "demonstrated their ineptitude in terms of the development of a moderate policy, sponsored by the state, and designed to confront the multiple dislocations born of urbanization, growing unemployment, and economic instability."[12]

Any sign of the liberal state as initiator of a positivist social policy has been lost in the overlapping shadows cast by these two bodies of historiography. The shadows fall across the pages of a work written in 1913 by lawyer, criminologist, and legislator Luis Castro Saborío, an ardent reformer who was much less confused about the possible marriage of positivism and humanism than are current scholars of the liberal era and well aware that social policy need not be confused with socialism. In a series of articles concerning various aspects of criminology which occupied one entire issue of the Ateneo de Costa Rica's journal, he meditated on the modern role of penology and updated with Comte and Lombroso the Benthamite suppositions of the 1884 dissertation of his patron, Cleto González Víquez: "from the idea of vengeance, we move to that of recovery, and from that to the idea of social protection. Altruism has successfully imposed itself."[13]

Given the scarcity of modern historical writing on penitentiary and police reform in Costa Rica, the ambitions of this essay must remain modest.[14] What follows is based on the somewhat fragmentary evidence compiled to complement a study of cultural relations and differences within the working classes of San José. In researching a wave of heroin consumption among young artisans and prostitutes in San José in the late 1920s, I had to try to understand the origins and development of the police agencies, the prison system, and other state institutions which identified, apprehended, punished, and treated these young workers through recourse to a very generalized discourse of social hygiene and social protection.[15] In discussing the beginnings of a carceral plan, a criminological knowledge, and a judicial police in Costa Rica, I will try to show that these were crucial pieces of an embryonic social policy developed by positivist reformers working from the privileged, if not always powerful, position of a vanguard within the liberal state.

As Ricardo Salvatore has pointed out for the case of Buenos Aires, positivist criminology involved more than simply the offering of clinical advice for the rehabilitation of inmates. It also provided "the rhetorical devices and images within which the newly formed working class could be comprehended, classified, and ordered."[16] Costa Rican social reformers grasped theories and techniques of penology, criminology, sociology, public health, and child protection from an expanding international web of agencies and publications devoted to these matters and adapted them to the Costa Rican setting. This helped the liberal state, especially after 1910, to anticipate and define the social question rather than merely to respond to working-class agitation for social reform. That is, a social technology was self-consciously advanced not only to interfere with the growing coherence of the working classes as a community but also to provide the state with some ability to shape the morality and behavior of this community. I will also suggest that police and penitentiary were the central figures around which there began to proliferate, in a paradigmatic fashion, an apparatus of social protection and social hygiene. This is most obvious in the "scientization" of philanthropy and the development of public health institutions which occurred alongside of, and intertwined with, the reforms of prison and police. These must be understood as processes that complemented each other's concentration on the urban laboring classes, inculcating in them bourgeois perspectives on self-discipline, honest work, and moral and racial purity.

### The City of San José and Its Workers

San José began to assume an urban character in the 1850s. The political capital, it also lay in the heart of the richest coffee-producing lands of the

Central Valley. The most important members of the coffee oligarchy, often with *fincas* (coffee estates) close by, displayed their preeminence with increasingly sumptuous homes in the center of the city. San José became both provider and emblem of the trappings of bourgeois urbanity, with an expanding commercial service sector, a presidential palace, a legislature, theaters, hotels, paved streets, gas lamps, and sewer and water systems that were the minimum requisites of modernity. A second phase of development occurred during the final two decades of the nineteenth century with the connection of the capital to the completed Atlantic and Pacific railways, electrification, and a tramline as well as the creation of a national archive, national museum, national monument, national library, and—the crowning glory—a national theater into which a state and an oligarchy with pretensions to high civilization poured a significant amount of public money.[17]

In this, Costa Rica's *belle époque*, the city also acquired a new complexity. With the drainage of a swamp adjacent to the northern sector of the city center and the building of a pleasant park in its place, the oligarchy now shifted their residences to the exclusive sector on the northern side of the park, Barrio Amon. On the other end of the social spectrum, La Puebla, which had formerly been a slightly removed suburb to the south where the poorer folk lived, now expanded and began to link up with the city proper. The entire southern and western portion of San José began to assume a popular flavor: El Laberinto, El Paso de la Vaca, Hospital. Here, around the market, the hospital, and the insane asylum, working-class San José began to take shape. The penitentiary would be erected on its northernmost fringe.

In 1864 the city proper had a population of almost 9,000; by the census of 1892, this figure had slightly more than doubled to 19,000. Between the urban census of 1904 and the national census of 1927, the city's population again more than doubled, from 24,000 to 51,000.[18] The scale of urbanization is underscored by the fact that, as late as 1892, the city accounted for only 50 percent of the population of the Canton of San José, which included the outlying rural settlements, many of which marked the site of important coffee *beneficios* (processing centers), whereas by 1927, the streets of San José accounted for almost 80 percent of the bodies resident in the canton. Though the country as a whole remained overwhelmingly rural, and though San José's population of 50,000 seems rather provincial by comparison with the millions of the world's great metropolises, the city nonetheless accounted for 10.8 percent of the country's populace in 1927. This is comparable to the proportion of national population accounted for by Santiago and Havana and much higher than that accounted for by Mexico City, if still, of course, far from the extreme concentration of Argentina's peoples within its capital.[19]

Due to the ambiguity of the census data available for these years, it is not possible to tell what percentage of urban dwellers were artisans or proletarians and what percentage casual laborers. By 1927, however, there is a clear rise in the kinds of occupations characteristic of a casual labor sector: municipal peons, watchmen, messengers, shoeshiners, and lottery ticket, newspaper, fruit, and other street vendors (16 percent of the respondents from the Hospital quadrant, the most populous and poorest of San José, declared their workplace to be the street). The feminization of the labor process is also apparent in the growth of piecework done in the home and a rise in the number of nannies and domestic servants. The first three decades of the century gave rise to the world of the *pulpería* (corner store), the bar and billiard hall, the lunchroom, and the dancehall, which became the points of concentration of a new public space, and a new popular culture shared by skilled and unskilled laborers.[20] Mario Samper and Víctor Hugo Acuña have also demonstrated a process of proletarianization among formerly independent artisans during the first two decades of the century, whereby larger workshops consolidated and some small industry appeared.[21] The era also saw a process of partial proletarianization in the countryside, with large coffee estates initiating a period of expansion at the expense of many smallholders. This did not end a continued access to land for many wage laborers, and the agricultural frontier continued to absorb dispossessed peasants. Still, it produced some migration into the city, though many of these recent arrivals continued to return to the nearby coffee-growing areas during the harvest.[22]

Acuña has shown that though urban employees, skilled workers, and laborers never accounted for more than 15 percent of the country's economically active populace prior to 1930, their political weight acquired a significance far outweighing their numbers. This was due to their concentration in the capital city and to the efforts of the working class, especially after 1890, to band together in mutualist associations, guilds, and eventually unions and parties. It was also due to their strategic political and ideological position vis-à-vis the liberal state. Commercial employees and skilled workers were the first groups from among the popular classes to acquire literacy and to participate in the electoral competitions of the oligarchy. They initially sought sanction from the state for their mutualist organizations and backed particular candidates in elections in order to receive a minimum of influence in the running of political affairs. This, in turn, bestowed legitimacy on the oligarchic system.[23]

The first two decades of the century saw the spread of anarchist and socialist radicalism among some sectors of the urban working class, increasingly militant strike activity, and the formation of the

Confederación General de Trabajadores (General Confederation of Workers, CGT), culminating, in 1920, in a successful general strike over the eight-hour day. Though still largely moderate rather than revolutionary, urban workers increasingly defined themselves, culturally and institutionally, in class terms.[24] An embrace of broadly socialist ideals reached one threshold in 1923, with the CGT dissolving itself into the populist Partido Reformista of Jorge Volio, and a second at the beginning of the 1930s, with growing support among important sectors of the San José working class for the nascent Communist Party.[25] The tensions of the 1920s, though never reaching the point of rupture with the liberal order, complicated the symbiotic relationship between the oligarchy and urban workers. This is the general context within which the liberal program of social hygienization must be understood.

### Confinement

The regime of Tomás Guardia took the first systematic steps to modernize the punitive role of the state. The death penalty was eliminated, and the "scandalous" use of chain gangs for public works in and around San José was ended. In 1880 a new penal code was enacted. It was a virtual copy of the Chilean code of 1875 and would prove a source of discontent to reformers, especially after plans for the new penitentiary had been drawn up, since its regime of punishments failed to make provisions for this type of confinement. As Mayela Solano and Carlos Naranjo point out, the main autochthonous elements in the 1880 code concerned draconian punishments for crimes against agricultural property (the theft of coffee and cattle in particular).[26] Costa Rica was still riding the wave of an expanding coffee economy, and the state was charged with extending the frontiers of productive (and ideally export-oriented) land use. The intuitions of those in charge of penal planning during the Guardia regime therefore led to attempts to make criminals and other deviants agriculturally productive and, as a corollary, to banish them from the city.

In the early 1870s two penal colonies for those convicted of serious crimes were established at San Lucas and Coco, both islands off the Pacific coast. Lesser crimes could be punished by exile from the Central Valley and confinement to insalubrious frontier towns like Matina and Moin. The Vagrancy Law of 1878 destined itinerants for work on the railroad to the Atlantic, the obsession of the Guardia regime.[27] At the heart of the penal plan of this era was an assumption that agricultural labor was the path to national expansion and a bucolic faith in the power of the land to rejuvenate the detritus of urban society.[28]

In a sense this was Costa Rica's experiment with transportation as a principle of correction. Its kinship with European systems of transportation is underscored by the fact that Costa Rican authorities saw such penal outposts fulfilling a quasi-colonial mission by bringing savage land under production and, in the process, establishing effective national sovereignty over areas which were only part of Costa Rica on government maps. In 1876 Eusebio Figueroa, a senior advisor to Guardia, submitted a report on how best to maximize the benefits of the railroad to the Atlantic. He recommended establishing along the more remote sections of the line colonies that would be populated with criminals, vagrants, and the insane, along with their families. The government could then make land grants to large growers desirable by providing them a solution to the country's chronic shortage of labor. In time those confined to the colonies, by now rehabilitated by discipline and work, would receive plots of land with their freedom. Figueroa described the project as the realization of "Costa Rica's manifest destiny." In a bizarre conclusion, he imagined a figure of authority, possibly Guardia, explaining their imperial mission to these assembled social outcasts in the following terms: "To these groups full of faith and life [!] could be said that which Napoleon III said to the advance troops marching off to Cochinchina: Go in small numbers, but carry the flag behind which follows a great people."[29]

The advent to power of the zealously reforming liberals of the 1880s, however, marked a move toward articulating the centrality of the urban space in terms of both penitentiary and police reform. In 1885, attempting to put their theories into practice, Jiménez and González Víquez would participate in the raising of a public subscription to get the model penitentiary under way. The minister of justice, Ascención Esquivel, joined the chorus demanding the adoption of new penal techniques to morally regenerate the inmates.[30] In 1890 a young lawyer, Octavio Beeche, was dispatched to Europe to study penal architecture and procedures and to report on their applicability to Costa Rica. His findings were praised by the minister of justice, and the regime approved the building of a panoptic penitentiary close to the Palace of Justice. Overseeing the team of engineers charged with the drawing up of the plans was González Víquez.[31]

It is not yet possible to advance a precise explanation for this shift from a rural to an urban locus of correction. Solano and Naranjo have shown that the high hopes for the island colonies on Coco and San Lucas were dashed in fairly short order. The authorities had intended to make San Lucas self-sufficient by selling in Puntarenas the surplus from the harvests of convict labor. By the end of the 1880s they realized that the island's soil and rainfall were poor and the place was plagued by locusts. Convicts had to be fed by purchasing goods from the mainland at inflated prices, and the maintenance of the facility became increasingly expensive. Still, these depressing conclusions were apparently drawn after the initial liberal expression of an urgent need for a penitentiary, and Solano and Naranjo see the rise of interest in such a penitentiary as a further cause of the decline in attention paid to San Lucas, rather than the other way around.[32]

It is possible that the failure of the penal colony model was obvious to liberals earlier than the late 1880s. There may, however, be more important reasons for the genesis of this obsession with the city in general and the penitentiary in particular. On top of the fact that San José continued to grow at a significant rate throughout this period, there was a growing awareness among a new generation of liberals that the penitentiary model had triumphed in Europe and North America—that it had become a figure of modernity. This was clear in the aforementioned writings of Jiménez and González Víquez. These liberals would have considered it imperative to construct a like beacon of modernity as part of an architecture of civilization that, for reasons of expedience and ideology, was concentrated in the capital city.

It is also worth considering Richard Morse's identification of a rise, from the middle of the nineteenth century onward, of "organicist" precepts in the thought of Latin American positivists confronting the growth of cities. No longer guaranteed to exude civilized values, cities were now considered the most likely breeding grounds for parasitic classes who fed upon and weakened the "body social of the whole nation."[33] As the organicist imagery was incorporated into Costa Rican liberalism, the idea of dispersing such parasites throughout the rural areas may have begun to seem rather misguided. Indeed, the allegedly superior rehabilitative character of the penitentiary would now be seen to be enhanced by its capacity to morally and physically remove such parasites from the workers in both rural and urban areas.

In any case, the impetus toward the building of a penitentiary appears to have been arrested during the anti-Olympian (if not really antiliberal) interregnum of José Joaquín Rodríguez and Rafael Yglesias (1890–1902). While these years saw the maintenance of the essential program of the liberal state, Rodríguez and Yglesias effectively marginalized figures such as Jiménez, González Víquez, and Esquivel from the direction of state policy. It is not really until the Olympian clique succeeded in retaining access to the upper echelons of political power in 1902 that the wheels of penal and police reform began to turn again.

As president between 1902 and 1906, Esquivel voiced concern about the need of a penitentiary to advance the program of "social hygiene against crime" and had new plans drawn up by Lucas Fernández, his chief of public works and one of the engineers involved in the plans of 1890. Fernández claimed to have refined his ideas on correctional engineering during trips to the United States and Europe. His new architectural vision was of a total correctional facility with one central panoptic location to survey the distinct departments destined for women, female minors, male minors, detainees, prisoners with a trial pending, and hardened criminals. He confidently asserted that the layout adopted "a combination of the radial and the circular panoptic, meshes well . . . and lends itself, what's more, to a greater subdivision of classes of prisoners than that previously planned, without in any way diminishing the efficacy of the central vigilance which will prove to be complete."[34]

It was during his first tenure as president (1906–1910) that González Víquez saw his youthful wish fulfilled. The prison was inaugurated in 1909, although it had yet to be completed, and the labor of inmates was employed to finish the job and then subsequently to reconstruct major portions of the edifice after it suffered extensive damage in the earthquake of 1910. The total cost, according to González Víquez, had been 600,000 colones (the average daily wage for an artisan at the time was about 3 colones). Authority for the penitentiary lay with the Ministry of War, though it was staffed in part by the Ministry of Government and Police.

Of conditions inside the penitentiary, only a sketchy idea can be provided.[35] The main entrance and offices were located in a building which faced the city and served, along with the walls and exterior guard towers, as the penitentiary's public facade. An enclosed walkway connected this to the inside of the prison proper, where a central observation tower overlooked a semicircular inner edifice which gave onto three brick cell blocks. On the north side of this factorylike complex was a pavilion which served as the prison hospital and was initially intended to house minors as well. The penitentiary had a small chapel and, supposedly, a library. Nursing care and some maintenance work was provided for by prisoners chosen on the basis of good conduct. A section of the prison was reserved for the installation of shops where inmates worked at shoemaking, carpentry, painting, tailoring, and hat washing. All those incarcerated, other than minors and political prisoners, had to work for their food and clothing, unless they deposited on a weekly basis a sum of money equivalent to the cost of their keep.

The general regulations of the penitentiary, enacted in 1915, offer some idea of the internal functioning of the prison. The director was charged with classifying the prisoners, insuring they worked at an appropriate trade, facilitating the sale of their products, offering each one the chance to meet with him once a week, authorizing visits of the doctor or chaplain to individual prisoners, overseeing sanitary conditions, and applying punishments. A secretary was to act as a kind of general monitor, keeping a registry of the moral conduct of the prisoners as well as a notebook detailing the behavior of the employees. The chaplain was to provide lectures on morality after the Mass. The guards, or inspectors, were responsible for enforcing a petty code of conduct which included prohibitions against shouting, singing vulgar songs, and using sign language. Special punishments included private or public dressings down, withholding credit for work or prohibiting work in the shops, confinement in the cell, and curtailing tobacco supply, correspondence, unsupervised visits, and library privileges. Copies of the obligations of prisoners were to be posted in every part of the prison, including in each cell. Collective protests were prohibited. The new penal code of 1924 supplemented these guidelines by making mandatory a daily registry of the inmates, their "conduct, disposition and determination to work, the character they reveal, and other observations on their mental state." These reports were to be archived in the newly created registry of delinquents.[36]

So it was decreed. How the penitentiary actually functioned is a question that awaits further research. It is known, however, that prisoners were occasionally subjected to visits from judges, politicians, and other dignitaries, whereupon they had to line up in military formation and, when asked, voice their complaints about the penitentiary. The prison population also received visits from Catholic and secular philanthropic groups. By 1914, one senior politician declared that the penitentiary's regime was too soft and comfortable, thereby promoting recidivism. Harsher treatment was urged, including a strict diet of bread and water for those who refused to work diligently, in order to promote contrition. Also in 1914 the state dispatched another lawyer to Europe to study the latest methods and principles of penitentiary systems. Politicians and prison reformers continued to insist that the penitentiary should be capable of moral correction, but indicators are that the conditions under which it operated fell abysmally short of the minimal standards that González Víquez might have imagined necessary for the "profoundly loving mother" to rehabilitate her foster children.

A 1932 report by the Patronato Nacional de la Infancia (PANI) found that although male minors (who were incarcerated in the penitentiary until 1935) were separated from adults, "the department of the penitentiary that is reserved for them is unhygienic and lacking in security" and does not prevent them from receiving the "bad influence of moral contagion" from the adult inmates. The boys were lacking in adequate clothing, bedding, primary instruction, and, generally, "the modern principles postulated by correctional pedagogy."[37] It seems unlikely that adult males enjoyed any better conditions. One reason for this probably towers over all others.

Almost from its inception, the facility departed radically from the penitentiary ideal in that the majority of prisoners at any one time were almost certainly juveniles and adults convicted of misdemeanors and unable to pay the corresponding fine. A 1914 report noted that there were 155 such prisoners on an average day in the penitentiary. The penitentiary, therefore, was overcrowded almost from the beginning, its population constantly being cycled through on short sentences. This could not but undermine the penitentiary's ostensible goal of morally correcting prisoners through concerted, prolonged, and individualized attention. I will have more to say about this tendency of the Costa Rican penitentiary system below, but it should be noted that until more sound research on the movement and status of inmates has been done, the above line of thought must remain at the level of a hypothesis.

The same report of the PANI outlined a different picture for female minors. Women were housed in the penitentiary until 1914, when a new women's prison was inaugurated for both minors and adults. Its administration was taken over by the Sisters of the Good Shepherd, a religious order that had run the previous correctional facility for female minors. In 1925 a new women's prison was built outside the city proper on land adjacent to that designated for the boys' reformatory. There "the conditions of isolation mean that these minors can be found under the constant vigilance of the sisters who comfort them morally and in a persistent manner with religious instruction; furthermore, the hygienic conditions could not be better."[38] The prison mostly housed women who were in contravention of the prostitution laws, and especially those who suffered from venereal disease, though it also served as a house of detention for those convicted of misdemeanors unrelated to prostitution, as well as those who had committed serious criminal offenses. The 1925 breakdown of women who had spent some time in the prison noted 51 confined for crimes, 598 for misdemeanors, and 230 for venereal disease.[39] Due to the emphasis on medical treatment, its supreme director was the official doctor of prisons. A 1921 report stated that the facility lacked basic bedding and a nursing infrastructure. By 1931, however, conditions had been improved through a regular budget, and the staff included the director (the mother superior), eight women jailers, four police officers, a nurse, a chaplain, and administrative and cleaning staff.[40]

The fascinating story of this prison—the site, surely, of a great many revealing confrontations between two opposite constructions of women, the pious Catholic mother and the vice-ridden prostitute—remains to be told. It is noteworthy, however, that the otherwise vehemently anticlerical Olympians (whose 1884 banishment of the archbishop and religious orders and attendant anticlerical legislation were sparked by the recruitment of a preeminent merchant's daughter into a convent), while eliminating the hand of religious orders in the primary education of girls, would introduce a new religious order into the country specifically to deal with female deviance. Though the sisters were now, of course, subordinated to state funding and the oversight of a secular, state physician, the prison of the Sisters of the Good Shepherd was surely an unusual incarnation of González Víquez's metaphor of the prison as profoundly loving mother. As much as anything else, it probably marks the point of positivist surrender, at the gates of female sin and deviance, to the master organizers of unreason.

## Criminology

The state's capacity to provide these new facilities with a clientele had been given a boost in the new general code for San José's Police of Order and Security of 1908.[41] Among its provisions was the creation of a special "investigation unit" to be filled by the "most expert, intelligent and able policemen." They would be responsible not only for investigating crimes but also for "making lists of the vagrants, professional gamblers, prostitutes, petty thieves, people of bad character, escaped prisoners, confirmed drunks, the insane and demented, and other suspicious people at large in the city." They were also to gather and centralize similar information provided by police agents throughout the country.[42] While a general concern with these types of social deviance was not new, the novelty of the 1908 code lay in its provisions for a specialized agency which would dedicate itself to the task of producing, accumulating, and centralizing the knowledge of a plebeian criminal element identified specifically as urban in nature.

It was Luis Castro Saborío who, with the patronage and support of President González Víquez, opened a training school in scientific judicial policing in early 1910. In the preamble justifying the need for the school, in a report submitted to the director of police, Castro Saborío remarked that "the series of events of different penal denomination, which in recent times have occurred in the country, some of them manifestations of grave social danger, made me see the alarming advances that the criminal element has achieved [in our society]." The school offered courses in judicial policing, criminal law procedures, criminal anthropology, legal medicine, and the equipping of a modern investigation unit.[43]

Though there are no other known records of this school, we can get a reasonable idea of the content of the courses by looking at the collection of articles on criminology that Castro Saborío wrote for the *Anales del Ateneo de Costa Rica* in 1913. Positivist criminology had been introduced to Costa Rica by Octavio Beeche, who had studied under Francisco Carrara at the University of Pisa during his 1890 sojourn to examine European penitentiaries.[44] Beeche's Italian experience was imparted in the College of Law, and its dominant influence is obvious in the writings of Castro Saborío. Costa Rica's extant penal code is declared to be archaic and not up to the modern standards of the United States, in practice, and Italy, in theory. Reform is needed because "criminality is evolving in Costa Rica, its path obeying the circumstances of the historical moment the country is going through." Crimes of blood are now being surpassed by crimes of guile, "which are products of the struggle for existence in an anguished environment due to the increase in population and the current stunted economic situation." What is needed now is the most modern penology that fuses social work and psychiatry with law and moral instruction.[45]

Castro Saborío goes on to outline the most prominent criminological theories, with special emphasis on those of Ferri and Lombroso. While not a dogmatic follower of any of them, he does accept the premise that there are "criminal classes" who are, "in the main, examples of the results of the laws of evolution, or natural selection, discovered by Darwin." He furthermore accepts that crime is often transmissible by hereditary means and can be produced by alcoholism and other vices. The argument comes full circle in a concluding statement:

> There is a final cause that produces degeneration, one that is not personal vice, but rather one of poor social structure. I refer to poverty . . . which tends necessarily to impede the normal development of the individual and produce beings who are weak and badly formed to struggle for existence, and excellent agents, without a doubt, for the production of crime.[46]

Castro Saborío nicely folds biological causality into sociological causality and in so doing suggests that a criminal class must inevitably take shape in a Costa Rica increasingly experiencing the dire consequences of a dependent agro-export capitalism.

Two other criminological studies of note also appeared in this juncture. The first, Anastasio Alfaro's *Arqueología criminal americana* (1908), was a descriptive account of various interesting crimes committed in Costa Rica during the colonial era. Its interest lies more in the mere fact of its compilation, since it displays a growing fascination with the world of "national" crime. Of more significance was the 1914 publication of the winning entry in the category of sociology of a national literary competition, Ramón Rojas Corrales's *La infancia delincuente en Costa Rica* (the competition had been adjudicated by the ubiquitous González Víquez). He declares juvenile delinquency to be a social problem which has arisen in Costa Rica "in recent times": "from people's lips one hears little else but the cry of 'watch out!,' certain of the danger posed by this sickness which threatens to invade the entire social organism like a voracious fire."[47]

This incendiary cry and the subsequent statistics used to justify it bear some comment. First of all, the only existing historical study of delinquency in San José prior to 1900 does not demonstrate a rise in criminal activity proportionately greater than the increase in population.[48] While further research is certainly required to determine whether crime or juvenile delinquency was highlighted during this era through some specific "moral panic," Rojas's introduction either indicates that such a panic had occurred or itself attempts to incite one. This is confirmed by a willful misreading of his own statistical evidence (another aspect common to the moral panic, as Jennifer Davis has shown), suggesting a "grave increase" in the numbers of convicted delinquents between 1908 and 1913, when in fact the absolute numbers in the first year remained almost identical to those in the last year, despite wild fluctuations in the interim.[49]

Curiously, in the opening essay of his collection in the *Anales*, Castro Saborío had argued that Costa Rica must prepare for modern penal practices not because of an actual increment in criminal activity but because it must anticipate the kinds of criminal behavior found in the growing metropolises of the world (he conjured the specter of such moral decadence not through literary reference to Sue or Zola but through reference to film images of the masses in the great cities).[50] I suggest that Rojas and Castro Saborío must be considered, along with González Víquez himself, "moral entrepreneurs" of sorts, achieving personal and political self-aggrandizement, as well as the imposition of an ideological plan, through the promotion of an alleged mortal public danger.[51] According to the figures in another source, the number of crimes prosecuted in San José had actually dropped significantly between 1912 and 1913 (from 650 to 401).[52] It is worth considering the possibility that these moral entrepreneurs now made a conscious decision to blur the distinction between petty crime (*faltas*, roughly equivalent to a misdemeanor) and serious crime. The petty delinquent was thus refashioned as an immanent criminal, and the mortal danger could be shown by pointing to a much greater pool of dangerous types looming out of the mass of the urban laboring poor.

Indeed, Rojas's study also demonstrates that the conceptualization of crime and delinquency as social pathology had become firmly implanted in the minds of those who aspired to the status of the social scientist. Citing a variety of sources, from Lombroso to recent international conferences on child protection, Rojas postulates a hodgepodge of "causes" of juvenile delinquency in Costa Rica—alcoholism, tobacco usage, physiological degeneration due to poor nutrition and disease, prostitution, consanguineous marriages, pauperism, abandonment, the erosion of the family and the home—that add up to a composite picture of the lower strata of the urban laboring classes.[53] Moral, economic, social, and biological categories are subsumed by an overriding metaphor of the polity as organism in which symptoms of illness are themselves agents of further infection. Rojas's solution to this question of social hygiene was to propose that the state focus on youth and maternity as a critical realm of both potentially healthy cellular growth within the social organism and potentially disastrous vulnerability to infections that would perpetuate the disease in the body politic.

## Detection

In August 1917, during the short-lived Tinoco dictatorship, the special investigation unit of the 1908 code was designated a Detective Corps and equipped with a National Cabinet of Identification, both now, along with the penitentiary itself, under the jurisdiction of the Ministry of War rather than Government and Police.[54] This change was not due to the "anomalous" Tinoco dictatorship. Rather, it formed part of a general tendency cemented during the administration of Julio Acosta (1920–1924), when his brother Aquiles took charge of the Ministries of Government and War and reordered the police apparatus to achieve a better coherence within a new Ministry of Public Security. According to Mercedes Muñoz, it was in this same year, 1922, that the number of police first outstripped the number of soldiers in Costa Rica.[55]

The corps varied in size between 1917 and 1935 from as low as twelve agents to as many as thirty, though it always included a director, a subdirector and secretary in charge of office administration, and eventually a photographer. The job of director was a political appointment, and even the detective jobs were occasionally given as part of the petty patronage that permeated the Costa Rican state. The need to reform the force was consistently expressed by various public figures, and the minister of public security even went as far as contracting Samuel Roe, a policeman from the Panama Canal Zone, to retrain the force and draw up a program for reform in 1928. While nothing is known about Roe, his correspondence with the minister reveals a young detective instilled with the new professionalism of U.S. policing. This was the central thrust of his report, which urged the state to provide funds that would allow a professional ethic to take root. He praised the dedication of many on the force but noted that the detectives were underpaid and as a result could not carry out certain tasks, took second jobs, got into debt with shady characters, and were vulnerable to bribery and other forms of corruption (not to mention poorly dressed and unkempt). His recommendations were warmly received but never implemented.[56]

Although the Detective Corps carried out political tasks from its inception, the force put most of its emphasis on regulating the growing urban center and particularly the real and expected increase in property crimes. In this sense it followed a general tendency evident in the police function in the entire Western world during this era.[57] The manner in which José María Pinaud, the director of detectives between 1920 and 1928, measured the success of the squad through a straight accounting of percentage of stolen goods subsequently recovered reached comic proportions.[58] The focus of the corps on petty crime swelled the ranks of penitentiary inmates and thus drastically expanded the pool of delinquents; moreover, this appears to have been part of a conscious strategy on the part of the state.

Arguably the most significant change in the new penal code of 1924 was that the maximum amount of incarceration allowable for *faltas*, and for "police contraventions," which included moral crimes such as vagrancy, was tripled from 60 to 180 days. The fine equivalent to this time was doubled from 1 to 2 colones per day, thus making it that much more likely that an accused of the poorer classes would be unable to pay the fine and would have to spend time in the penitentiary for any number of lesser contraventions against the law.[59] Responsibility for prosecuting these contraventions lay outside the courts, resting instead with the country's principal police agents. The rules of evidence established in the code of penal procedure and by the Supreme Court played little or no role here. It was enough to be a "known" delinquent and be found in "suspicious places" or with "bad company" to pass up to six months in the penitentiary.

As I have demonstrated elsewhere in an analysis of the trials of artisans charged with drug consumption between 1929 and 1934, there did not have to exist any material evidence against the accused, only circumstantial (the word of a detective, a previous conviction, or suspicious activities), for the respective police agent to pass a guilty sentence.[60] Those convicted of misdemeanors had the right to appeal their sentence before the governor of San José, and many did. They lost, however, without exception, for the simple reason that, in the words of the governor with respect to the appeal of two prostitutes convicted of heroin use, "in this class of trials" there exists a "juris tantum" assumption, whereby "the guilt of the accused is presumed, and it is up to them to destroy that presumption." To destroy it was virtually impossible, given that in this case, for example, the convicted women presented a sworn retraction of testimony by the principal witness who had testified against them.[61]

Those detained for trial who could finance a writ of habeas corpus before the court appeared to have some success in getting their charge dismissed for lack of evidence. Of course, those convicted of misdemeanors and contraventions could pay a fine of between 60 and 360 colones (that is, between one and six months' wages for the average artisan) to avoid a stay in prison.[62] Obviously, the majority could not do so. This fact calls into question the functioning of the juridical process in Costa Rica and points toward the necessity of studying more closely the trials and convictions for misdemeanors as a mechanism for control of the laboring classes. Although such research has not yet begun, some idea of the extent of this subjuridical system administered almost wholly by the police can be gained by the following figures: in 1925, the principal agent of the judicial police in San José processed over 4,000 *faltas;* in 1929 the figure was almost 3,000.[63] These trials, which can only be described as "extraconstitutional," gave the police a large measure of autonomy in supervising the popular classes through the use of "micropunishments" (they were, literally, *sanciones administrativas*).

That this practice was condoned and given new impetus in the 1924 code would seem to indicate official recognition that, in practice, the penitentiary was not to function according to the ideal of correction for serious criminals (though this ideal role may have been retained at the symbolic level in political discourse for public consumption). Rather, it is my sense that the primary role of the penitentiary was now to be that of registry, holding tank, and clearinghouse of an expanded network of police surveillance of the popular classes that itself demanded a constant and fresh flow of delinquency for self-justification.

While a utopian theorist such as Castro Saborío or even a pedantic professional like Roe might well have been appalled by the inability of the judicial police to effect a scientific plan, by their lack of state funding, and by their inefficiency, corruption, and petty patronage, it would be a mistake to conclude that the basic postulates of positivist criminology played no role in the administration of the laboring classes. Beyond theory and ideals, the Detective Corps began to infiltrate into the world of artisans and plebeians and to know them as objects of study, documentable and documented, supervisable and supervised. This world, in the words of the minister of public security in 1928, "the Apacheism [*apachismo*] that makes daily strikes against property," was conceived as a pool of real and latent delinquency, barbarism in the very heart of civilization which justified a perpetual supervision of the popular classes.[64] The terminology is interesting in that it reveals a superimposition, at the official level, of French conceptions of delinquency on the Costa Rican urban landscape, even as a detective from the United States was laboring to reform the force (the label "Apache" had been coined in 1902 by a Parisian mass daily newspaper for two warring youth gangs of the working-class suburbs).[65]

Despite their shortcomings, detectives had a significant presence within the popular quarters of the city. Informants and spies were used on a regular basis, recruited from the known delinquents. Agents were apparently able to keep a suspect under surveillance for days at a time and had compiled a great deal of information on the recidivists and their acquaintances.[66] Moreover, the category of delinquency was internalized by the laboring classes themselves to mark the delicate dividing line between the honest working class and the vice-ridden poor. This is reflected in the fact that working-class families would avail themselves of the system of micropunishment to effect the moral rehabilitation of family members in danger of falling, as in the case of the mother of an apprentice tailor suspected of drug consumption. She turned him in to the authorities and requested his incarceration for three months "in the hope that, once this time is over, he might come out and return to work in the manner that he did prior to having this vice."[67]

## Social Protection

The first decade of the twentieth century saw a general elite preoccupation with the high levels of infant mortality and disease among the laboring classes, both urban and rural. Despite diminished rates of economic growth, labor power remained in short supply, and the oligarchy was convinced that immigration was not the answer to this problem. This was so largely because the desired influx of Europeans had never materialized, and those who did arrive after 1870, and those likely to arrive in the future, were mostly West Indians, Chinese, East Indians, and Nicaraguans, perceived as "inappropriate" aliens who threatened the purity and health of the Costa Rican "race." The solution advanced was what González Víquez called "autoimmigration": more Costa Ricans through a lowering of infant mortality and a healthy infancy and childhood.[68] Since disease and ill health were endemic to the poorer of the laboring classes, hygienicist discourse could not avoid a metaphorical merger of the physical pathology of malnutrition and intestinal infection with the moral pathology of delinquency, sloth, and vice. Institutions of philanthropy, receiving increasing proportions of their funding from the state and incorporating "scientific" techniques and goals into their practices, assumed a parallel police function of moral and physical hygienization in the lives of the urban laboring groups.

As early as 1905, an infants' asylum was established in San José where domestic servants with illegitimate children could leave their babies during their twelve-hour workday. Only those whose employers would certify the illegitimate state of the child and the disposition to work of the mother were allowed this privilege (which cost them 20 percent of their wages). The asylum created a corps of female wardens (*celadoras*) whose task was to investigate the conduct of the mothers and report any irregularities at each meeting of the board of directors "so that they might impose the appropriate corrective measures."[69] This is almost certainly the origin of social work in Costa Rica.

The directors no doubt included society women such as Amparo de Zeledón, the owner of the country's premier pharmacy and founding member and director of the highly respected Drop of Milk program established in 1913. The bylaws of the society set out as its aims "to help mothers with few resources, regardless of religion, to nourish their children from one day up to two years of age. No distinction will be made between married and unmarried mothers, since the primary goal of the society is to *conserve children for the country*."[70] In her first annual report, Zeledón made clear that she saw her work not in religious terms but as part of the "magnum opus of social improvement"; likewise, the goal was not simply to ensure physically robust children but also "to teach the mothers and to raise the moral level of both [mother and child]." The moral policing function of the social worker was also present here, as was the task of accumulating a body of knowledge about these women. All the mothers involved in the partially state-funded program had to contribute some money, thus avoiding the bad moral habits believed to be instilled by the receipt of pure charity. Each received a visit from the director herself so that Zeledón might "proceed in this terrain with a knowledge of causes and with justice." The first visit allowed her "to judge the accuracy of the facts received regarding their conditions of poverty and to appreciate certain details that confirm or modify the first impression." The home of the destitute mother becomes a cell, open to the panoptic gaze of the elite woman, and not just once: "successive visits have more the character of vigilance than of anything else, because I undertake them with the exclusive objective of seeing how they are following our counsel." Impoverished mothers participating in the program were also visited by other well-to-do members of the society.[71]

This appropriation of the social inspection task by preeminent members of society surely bespeaks, on the one hand, a sense of urgency in the face of a perceived degeneration of the national race and, on the other hand, the fear of this unknown class of poor hidden from their view beyond the frontiers of urban decency. The mediating petty functionary role of the social worker would not be long in coming, however. By the end of the 1920s, the state was ready to support an agency devoted solely to the problems of maternity and child protection. The Patronato Nacional de la Infancia was promoted and directed by Luis Felipe González Flores, brother of former deposed president Alfredo González Flores and the minister of education during that ill-fated government. The PANI finally came to life in 1930 to tackle "two transcendental problems that present themselves to the perspicacious pupils of the statesman and to the scrutinizing mind of the sociologist: the problem of the quantity of our population . . . and that of its quality, or the improvement of our race." Motherhood and childhood were now to be preserved, analyzed, and made purer and more productive through the agency of an institution of experts working in close conjunction with the authorities of education, police, courts, prisons, reformatories, and public health. Many of the goals of the PANI, as articulated by González Flores, had a clear eugenicist bent: "the control of natality among families immersed in the poor classes; the fight against *mestizaje* to improve racial selection, and the restriction of undesirable immigration for the same reason; and finally, the promotion of any and all measures of social hygiene to protect childhood and motherhood."[72]

Though it is unclear how far the PANI was able to go in achieving its goals, by 1933 the agency was combatting delinquency among minors through the use of *visitadoras*, female social workers drawn from among the ranks of locally trained nurses. In the words of González Flores, the visitors "perform a double function of great utility: they observe and inform on those social phenomena that it is our job to study, and they make social assistance effective by expurgating from its midst any parasitism that would make it noxious." By 1933, these social workers had accumulated files on 4,000 families in San José and surrounding areas.[73] Estimating conservatively, this would mean that they had collected data on the most intimate aspects of the lives of some 15,000 of the canton's 65,000 people. This is not to ignore that the plan of the PANI also included measures such as maternity leave, a stricter enforcement of child support payments, gentler treatment of juvenile delinquents, and the removal of children and women from abusive situations. It is quite likely that some women and youth found ways to turn the institution to their advantage. This humanism, however, was part and parcel of a positivist and racist design intended to guide procedures of state intervention in, and manipulation of, the lives of the laboring poor and to accumulate a body of knowledge about them that would expedite and make more effective the action of expert functionaries.

Arguably the most effective of interventions by the liberal state in the magnum opus of social hygienization, however, was in the area of public health itself. While in the minds of the elite the more seamy and threatening expressions of popular vice were born of urban living, the lack of physical hygiene was a problem endemic to both rural and urban laborers. Hookworm disease, the "germ of laziness," was widespread in Costa Rica due to poor sanitation systems and unclean water supplies; it was seen to be responsible for the high level of infant mortality that was depriving the country of sufficient laborers and to be diminishing the productivity of those laborers there were. Costa Rica's first nationally functional public health program, begun in 1914, was undertaken under the direction of a Rockefeller Foundation physician charged with eradicating hookworm disease in the countryside.[74] The local team he assembled around him, led by Dr. Solón Núñez, would go through various transformations on its way to becoming the Ministry of Public Health in 1927.

The ministry was grafted onto a rather piecemeal system of health inspection that, nonetheless, did already have a significant presence in the municipality of San José (again largely due to the efforts of González Víquez during his tenure as president of the municipal council). Despite constant cries that it was an ineffective agency, the chief of sanitation in the city reported in 1913 that his department had made almost 30,000 inspections during the year and his agents had ordered almost 2,000 repairs and modifications.[75] The Rockefeller team extended this in dramatic fashion into other cities and towns and into the countryside. By 1916, the head of the mission, Louis Schapiro, claimed that, despite having to combat the "deaf opposition" of curanderos (rural medicine men and women), over 100,000 people had attended public and private conferences given by his staff on matters of personal and community hygiene.[76]

The Rockefeller-sponsored mission almost immediately began to work through the school system (Núñez had been a school inspector prior to training as a physician), issuing a series of popularly written pamphlets on hygiene and the nature of various diseases and especially targeting schoolteachers as agents of enlightenment in the rural and urban backwaters. Schapiro's 1915 booklet, *Mission of the Primary School Teacher in the Service of School Sanitary Inspection*, included a workbook wherein teachers could take meticulous notes on each individual student. These included not only physical details such as the number of baths taken per week and the state of eyesight, but also questions of "moral condition, extrascholarly work, family history," and grades.[77]

With the end of Rockefeller aid in 1921, Núñez converted the team into the Subsecretariat of Public Health. He began to consolidate all public health–related agencies under his central authority and carried on a strong campaign to subordinate the philanthropic groups which controlled the hospitals, important preserves of oligarchic prestige, to the jurisdiction of the state. He was on the cutting edge of the promotion of a state policy of social protection governed by the scientific principles embodied in the 1923 code of public health. During the 1920s the agency deepened its activity among urban laborers, hiring a trained statistician to elaborate a statistical picture of "the sanitary problem of the working classes." The Subsecretariat also established a Public Health and Hygiene Police, which, on top of enforcing basic sanitary regulations, worked closely with the Detective Corps to eradicate the popular medicine of empirics and midwives and to suppress the growing use of heroin and marijuana among young artisans and casual laborers.[78] Though it is unknown how many teachers took to heart the 1915 suggestion of Schapiro to perform the tasks of the social worker, whatever hesitation they might have shown was at least partially overcome in 1927 by the ministry's hiring of some twenty-one women sanitary assistants to perform health inspections of students in the country's schools.[79]

## Conclusion

It would be rash to posit a direct causal relationship between the presence of this dispersed network of social hygiene and scientific policing and the Costa Rican oligarchy's ability, unique among Central American countries, to weather the depression without recourse to military dictatorship. Neither, however, should the history of these institutions be ignored in the equation of what might be called, in a general way, the growth of effective government in Costa Rica. Much of this growth involved an unprecedented appropriation of maternal roles by the state: the penitentiary as loving mother, the women's prison as loving mother superior, the Ministry of the Interior and women of the oligarchy as surrogate providers of mother's milk and regulators of maternity and childhood. It also involved the training of a caste of women teachers, nurses, and social workers to advance the national quest for improved moral and physical hygiene. The state also expanded its "masculine" wardrobe to include a more refined policeman's uniform and the respective garb of the inspector, the criminology professor, and the physician.

If this reads like an overly poetic and dubious exercise in personification, it should be recalled that what held these disparate state activities together and assigned them functions in a common plan was a metaphor of the society as organism. The importance of this image within dominant ideology was first established by positivist reformers obsessed by questions of criminology and the raising of a penitentiary. Though that facility, once constructed, does not seem to have had much success as a model prison setting wretched souls back on the path to duty, it did play a central role in the process of observing and confining workers and laborers who had been identified, by the diagnostic state, as the prime agents of moral and physical infection within the body politic. Increased vigilance was now called for, by the physician as well as by a more educated patient, in order to arrest the spread of the infection and ensure that it did not transform itself into even more dangerous forms of contagion.

In sum, the idea of social hygiene and prophylaxis began increasingly to govern the expansion of ethical activities by the liberal state. Institutions were created to mediate and diffuse class and political confrontation, to accumulate knowledge on the conditions of the laboring poor to serve as the basis for anticipating and preempting social crises, and to further the state's capacity to educate the laboring groups in questions of moral decency, honest toil, racial hierarchies, and national productivity. In doing so they pioneered techniques of policing, inspection, and social work that prefigured and marked the later (and, by Central American standards, precocious and ambitious) creation of a "welfare state" traditionally seen to have had its beginnings in the social reform of the Calderón Guardia administration of 1940 to 1944.

The extent of continuity between the incipient social policy discussed here and the more expansive reforms of the 1940s is something that cannot be dealt with in this essay. Nonetheless, it is worth noting that Calderón's pioneering social security legislation (1941) was essentially the product of close consultations with a small group of socially progressive members of the preeminent classes. Mark Rosenberg cites as prime influences Calderón's father, a physician, who had had daily contact with San José's laboring poor during the first three decades of the century; Guillermo Padilla Castro, the director of the PANI, who wrote the legislation; and Dr. Mario Luján, the new minister of health and long a reformist crusader within the ranks of the political class. In 1943, with the system ready to be set in motion, Solón Núñez was invited back to take over the Ministry of Health.[80] These connections, superficial though they might be, are the scent on a trail that probably leads to the elusive soul of Costa Rican social democracy.

The penitentiary was closed down in 1979 and sat empty for over a decade. In 1990 Rafael Ángel "Junior" Calderón Fournier, the son of the great reformer of the 1940s, was elected to the presidency. His wife, Margarita Penón, has taken on a great philanthropic project (as first ladies are wont to do): to renovate the penitentiary and transform it into the Costa Rican Center for Science and Culture. In one of the old cell blocks will be a Museo de los Niños, in another a Museo Penitenciario.

## Notes

I would like to thank the Social Sciences and Humanities Research Council of Canada for generous postdoctoral fellowship assistance during the research phase of this work.

1. Luis Castro Saborío, "Examinando el código penal," *Anales del Ateneo de Costa Rica* 2, no. 5 (1913): 371.

2. Published as Cleto González Víquez, "La irresponsabilidad criminal," in *Casos prácticos del código penal* (San José: Imprenta Alsina, 1910), pp. 118–119.

3. Ricardo Jiménez Oreamuno, "Disertación leída por el Sr. don Ricardo Jiménez, en el acto de dar principio a su examen público para recibir el título de abogado," in Eugenio Rodríguez Vega, ed., *Ricardo Jiménez Oreamuno: su pensamiento* (San José: Editorial Costa Rica, 1980), pp. 11–19.

4. The reform involved the passing of anticlerical legislation designed to subordinate Church to state, the enactment of a civil code to regularize and legitimize the jumbled legal framework of a coffee-based capitalism by then almost fifty years in the making, and an ambitious program of universal primary education. In 1882, González Víquez and Jiménez had begun to serve in the capacity of collaborators in the writing of the civil code.

5. Surprisingly little biographical attention has been given these two titans; unsatisfying to one degree or another are Luis Felipe González Flores, *Biografía del Lic. Cleto González Víquez* (San José: Lehmann, 1958); Enrique Martínez Arias, "Cleto González Víquez en la primera década del siglo XX," Licenciatura thesis, University of Costa Rica, 1971; and Eugenio Rodríguez Vega, *Los días de don Ricardo*, 5th ed. (San José: Editorial Costa Rica, 1980).

6. Patricia Badilla G., "Ideología y derecho: el espíritu mesiánico de la Reforma Jurídica costarricense (1882–1888)," *Revista de Historia* (Universidad de Costa Rica/Universidad Nacional) 18 (July–December 1988): 187–202. The past few years have seen research on the question of delinquency in San José and Heredia by a group based at the Universidad Nacional, but systematic exposition of the results has not yet occurred. Some examples are Carlos Naranjo G. and Mayela Solano Q., "El delito en San José: 1870–1900," *Revista de Historia* (UCR/UNA) 20 (July–December 1989): 81–104; Carlos Naranjo G., "Pilar Jiménez, bandolero: el bandolerismo en el Valle Central de Costa Rica (1850–1890)," and Juan José Marín H., "Prostitución y pecado en la bella y próspera ciudad de San José (1850–1930)," in Iván Molina J. and Steven Palmer, eds., *El paso del cometa: estado, política social y culturas populares en Costa Rica (1800–1950)* (San José: Editorial Porvenir/Plumsock Mesoamerican Studies, 1994).

7. By far the best historical account of this process, which also has the

virtue of demythologizing it, is Mario Samper K., "Fuerzas sociopolíticas y procesos electorales en Costa Rica, 1921–1936," *Revista de Historia*, número especial (1988): 157–221. See also the pioneering approach of Fabrice Edouard Lehoucq, "The Origins of Democracy in Costa Rica in Comparative Perspective," Ph.D. diss., Duke University, 1992, esp. pp. 56–117.

8. According to Eugenio Rodríguez Vega, for example, "Costa Rican liberals had very open minds, which distinguishes them from liberals in other areas." *El pensamiento liberal: antología* (San José: Editorial Costa Rica, 1979), p. 9.

9. Mercedes Muñoz G., *El estado y la abolición del ejército en Costa Rica, 1914–1949* (San José: Editorial Porvenir, 1990). Though Muñoz displays a keen awareness of some of the issues of coercion and police reform and is skeptical of the dominant mythology concerning the "unarmed democracy," the very focus of her study indicates the power of this mythology to circumscribe the historian's endeavor.

10. This is the general argument of Orlando Salazar Mora, *El apogeo de la República Liberal en Costa Rica, 1870–1914* (San José: Editorial de la Universidad de Costa Rica, 1990), an attempt to synthesize the sum of knowledge about the political history of the rise of the Liberal state.

11. The social reforms involved four main components: social security (including free health care, accident insurance, and pensions), the incorporation of a series of social guarantees into the constitution, a labor code, and the opening of the University of Costa Rica.

12. Mark Rosenberg, *Las luchas por el Seguro Social en Costa Rica* (San José: Editorial de Costa Rica, 1980), p. 19. The classic formulation of this critique of the liberal state was Rodrigo Facio's *Estudio sobre economía costarricense* (San José: Editorial "Soley y Valverde," 1942), which predated the social reforms and which would become the foundational treatise of Costa Rican social democracy.

13. Castro Saborío, "Estudios penales," *Anales del Ateneo de Costa Rica* 2, no. 5 (1913): 362.

14. The closest thing to a history of this kind is the valuable 1924 compendium of developments within the field of penology by Ricardo Jinesta, *La evolución penitenciaria en Costa Rica*, 2d ed. (San José: Imprenta Falco Hermanos, 1940). I have unfortunately been unable to consult Mónica Granados, "Estudio exploratorio para la construcción de una teoría política-económica de la pena en la Costa Rica del Siglo XIX," Master's thesis, Instituto Nacional de Ciencias Penales, Mexico City, 1986.

15. Steven Palmer, "Pánico en San José: el consumo de heroína, la cultura plebeya y la política social en 1929," in Molina and Palmer, eds., *El paso del cometa*.

16. Ricardo D. Salvatore, "Criminology, Prison Reform, and the Buenos Aires Working Class," *Journal of Interdisciplinary History* 23, no. 2 (autumn 1992): 280.

17. Steven Palmer, "Prolegómenos a toda futura historia de San José, Costa Rica (1750–1900)," *Mesoamérica*, forthcoming; Patricia Fumero V., "La ciudad en la aldea: actividades y diversiones urbanas en San José a mediados del siglo XIX," in Iván Molina J. and Steven Palmer, eds., *Héroes al gusto y libros de moda: sociedad y cambio cultural en Costa Rica (1750–1900)* (San José: Editorial

Porvenir/Plumsock Mesoamerican Studies, 1992), pp. 77–105; José Luis Vega C., "San José: tenencia de la tierra y nuevos grupos sociales en el siglo XIX," in Rodrigo Fernández and Mario Lungo, eds., *La estructuración de las capitales centroamericanas* (San José: EDUCA, 1988), pp. 161–182.

18. Cleto González Víquez, *Apuntes estadísticos sobre la ciudad de San José* (San José: Imprenta Alsino, 1905), p. 4; Mario Samper K., ed., *El censo de la población de 1927: creación de una base nominal computarizada* (San José: Oficina de Publicaciones de la UCR, 1991), p. 63.

19. Naranjo and Solano, "El delito en San José," p. 89; Samper, *El censo de 1927*, p. 63; Richard M. Morse, "Latin American Cities in the 19th Century: Approaches and Tentative Generalizations," in Morse, ed., *The Urban Development of Latin America, 1750–1920* (Stanford, Calif.: Center for Latin American Studies, 1971), p. 5a.

20. Centro de Investigaciones Históricas, "Base de datos: el Censo de 1927," information processed by Saray Castro.

21. Mario Samper K., "Evolución de la estructura socio-ocupacional costarricense: labradores, artesanos y jornaleros, 1864–1935," Licenciatura thesis, University of Costa Rica, 1979, pp. 146–147; Víctor Hugo Acuña O., *Los orígenes de la clase obrera en Costa Rica: las huelgas de 1920 por la jornada de ocho horas* (San José: CENAP-CEPAS, 1986), pp. 9–13.

22. Naranjo and Solano, "El delito en San José," pp. 96–98.

23. Acuña O., *Orígenes de la clase obrera en Costa Rica*, pp. 11–20; and idem, "Nación y clase obrera en Centroamérica durante la época Liberal (1870–1930)," in Molina and Palmer, eds., *El paso del cometa*.

24. Mario Oliva Medina, *Artesanos y obreros costarricenses, 1880–1914* (San José: Editorial Costa Rica, 1985), passim.

25. Victoria Ramírez A., *Jorge Volio y la revolución vigente* (San José: Editorial Guayacán, 1989), pp. 65–84; Rodolfo Cerdas C., *La hoz y el machete: la Internacional Comunista, América Latina y la revolución en Centroamérica* (San José: Editorial Universidad Estatal a Distancia, 1986), pp. 323–343.

26. Mayela Solano Q. and Carlos Naranjo G., "El delito en la provincia de San José, 1870–1900," Licenciatura thesis, Universidad de Costa Rica, San José, 1989, p. 123.

27. Solano and Naranjo, "El delito en la provincia de San José," p. 129; Jinesta, *La evolución penitenciaria*, pp. 163–184.

28. Jinesta, *La evolución penitenciaria*, pp. 163–184.

29. Eusebio Figueroa, "Informe," in Rodríguez Vega, ed., *El pensamiento liberal*, pp. 119, 11–119 passim.

30. Jinesta, *La evolución penitenciaria*, p. 185.

31. Ibid., pp. 201–203.

32. Solano and Naranjo, "El delito en la provincia de San José," pp. 133–134.

33. Richard M. Morse, "Latin American Intellectuals and the City, 1860–1940," *Journal of Latin American Studies* 10, no. 2 (1978): 227, 219–238 passim.

34. Jinesta, *La evolución penitenciaria*, pp. 216, 221–222.

35. Unless otherwise indicated, what follows has been compiled from ibid., pp. 232–251.

36. Articles 97 and 239, *Código penal de la República de Costa Rica* (San José: Trejos Hnos., 1924).

37. "Informe of the President of the PANI," in *Memoria de gobernación, policía, trabajo y previsión social correspondiente al año 1932* (San José: Imprenta Nacional, 1934), pp. 193–194.

38. Ibid., p. 194.

39. *Memoria de gobernación y policía, año 1925* (San José: Imprenta Nacional, 1926), p. 391.

40. "Informe del gobernador de San José," *Memoria de gobernación y policía correspondiente al año 1921* (San José: Imprenta Nacional, 1922), p. 86; Archivo Nacional de Costa Rica, Congreso 15.962.

41. The first systematic effort at police reform had occurred in San José between 1885 and 1887. Due to the expansion of the city, the force's numbers were doubled and its organization revamped to the point where the municipality was incapable of maintaining it and had to cede control to González Víquez's Ministry of the Interior. It now became the nucleus of the state's Police of Order and Security. Though ostensibly the new police were to keep surveillance on the population of itinerants and vagrants, Naranjo and Solano have shown that the emphasis of the police was to patrol and protect the property of the more posh streets of the capital; see "El delito en San José," p. 87.

42. *La Gaceta*, July 28, 1908, p. 125 (articles 64–66).

43. Jinesta, *La evolución penitenciaria*, pp. 236–237.

44. Ibid., p. 201.

45. Castro Saborío, "Examinando el código penal," pp. 369–371.

46. Castro Saborío, "Entre líneas," pp. 470–472.

47. Ramón Rojas Corrales, *La infancia delincuente en Costa Rica* (San José: Tipografía Nacional, 1914), p. 17.

48. The study of Naranjo and Solano, which only extends to 1900, actually indicates that in the thirty-year period between 1870 and 1900 the median number of property crimes in San José remained constant. "El delito en San José," p. 97.

49. Rojas, *La infancia delincuente*, pp. 69–71. Jennifer Davis, "The London Garrotting Panic of 1862: A Moral Panic and the Creation of a Criminal Class in Mid-Victorian England," in V. A. C. Gatrell et al., *Crime and the Law: The Social History of Crime in Western Europe since 1500* (London: Europa Publications, 1980), p. 191, offers an excellent, and apropos, application of the model of the moral panic, originally developed in Stanley Cohen, *Folk Devils and Moral Panics: The Creation of the Mods and the Rockers*, 2d ed. (New York: St. Martin's Press, 1980).

50. Castro Saborío, "Estudios penales," p. 361.

51. Davis, "The London Garrotting Panic of 1862," p. 199.

52. Jinesta, *La evolución penitenciaria*, p. 241.

53. Rojas, *La infancia delincuente*, pp. 24–35.

54. Jinesta, *La evolución penitenciaria*, p. 249. The extraordinary decree creating the force was ratified by Congress, upon urging from the executive, in 1923, with the justification that the corps had been "already sufficiently tried out with excellent results." ANCR, Congreso 12.800.

55. Muñoz, *El estado y la abolición del ejército*, pp. 103–104.

56. "Proyecto para organizar el Cuerpo de Policía de Investigación," and accompanying documents, ANCR, Guerra 9571.

57. Julia Kirk Blackwelder, "Urbanization, Crime, and Policing: Buenos Aires, 1870–1914," in Lyman L. Johnson, ed., *The Problem of Order in Changing Societies: Essays on Crime and Policing in Argentina and Uruguay, 1750–1940* (Albuquerque: University of New Mexico Press, 1990), pp. 65–67.

58. See, for example, his "Informe" of 1920 in ANCR, Guerra 9223.

59. Iván Ávila F., "Apuntes sobre faltas de policía," Licenciatura thesis, University of Costa Rica, 1969, p. 8; *Código penal . . . 1924*, articles 542–556.

60 . Palmer, "El consumo de heroína entre los artesanos de San José."

61 . ANCR, Salubridad Pública 131.

62 . I am grateful to José Manuel Cerdas for this information on approximate wage scales of artisans during this era.

63. *Memoria de la Secretaría de Gobernación y Policía correspondiente al año 1925* (San José: Imprenta Nacional, 1926), p. 391; *Memoria de la Secretaría de Gobernación y Policía correspondiente al año 1929* (San José: Imprenta Nacional, 1931), p. 307.

64. "Proyecto de ley para organizar el Cuerpo de Detectivos," September 1928, ANCR Guerra 9571. On this point, see Michel Foucault, *Discipline and Punish: The Birth of the Prison*, trans. Alan Sheridan (New York: Pantheon, 1977), p. 281.

65. Robert A. Nye, *Crime, Madness and Politics in Modern France: The Medical Concept of National Decline* (Princeton, N.J.: Princeton University Press, 1984), p. 197.

66. ANCR, Salubridad Pública 2 and 43.

67. Ibid., Salubridad Pública 102.

68. "Mensaje del presidente de la república al Congreso Constitucional [1929]," in Carlos Meléndez Ch., ed., *Mensajes presidenciales, 1928–1940* (San José: Academia de Geografía e Historia, 1987), p. 31. Ironically, González Víquez's own father was a Nicaraguan immigrant of relatively humble extraction.

69. Rojas, *La infancia delincuente*, pp. 143–144.

70. Ibid., p. 149; emphasis in the original.

71. *La Gota de Leche: memoria relativa a la actuación del año 1913–14* (San José: Tipografía Nacional, n.d.), n.p.

72. Luis Felipe González Flores, "Conferencia del Profesor Luis Felipe González Flores," *Boletín del Patronato Nacional de la Infancia* 1, no. 2 (1930): 34.

73. "Informe del presidente del PANI relativo a los labores del año 1933," *Boletín del Patronato Nacional de la Infancia* 5, no. 25 (1934): 1136–1137.

74. On the origins of the Rockefeller involvement in the campaign against this disease, see John Ettling, *The Germ of Laziness: Rockefeller Philanthropy and Public Health in the New South* (Cambridge and London: Harvard University Press, 1981).

75. "Informe del jefe de sanitación," *Memoria de gobernación y policía, año 1913* (San José: Tipografía Nacional, 1914), pp. 341–342.

76. *Memoria del Ministerio de Gobernación y Policía, año 1916* (San José: Tipografía Nacional, 1917), p. lxii.

77. Louis Schapiro, *Misión del maestro de escuela en el servicio de la inspección sanitaria escolar* (San José: Tipografía Nacional, 1915).

78 . The only thing resembling a historical account of the Ministry of Public Health is Núñez's own account of it in the *Memoria de la Secretaría de Salubridad Pública y protección social correspondiente a los años 1930–1931* (San José: Imprenta Nacional, 1932).

79 . Ibid. I feel compelled to note here that Costa Ricans are the most fanatical people about questions of personal hygiene that I have ever encountered, to the point that the taking of a shower is a near religious ritual, and a day passed without at least one produces feelings of self-disgust and guilt akin to those of a devout Catholic who has neglected Mass and confession.

80 . Mark Rosenberg, "Social Reform in Costa Rica: Social Security and the Presidency of Rafael Ángel Calderón," *Hispanic American Historical Review* 61, no. 2 (1981): 279–284.

# Selected Bibliography

This bibliography contains those materials quoted in the essays that are most relevant to the study of criminal justice history in Latin America.

## Contemporary Accounts on Crime, Prisons, and Criminology in Modern Latin America

Albarracín, Augusto S. "Memoria presentada por el presidente de la Junta Inspectora del Panóptico, Dr. D. Augusto S. Albarracín al Ministerio de Justicia, Culto, Instrucción y Beneficencia." In *Memoria que presenta el Ministro de Justicia, Culto, Instrucción y Beneficencia al Congreso Ordinario de 1890* (Lima: Imprenta de Torres Aguirre, 1890).

Alcover, Antonio Miguel. "Necesidad de una nueva cárcel pública en Sagua y como su construcción puede servir de modelo para nuevas penitenciarías en Cuba." In *Memoria oficial: octava conferencia nacional de beneficencia y corrección de la Isla de Cuba* (Havana: Librería e Imprenta "La Moderna Poesía," 1911).

Altmann Smythe, Julio. *Reseña histórica de la evolución del derecho penal, con conclusiones sobre la futura política criminal del Perú* (Lima: Sanmartí y Cía, 1944).

Barbosa, Orestes. *Na prisão* (Rio de Janeiro: Jacintho Ribeiro dos Santos, 1922).

Barreto de Menezes, Tobias. *Menores e loucos em direito criminal* (Rio de Janeiro: Laemert, 1884).

Beeche, Octavio. *Estudios penitenciarios: informe presentado al gobierno de Costa Rica* (San José: Tipografía Nacional, 1890).

Bevilaqua, Clovis. *Criminologia e direito* [1896] (Rio de Janeiro: Ed. Rio, 1983).

——. *Estudos de direito e economia política* [1901] (Rio de Janeiro and Paris: H. Garnier, 1902).

Brockway, Zebulon, and J. R. Bittanger. *La cuestión penal* (Toluca, Mexico: Martínez, 1871).

Calle, Juan José, et al. "Informe que la comisión encargada de examinar el estado administrativo y técnico de la penitenciaría de Lima, ha presentado al ministerio de justicia" [1915]. *La Revista del Foro* 7, no. 12 (1920) and 8, no. 13 (1921).

Carranza, Adolfo S. "Cárceles argentinas y chilenas." *Revista Argentina de Ciencias Políticas* 10 (1915): 57–59.

——. *Estado de algunas cárceles en Europa. Informe* (Tucumán: N.p., 1921).

Castro Saborío, Luis. "Estudios penales." *Anales del Ateneo de Costa Rica* 2, no. 5 (1913).

Claros, Armando. *Informe del delegado al Congreso Penitenciario de Washington* (Buenos Aires: N.p., 1911).

Colombia, Departamento de Prisiones. *La reforma carcelaria y penitenciaria en Colombia* (Bogotá: Imprenta Nacional, 1936).

——. *Realizaciones y proyectos para la reforma carcelaria y penitenciaria, 1938–1939* (Bogotá: Imprenta Nacional, 1939).

Cueto, Casimiro. "Consideraciones generales y apuntes para la crítica estadística de la criminalidad habida en el Distrito Federal durante el año de 1922." *Boletín de la Sociedad Mexicana de Geografía y Estadística* 37, nos. 1–6 (1928).

de Almeida Leite Moraes, Jr., Joaquim. "Qual o melhor dos sistemas penitenciários conhecidos?" *O Direito* 11, no. 32 (December 1883).

de Barros, Alfredo. *Notas e apontamentos sobre minha prisão na fortaleza da conceição, na Casa de Correção e em minha residência (sob palavra) desde 4 de novembro de 1893 até 14 de agosto de 1894* (Rio de Janeiro: Oficina de Obras do Jornal do Brasil, 1895).

de Córdoba, Federico. "El nuevo sistema penitenciario cubano." *Revista Penal y Penitenciaria* 18 (October–November 1940).

de Moraes, Evaristo. *A campanha abolicionista 1879–1888* [1924] (Brasília: Ed. Universitária de Brasília, 1986).

——. *Minhas prisões e outros assuntos contemporâneos* (Rio de Janeiro: Edição do Autor, 1924).

——. *Prisões e instituições penitenciárias no Brasil* (Rio de Janeiro: Liv. Cândido de Oliveira, 1923).

de Oliveira, Elias. *Criminologia das multidões.* 2d ed. (São Paulo: Ed. Saraiva, 1966).

de Veyga, Francisco. *Los auxiliares de la delincuencia* (Buenos Aires: Talleres Gráficos de la Penitenciaría Nacional, 1910).

——. *Los lunfardos: psicología de los delincuentes profesionales* (Buenos Aires: Talleres Gráficos de la Penitenciaría Nacional, 1910).

Dellepiani, Antonio. *El idioma del delito* [1894] (Buenos Aires: Los Libros del Mirasol, 1967).

Dias, Everardo. *Bastilhas modernas* (São Paulo: Edit. de Obras Sociais e Literárias, 1926).

Dr. Antonio. *Memórias de um rato de hotel: a vida do Dr Antonio narrada por ele mesmo* (Rio de Janeiro: N.p., 1912).

Drago, Luis M. *Los hombres de presa* (Buenos Aires: Félix Lajouane, 1886).

Escudero, Félix. "Vagancia y mendicidad." Memoria de prueba, Facultad de Leyes y Ciencias Políticas, Universidad de Chile, Santiago, 1899.

Ferreira de Souza Pitanga, Antonio. *Organização penitenciária nos países latino-americanos: memória jurídica* (Rio de Janeiro: Imprensa Nacional, 1907).

Fuentes, Manuel Atanasio, and M. A. de la Lama. *Diccionario de jurisprudencia y de legislación peruana: parte criminal* (Lima: Imprenta del Estado, 1877).

Galdamés, Luis. *La lucha contra el crimen* (Santiago: Imprenta de E. Blanchard, 1903).

García Ramírez, Sergio. *El artículo 18 constitucional: prisión preventiva, sistema penitenciario, menores infractores* (Mexico City: UNAM, 1967).

Gómez, Eusebio. *La mala vida en Buenos Aires* (Buenos Aires: J. Roldán, 1908).

Guerrero, Julio. *El génesis del crimen en México: estudio de psiquiatría social* (Mexico City: Librería de la Viuda de Ch. Bouret, 1901).

Ingenieros, José. *Criminología* (Madrid: D. Jorro, 1913).

Jinesta, Ricardo. *La evolución penitenciaria en Costa Rica.* 2d ed. (San José: Imprenta Falco Hermanos, 1940).

León, Carlos Aurelio. *Nuestras cárceles* (Lima: Librería e Imprenta Gil, 1920).

Macedo, Miguel S. "Los establecimientos penales." *Criminalia* 20, no. 7 (July 1954).

Macedo Soares, Gerson. *Quinze dias nas prisões do estado* (Rio de Janeiro: Benjamin Costallat & Miccolis, 1924).

Mora, José María Luis. "Memoria sobre cárceles inglesas." In *Obras completas*, vol. 7, *Obra diplomática* (Mexico City: Secretaría de Educación Pública, 1988).

Moyano Gacitúa, Carlos. *La delincuencia argentina ante algunas cifras y teorías* (Córdoba: F. Domeneci, 1905).

Nina Rodrigues, Raymundo. *As raças humanas e a responsabilidade penal no Brasil* [1894] (Bahia: Liv. Progreso, 1957).

Otero, Mariano. "Indicaciones sobre la importancia y necesidad de la reforma de las leyes penales (1844)." In Mariano Otero, *Obras*, vol. 2 (Mexico City: Editorial Porrúa, 1967).

———. "Iniciativa dirigida a la Cámara de Diputados, por el Ministerio de Relaciones sobre la adopción y establecimiento del régimen penitenciario en el Distrito y territorios (1848)." In Mariano Otero, *Obras*, vol. 2. (Mexico City: Editorial Porrúa, 1967).

Paz Soldán, Mariano Felipe. *Examen de las penitenciarías de los Estados Unidos: informe que presenta al Supremo Gobierno del Perú* (New York: S. W. Benedict, 1853).

———. *Reglamento para el servicio interior de la prisión penitenciaria de Lima* (Lima: Imprenta de José Masías, 1863).

Peixoto, Afrânio. *Psico-patologia forense* (São Paulo and Rio de Janeiro: Francisco Alves, 1916).

Peña, Francisco Javier. "Cárceles en México en 1875." *Criminalia* 25, no. 5 (August 1959).

Pichardo y Moya, Gabriel. "Nuestras cárceles." In *Memoria oficial: tercera conferencia nacional de beneficencia y corrección de la Isla de Cuba* (Havana: Librería e Imprenta "La Moderna Poesía," 1904), 261–265.

Ribeiro, Israel. *As minhas prisões: episódios de 34 dias de exílio* (Bahia: N.p., 1926).

Riviera Cambas, Manuel. "Estado de la Cárcel Nacional conocida como Cárcel de Belén en el año de 1882." *Criminalia* 25, no. 8 (August 1959).

Rocafuerte, Vicente. "Ensayo sobre el nuevo sistema de cárceles." In Neptalí Zúñiga, ed., *Colección Rocafuerte*, vol. 9, *Rocafuerte y las doctrinas penales* (Quito: Gobierno de Ecuador, 1947).

Rojas Corrales, Ramón. *La infancia delincuente en Costa Rica* (San José: Tipografía Nacional, 1914).

Roumagnac, Carlos. *Los criminales en México: ensayo de psicología criminal* (Mexico City: Tipografía "El Fénix," 1904).

Ruiz-Funes, Mariano. "La antropología penitenciaria en Cuba." In *El delincuente y la justicia* (Buenos Aires: Librería La Facultad, 1944), 114–119.

Senna, Ernesto. *Através do cárcere* (Rio de Janeiro: Imprensa Nacional, 1907).

Silva Riestra, Juan. "La cárcel modelo de São Paulo." *Archivos de Medicina Legal e Identificação* 6, no. 13 (June 1936).

Simões, Pereira, and Herculano Ramos. *Uma visita a Casa de Detenção por um arquiteto e um engenheiro civil* (Pernambuco: Tipografia do Jornal do Recife, 1882).

Souza Bandeira Filho, Antônio H. "A questão penitenciária no Brasil." *O Direito* 31 (May 1881).

Ulloa, José Casimiro. "Higiene de las prisiones." *Gaceta Médica de Lima* 67 (1859).

Viana de Almeida Vale, Luís. *Relatório do diretor da Casa de Correção da corte* (Rio de Janeiro: Imprensa Nacional, 1870).

Valdovinos, Mucio. *Ensayo sobre los diversos sistemas de cárceles conocidos bajo el nombre de penitenciarías y algunas reflexiones respecto al que debe adoptarse en la República Mexicana* (Mexico City: Imprenta de Cumplido, 1852).

Vicuña Mackenna, Benjamín. *Memoria sobre el sistema penitenciario en jeneral i su mejor aplicación en Chile* (Santiago: Imprenta del Ferrocarril, 1857).

———. *Un año en la intendencia de Santiago: lo que es la capital y lo que debería ser* (Santiago: Imprenta de la Librería del Mercurio, 1873).

Villavicencio, Víctor M. *La reforma penitenciaria en el Perú* (Lima: Imprenta A. J. Rivas Berrio, 1927).

**Secondary Bibliography on Crime and Punishment in Latin American History**

Adamo, Samuel. "The Broken Promise: Race, Health and Justice in Rio de Janeiro 1890–1940." Ph.D. dissertation, University of New Mexico, Albuquerque, 1983.

Aguirre, Carlos. "Disciplina, castigo y control social: estudio sobre conductas sociales y mecanismos punitivos, Lima, 1821–1868." Licenciatura thesis, Universidad Nacional Federico Villarreal, Lima, 1990.

Aguirre, Carlos, and Charles Walker, eds. *Bandoleros, abigeos y montoneros: criminalidad y violencia en el Perú, siglos XVIII–XX* (Lima: Instituto de Apoyo Agrario, 1990).

Argüello, Santiago. *Prisiones: estado de la cuestión* (Quito, Ecuador: El Conejo, 1991).

Aufderheide, Patricia A. "Order and Violence: Social Deviance and Social Control in Brazil, 1780–1840." Ph.D. dissertation, University of Minnesota, Minneapolis, 1976.

Ávila F., Iván. "Apuntes sobre faltas de policía." Licenciatura thesis, Universidad de Costa Rica, San José, 1969.

Beattie, Peter. "Discipline and Progress: Brazilian Army Reform and Changing Strategies of Social Control, 1870–1916." Paper presented to the Brazilian Studies Meeting at the American Historical Association Conference, San Francisco, January 1993.

Belbey, José. "Antonio Ballvé, un precursor del moderno tratamiento de los delincuentes." *Archivos de Medicina Legal* (1950): 51–72.

Blackwelder, Julia Kirk. "Urbanization, Crime, and Policing: Buenos Aires, 1870–1914." In Lyman L. Johnson, ed., *The Problem of Order in Changing Societies: Essays on Crime and Policing in Argentina and Uruguay, 1750–1940* (Albuquerque: University of New Mexico Press, 1990), 65–67.

Carrara, Sérgio Luís. "Crime e loucura: o aparecimento do manicômio judiciário na passagem do século." M.A. thesis, Universidade Federal do Rio de Janeiro, Brazil, 1987.

Carrión Tizcareño, Manuel. *La cárcel en México* (Mexico City: N.p., 1975).

Cavieres, Eduardo. "Aislar el cuerpo y sanar el alma: el régimen penitenciario chileno, 1843–1928." Unpublished manuscript.

Cruz Barrera, Nydia E. "Confines: el desarrollo del sistema penitenciario poblano en el siglo XIX." Tesis de maestría en Ciencias Sociales, Universidad Autónoma de Puebla, Mexico, 1989.

———. "Los encierros de los ángeles: las prisiones poblanas en el siglo XIX." In Carlos Contreras, ed., *Espacio y perfiles: historia regional mexicana del siglo XIX* (Puebla, Mexico: Centro de Investigaciones Históricas y Sociales de la Universidad Autónoma de Puebla, 1989), 1: 223–242.

———. "Reclusión, control social y ciencia penitenciaria en Puebla en el siglo XIX." *Siglo XIX: Revista de Historia* (Instituto Mora, Mexico City) 12 (1992).

Del Olmo, Rosa. *América Latina y su criminología* (Mexico City: Siglo XXI, 1981).

Espinoza, Eduardo. "114 años del penal García Moreno." *Ruptura* (Quito, Ecuador) 32 (1988): 233–236.

Fausto, Boris. *Crime e cotidiano: a criminalidade em São Paulo (1880–1924)* (São Paulo: Ed. Brasiliense, 1984).

Fonseca, Guido. *Crimes, criminosos e a criminalidade em São Paulo (1870–1950)* (São Paulo: Ed. Resenha Tributária, 1988).

García, Francisco J. "El edificio de la Real Cárcel de San Juan (1800–1898)." *Plural* 3, no. 2 (1984).

García Basalo, J. Carlos. *La colonización penal de la Tierra del Fuego* (Buenos Aires: Marymar, 1988).

———. *Historia de la Penitenciaría de Buenos Aires, 1869–1880* (Buenos Aires: Servicio Penitenciario Federal, 1979).

———. *San Martín y la reforma carcelaria: aporte a la historia del derecho penal argentino y americano* (Buenos Aires: Ediciones Arayú, 1954).

Geli, Patricio. "Los anarquistas en el gabinete antropométrico: anarquismo y criminología en la sociedad argentina del 900." *Entrepasados* 2, no. 2 (1992): 7–24.

Goetschel, Ana María. "El discurso sobre la delincuencia y la constitución del estado ecuatoriano en el siglo XIX (períodos Garciano y Liberal)." Master's thesis, Facultad Latinoamericana de Ciencias Sociales (FLACSO), Quito, Ecuador, 1992.

Granados, Mónica. "Estudio exploratorio para la construcción de una teoría política-económica de la pena en la Costa Rica del Siglo XIX." Master's thesis, Instituto Nacional de Ciencias Penales, Mexico City, 1986.

Guy, Donna. "Prostitution and Female Criminality in Buenos Aires, 1875–1937." In Lyman L. Johnson, ed., The Problem of Order in Changing Societies: Essays on Crime and Policing in Argentina and Uruguay, 1750–1940 (Albuquerque: University of New Mexico Press, 1990), 89–115.

———. Sex and Danger in Buenos Aires: Prostitution, Family, and Nation in Argentina (Lincoln: University of Nebraska Press, 1991).

———. "White Slavery, Public Health, and the Socialist Position on Legalized Prostitution in Argentina, 1913–1936." Latin American Research Review 23, no. 3 (1988): 60–80.

Holloway, Thomas. Policing Rio de Janeiro: Resistance and Repression in a 19th-Century City (Stanford, Calif.: Stanford University Press, 1993).

Huggins, Martha K. From Slavery to Vagrancy in Brazil: Crime and Social Control in the Third World (New Brunswick, N.J.: Rutgers University Press, 1985).

Johnson, Lyman L., ed. The Problem of Order in Changing Societies: Essays on Crime and Policing in Argentina and Uruguay, 1750–1940 (Albuquerque: University of New Mexico Press, 1990).

Linares Alemán, Myrla. El sistema penitenciario venezolano (Caracas: Instituto de Ciencias Penales, 1977).

Marín, Thelvia. Condenados: del presidio a la vida (Mexico City: Siglo XXI, 1976).

Marín H., Juan José. "Prostitución y pecado en la bella y próspera ciudad de San José (1850–1930)." In Iván Molina J. and Steven Palmer, eds., El paso del cometa: estado, política social y culturas populares en Costa Rica (1800–1950) (San José: Editorial Porvenir/Plumsock Mesoamerican Studies, 1994).

Muñoz Gómez, Jesús A. "Notes toward a Historical Understanding of the Colombian Penal System." Crime and Social Justice 30 (1987): 60–77.

Naranjo G., Carlos. "Pilar Jiménez, bandolero: el bandolerismo en el Valle Central de Costa Rica (1850–1890)." In Iván Molina J. and Steven Palmer, eds., El paso del cometa: estado, política social y culturas populares en Costa Rica (1800–1950) (San José: Editorial Porvenir/Plumsock Mesoamerican Studies, 1994).

Naranjo G., Carlos, and Mayela Solano Q. "El delito en San José: 1870–1900." Revista de Historia 20 (July–December 1989).

Palmer, Steven. "Pánico en San José: el consumo de heroína, la cultura plebeya y la política social en 1929." In Iván Molina J. and Steven Palmer, eds., El paso del cometa: estado, política social y culturas populares en Costa Rica (1800–1950) (San José: Editorial Porvenir/Plumsock Mesoamerican Studies, 1994).

Pearson, Jennifer M. "Centro Femenil: A Women's Prison in Mexico." Social Justice 20, nos. 3–4 (1993): 85–128.

Pereira de Queiroz, Maria Isaura. História do Cangaço (São Paulo: Global, 1982).

Pereira Machado, Maria H. Crime e escravidão: trabalho, luta e resistência nas *lavouras paulistas, 1830–1888* (São Paulo: Brasiliense, 1987).

Pérez Guadalupe, José Luis. *Faites y atorrantes: una etnografía del penal de Lurigancho* (Lima: Centro de Investigaciones Teológicas, 1994).

Picó, Fernando. *El día menos pensado: historia de los presidiarios de Puerto Rico* (Río Piedras: Ed. Huracán, 1994).

Poole, Deborah. "Ciencia, peligrosidad y represión en la criminología indigenista peruana." In Carlos Aguirre and Charles Walker, eds., *Bandoleros, abigeos y montoneros: criminalidad y violencia en el Perú, siglos XVIII–XX* (Lima: Instituto de Apoyo Agrario, 1990), 335–367.

Rago, Margareth. *Do cabaré ao lar: a utopia da cidade disciplinar* (Rio de Janeiro: Paz e Terra, 1987).

Rohlfes, Laurence. "Police and Penal Correction in Mexico City, 1876–1911: A Study of Order and Progress in Porfirian Mexico." Ph.D. dissertation, Tulane University, New Orleans, Louisiana, 1983.

Ruibal, Beatriz. *Ideología del control social: Buenos Aires, 1880–1920* (Buenos Aires: Centro Editor de América Latina, 1993).

Salvatore, Ricardo D. "Criminology, Prison Reform, and the Buenos Aires Working Class." *Journal of Interdisciplinary History* 23, no. 2 (autumn 1992): 279–299.

———. "Reclutamiento militar, disciplinamiento y proletarización en la era de Rosas." *Boletín de Historia Argentina y Americana Dr. E. Ravignani* 5 (1992): 25–47.

Santiago-Valles, Kelvin. *"Subject People" and Colonial Discourses: Economic Transformation and Social Disorder in Puerto Rico, 1898–1947* (Albany: State University of New York Press, 1994).

Slatta, Richard W., ed. *Bandidos: The Varieties of Latin American Banditry* (New York: Greenwood Press, 1987).

Solano Q., Mayela, and Carlos Naranjo G. "El delito en la provincia de San José, 1870–1900." Licenciatura thesis, Universidad de Costa Rica, San José, 1989.

Teeters, Negley K. *Penology from Panama to Cape Horn* (Philadelphia: University of Pennsylvania Press, 1946).

Troconis de Veracoechea, Emilia. *Historia de las cárceles en Venezuela (1600–1890)* (Caracas: Academia Nacional de Historia, 1983).

Trotman, David. *Crime in Trinidad: Conflict and Control in a Plantation Society, 1838–1900* (Knoxville: University of Tennessee Press, 1986).

Valenzuela, Jaime. *Bandidaje rural en Chile central* (Santiago: Centro de Investigaciones D. Barros Arana, 1991).

Vanderwood, Paul J. *Disorder and Progress: Bandits, Police, and Mexican Development.* 2d ed. (Wilmington, Del.: Scholarly Resources, 1992).

Vivalda, Graciela, and Gabriela Dalla Corte. "La mujer y el Asilo del Buen Pastor en Rosario, 1898–1911." Paper presented to the Jornadas sobre los Trabajadores en la Historia del Siglo XX, Fundación Simón Rodríguez, Buenos Aires, July 17–18, 1991.

Walker, Charles. "Montoneros, bandoleros, malhechores: criminalidad y política en las primeras décadas republicanas." In Carlos Aguirre and Charles Walker, eds., *Bandoleros, abigeos y montoneros: criminalidad y violencia en el Perú, siglos XVIII–XX* (Lima: Instituto de Apoyo Agrario, 1990), 105–136.

**Theoretical and Comparative Work on Criminal Justice History**

Arnold, David. "The Colonial Prison: Power, Knowledge and Penology in Nineteenth-Century India." In David Arnold and David Hardiman, eds., *Subaltern Studies* (Delhi: Oxford University Press, 1994), 8: 148-187.

——. *Police Power and Colonial Rule: Madras, 1859-1947* (Delhi and New York: Oxford University Press, 1986).

Beirne, Piers. *Inventing Criminology. Essays on the Rise of Homo Criminalis* (Albany: State University of New York Press, 1993).

Bender, John B. *Imagining the Penitentiary: Fiction and the Architecture of Mind in Eighteenth-Century England* (Chicago: University of Chicago Press, 1987).

Callahan, William. "The Problem of Confinement: An Aspect of Poor Relief in Eighteenth-Century Spain." *Hispanic American Historical Review* 51, no. 1 (February 1971).

Chevalier, Louis. *Laboring Classes and Dangerous Classes in Paris during the First Half of the Nineteenth Century* (New York: Howard Fertig, 1973).

Chisholm, Linda. "Education, Punishment and the Contradictions of Penal Reform: Klan Paton and Diepkloof Reformatory, 1934-1948." *Journal of Southern African Studies* 17, no. 1 (1991).

——. "The Pedagogy of Porter: The Origins of the Reformatory in the Cape Colony, 1882-1910." *Journal of African History* 27, no. 3 (1986).

Cohen, Stanley. *Folk Devils and Moral Panics: The Creation of the Mods and the Rockers.* 2d ed. (New York: St. Martin's Press, 1980).

Cohen, Stanley, and Andrew Scull, eds. *Social Control and the State: Historical and Comparative Essays* (Oxford: Basil Blackwell, 1985).

Crummey, Donald, ed. *Banditry, Rebellion, and Social Protest in Africa* (London: James Currey, 1986).

Dandeker, Christopher. *Surveillance, Power, and Modernity: Bureaucracy and Discipline from 1700 to the Present* (New York: St. Martin's Press, 1990).

Davidson, Alastair. *The Invisible State: The Formation of the Australian State, 1788-1901* (Cambridge, England: Cambridge University Press, 1991).

Davies, Ioan. *Writers in Prison* (Oxford: Basil Blackwell, 1990).

Davis, Jennifer. "The London Garrotting Panic of 1862: A Moral Panic and the Creation of a Criminal Class in Mid-Victorian England." In V. A. C. Gatrell et al., *Crime and the Law: The Social History of Crime in Western Europe since 1500* (London: Europa Publications, 1980).

Donzelot, Jacques. *The Policing of Families* (London: Hutchison, 1979).

Dumm, Thomas. *Democracy and Punishment: Disciplinary Origins of the United States* (Madison: University of Wisconsin Press, 1987).

Emsley, Clive. *Crime and Society in England 1750-1900* (London: Longman, 1987).

Evans, Robin. *The Fabrication of Virtue: English Prison Architecture 1750-1840* (Cambridge, England: Cambridge University Press, 1982).

Forsythe, William J. *Penal Discipline, Reformatory Projects, and the English Prison Commission, 1895-1939* (Exeter, England: University of Exeter Press, 1991).

——. *The Reform of Prisoners, 1830-1900* (New York: St. Martin's Press, 1987).

Foucault, Michel. *Discipline and Punish: The Birth of the Prison,* trans. Alan Sheridan (New York: Pantheon Books, 1977).

——. *Power/Knowledge: Selected Interviews & Other Writings, 1972–1977,* ed. Colin Gordon (New York: Pantheon Books, 1972).

Frese Witt, Mary Ann. *Existential Prisons: Captivity in Mid-Twentieth-Century French Literature* (Durham: Duke University Press, 1985).

Friedman, Lawrence M. *Crime and Punishment in American History* (New York: Basic Books, 1993).

García Valdés, Carlos. *Régimen penitenciario de España (Investigación histórica y sistemática)* (Madrid: Publicaciones del Instituto de Criminología, Universidad de Madrid, 1975).

Garland, David. *Punishment and Modern Society: A Study in Social Theory* (Chicago: University of Chicago Press, 1990).

——. *Punishment and Welfare: A History of Penal Strategies* (Aldershot, England: Gower, 1985).

Gatrell, V. A. C. "Crime, Authority and the Policeman- State." In *The Cambridge Social History of Britain, 1750–1950,* vol. 3 (Cambridge, England: Cambridge University Press, 1990).

Goffman, Erving. "On the Characteristics of Total Institutions." In Donald R. Cressy, ed., *The Prison: Studies in Institutional Organization and Change* (New York: Holt, Rinehart and Winston, 1961).

Grunhüt, Max. *Penal Reform: A Comparative Study* (Oxford: Clarendon Press, 1948).

Henriques, U. R. Q. "The Rise and Decline of the Separate System of Prison Discipline." *Past and Present* 54 (1972).

Hindus, Michael S. *Prison and Plantation* (Chapel Hill: University of North Carolina Press, 1980).

Hirsch, Adam J. *The Rise of the Penitentiary: Prisons and Punishment in Early America* (New Haven: Yale University Press, 1992).

Hogg, Russell. "Imprisonment and Society under Early British Capitalism." In Anthony Platt and Paul Takagi, eds., *Punishment and Penal Discipline: Essays on the Prison and the Prisoners' Movement* (Berkeley: Crime and Social Justice Associates, 1980).

Howe, Adrian. *Punish and Critique: Towards a Feminist Analysis of Penality* (London and New York: Routledge, 1994).

Ignatieff, Michael. "Historiographie critique du système pénitentiaire." In Jacques G. Petit, ed., *La Prison, le bagne et l'histoire* (Geneva: Librairie des Méridiens, 1984), 9–17.

——. *A Just Measure of Pain: The Penitentiary in the Industrial Revolution, 1750–1850* (New York: Pantheon Books, 1978).

——. "State, Civil Society, and Total Institutions: A Critique of Recent Social Histories of Punishment." In Stanley Cohen and Andrew Scull, eds., *Social Control and the State: Historical and Contemporary Essays* (Oxford: Basil Blackwell, 1985), 75–105.

Innes, Joanna. "Prisons for the Poor: English Bridewells, 1555–1800." In Francis Snyder and Douglas Hay, eds., *Labour, Law, and Crime: An Historical Perspective* (London: Tavistock Publications, 1987), 42–122.

Killingray, David. "The 'Rod of Empire': The Debate over Corporal Punishment in British African Colonial Times, 1886–1946," *Journal of African History* 35, no. 2 (1994).

Leps, Marie-Christine. *Apprehending the Criminal: The Production of Deviance in Nineteenth-Century Discourse* (Durham: Duke University Press, 1992).

Linebaugh, Peter. *The London Hanged: Crime and Civil Society in Eighteenth-Century London* (Cambridge, England: Cambridge University Press, 1992).

Mannheim, Hermann. *Pioneers in Criminology* (London: Stevens, 1960).

Maristany, Luis. *El gabinete del Doctor Lombroso (delincuencia y fin de siglo en España)* (Barcelona: Editorial Anagrama, 1973).

Masur, Louis P. *Rites of Execution: Capital Punishment and the Transformation of American Culture, 1776–1865* (New York: Oxford University Press, 1989).

Melossi, Dario, and Massimo Pavarini. *The Prison and the Factory: Origins of the Penitentiary System* (Totowa, N.J.: Barnes and Noble, 1981).

Miller, Martin B. "At Hard Labor: Rediscovering the 19th Century Prison." In Anthony Platt and Paul Takagi, eds., *Punishment and Penal Discipline: Essays on the Prison and the Prisoners' Movement* (Berkeley: Crime and Social Justice Associates, 1980).

Nicholas, Stephen, ed. *Convict Workers: Reinterpreting Australia's Past* (Cambridge, England: Cambridge University Press, 1988).

Nye, Robert A. *Crime, Madness and Politics in Modern France: The Medical Concept of National Decline* (Princeton, N.J.: Princeton University Press, 1984).

O'Brien, Patricia. *The Promise of Punishment: Prisons in Nineteenth-Century France* (Princeton, N.J.: Princeton University Press, 1980).

Pashukanis, Evgenii. *Law and Marxism: A General Theory* (London: Ink Links, 1978).

Pasquino, Pasquale. "Criminology: The Birth of a Special Savoir." *Ideology and Consciousness* 7 (autumn 1980).

Pérez Estévez, Rosa María. *El problema de los vagos en la España del siglo XVIII* (Madrid: Confederación Española de Cajas de Ahorro, 1976).

Perrot, Michelle. "Delinquency and the Penitentiary System in Nineteenth-Century France." In Robert Forster and Orest Ranum, eds., *Deviants and the Abandoned in French Society: Selections from the Annales, Economies, Societies, Civilisations* (Baltimore, Md.: Johns Hopkins University Press, 1978).

——, ed. *L'Impossible Prison: recherches sur le système pénitentiaire aux XIXe siècle* (Paris: Editions du Seuil, 1980).

Peset, José Luis. *Ciencia y marginación: sobre negros, locos y criminales* (Barcelona: Editorial Crítica, Grupo Editorial Grijalbo, 1983).

Pike, Ruth. *Penal Servitude in Early Modern Spain* (Madison: University of Wisconsin Press, 1983).

Pisciotta, Alexander W. *Benevolent Repression: Social Control and the American Reformatory-Prison Movement* (New York and London: New York University Press, 1994).

Platt, Anthony M. *The Child Savers: The Invention of Delinquency* (Chicago and London: University of Chicago Press, 1969).

Priestley, Philip. *Victorian Prison Lives: English Prison Biography 1830–1914* (London: Methuen, 1985).

Rafter, Nicole. *Partial Justice: Women, Prisons, and Social Control*. 2d ed. (New Brunswick, N.J.: Transaction Publishers, 1990).

Rejali, Darius M. *Torture and Modernity: Self, Society, and State in Modern Iran* (Boulder, Colo.: Westview Press, 1994).

Rothman, David. *Conscience and Convenience: The Asylum and Its Alternatives in Progressive America* (Boston: Little, Brown and Company, 1980).

———. *The Discovery of the Asylum: Social Order and Disorder in the New Republic* (Boston: Little, Brown and Company, 1971).

Rudé, George. *Protest and Punishment: The Story of Social and Political Protesters Transported to Australia 1788–1868* (Oxford: Clarendon Press, 1978).

Rusche, George, and Otto Kirchheimer. *Punishment and Social Structure* (New York: Columbia University Press, 1939).

Sellin, Thorstein. *Pioneering in Penology: The Amsterdam Houses of Correction in the Sixteenth and Seventeenth Centuries* (Philadelphia: University of Pennsylvania Press, 1944).

Semple, Janet. *Bentham's Prison: A Study of the Panopticon Penitentiary* (Oxford: Oxford University Press, 1993).

Serna Alonso, Justo. *Presos y pobres en la España del siglo XIX* (Barcelona: PPU, 1988).

Shaw, A. G. L. *Convicts and the Colonies* (London: Faber and Faber, 1966).

Sim, Joe. *Medical Power in Prisons: The Prison Medical Service in England 1774–1989* (Milton Keynes, England: Open University Press, 1990).

Spierenburg, Pieter. *The Prison Experience: Disciplinary Institutions and Their Inmates in Early Modern Europe* (New Brunswick, N.J.: Rutgers University Press, 1991).

———. *The Spectacle of Suffering: Executions and the Evolution of Repression: From a Preindustrial Metropolis to the European Experience* (Cambridge, England: Cambridge University Press, 1984).

Spitzer, Steven. "Notes toward a Theory of Punishment and Social Change." *Research in Law and Sociology* 2 (1979).

Spitzer, Steven, and Andrew Scull. "Social Control in Historical Perspective: From Private to Public Responses to Crime." In David F. Greenberg, ed., *Corrections and Punishment* (Beverly Hills, Calif.: Sage Publications, 1977).

Staples, William G. *Castles of Our Conscience: Social Control and the American State, 1800–1985* (New Brunswick, N.J.: Rutgers University Press, 1991).

Taylor, Ian, Paul Walton, and Jock Young. *The New Criminology* (London: Routledge & Kegan Paul, 1973).

Watson, Stephen. "Malingerers, the 'Weakminded' Criminal and the 'Moral Imbecile': How the English Prison Medical Officer Became an Expert in Mental Deficiency, 1880–1930." In Michael Clark and Catherine Crawford, eds., *Legal Medicine in History* (Cambridge, England: Cambridge University Press, 1994), 223–241.

Weiss, Robert P. "Humanitarianism, Labor Exploitation, or Social Control: A Critical Survey of Theory and Research on the Origins and Development of Prisons." *Social History* 12, no. 3 (October 1987): 331–350.

Weisser, Michael. "Crime and Punishment in Early Modern Spain." In V. A. C. Gatrell et al., eds., *Crime and the Law: The Social History of Crime in Western Europe since 1500* (London: Europa Publications Ltd., 1980), 76–96.
Zedner, Lucia. *Women, Crime, and Custody in Victorian England* (Oxford: Clarendon Press, 1991).

# Contributors

**Carlos Aguirre.** MacArthur Fellow at the University of Minnesota and member of the Instituto Pasado y Presente (Lima, Peru). Author of *Agentes de su propia libertad. Los esclavos de Lima y la desintegración de la esclavitud, 1821–1854* (Lima, 1993) and several articles on the social history of nineteenth-century Peru. His forthcoming dissertation is a study of crime and punishment in Lima from 1860 to 1930.

**Marcos Luiz Bretas.** Researcher at the History Department of the Fundação Casa de Rui Barbosa in Rio de Janeiro. He obtained his doctoral degree at the Open University, Milton Keynes, Great Britain, with a dissertation entitled "You Can't! The Daily Exercise of Police Authority in Rio de Janeiro, 1907–1930." He has published various articles on policing and crime in Rio de Janeiro.

**Robert Buffington.** Assistant Professor of Latin American History at St. John's University (Collegeville, Minnesota). He obtained his Ph.D. at the University of Arizona, Tucson, with a dissertation entitled "Forging the Fatherland: Criminality and Citizenship in Modern Mexico."

**Steven Palmer.** Currently a Visiting Professor in History at the University of Costa Rica. He has worked on the origins of nationalism in the Central American countries and on the beginnings of social policy in Costa Rica. He coedited, with Iván Molina, *El paso del cometa: Estado, política social y culturas populares en Costa Rica (1800–1950)* (San José, 1994).

**Ricardo D. Salvatore.** Professor at the Universidad Torcuato di Tella (Buenos Aires). He previously taught at the Universidad de Córdoba, Southern Methodist University, and the University of Minnesota, and was a Fellow at the Institute of Agrarian Studies (Yale) and the Institute of Advanced Studies (Princeton). His articles have appeared in the

*Journal of Interdisciplinary History, Economic History Review*, and *Social Science History*, among others. He is currently finishing a book about markets, coercion, and rural workers' identity in an early nineteenth–century Buenos Aires province.

**Kelvin Santiago-Valles.** Associate Professor of Sociology, Africana Studies, and Latin American and Caribbean Area Studies at SUNY-Binghamton. He is the author of *"Subject People" and Colonial Discourses: Economic Transformations and Social Disorder in Puerto Rico, 1898–1947* (New York, 1994). He has held a Rockefeller Foundation Humanities Fellowship at SUNY-Buffalo.

**María Soledad Zárate.** Assistant Professor of History and Gender Studies at the Pontificia Universidad Católica de Chile (Santiago). Her current research focuses on sexuality and gender in twentieth-century Chile. She is coeditor of the forthcoming volume *New Histories. Male and Female Identities in Chilean History.*

# Index

Acuña, Victor Hugo: on political weight of working class, 229

Africa, penal regimes in, xxn.4

Agricultural colonies: in Argentina, 12; in Chile, 10; in Colombia, 14; in Costa Rica, 14; in Ecuador, 11

Aguirre, Carlos, 34n.1, 71nn.21, 27, 72nn.39, 45, 73n.63, 74n.65

Alcover, Antonio Miguel: on role of penitentiaries in reflecting Cuban image, 40n.56

Alfaro, Anastasio: on crimes in Costa Rica in colonial period, 237

Almeida Vale, Luis Vianna de: as director of Casa de Correção (Brazil), 106–107; description of new prisoners, 107–108; 1870 report of, 107; on length of sentence, 109; on physical characteristics of prisoners, 108; on prisoner reform, 107

Argentina: xiv–xv, 11–12, 19, 22, 28, 30; Association for Juridical Anthropology of, 196; Auburn system in, 196, 197; Buenos Aires, 11–12, 14; corporal punishment in, 16; Correccional de Mujeres in, 12; criminal anthropology association in, 20–21; criminologists in, xv, 22; and delinquents, 22; and export economy, 199; Instituto de Criminología of, 11; Italian positivism in, 196; labor movement in, 199; *mala vida*

(criminal class), 22; Penal de Tierra del Fuego, 12; Penitenciaría de Córdoba of, 12; Penitenciaría Nacional de Buenos Aires, 11–12, 28, 194–195, 197; prison reform in, 194–200. *See also* Agricultural colonies

Association for Juridical Anthropology. *See* Argentina

Auburn penitentiary, 6, 27

Auburn system, 6, 10, 56, 58; in Argentina, 196, 197; in Brazil, 105, 202

Australia, penal regimes in, xxn.4

Ávila, Ignacio ("El Águila"), 140

Badilla, Patricia: on lawyer-statesmen, 225

Bahia. *See* Brazil

Bailey, David C.: on revisionist historiography, 188n.9

Baily, Samuel S., 218–219n.15

Baker, Keith Michael: on definition of discourse, 188n.5

Ballvé, Antonio, 197

Ballvé, J. A.: as positivist reformer, 11

Bandeira, Souza: on use of shackles, 210

Barbagelata, José: on penitentiary as part of city, 75n.86

Barbosa, Orestes, 105; as inmate, 115; on prison as a city, 115–116

Barreto, Tobias: on atavism, 202; on female incapacity extended to

CPSIA information can be obtained
at www.ICGtesting.com
Printed in the USA
LVOW03s1039180817
545301LV00001B/57/P